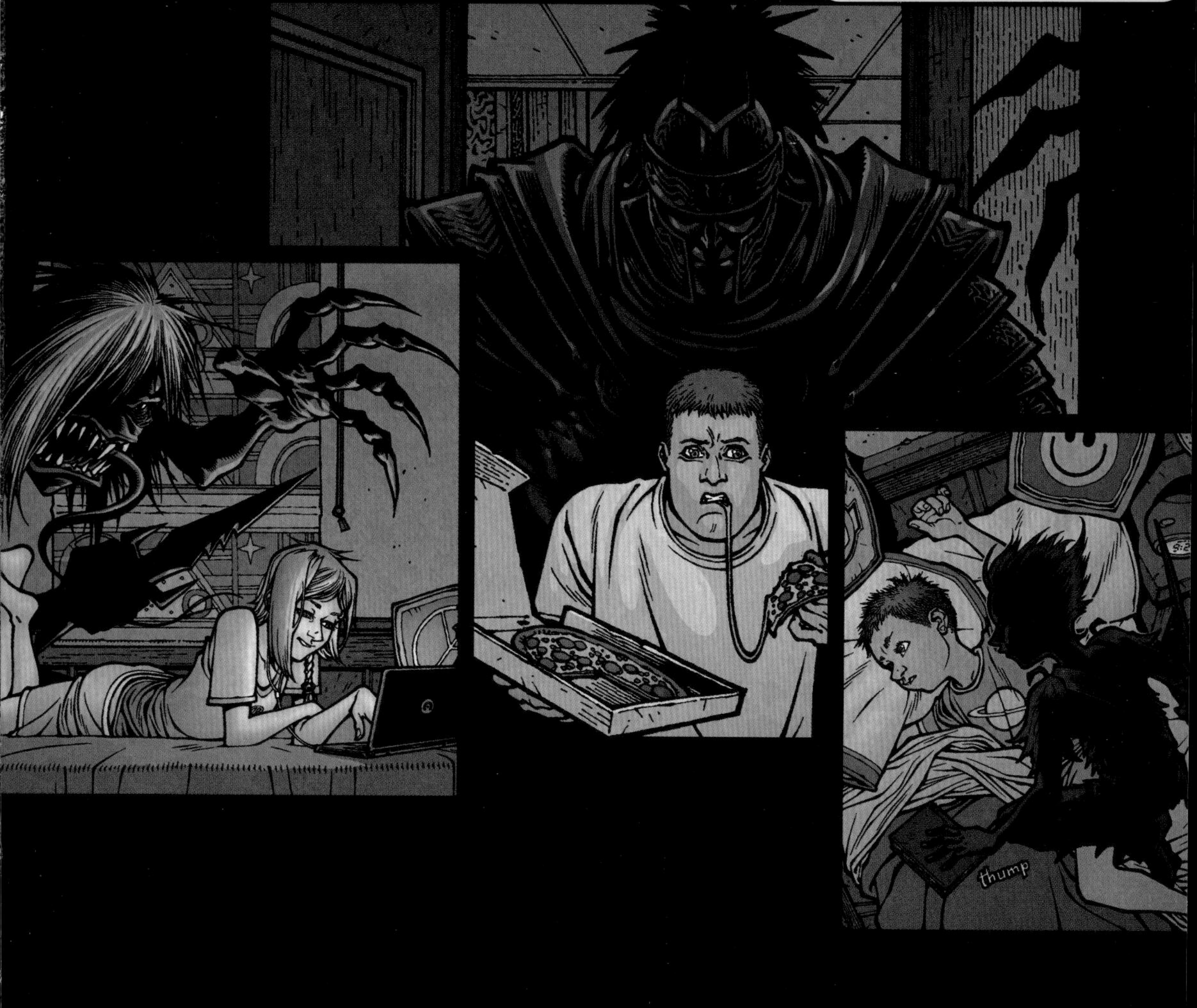
thump

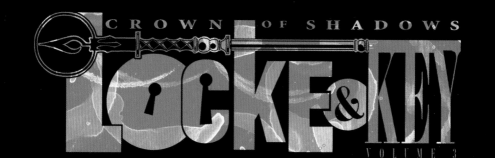

CROWN OF SHADOWS

LOCKE & KEY

VOLUME 3

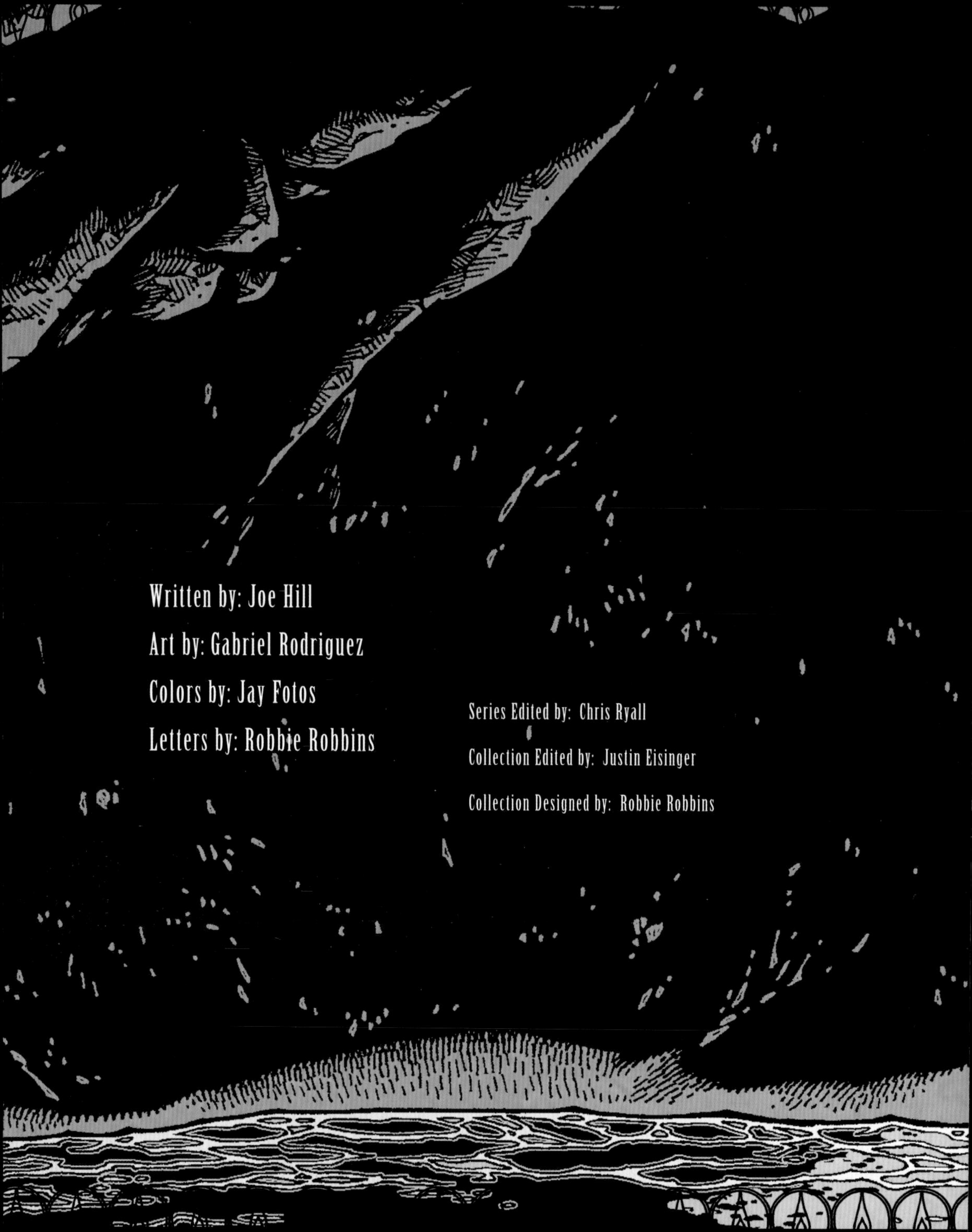

Written by: Joe Hill

Art by: Gabriel Rodriguez

Colors by: Jay Fotos

Letters by: Robbie Robbins

Series Edited by: Chris Ryall

Collection Edited by: Justin Eisinger

Collection Designed by: Robbie Robbins

Locke & Key created by Joe Hill and Gabriel Rodriguez

ISBN: 978-1-60010-953-9

14 13 12 11 1 2 3 4

IDW™

Ted Adams, CEO & Publisher
Greg Goldstein, Chief Operating Officer
Robbie Robbins, EVP/Sr. Graphic Artist
Chris Ryall, Chief Creative Officer/Editor-in-Chief
Matthew Ruzicka, CPA, Chief Financial Officer
Alan Payne, VP of Sales

Become our fan on Facebook **facebook.com/idwpublishing**
Follow us on Twitter **@idwpublishing**
Check us out on YouTube **youtube.com/idwpublishing**
www.IDWPUBLISHING.com

Originally published as LOCKE & KEY: KEYS TO THE KINGDOM Issues #1–6.

JOE HILL:
To Ethan, Aidan, and Ryan.
Your Dad loves you.

GABRIEL RODRIGUEZ:
To José Manuel, Benjamin, and Matias.
With love from Dad.

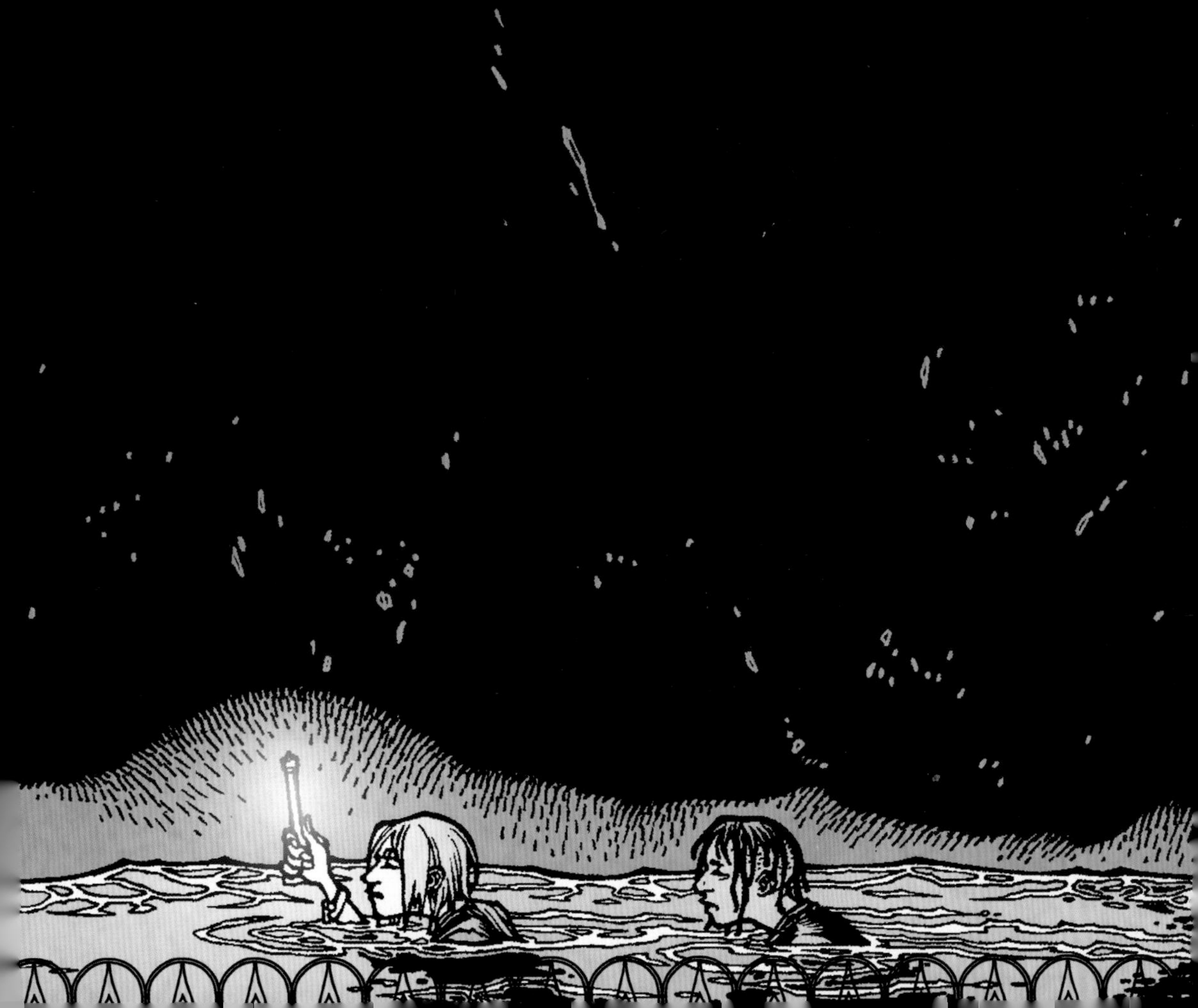

introduction
by Brian K. Vaughan

Wait, you're just reading Crown of Shadows *now*?

What the hell took you so long?

Look, I fully understand the appeal of "waiting for the trade," and IDW puts together some lovely compilations, but *Locke & Key* is one of the few ongoing comics that demands to be read the day a new issue is released. Since the first page of the first installment, it's been a top-of-the-pile series for me every single month it's come out.

(Incidentally, way back when I still had hair, I used to put my favorite comics from that week's purchases on the *bottom* of my to-read pile, as a little reward for making it through whatever crap I was just buying out of habit. But now that I'm busy and old, I try to read the good stuff the second it's in my hands, and the crap never.)

Anyway, if you've already read the first two storylines of this epic-in-the-making, you know it's not good, it's fucking great. There's just not another book on the stands quite like this, is there? The mythology of the world is vast and imaginative, but the family at its core is so real, so relatable.

Like I said, I can never wait for these collections, so I don't know if any of my fellow introducers have already made this obvious connection, but Joe Hill and Gabriel Rodriguez fit together as elegantly as their title. Unlike most of us lowly funny-book writers, Joe is a first-rate novelist who doesn't need an artist to make him look good. And any silent panel in this collection is proof enough that Gabriel doesn't need a bunch of highfalutin words to tell a story beautifully. But man, together, these guys sing. I'm pretty sure this is their first collaboration, and already the bastards harmonize as well as seasoned duos like Gaiman & McKean, Morrison & Quitely, and Ennis & Dillon.

I mean, just look at how perfectly each scene is paced, how thoughtfully every single page is constructed. I once told another writer that while comics can be creepy or unsettling, they're almost never frightening. Without the benefit of music, sound design, and editing, I think it's tough for most fiction to elicit genuine fear. But I'll be damned if there aren't a few moments in this arc (particularly during the haunting stand-alone coda) that rank right up there with some of the scariest scenes from those early Moore/Bissette/Totleben issues of *Swamp Thing*.

And while the supernatural stuff is brilliant (I will never tire of learning about new keys), the reason I'm afraid is because of how much I've come to care about Tyler, Kinsey, and especially Bode. Those kids aren't characters, they're people.

Readers love fantasy, but we *need* horror. Smart horror. Truthful horror. Horror that helps us make sense of a cruelly senseless world. *Locke & Key* is all of those things… and somehow, every so often, it's also really goddamn funny. Now that's just showing off.

Whatever, we've wasted too much time already. What the hell are you waiting for? Come on in.

Door's open.

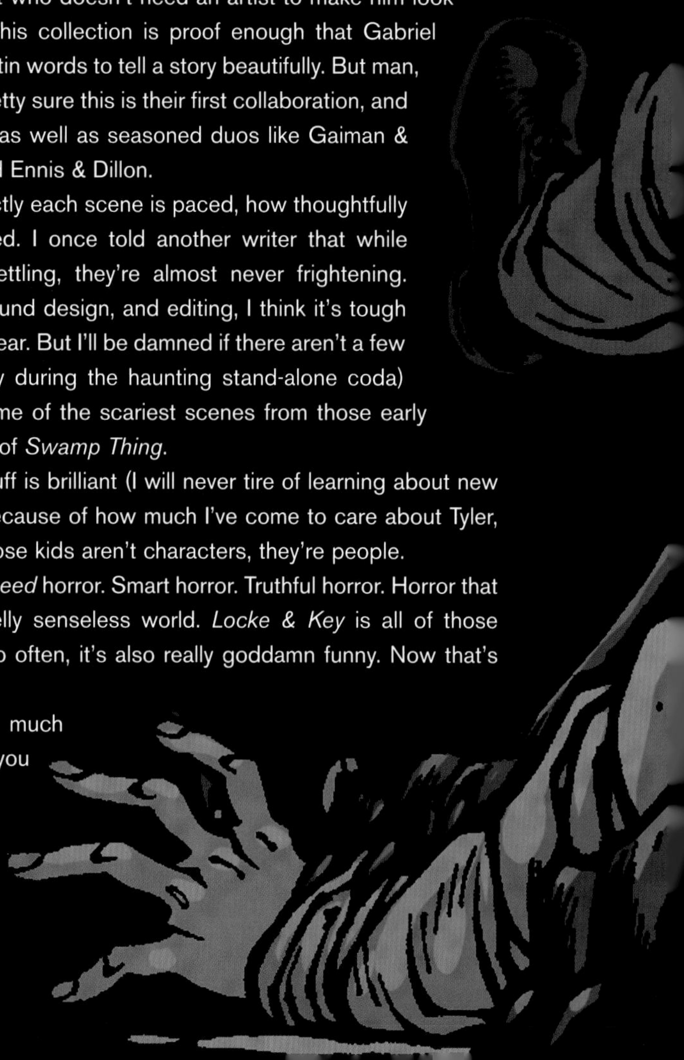

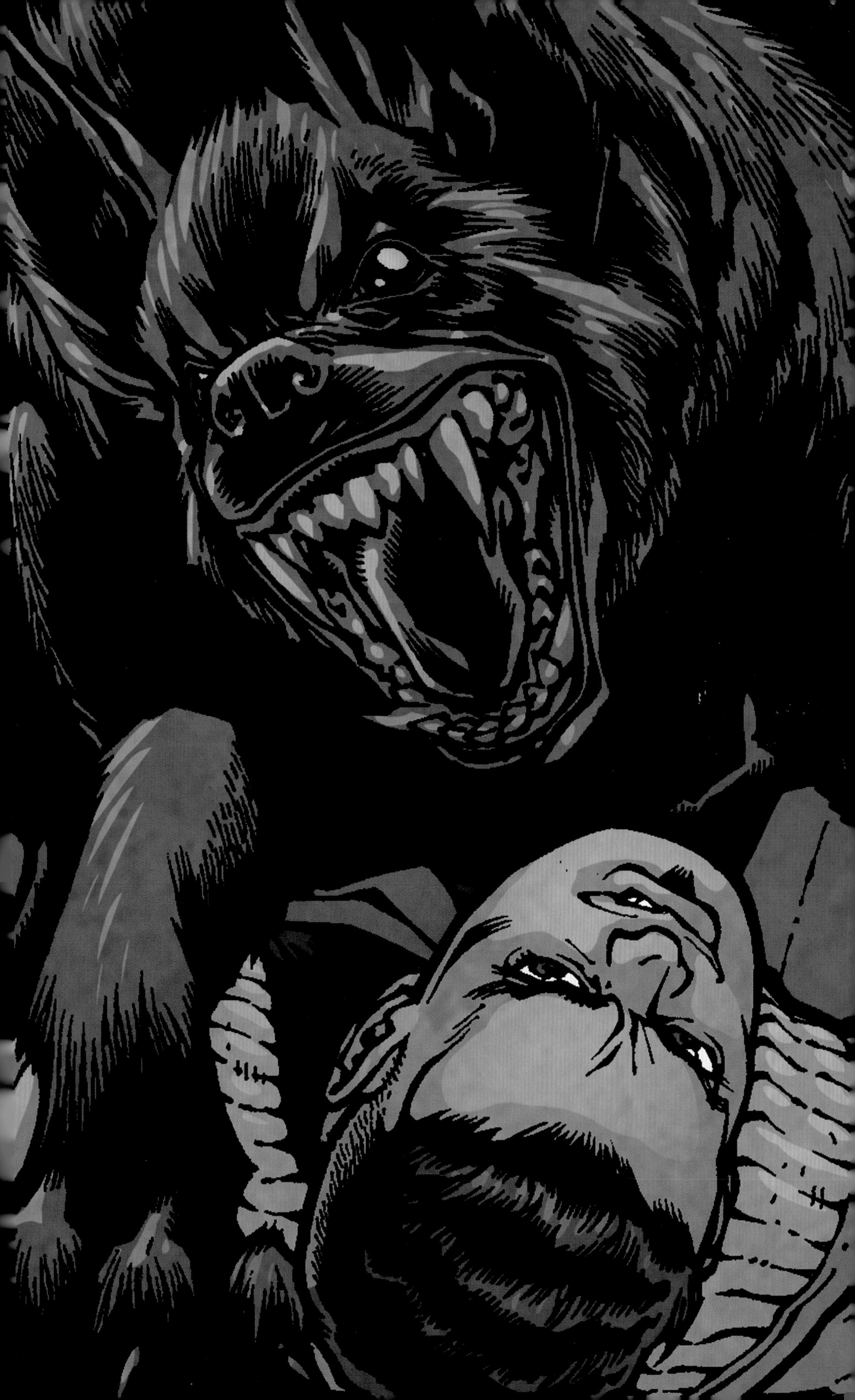

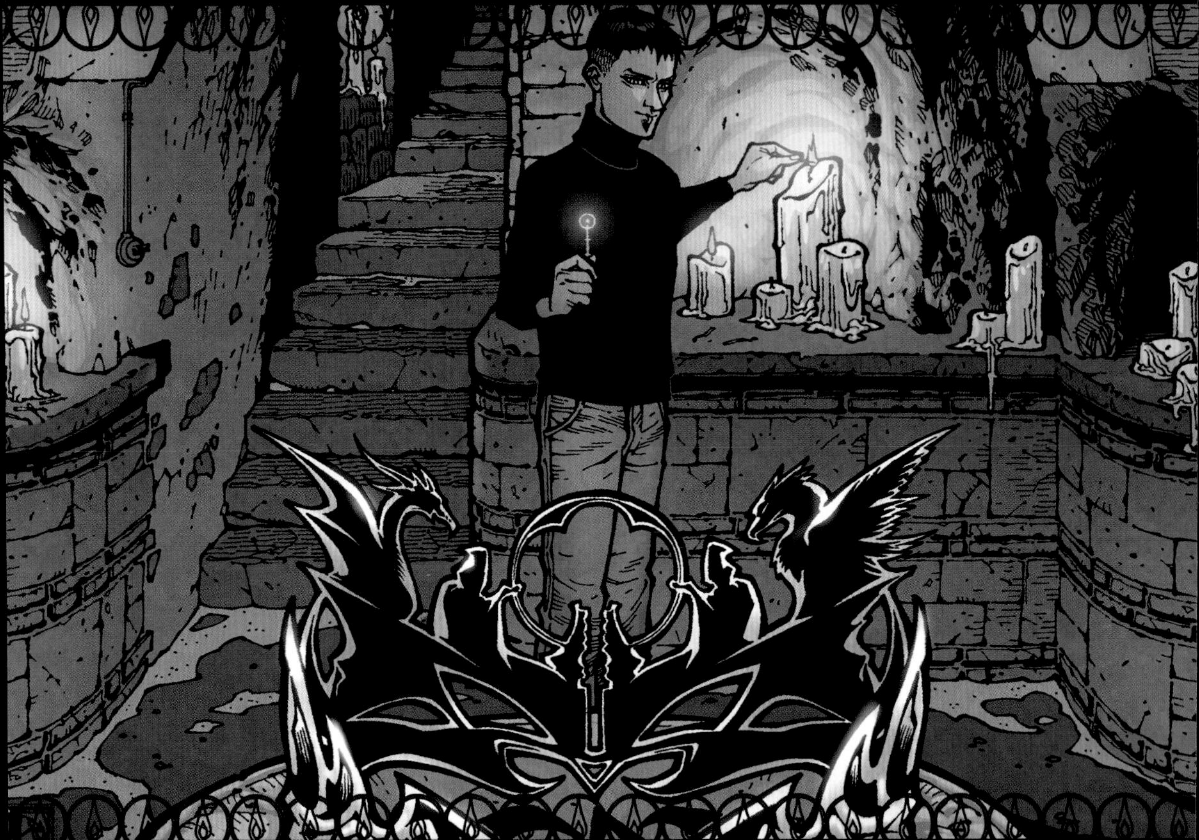

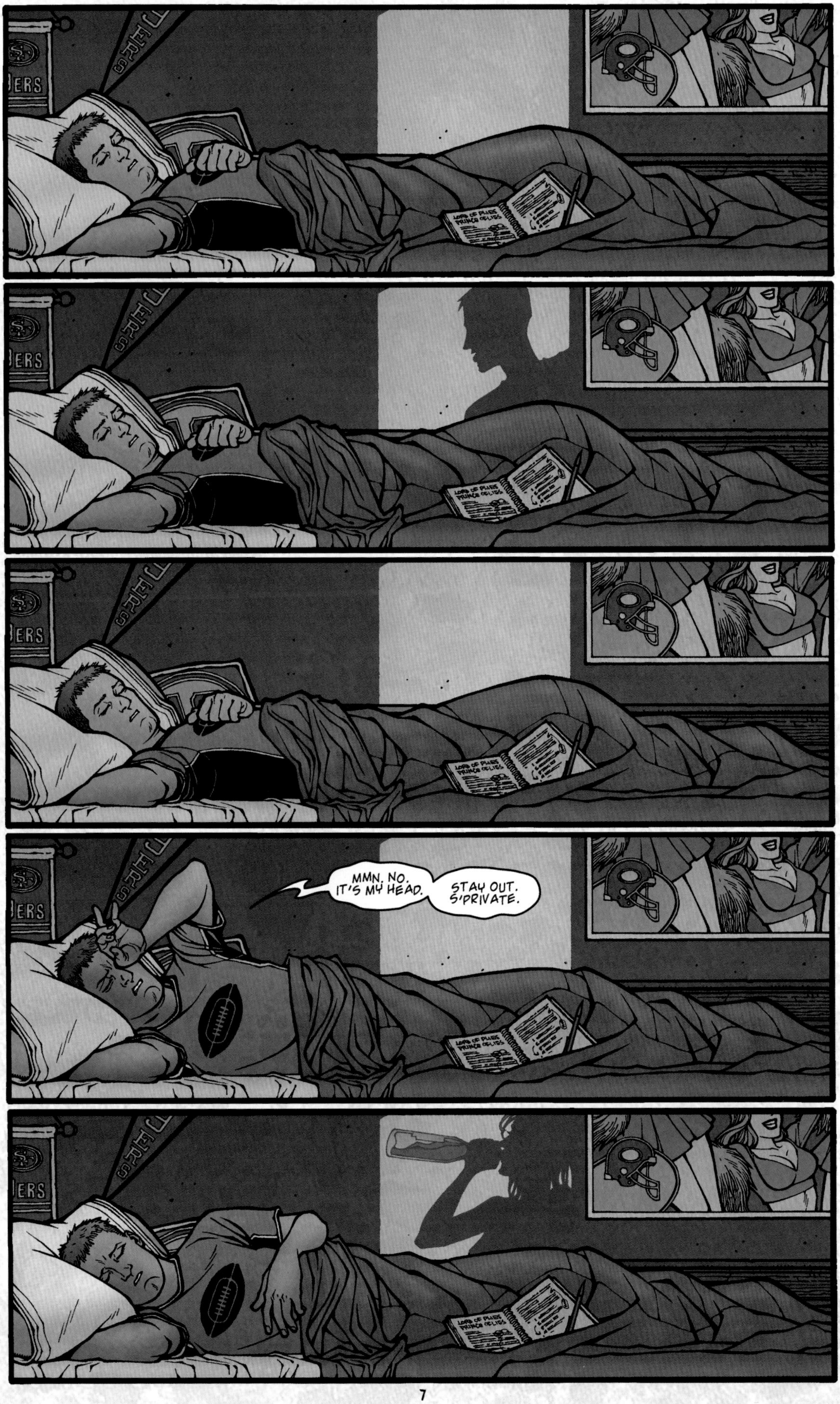
MMN. NO. IT'S MY HEAD.
STAY OUT. S'PRIVATE.

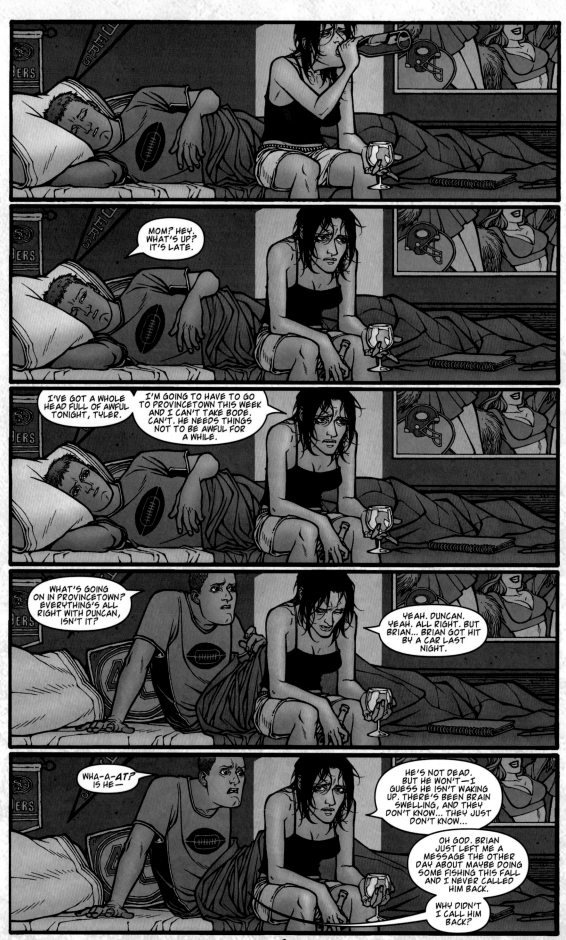

MOM? HEY. WHAT'S UP? IT'S LATE.

I'VE GOT A WHOLE HEAD FULL OF AWFUL TONIGHT, TYLER.

I'M GOING TO HAVE TO GO TO PROVINCETOWN THIS WEEK AND I CAN'T TAKE BODE. CAN'T. HE NEEDS THINGS NOT TO BE AWFUL FOR A WHILE.

WHAT'S GOING ON IN PROVINCETOWN? EVERYTHING'S ALL RIGHT WITH DUNCAN, ISN'T IT?

YEAH. DUNCAN. YEAH. ALL RIGHT. BUT BRIAN... BRIAN GOT HIT BY A CAR LAST NIGHT.

WHA-A-AT? IS HE—

HE'S NOT DEAD. BUT HE WON'T—I GUESS HE ISN'T WAKING UP. THERE'S BEEN BRAIN SWELLING, AND THEY DON'T KNOW... THEY JUST DON'T KNOW...

OH GOD. BRIAN JUST LEFT ME A MESSAGE THE OTHER DAY ABOUT MAYBE DOING SOME FISHING THIS FALL AND I NEVER CALLED HIM BACK.

WHY DIDN'T I CALL HIM BACK?

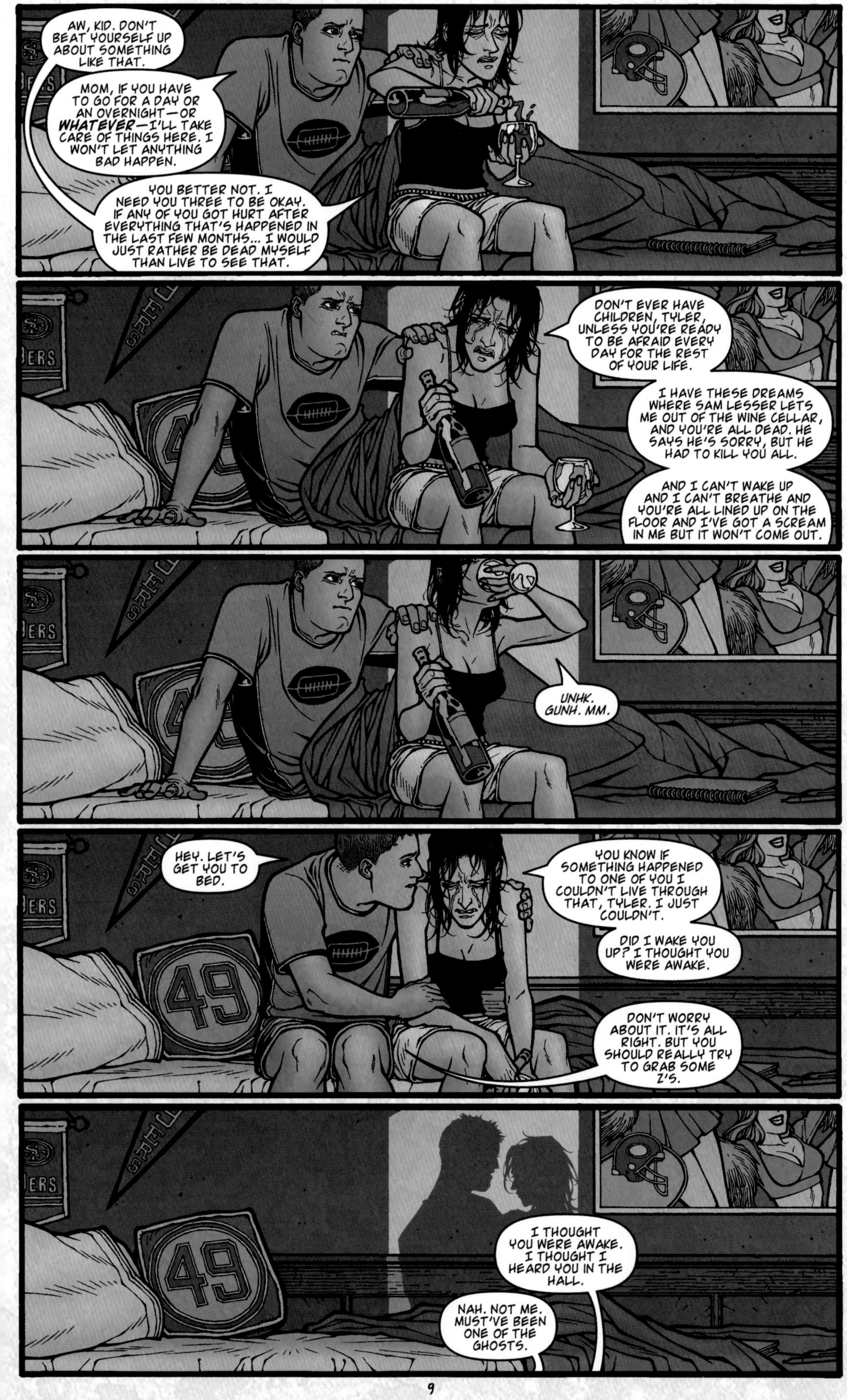

AW, KID. DON'T BEAT YOURSELF UP ABOUT SOMETHING LIKE THAT.
MOM, IF YOU HAVE TO GO FOR A DAY OR AN OVERNIGHT—OR *WHATEVER*—I'LL TAKE CARE OF THINGS HERE. I WON'T LET ANYTHING BAD HAPPEN.
YOU BETTER NOT. I NEED YOU THREE TO BE OKAY. IF ANY OF YOU GOT HURT AFTER EVERYTHING THAT'S HAPPENED IN THE LAST FEW MONTHS... I WOULD JUST RATHER BE DEAD MYSELF THAN LIVE TO SEE THAT.
DON'T EVER HAVE CHILDREN, TYLER, UNLESS YOU'RE READY TO BE AFRAID EVERY DAY FOR THE REST OF YOUR LIFE.
I HAVE THESE DREAMS WHERE SAM LESSER LETS ME OUT OF THE WINE CELLAR, AND YOU'RE ALL DEAD. HE SAYS HE'S SORRY, BUT HE HAD TO KILL YOU ALL.
AND I CAN'T WAKE UP AND I CAN'T BREATHE AND YOU'RE ALL LINED UP ON THE FLOOR AND I'VE GOT A SCREAM IN ME BUT IT WON'T COME OUT.
UNHK. GUNH. MM.
HEY. LET'S GET YOU TO BED.
YOU KNOW IF SOMETHING HAPPENED TO ONE OF YOU I COULDN'T LIVE THROUGH THAT, TYLER. I JUST COULDN'T.
DID I WAKE YOU UP? I THOUGHT YOU WERE AWAKE.
DON'T WORRY ABOUT IT. IT'S ALL RIGHT. BUT YOU SHOULD REALLY TRY TO GRAB SOME Z'S.
I THOUGHT YOU WERE AWAKE. I THOUGHT I HEARD YOU IN THE HALL.
NAH. NOT ME. MUST'VE BEEN ONE OF THE GHOSTS.

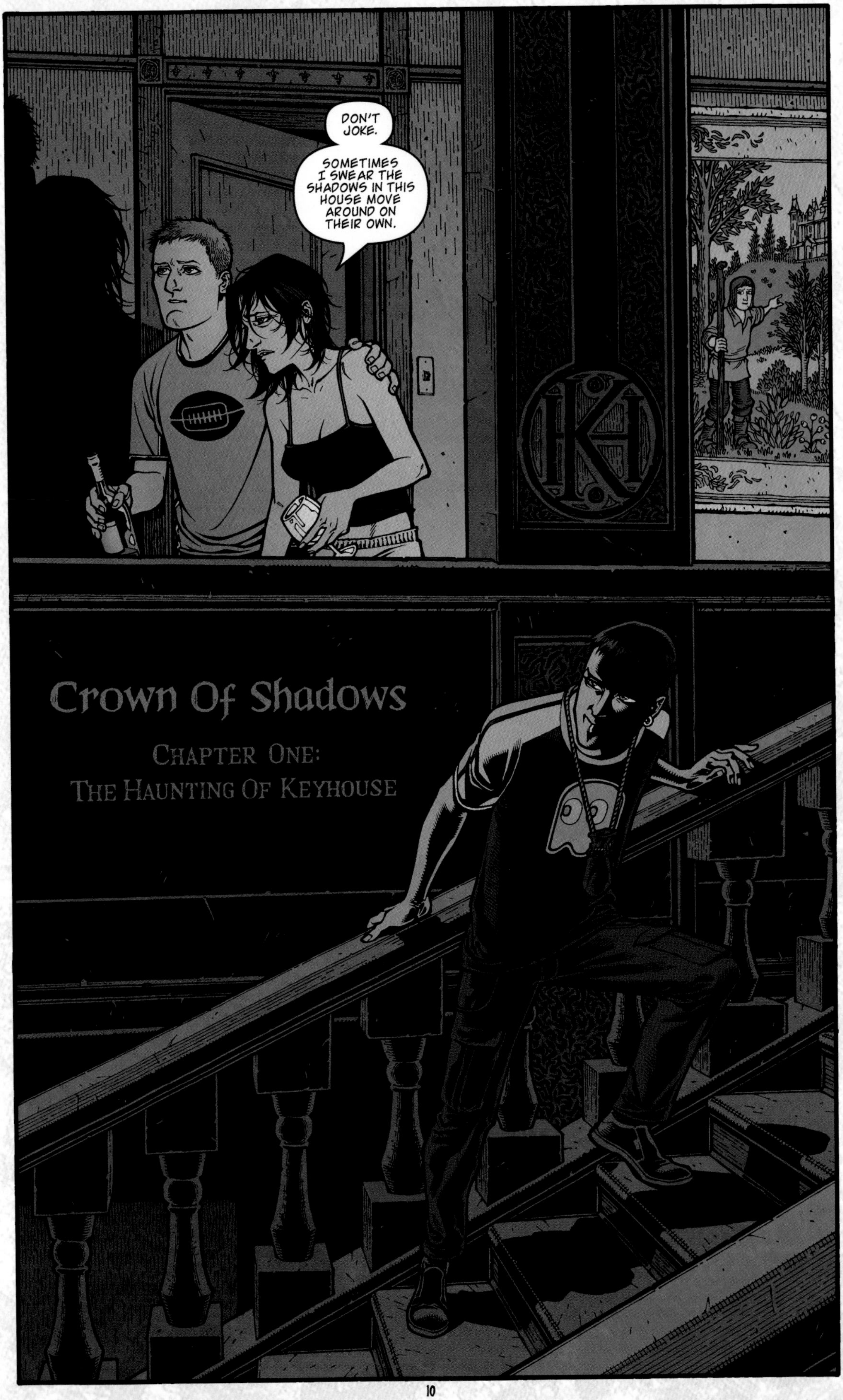
DON'T JOKE.
SOMETIMES I SWEAR THE SHADOWS IN THIS HOUSE MOVE AROUND ON THEIR OWN.
Crown Of Shadows
Chapter One: The Haunting Of Keyhouse

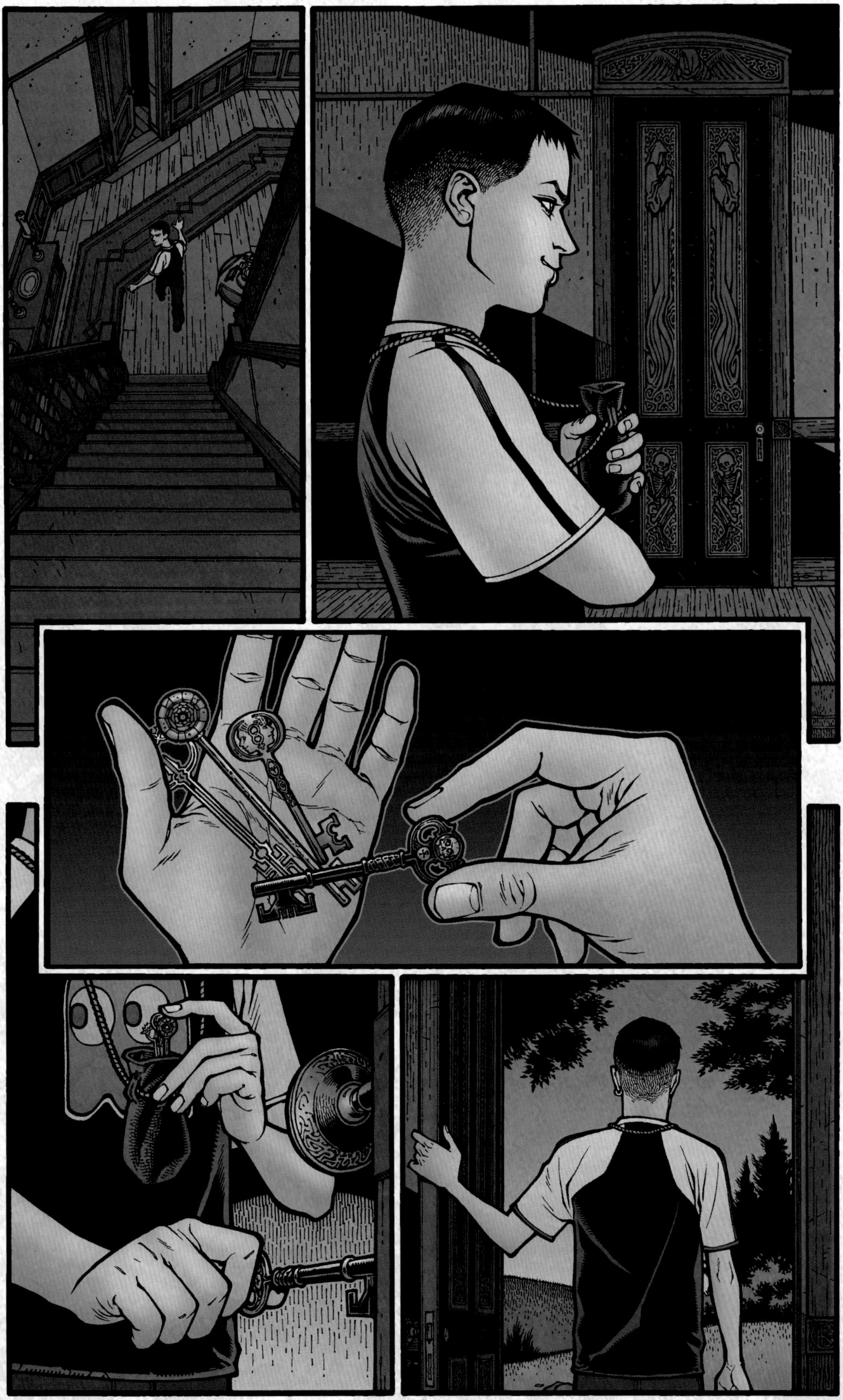

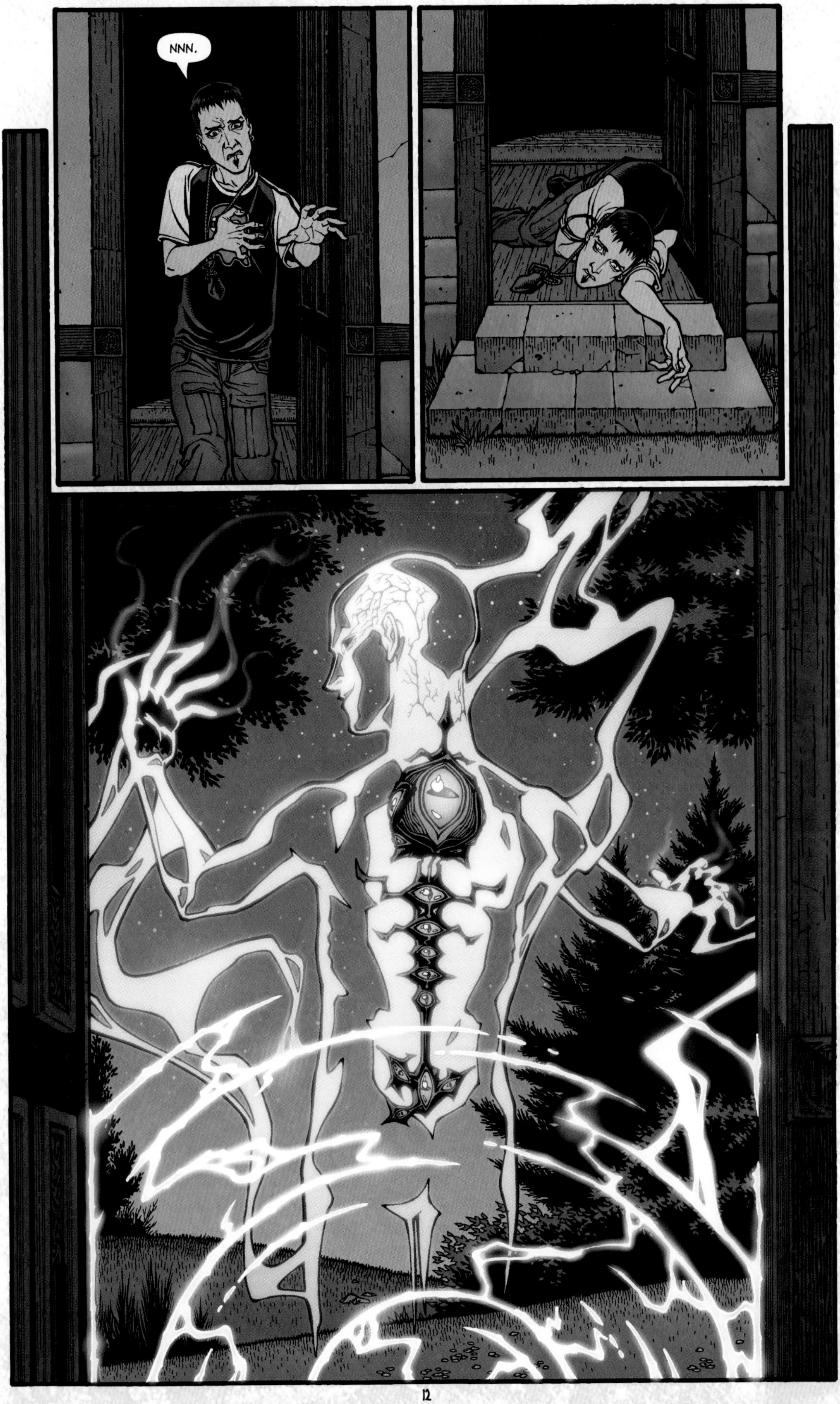
NNN.

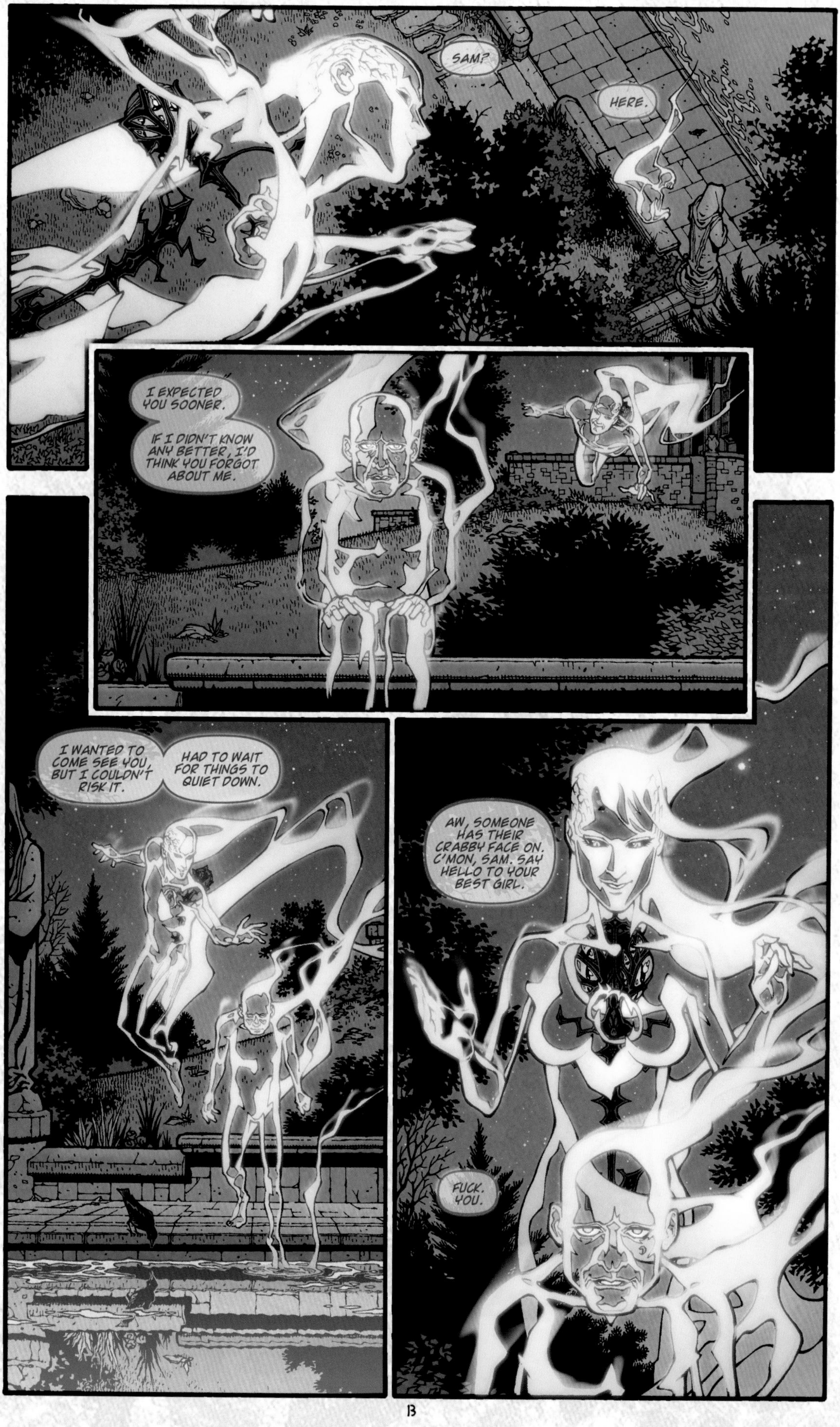
SAM?
HERE.
I EXPECTED YOU SOONER.
IF I DIDN'T KNOW ANY BETTER, I'D THINK YOU FORGOT ABOUT ME.
I WANTED TO COME SEE YOU, BUT I COULDN'T RISK IT.
HAD TO WAIT FOR THINGS TO QUIET DOWN.
AW, SOMEONE HAS THEIR CRABBY FACE ON. C'MON, SAM. SAY HELLO TO YOUR BEST GIRL.
FUCK. YOU.

YEAH, SORRY ON THAT. I'M NOT SURE GHOSTS CAN. FUCK, I MEAN. SOULS DON'T EVEN HAVE A GENDER.

THEY DON'T HAVE—CREATURES—STUCK INTO THEM EITHER. WHAT IS THAT THING... THAT FUCKING THING IN YOUR BACK?

THIS? BELIEVE IT OR NOT, SAM, IT'S ANOTHER KIND OF KEY. IT'S THE KEY TO UNLOCKING PERFECT HAPPINESS.

ONCE UPON A TIME, I WAS SUCH AN UNHAPPY PERSON. BUT I'M ALL BETTER NOW. I'M NEVER SAD, OR LONELY. NOT ANYMORE.

IT'S NOT THE ONLY ONE, EITHER. THERE ARE MORE KEYS JUST LIKE IT. I WANT YOU TO HAVE ONE, SAM.

WHAT ABOUT WHAT I WANT?

WHAT'S THAT?

I WANT YOUR BODY.

CAN'T HELP YOU WITH THAT, SAM. I'M AFRAID I'M FAIRLY ATTACHED TO MY BODY.

NOT AT THE MOMENT.

YOU KNOW WHAT I MEAN.

I CAN GET YOU A BODY IF THAT'S WHAT YOU WANT. IT WOULDN'T BE HARD. BUT LET'S NOT GET AHEAD OF OURSELVES FIRST—HAVE YOU FOUND THE KEY TO THE BLACK DOOR?

DO YOU KNOW WHERE IT IS?

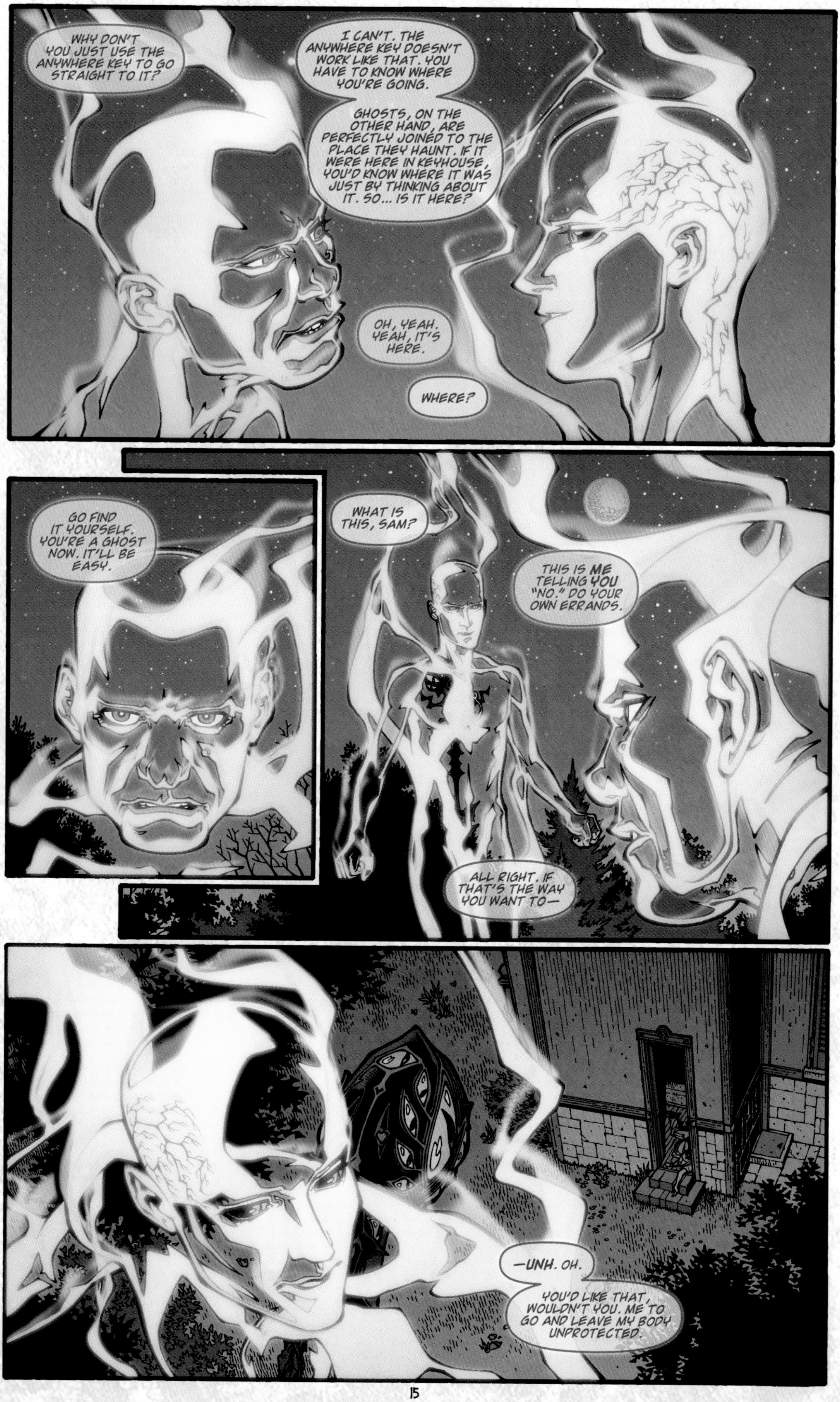
WHY DON'T YOU JUST USE THE ANYWHERE KEY TO GO STRAIGHT TO IT?
I CAN'T. THE ANYWHERE KEY DOESN'T WORK LIKE THAT. YOU HAVE TO KNOW WHERE YOU'RE GOING.
GHOSTS, ON THE OTHER HAND, ARE PERFECTLY JOINED TO THE PLACE THEY HAUNT. IF IT WERE HERE IN KEYHOUSE, YOU'D KNOW WHERE IT WAS JUST BY THINKING ABOUT IT. SO... IS IT HERE?
OH, YEAH. YEAH, IT'S HERE.
WHERE?
GO FIND IT YOURSELF. YOU'RE A GHOST NOW. IT'LL BE EASY.
WHAT IS THIS, SAM?
THIS IS ME TELLING YOU "NO." DO YOUR OWN ERRANDS.
ALL RIGHT. IF THAT'S THE WAY YOU WANT TO—
—UNH. OH.
YOU'D LIKE THAT, WOULDN'T YOU. ME TO GO AND LEAVE MY BODY UNPROTECTED.

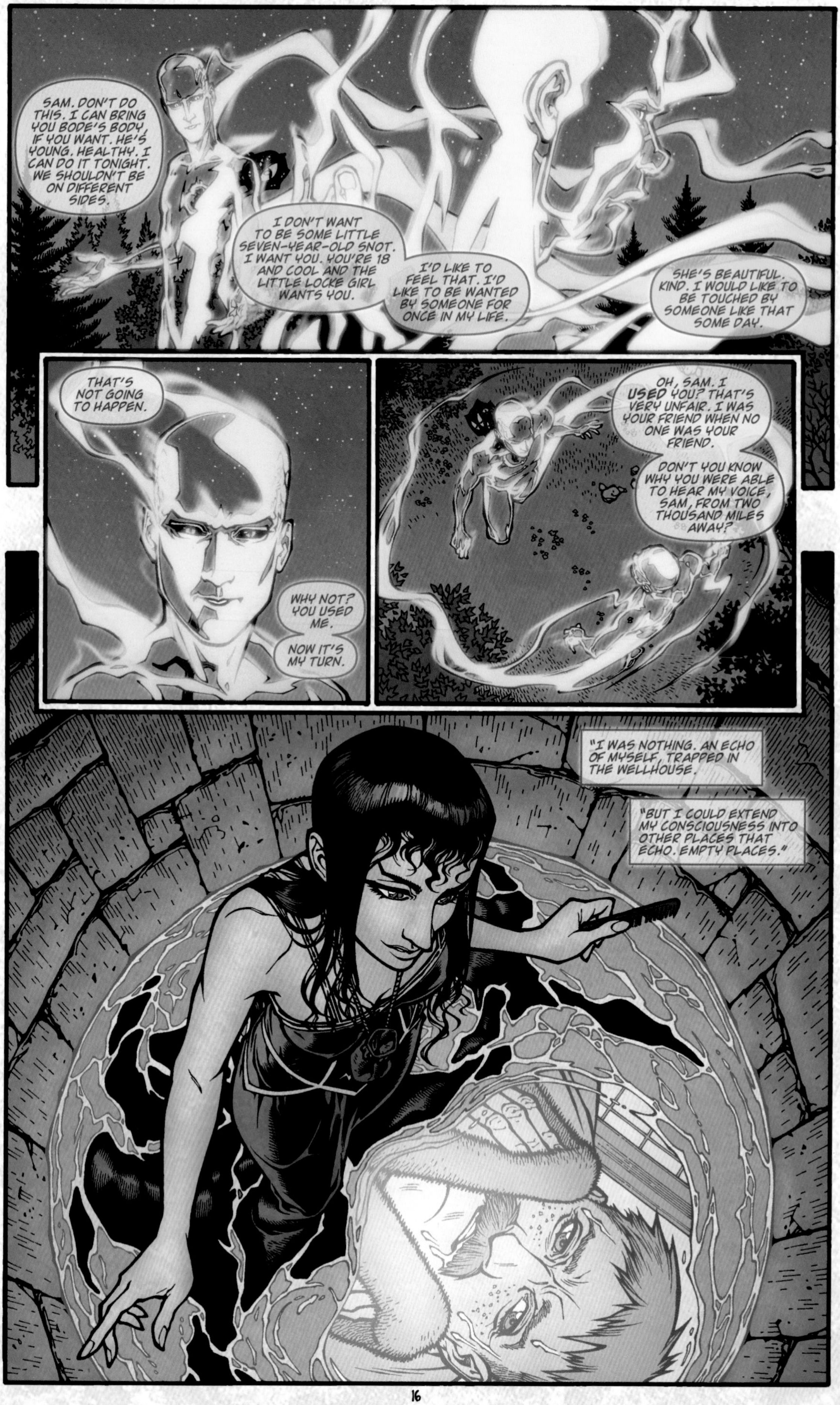
SAM. DON'T DO THIS. I CAN BRING YOU BODE'S BODY, IF YOU WANT. HE'S YOUNG. HEALTHY. I CAN DO IT TONIGHT. WE SHOULDN'T BE ON DIFFERENT SIDES.
I DON'T WANT TO BE SOME LITTLE SEVEN-YEAR-OLD SNOT. I WANT YOU. YOU'RE 18 AND COOL AND THE LITTLE LOCKE GIRL WANTS YOU.
I'D LIKE TO FEEL THAT. I'D LIKE TO BE WANTED BY SOMEONE FOR ONCE IN MY LIFE.
SHE'S BEAUTIFUL. KIND. I WOULD LIKE TO BE TOUCHED BY SOMEONE LIKE THAT SOME DAY.
THAT'S NOT GOING TO HAPPEN.
WHY NOT? YOU USED ME.
NOW IT'S MY TURN.
OH, SAM. I USED YOU? THAT'S VERY UNFAIR. I WAS YOUR FRIEND WHEN NO ONE WAS YOUR FRIEND.
DON'T YOU KNOW WHY YOU WERE ABLE TO HEAR MY VOICE, SAM, FROM TWO THOUSAND MILES AWAY?
"I WAS NOTHING. AN ECHO OF MYSELF, TRAPPED IN THE WELLHOUSE.
"BUT I COULD EXTEND MY CONSCIOUSNESS INTO OTHER PLACES THAT ECHO. EMPTY PLACES."

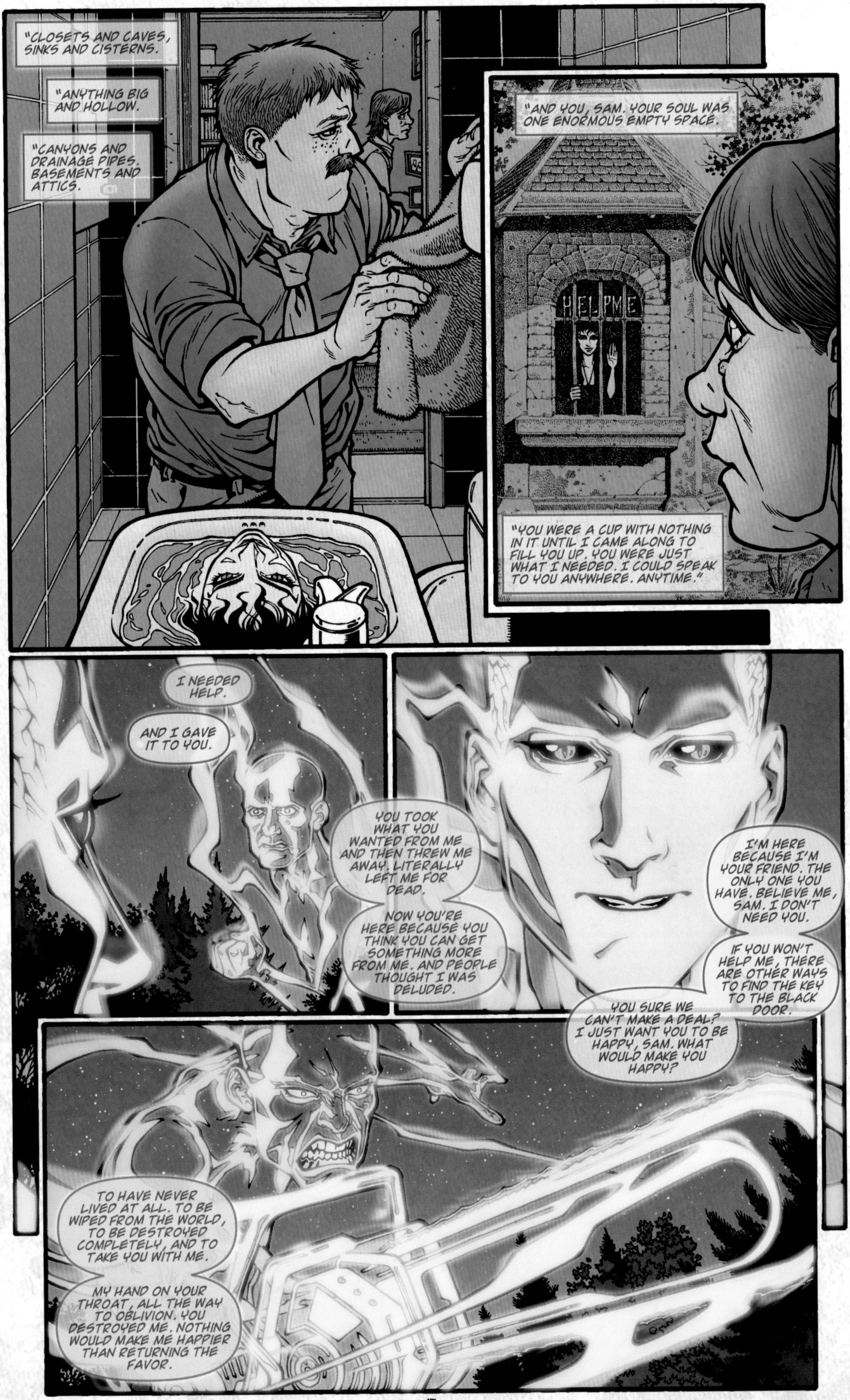
"CLOSETS AND CAVES, SINKS AND CISTERNS.
"ANYTHING BIG AND HOLLOW.
"CANYONS AND DRAINAGE PIPES. BASEMENTS AND ATTICS.
"AND YOU, SAM. YOUR SOUL WAS ONE ENORMOUS EMPTY SPACE.
HELPME
"YOU WERE A CUP WITH NOTHING IN IT UNTIL I CAME ALONG TO FILL YOU UP. YOU WERE JUST WHAT I NEEDED. I COULD SPEAK TO YOU ANYWHERE. ANYTIME."
I NEEDED HELP.
AND I GAVE IT TO YOU.
YOU TOOK WHAT YOU WANTED FROM ME AND THEN THREW ME AWAY. LITERALLY LEFT ME FOR DEAD.
NOW YOU'RE HERE BECAUSE YOU THINK YOU CAN GET SOMETHING MORE FROM ME. AND PEOPLE THOUGHT I WAS DELUDED.
I'M HERE BECAUSE I'M YOUR FRIEND. THE ONLY ONE YOU HAVE. BELIEVE ME, SAM. I DON'T NEED YOU.
IF YOU WON'T HELP ME, THERE ARE OTHER WAYS TO FIND THE KEY TO THE BLACK DOOR.
YOU SURE WE CAN'T MAKE A DEAL? I JUST WANT YOU TO BE HAPPY, SAM. WHAT WOULD MAKE YOU HAPPY?
TO HAVE NEVER LIVED AT ALL. TO BE WIPED FROM THE WORLD, TO BE DESTROYED COMPLETELY, AND TO TAKE YOU WITH ME.
MY HAND ON YOUR THROAT, ALL THE WAY TO OBLIVION. YOU DESTROYED ME. NOTHING WOULD MAKE ME HAPPIER THAN RETURNING THE FAVOR.

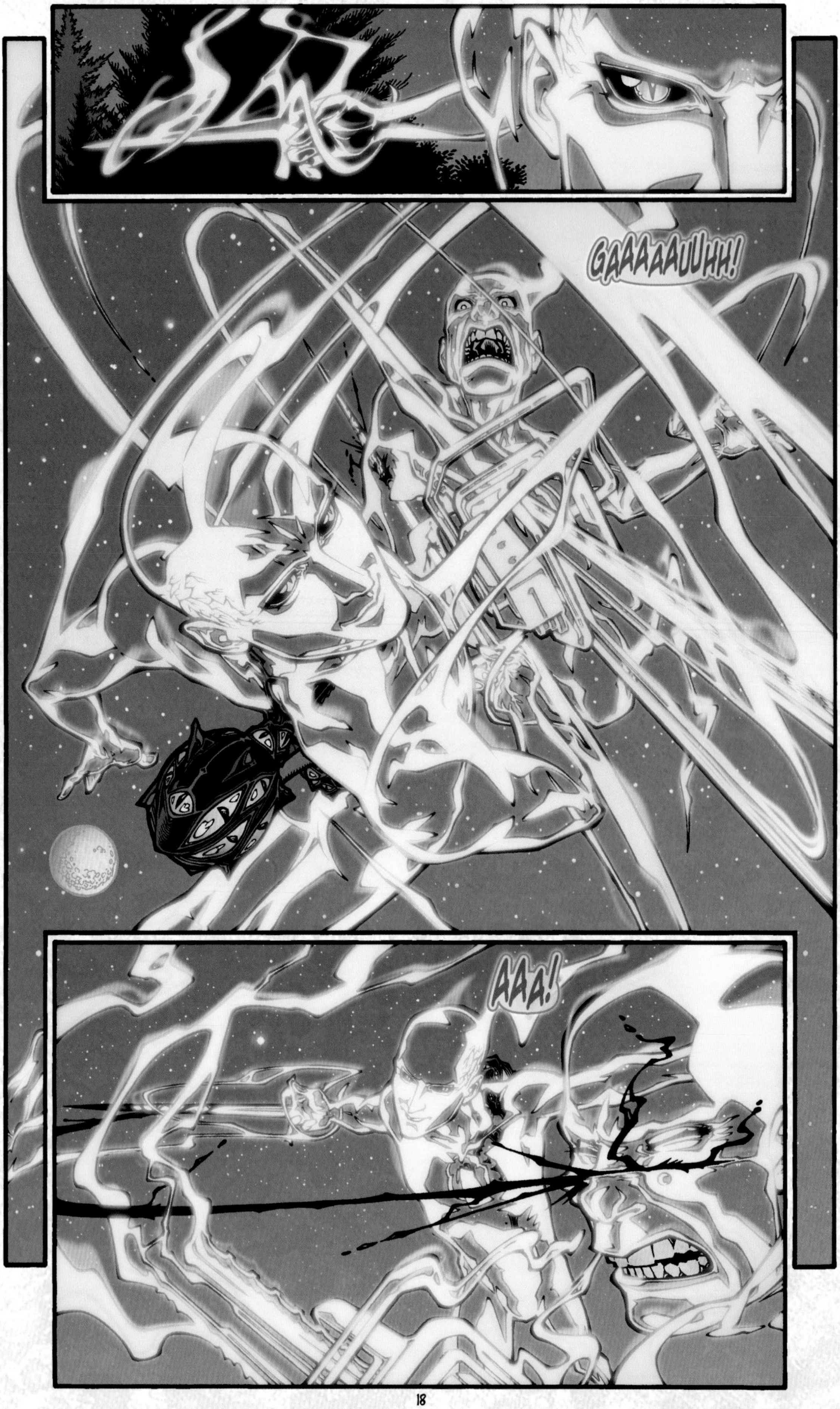
GAAAAAUUHH!
AAA!

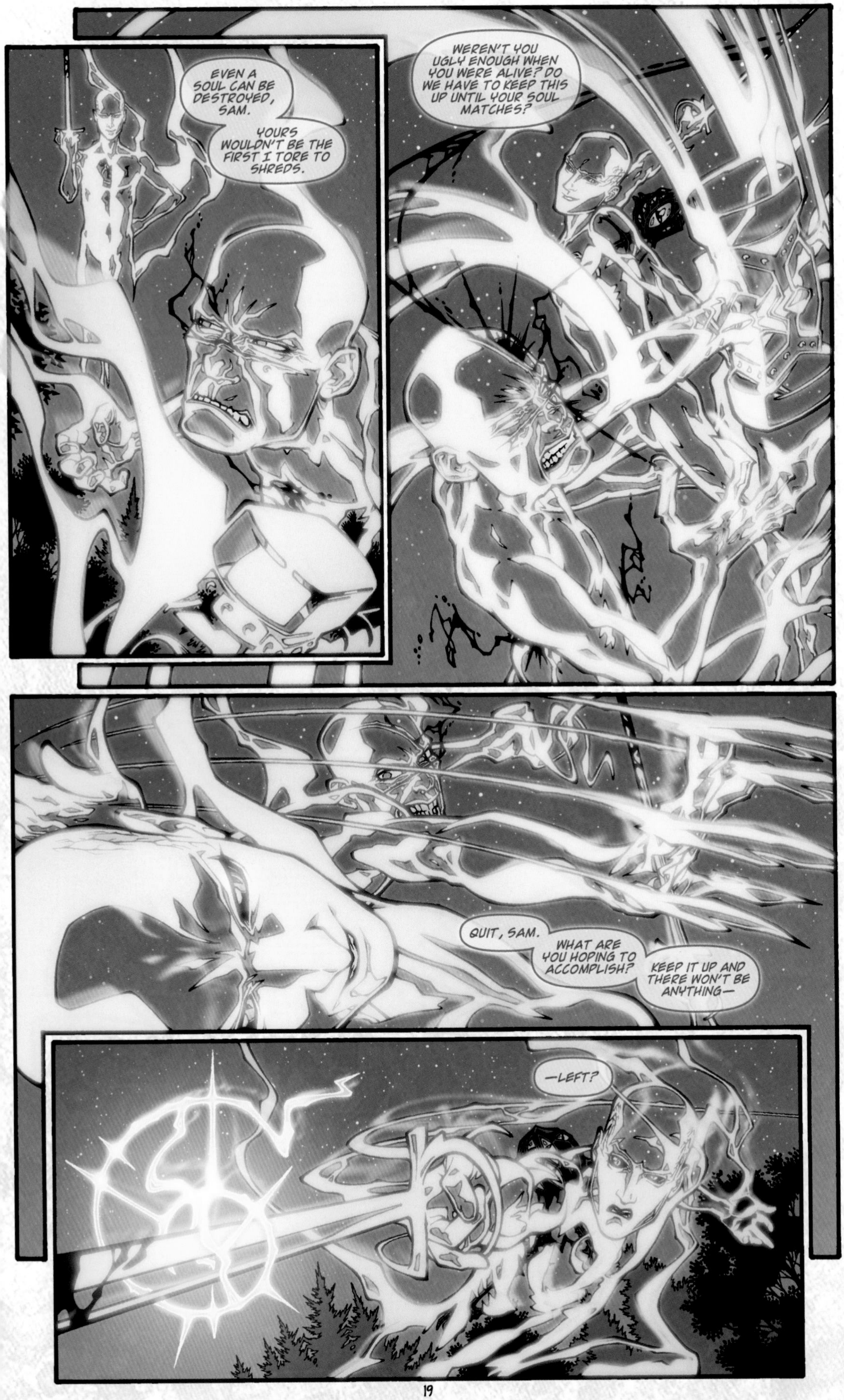
EVEN A SOUL CAN BE DESTROYED, SAM.
YOURS WOULDN'T BE THE FIRST I TORE TO SHREDS.
WEREN'T YOU UGLY ENOUGH WHEN YOU WERE ALIVE? DO WE HAVE TO KEEP THIS UP UNTIL YOUR SOUL MATCHES?
QUIT, SAM.
WHAT ARE YOU HOPING TO ACCOMPLISH?
KEEP IT UP AND THERE WON'T BE ANYTHING—
—LEFT?

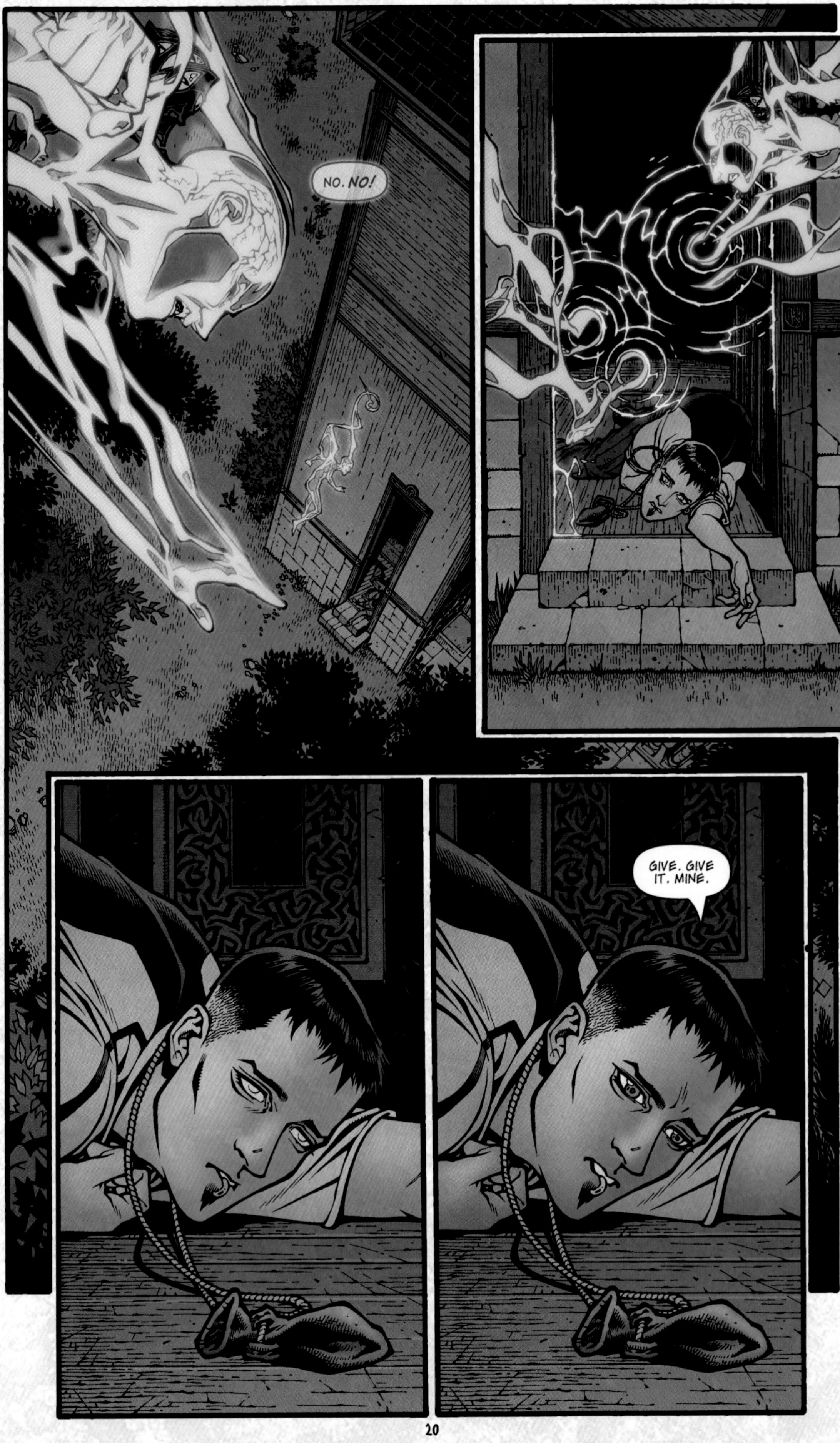
NO. NO!
GIVE. GIVE IT. MINE.

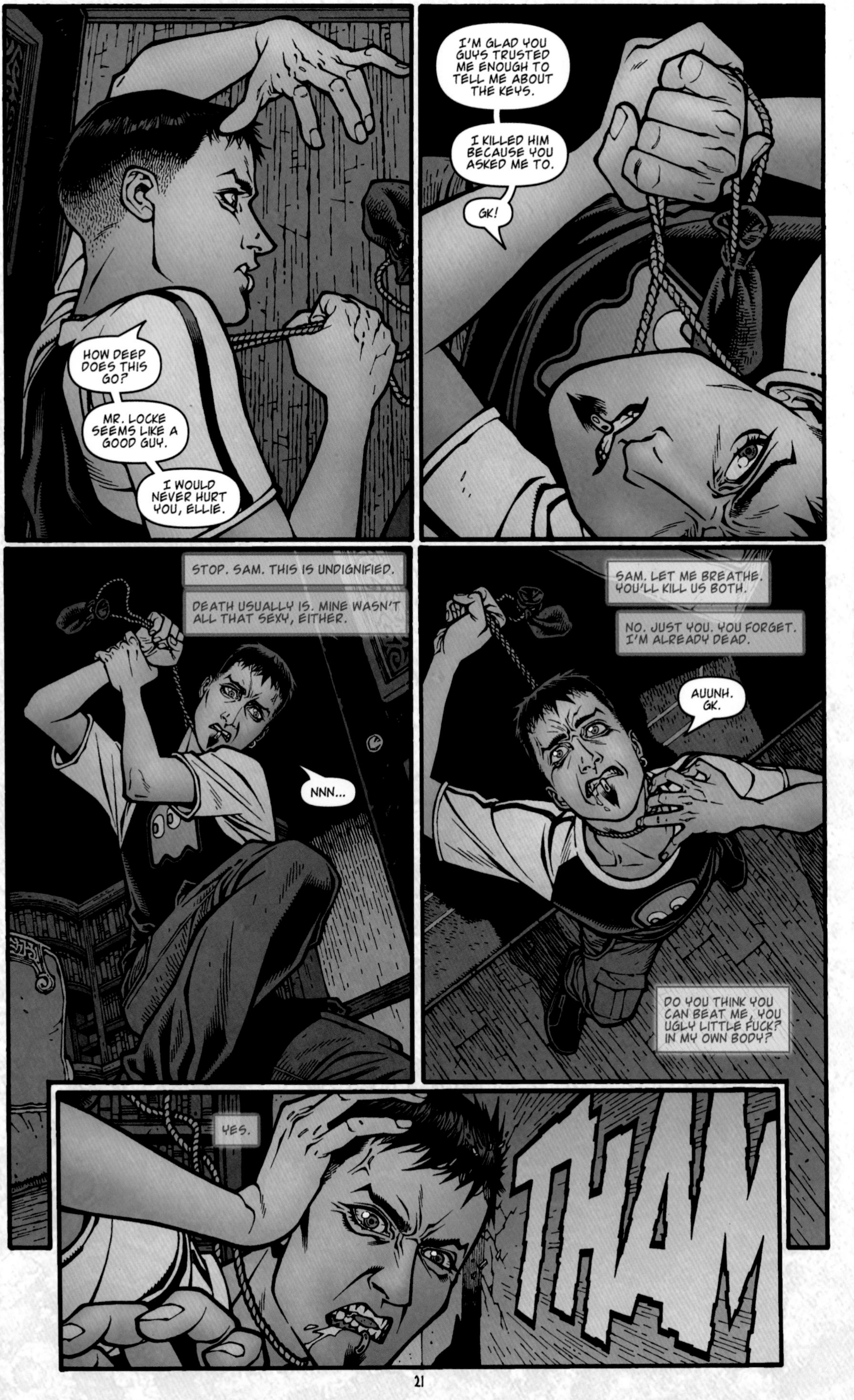
HOW DEEP DOES THIS GO?
MR. LOCKE SEEMS LIKE A GOOD GUY.
I WOULD NEVER HURT YOU, ELLIE.
I'M GLAD YOU GUYS TRUSTED ME ENOUGH TO TELL ME ABOUT THE KEYS.
I KILLED HIM BECAUSE YOU ASKED ME TO.
GK!
STOP. SAM. THIS IS UNDIGNIFIED.
DEATH USUALLY IS. MINE WASN'T ALL THAT SEXY, EITHER.
NNN...
SAM. LET ME BREATHE. YOU'LL KILL US BOTH.
NO. JUST YOU. YOU FORGET. I'M ALREADY DEAD.
AUUNH. GK.
DO YOU THINK YOU CAN BEAT ME, YOU UGLY LITTLE FUCK? IN MY OWN BODY?
YES.
THAM

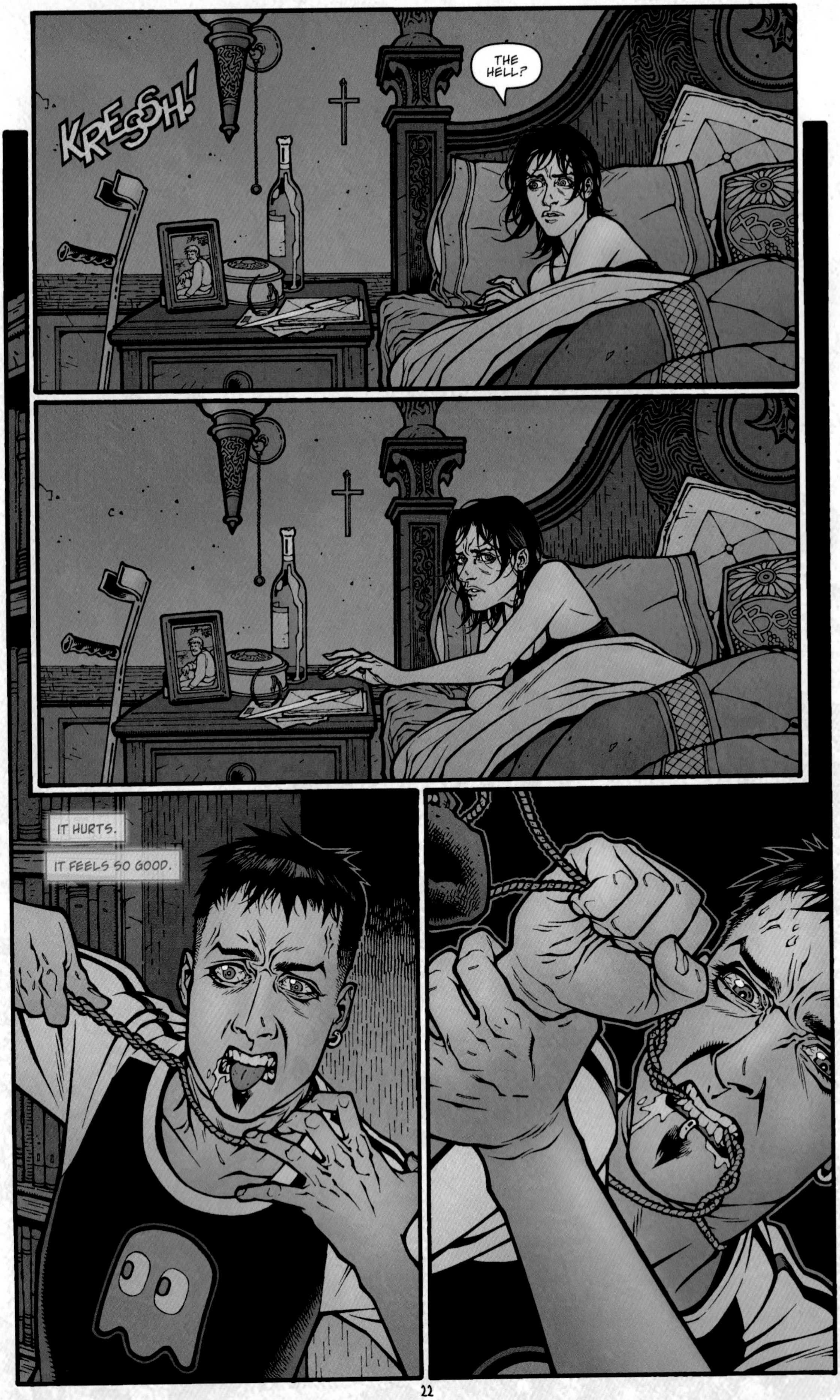
KRESSH!
THE HELL?
IT HURTS.
IT FEELS SO GOOD.

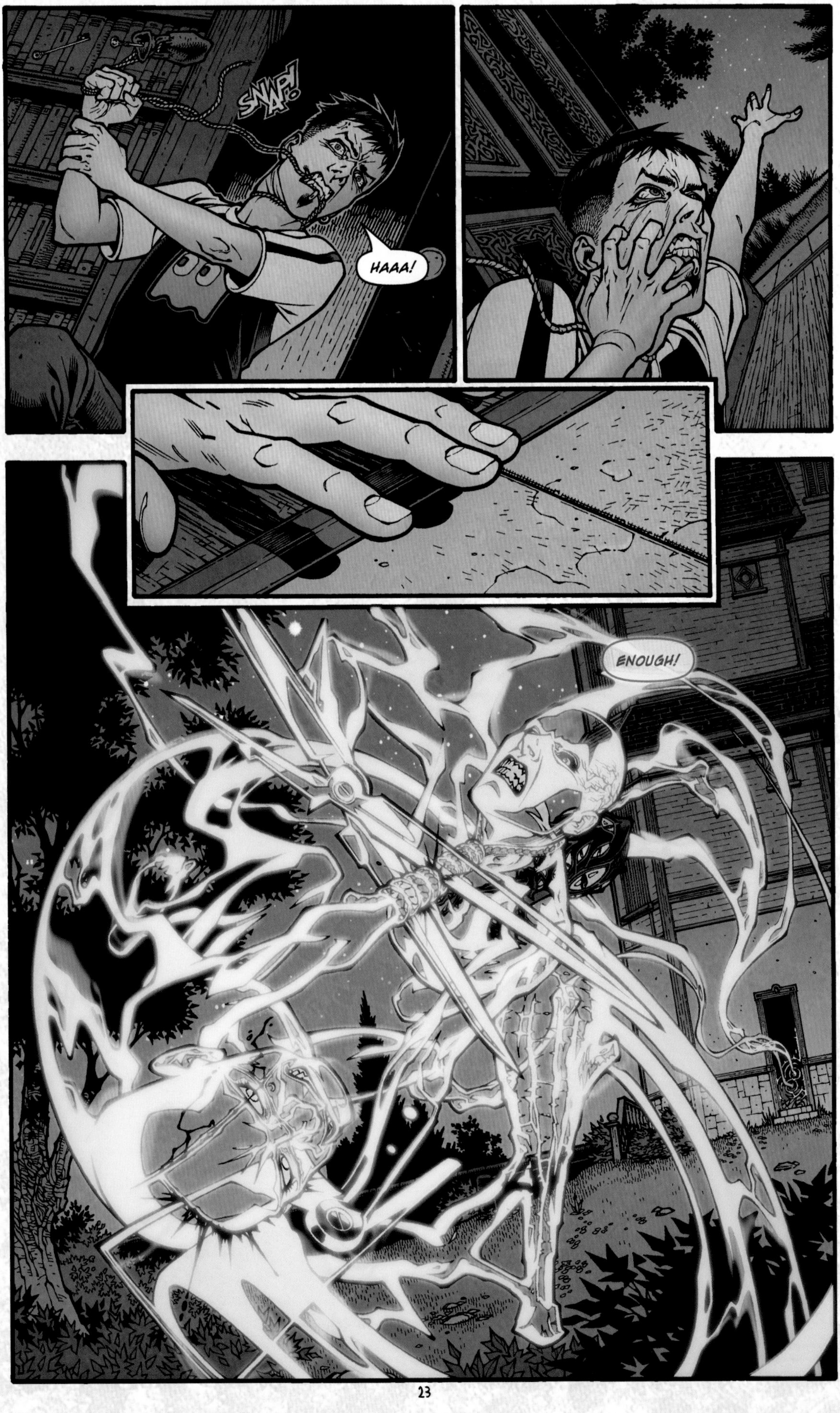
SNAP! A!
HAAA!
ENOUGH!

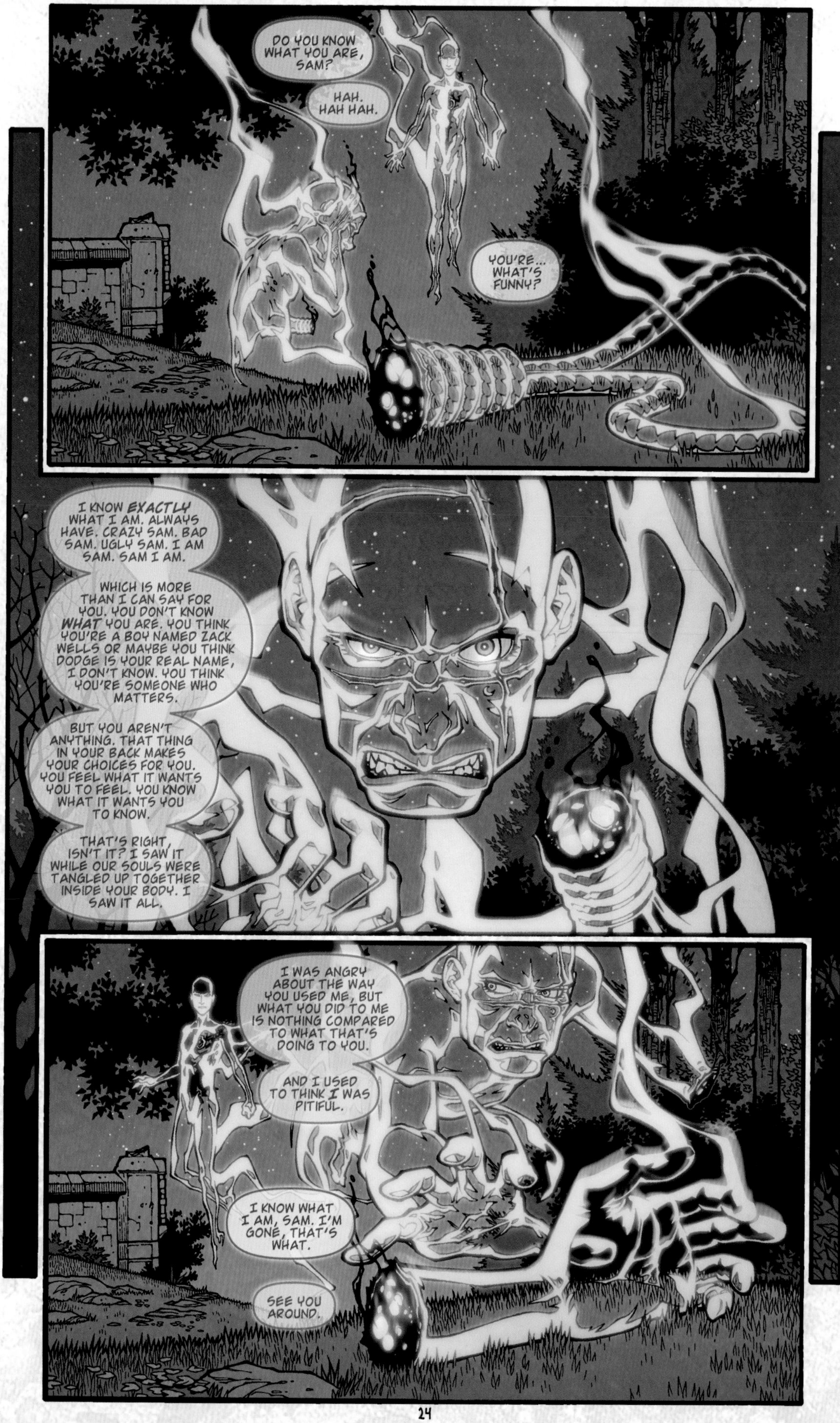

DO YOU KNOW WHAT YOU ARE, SAM?
HAH. HAH HAH.
YOU'RE... WHAT'S FUNNY?
I KNOW EXACTLY WHAT I AM. ALWAYS HAVE. CRAZY SAM. BAD SAM. UGLY SAM. I AM SAM. SAM I AM.
WHICH IS MORE THAN I CAN SAY FOR YOU. YOU DON'T KNOW WHAT YOU ARE. YOU THINK YOU'RE A BOY NAMED ZACK WELLS OR MAYBE YOU THINK DODGE IS YOUR REAL NAME, I DON'T KNOW. YOU THINK YOU'RE SOMEONE WHO MATTERS.
BUT YOU AREN'T ANYTHING. THAT THING IN YOUR BACK MAKES YOUR CHOICES FOR YOU. YOU FEEL WHAT IT WANTS YOU TO FEEL. YOU KNOW WHAT IT WANTS YOU TO KNOW.
THAT'S RIGHT, ISN'T IT? I SAW IT WHILE OUR SOULS WERE TANGLED UP TOGETHER INSIDE YOUR BODY. I SAW IT ALL.
I WAS ANGRY ABOUT THE WAY YOU USED ME, BUT WHAT YOU DID TO ME IS NOTHING COMPARED TO WHAT THAT'S DOING TO YOU.
AND I USED TO THINK I WAS PITIFUL.
I KNOW WHAT I AM, SAM. I'M GONE, THAT'S WHAT.
SEE YOU AROUND.

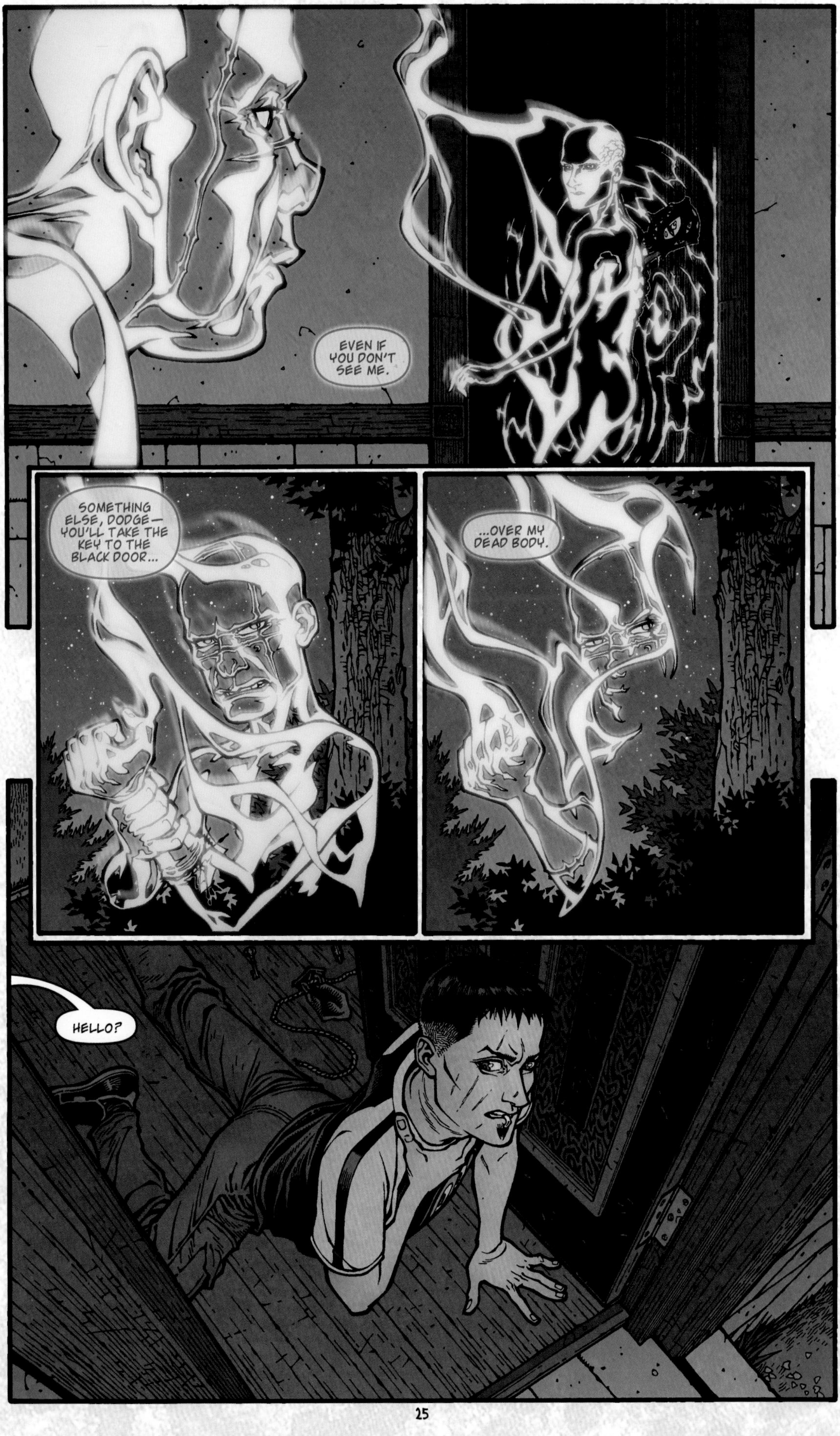
EVEN IF YOU DON'T SEE ME.
SOMETHING ELSE, DODGE— YOU'LL TAKE THE KEY TO THE BLACK DOOR...
...OVER MY DEAD BODY.
HELLO?

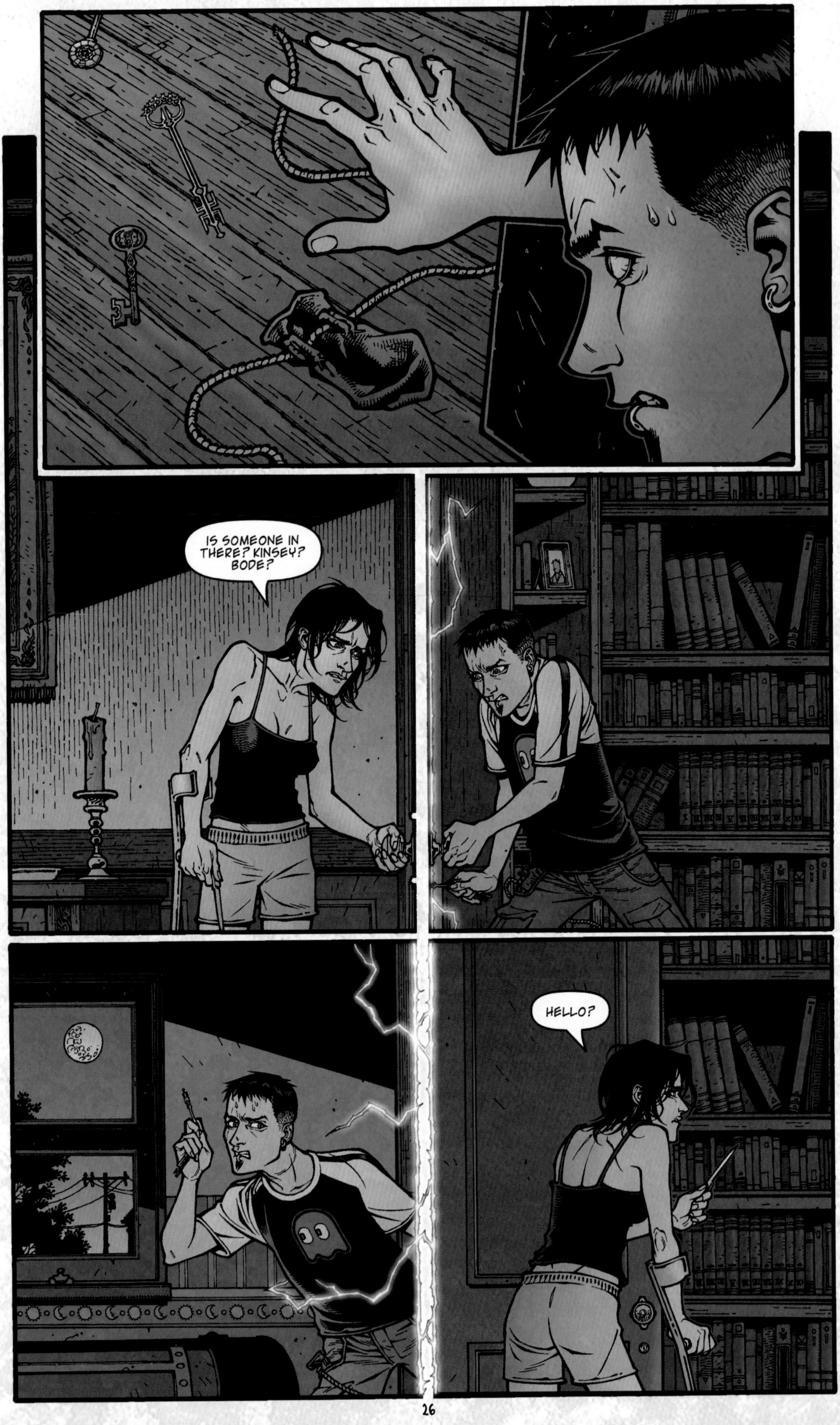
IS SOMEONE IN THERE? KINSEY? BODE?
HELLO?

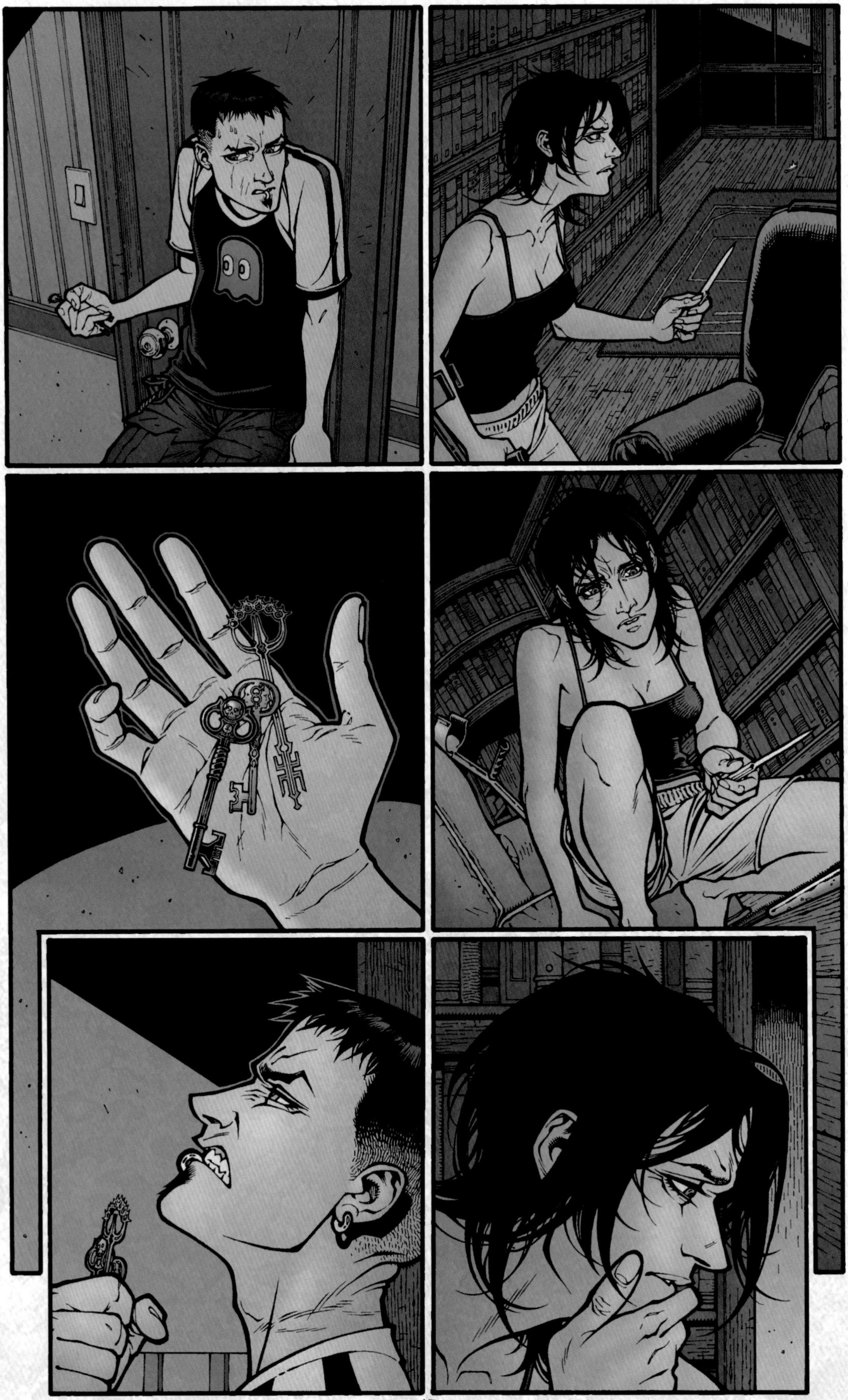

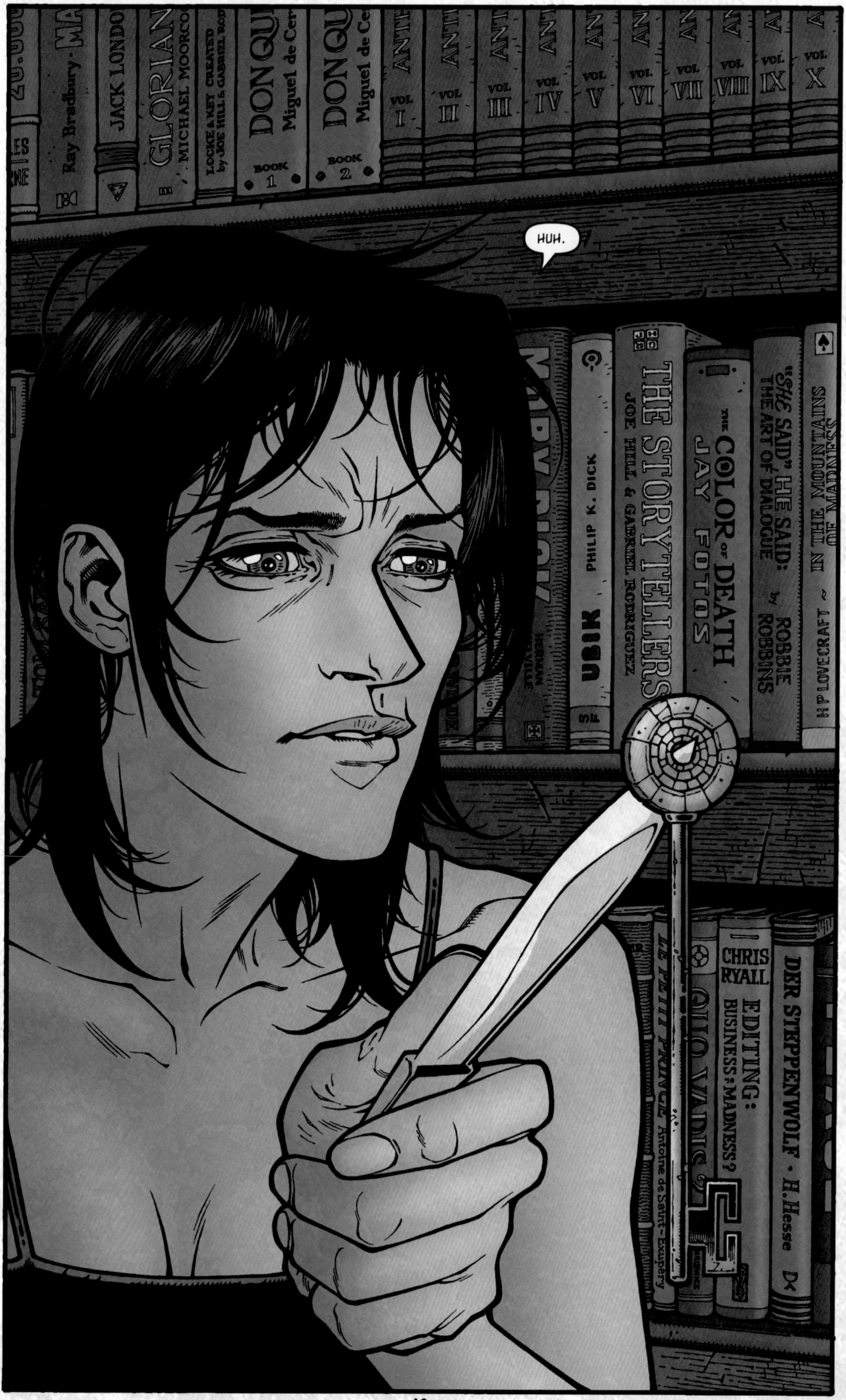

Ray Bradbury
JACK LONDON
GLORIANA
MICHAEL MOORCOCK
LOCKE & KEY CREATED by JOE HILL & GABRIEL RODRIGUEZ
DONQUIXOTE
Miguel de Cervantes
BOOK 1
BOOK 2
VOL I
VOL II
VOL III
VOL IV
VOL V
VOL VI
VOL VII
VOL VIII
VOL IX
VOL X
HUH.
UBIK
PHILIP K. DICK
SF
THE STORYTELLERS
JOE HILL & GABRIEL RODRIGUEZ
THE COLOR OF DEATH
JAY FOTOS
"SHE SAID" HE SAID:
THE ART OF DIALOGUE
by ROBBIE ROBBINS
H.P. LOVECRAFT
IN THE MOUNTAINS OF MADNESS
Antoine de Saint-Exupéry
QUO VADIS
CHRIS RYALL
EDITING: BUSINESS & MADNESS?
DER STEPPENWOLF · H. Hesse

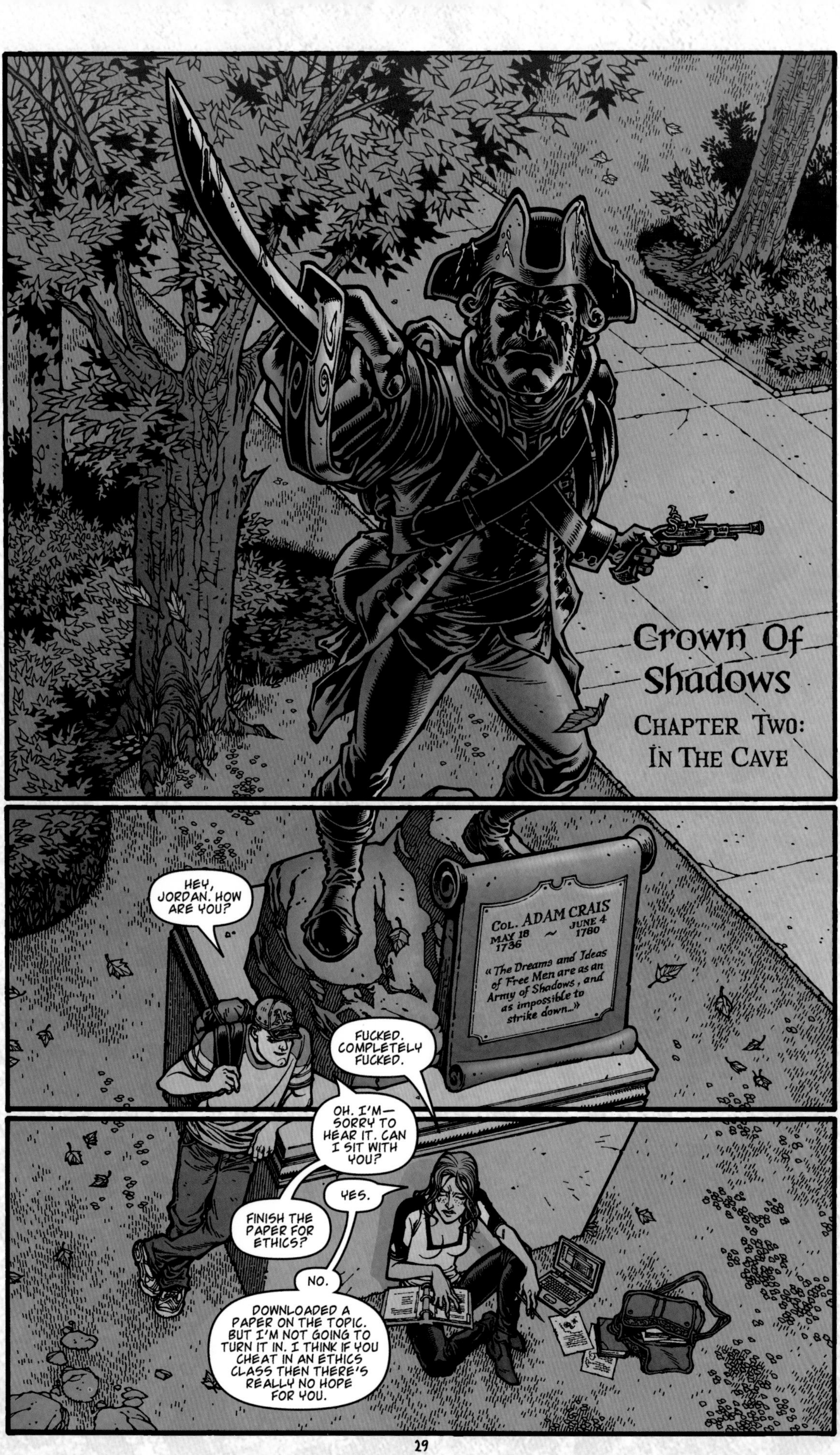

Crown Of Shadows
Chapter Two: In The Cave
Col. ADAM CRAIS
MAY 18 1736 ~ JUNE 4 1780
« The Dreams and Ideas of Free Men are as an Army of Shadows , and as impossible to strike down...»
HEY, JORDAN. HOW ARE YOU?
FUCKED. COMPLETELY FUCKED.
OH. I'M— SORRY TO HEAR IT. CAN I SIT WITH YOU?
YES.
FINISH THE PAPER FOR ETHICS?
NO.
DOWNLOADED A PAPER ON THE TOPIC. BUT I'M NOT GOING TO TURN IT IN. I THINK IF YOU CHEAT IN AN ETHICS CLASS THEN THERE'S REALLY NO HOPE FOR YOU.

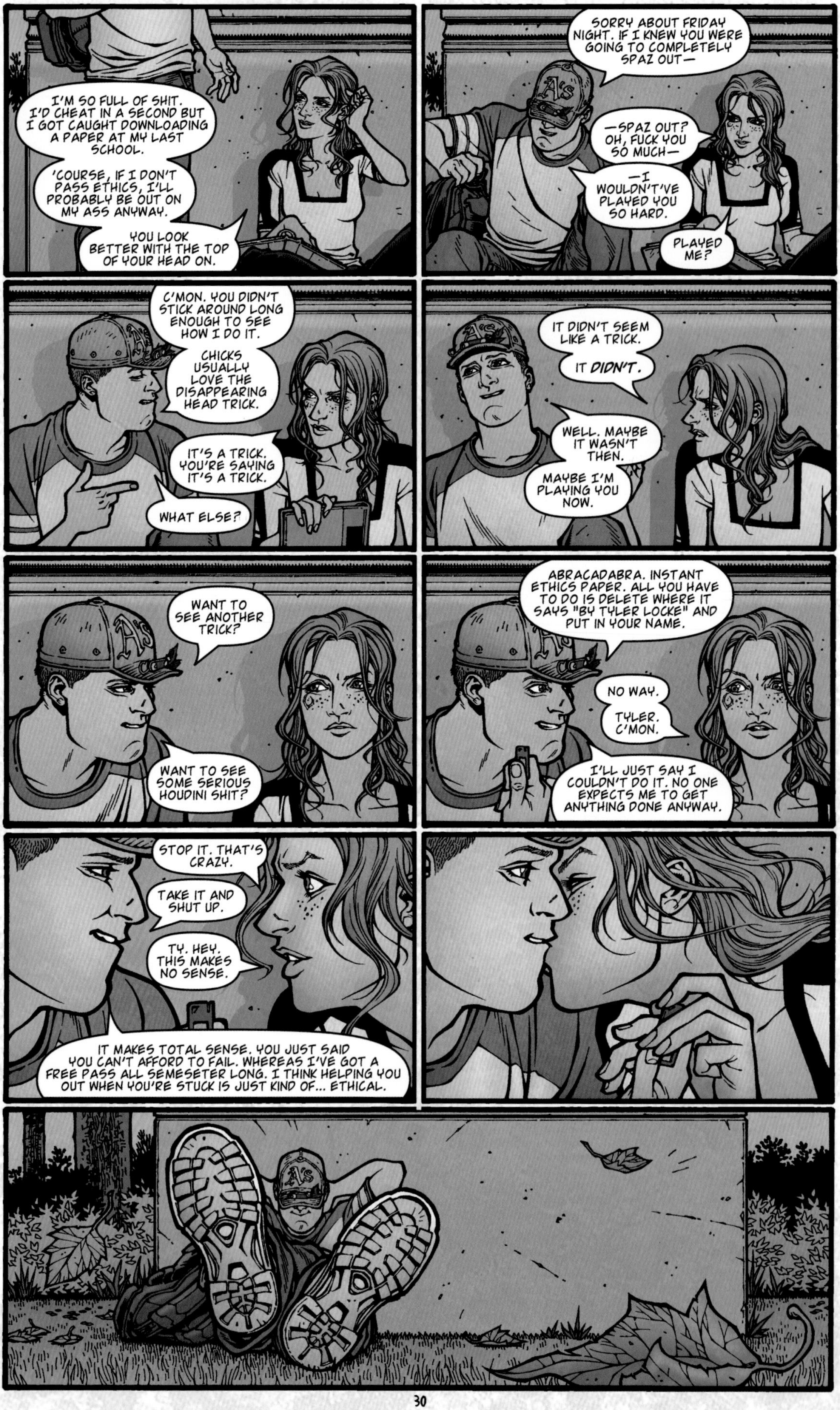
I'M SO FULL OF SHIT. I'D CHEAT IN A SECOND BUT I GOT CAUGHT DOWNLOADING A PAPER AT MY LAST SCHOOL.
'COURSE, IF I DON'T PASS ETHICS, I'LL PROBABLY BE OUT ON MY ASS ANYWAY.
YOU LOOK BETTER WITH THE TOP OF YOUR HEAD ON.
SORRY ABOUT FRIDAY NIGHT. IF I KNEW YOU WERE GOING TO COMPLETELY SPAZ OUT—
—SPAZ OUT? OH, FUCK YOU SO MUCH—
—I WOULDN'T'VE PLAYED YOU SO HARD.
PLAYED ME?
C'MON. YOU DIDN'T STICK AROUND LONG ENOUGH TO SEE HOW I DO IT.
CHICKS USUALLY LOVE THE DISAPPEARING HEAD TRICK.
IT'S A TRICK. YOU'RE SAYING IT'S A TRICK.
WHAT ELSE?
IT DIDN'T SEEM LIKE A TRICK.
IT *DIDN'T*.
WELL. MAYBE IT WASN'T THEN.
MAYBE I'M PLAYING YOU NOW.
WANT TO SEE ANOTHER TRICK?
WANT TO SEE SOME SERIOUS HOUDINI SHIT?
ABRACADABRA. INSTANT ETHICS PAPER. ALL YOU HAVE TO DO IS DELETE WHERE IT SAYS "BY TYLER LOCKE" AND PUT IN YOUR NAME.
NO WAY.
TYLER. C'MON.
I'LL JUST SAY I COULDN'T DO IT. NO ONE EXPECTS ME TO GET ANYTHING DONE ANYWAY.
STOP IT. THAT'S CRAZY.
TAKE IT AND SHUT UP.
TY. HEY. THIS MAKES NO SENSE.
IT MAKES TOTAL SENSE. YOU JUST SAID YOU CAN'T AFFORD TO FAIL. WHEREAS I'VE GOT A FREE PASS ALL SEMESETER LONG. I THINK HELPING YOU OUT WHEN YOU'RE STUCK IS JUST KIND OF... ETHICAL.

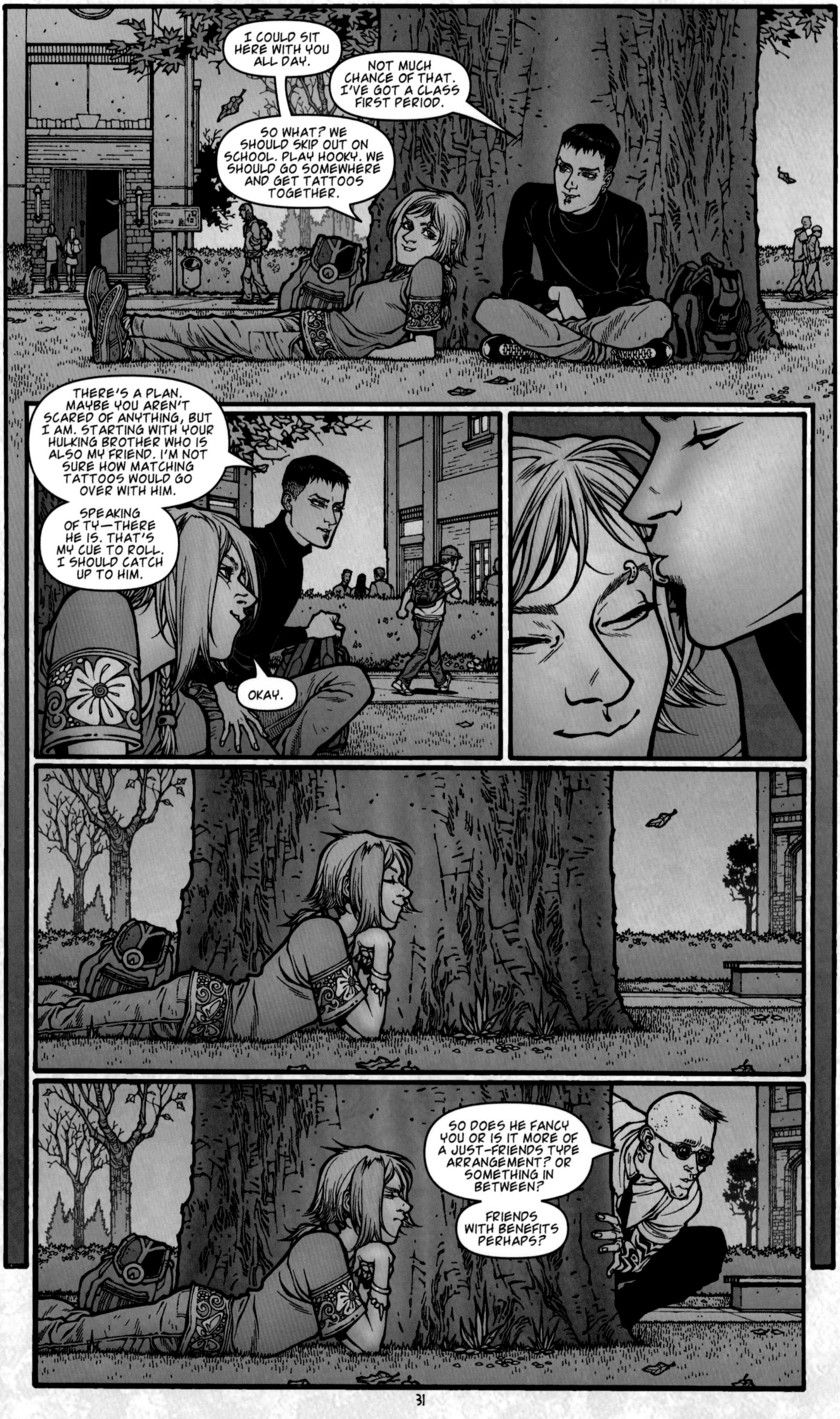
I COULD SIT HERE WITH YOU ALL DAY.
NOT MUCH CHANCE OF THAT. I'VE GOT A CLASS FIRST PERIOD.
SO WHAT? WE SHOULD SKIP OUT ON SCHOOL. PLAY HOOKY. WE SHOULD GO SOMEWHERE AND GET TATTOOS TOGETHER.
THERE'S A PLAN. MAYBE YOU AREN'T SCARED OF ANYTHING, BUT I AM. STARTING WITH YOUR HULKING BROTHER WHO IS ALSO MY FRIEND. I'M NOT SURE HOW MATCHING TATTOOS WOULD GO OVER WITH HIM.
SPEAKING OF TY—THERE HE IS. THAT'S MY CUE TO ROLL. I SHOULD CATCH UP TO HIM.
OKAY.
SO DOES HE FANCY YOU OR IS IT MORE OF A JUST-FRIENDS TYPE ARRANGEMENT? OR SOMETHING IN BETWEEN?
FRIENDS WITH BENEFITS PERHAPS?

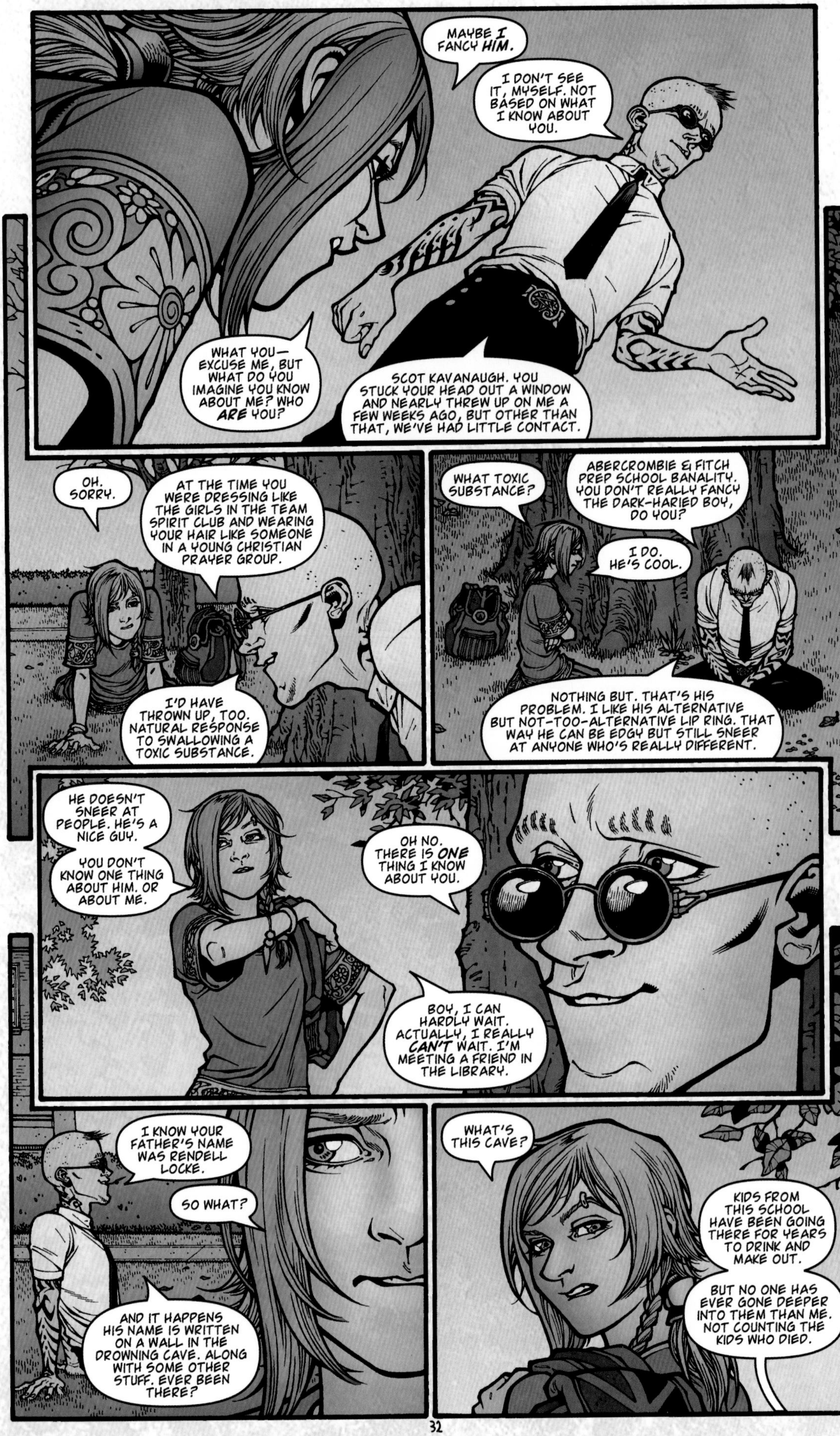
MAYBE I FANCY HIM.
I DON'T SEE IT, MYSELF. NOT BASED ON WHAT I KNOW ABOUT YOU.
WHAT YOU— EXCUSE ME, BUT WHAT DO YOU IMAGINE YOU KNOW ABOUT ME? WHO ARE YOU?
SCOT KAVANAUGH. YOU STUCK YOUR HEAD OUT A WINDOW AND NEARLY THREW UP ON ME A FEW WEEKS AGO, BUT OTHER THAN THAT, WE'VE HAD LITTLE CONTACT.
OH. SORRY.
AT THE TIME YOU WERE DRESSING LIKE THE GIRLS IN THE TEAM SPIRIT CLUB AND WEARING YOUR HAIR LIKE SOMEONE IN A YOUNG CHRISTIAN PRAYER GROUP.
I'D HAVE THROWN UP, TOO. NATURAL RESPONSE TO SWALLOWING A TOXIC SUBSTANCE.
WHAT TOXIC SUBSTANCE?
ABERCROMBIE & FITCH PREP SCHOOL BANALITY. YOU DON'T REALLY FANCY THE DARK-HARIED BOY, DO YOU?
I DO. HE'S COOL.
NOTHING BUT. THAT'S HIS PROBLEM. I LIKE HIS ALTERNATIVE BUT NOT-TOO-ALTERNATIVE LIP RING. THAT WAY HE CAN BE EDGY BUT STILL SNEER AT ANYONE WHO'S REALLY DIFFERENT.
HE DOESN'T SNEER AT PEOPLE. HE'S A NICE GUY.
YOU DON'T KNOW ONE THING ABOUT HIM. OR ABOUT ME.
OH NO. THERE IS ONE THING I KNOW ABOUT YOU.
BOY, I CAN HARDLY WAIT. ACTUALLY, I REALLY CAN'T WAIT. I'M MEETING A FRIEND IN THE LIBRARY.
I KNOW YOUR FATHER'S NAME WAS RENDELL LOCKE.
SO WHAT?
AND IT HAPPENS HIS NAME IS WRITTEN ON A WALL IN THE DROWNING CAVE. ALONG WITH SOME OTHER STUFF. EVER BEEN THERE?
WHAT'S THIS CAVE?
KIDS FROM THIS SCHOOL HAVE BEEN GOING THERE FOR YEARS TO DRINK AND MAKE OUT.
BUT NO ONE HAS EVER GONE DEEPER INTO THEM THAN ME. NOT COUNTING THE KIDS WHO DIED.

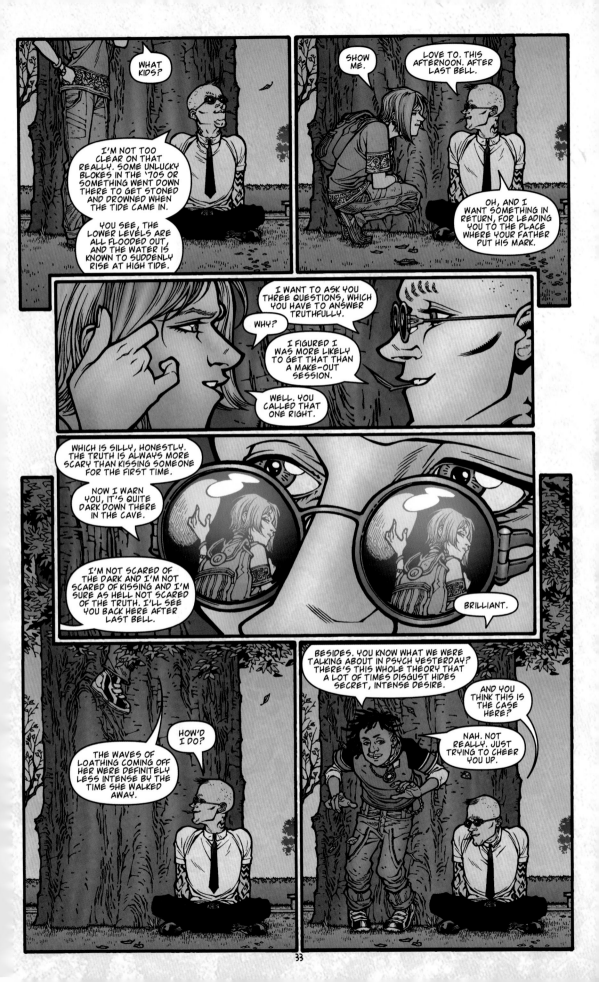

WHAT KIDS?

I'M NOT TOO CLEAR ON THAT REALLY. SOME UNLUCKY BLOKES IN THE '70S OR SOMETHING WENT DOWN THERE TO GET STONED AND DROWNED WHEN THE TIDE CAME IN.

YOU SEE, THE LOWER LEVELS ARE ALL FLOODED OUT, AND THE WATER IS KNOWN TO SUDDENLY RISE AT HIGH TIDE.

SHOW ME.

LOVE TO. THIS AFTERNOON. AFTER LAST BELL.

OH, AND I WANT SOMETHING IN RETURN, FOR LEADING YOU TO THE PLACE WHERE YOUR FATHER PUT HIS MARK.

I WANT TO ASK YOU THREE QUESTIONS, WHICH YOU HAVE TO ANSWER TRUTHFULLY.

WHY?

I FIGURED I WAS MORE LIKELY TO GET THAT THAN A MAKE-OUT SESSION.

WELL. YOU CALLED THAT ONE RIGHT.

WHICH IS SILLY, HONESTLY. THE TRUTH IS ALWAYS MORE SCARY THAN KISSING SOMEONE FOR THE FIRST TIME.

NOW I WARN YOU, IT'S QUITE DARK DOWN THERE IN THE CAVE.

I'M NOT SCARED OF THE DARK AND I'M NOT SCARED OF KISSING AND I'M SURE AS HELL NOT SCARED OF THE TRUTH. I'LL SEE YOU BACK HERE AFTER LAST BELL.

BRILLIANT.

HOW'D I DO?

THE WAVES OF LOATHING COMING OFF HER WERE DEFINITELY LESS INTENSE BY THE TIME SHE WALKED AWAY.

BESIDES. YOU KNOW WHAT WE WERE TALKING ABOUT IN PSYCH YESTERDAY? THERE'S THIS WHOLE THEORY THAT A LOT OF TIMES DISGUST HIDES SECRET, INTENSE DESIRE.

AND YOU THINK THIS IS THE CASE HERE?

NAH. NOT REALLY. JUST TRYING TO CHEER YOU UP.

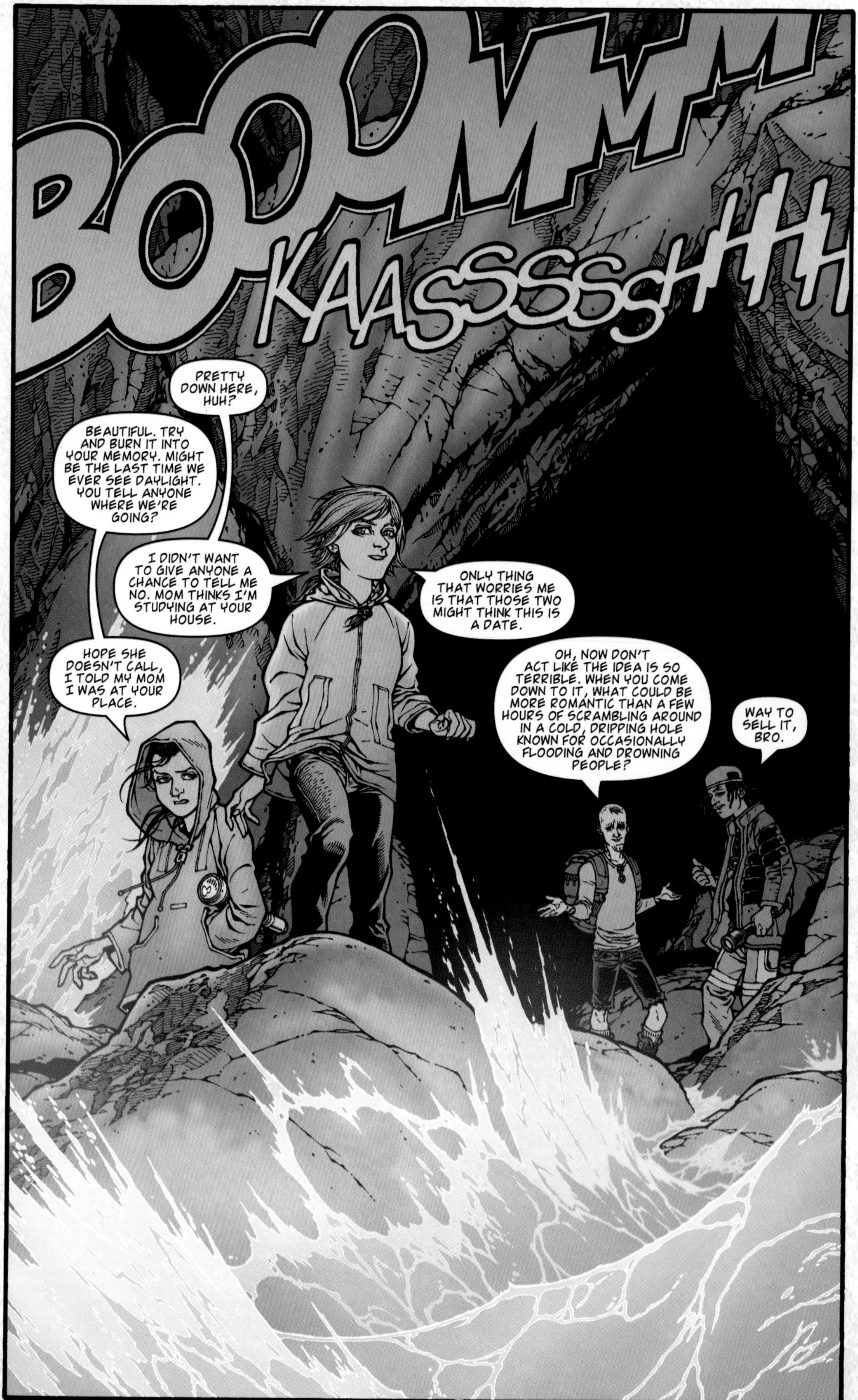
BOOMMM
KAASSSSSHHH
PRETTY DOWN HERE, HUH?
BEAUTIFUL. TRY AND BURN IT INTO YOUR MEMORY. MIGHT BE THE LAST TIME WE EVER SEE DAYLIGHT. YOU TELL ANYONE WHERE WE'RE GOING?
I DIDN'T WANT TO GIVE ANYONE A CHANCE TO TELL ME NO. MOM THINKS I'M STUDYING AT YOUR HOUSE.
HOPE SHE DOESN'T CALL, I TOLD MY MOM I WAS AT YOUR PLACE.
ONLY THING THAT WORRIES ME IS THAT THOSE TWO MIGHT THINK THIS IS A DATE.
OH, NOW DON'T ACT LIKE THE IDEA IS SO TERRIBLE. WHEN YOU COME DOWN TO IT, WHAT COULD BE MORE ROMANTIC THAN A FEW HOURS OF SCRAMBLING AROUND IN A COLD, DRIPPING HOLE KNOWN FOR OCCASIONALLY FLOODING AND DROWNING PEOPLE?
WAY TO SELL IT, BRO.

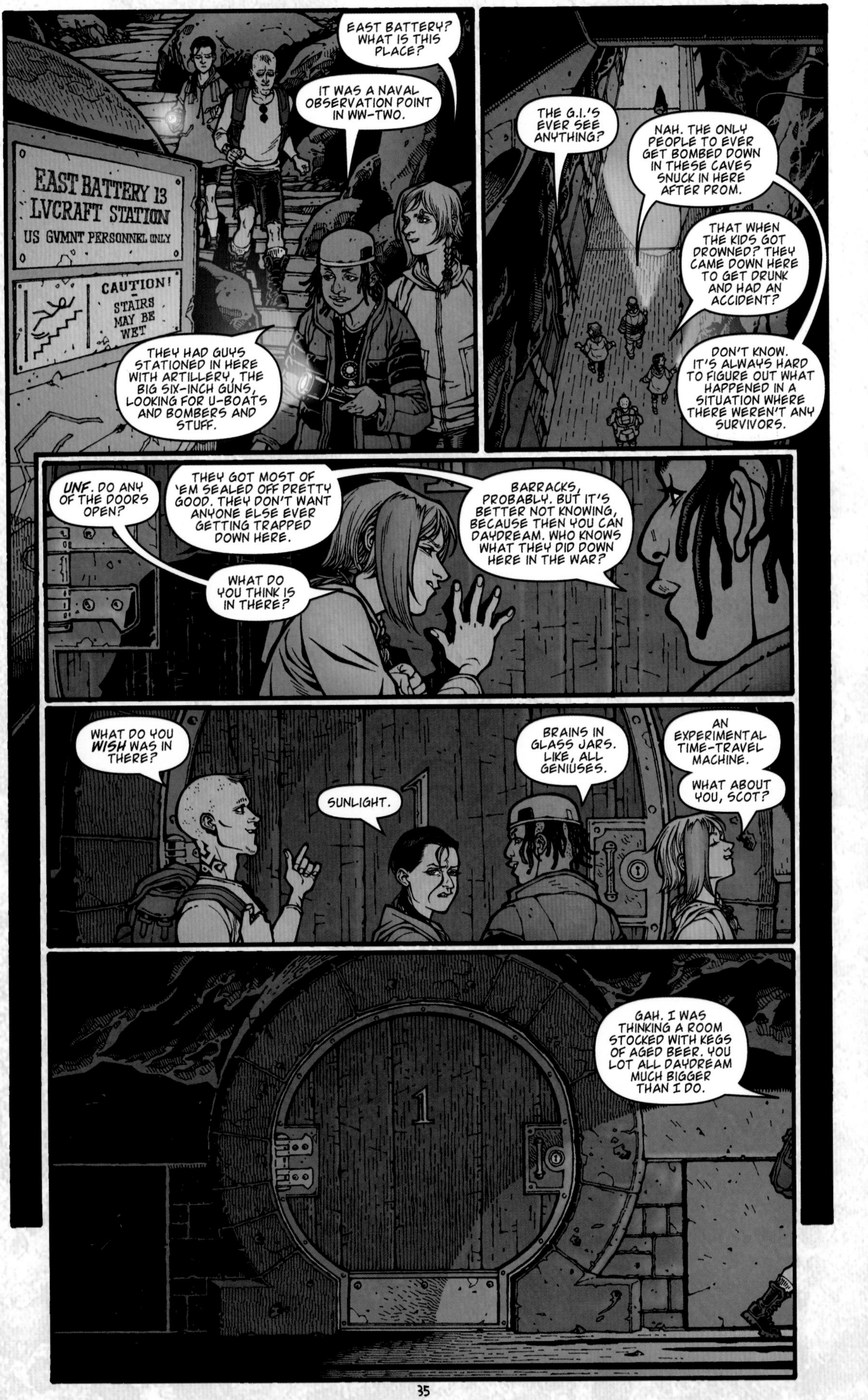
EAST BATTERY? WHAT IS THIS PLACE?
IT WAS A NAVAL OBSERVATION POINT IN WW-TWO.
EAST BATTERY 13 LVCRAFT STATION US GVMNT PERSONNEL ONLY
CAUTION! STAIRS MAY BE WET
THEY HAD GUYS STATIONED IN HERE WITH ARTILLERY, THE BIG SIX-INCH GUNS, LOOKING FOR U-BOATS AND BOMBERS AND STUFF.
THE G.I.'S EVER SEE ANYTHING?
NAH. THE ONLY PEOPLE TO EVER GET BOMBED DOWN IN THESE CAVES SNUCK IN HERE AFTER PROM.
THAT WHEN THE KIDS GOT DROWNED? THEY CAME DOWN HERE TO GET DRUNK AND HAD AN ACCIDENT?
DON'T KNOW. IT'S ALWAYS HARD TO FIGURE OUT WHAT HAPPENED IN A SITUATION WHERE THERE WEREN'T ANY SURVIVORS.
UNF. DO ANY OF THE DOORS OPEN?
THEY GOT MOST OF 'EM SEALED OFF PRETTY GOOD. THEY DON'T WANT ANYONE ELSE EVER GETTING TRAPPED DOWN HERE.
WHAT DO YOU THINK IS IN THERE?
BARRACKS, PROBABLY. BUT IT'S BETTER NOT KNOWING, BECAUSE THEN YOU CAN DAYDREAM. WHO KNOWS WHAT THEY DID DOWN HERE IN THE WAR?
WHAT DO YOU WISH WAS IN THERE?
SUNLIGHT.
BRAINS IN GLASS JARS. LIKE, ALL GENIUSES.
AN EXPERIMENTAL TIME-TRAVEL MACHINE.
WHAT ABOUT YOU, SCOT?
GAH. I WAS THINKING A ROOM STOCKED WITH KEGS OF AGED BEER. YOU LOT ALL DAYDREAM MUCH BIGGER THAN I DO.

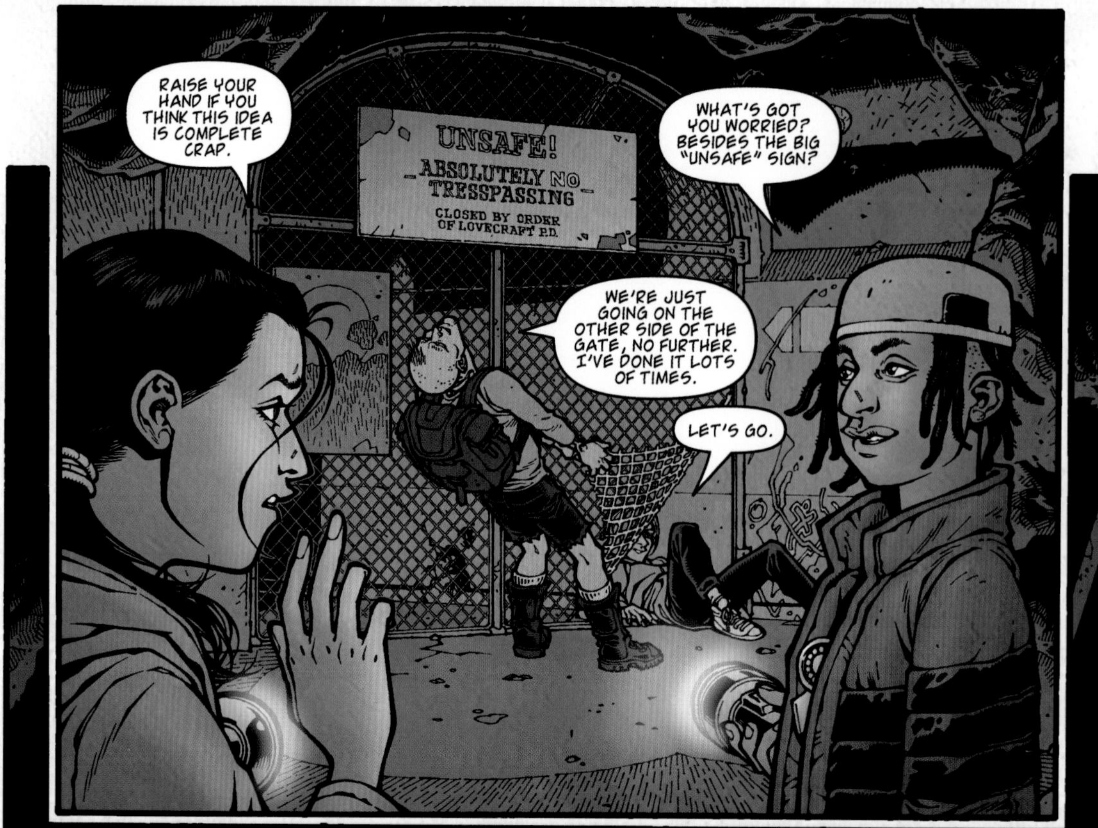
RAISE YOUR HAND IF YOU THINK THIS IDEA IS COMPLETE CRAP.
UNSAFE!
ABSOLUTELY NO TRESSPASSING
CLOSED BY ORDER OF LOVECRAFT P.D.
WHAT'S GOT YOU WORRIED? BESIDES THE BIG "UNSAFE" SIGN?
WE'RE JUST GOING ON THE OTHER SIDE OF THE GATE, NO FURTHER. I'VE DONE IT LOTS OF TIMES.
LET'S GO.

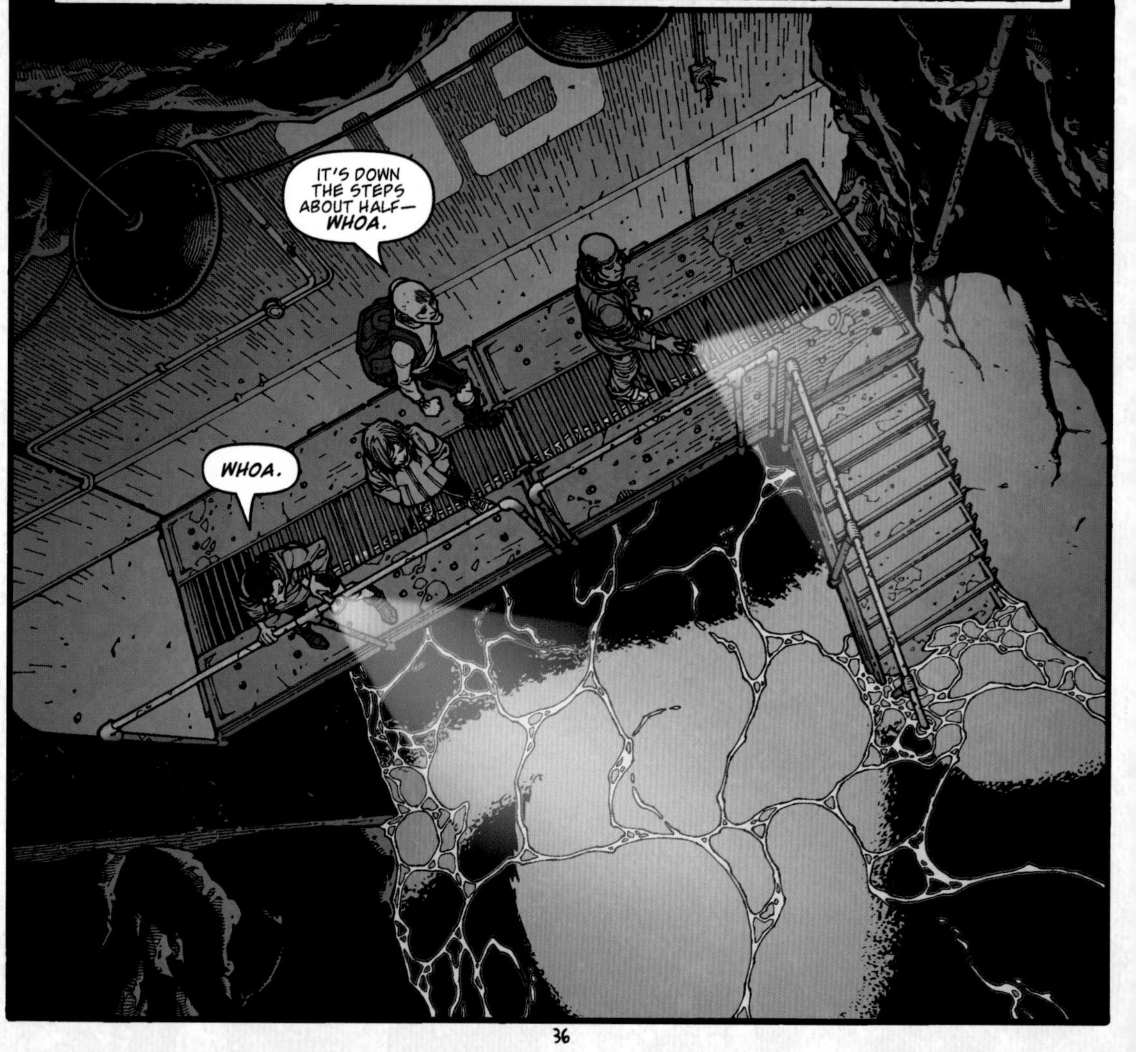
IT'S DOWN THE STEPS ABOUT HALF— WHOA.
WHOA.

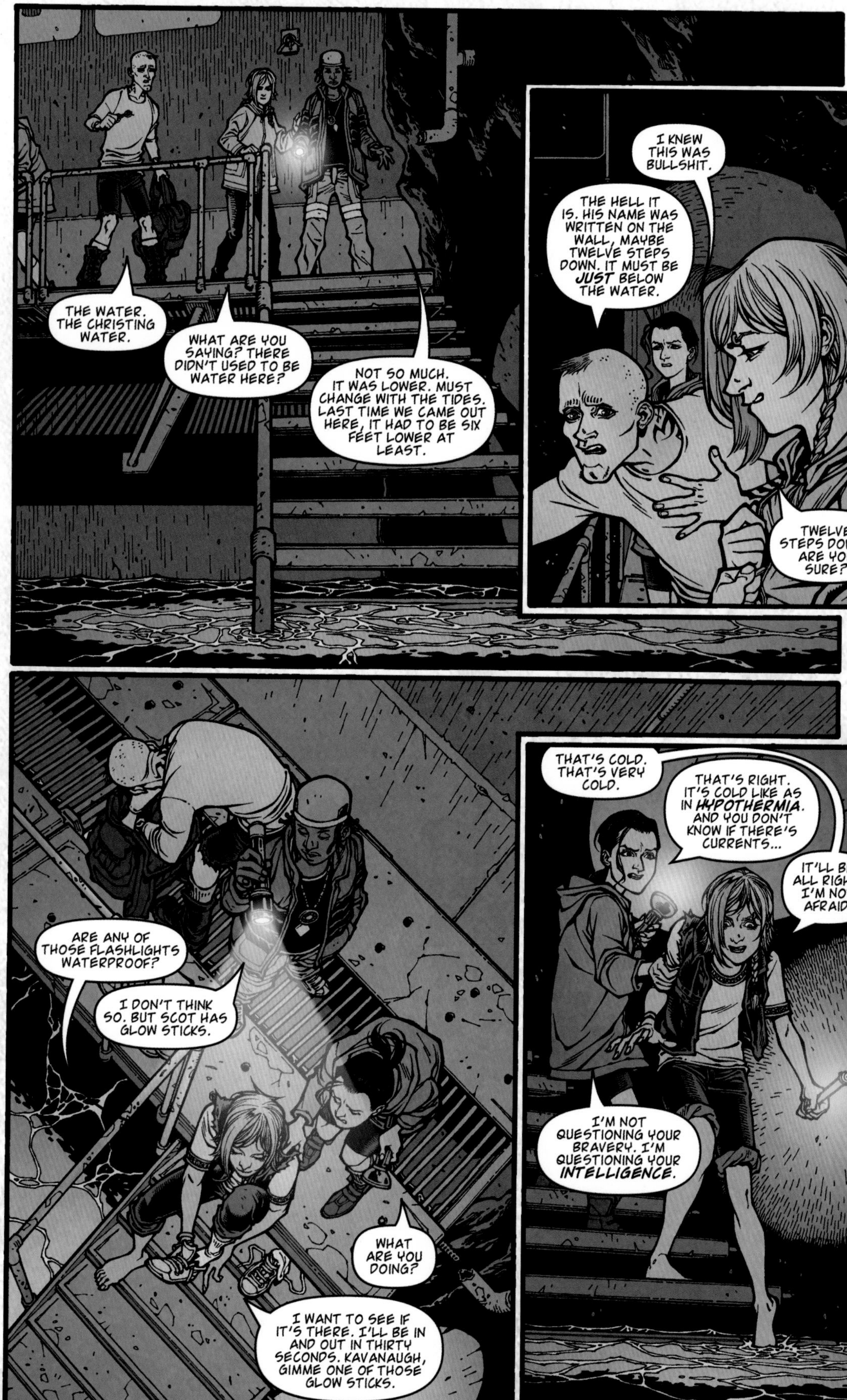
THE WATER. THE CHRISTING WATER.
WHAT ARE YOU SAYING? THERE DIDN'T USED TO BE WATER HERE?
NOT SO MUCH. IT WAS LOWER. MUST CHANGE WITH THE TIDES. LAST TIME WE CAME OUT HERE, IT HAD TO BE SIX FEET LOWER AT LEAST.
I KNEW THIS WAS BULLSHIT.
THE HELL IT IS. HIS NAME WAS WRITTEN ON THE WALL, MAYBE TWELVE STEPS DOWN. IT MUST BE JUST BELOW THE WATER.
TWELVE STEPS DOWN? ARE YOU SURE?
ARE ANY OF THOSE FLASHLIGHTS WATERPROOF?
I DON'T THINK SO. BUT SCOT HAS GLOW STICKS.
WHAT ARE YOU DOING?
I WANT TO SEE IF IT'S THERE. I'LL BE IN AND OUT IN THIRTY SECONDS. KAVANAUGH, GIMME ONE OF THOSE GLOW STICKS.
THAT'S COLD. THAT'S VERY COLD.
THAT'S RIGHT. IT'S COLD LIKE AS IN HYPOTHERMIA. AND YOU DON'T KNOW IF THERE'S CURRENTS...
IT'LL BE ALL RIGHT. I'M NOT AFRAID.
I'M NOT QUESTIONING YOUR BRAVERY. I'M QUESTIONING YOUR INTELLIGENCE.

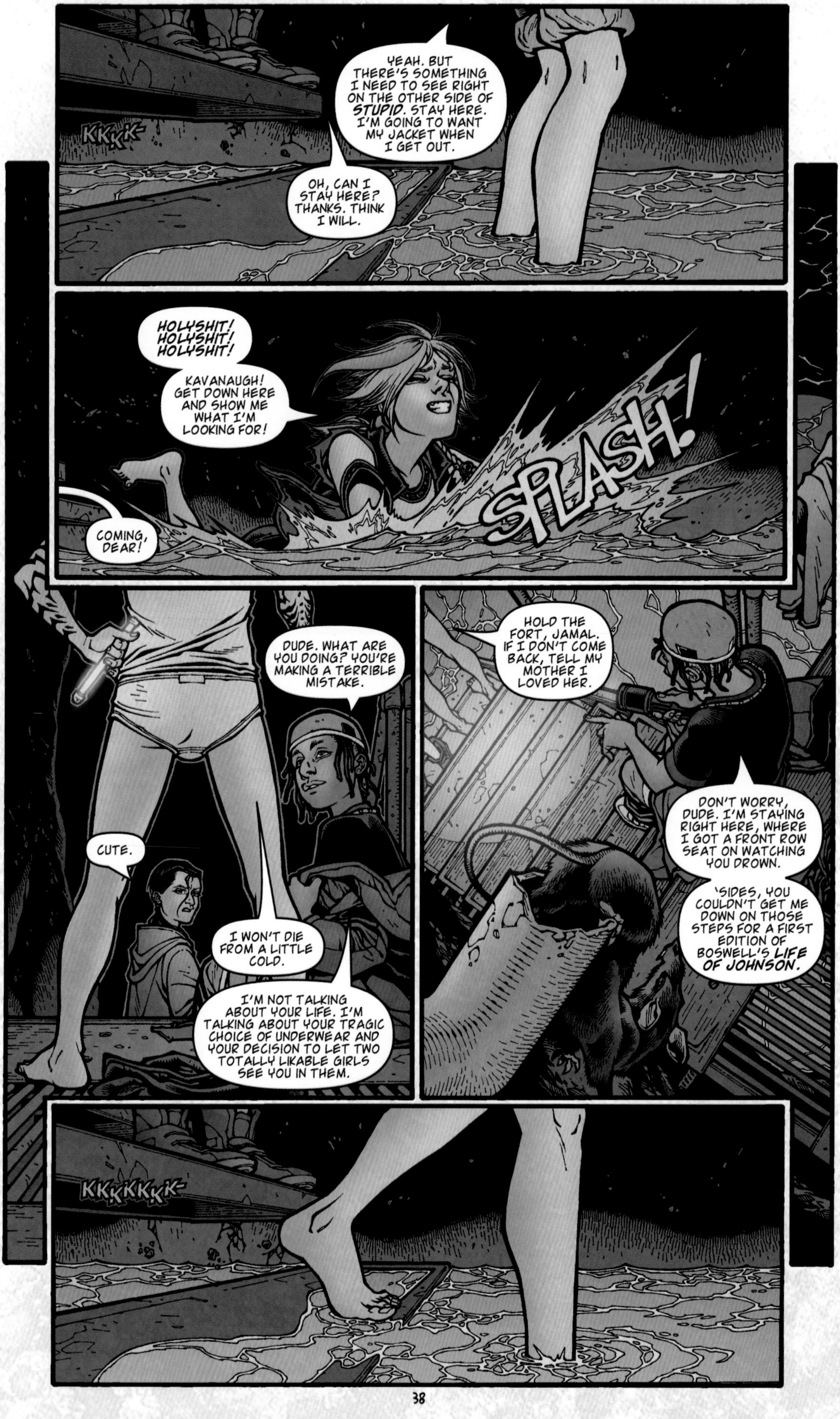
YEAH. BUT THERE'S SOMETHING I NEED TO SEE RIGHT ON THE OTHER SIDE OF STUPID. STAY HERE. I'M GOING TO WANT MY JACKET WHEN I GET OUT.
KKKK-
OH, CAN I STAY HERE? THANKS. THINK I WILL.
HOLYSHIT! HOLYSHIT! HOLYSHIT!
KAVANAUGH! GET DOWN HERE AND SHOW ME WHAT I'M LOOKING FOR!
SPLASH!
COMING, DEAR!
DUDE. WHAT ARE YOU DOING? YOU'RE MAKING A TERRIBLE MISTAKE.
CUTE.
I WON'T DIE FROM A LITTLE COLD.
I'M NOT TALKING ABOUT YOUR LIFE. I'M TALKING ABOUT YOUR TRAGIC CHOICE OF UNDERWEAR AND YOUR DECISION TO LET TWO TOTALLY LIKABLE GIRLS SEE YOU IN THEM.
HOLD THE FORT, JAMAL. IF I DON'T COME BACK, TELL MY MOTHER I LOVED HER.
DON'T WORRY, DUDE. I'M STAYING RIGHT HERE, WHERE I GOT A FRONT ROW SEAT ON WATCHING YOU DROWN.
'SIDES, YOU COULDN'T GET ME DOWN ON THOSE STEPS FOR A FIRST EDITION OF BOSWELL'S LIFE OF JOHNSON.
KKKKKKK-

GLUSSH!
WHEN I SAID GET DOWN HERE, I DIDN'T MEAN YOU HAD TO COME IN THE WATER. YOU COULD'VE JUST POINTED WHERE TO G-GO FROM THE STEPS.
I WAS SEIZED BY A SUDDEN FANTASY OF MYSELF AS LEONARDO DICAPRIO.
BESIDES, IT ISN'T SO BAD. LIKE BRIGHTON BEACH IN JULY. I THINK WE'RE CLOSE TO WHERE IT'S WRITTEN.
OKAY. I'M GOING DOWN FOR A LOOK.
I KNOW WHAT I'LL DO. I'LL SHOW HER HOW BIG MY BALLS ARE, JUMP RIGHT IN.
BLOODY BRILLIANT, KAVANAUGH. WHAT GOOD IS IT HAVING BALLS THE SIZE OF LORRIES IF YOU FREEZE THEM OFF?

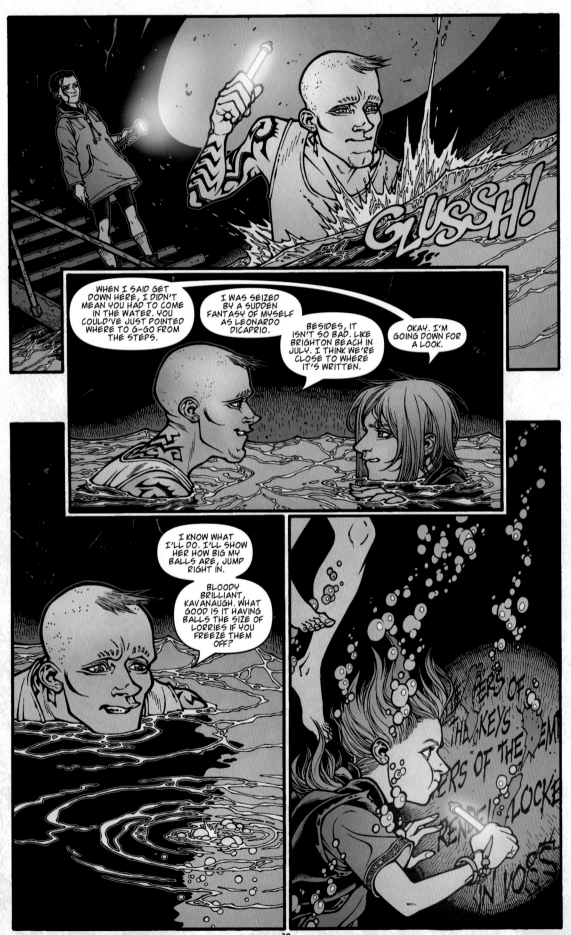

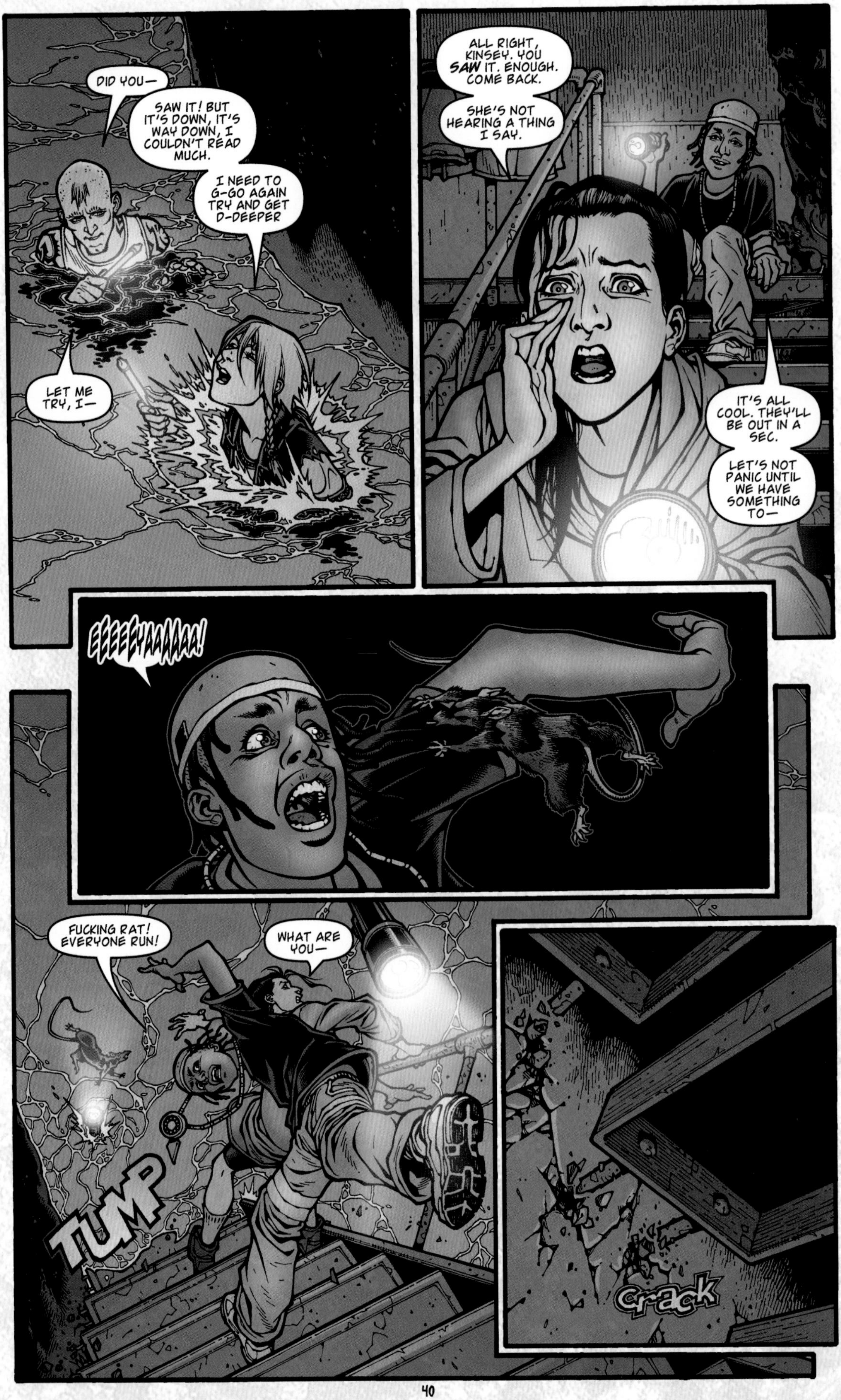
DID YOU—
SAW IT! BUT IT'S DOWN, IT'S WAY DOWN, I COULDN'T READ MUCH.
I NEED TO G-GO AGAIN TRY AND GET D-DEEPER
LET ME TRY, I—
ALL RIGHT, KINSEY. YOU SAW IT. ENOUGH. COME BACK.
SHE'S NOT HEARING A THING I SAY.
IT'S ALL COOL. THEY'LL BE OUT IN A SEC.
LET'S NOT PANIC UNTIL WE HAVE SOMETHING TO—
EEEEEYAAAAAA!
FUCKING RAT! EVERYONE RUN!
WHAT ARE YOU—
TUMP
CRACK

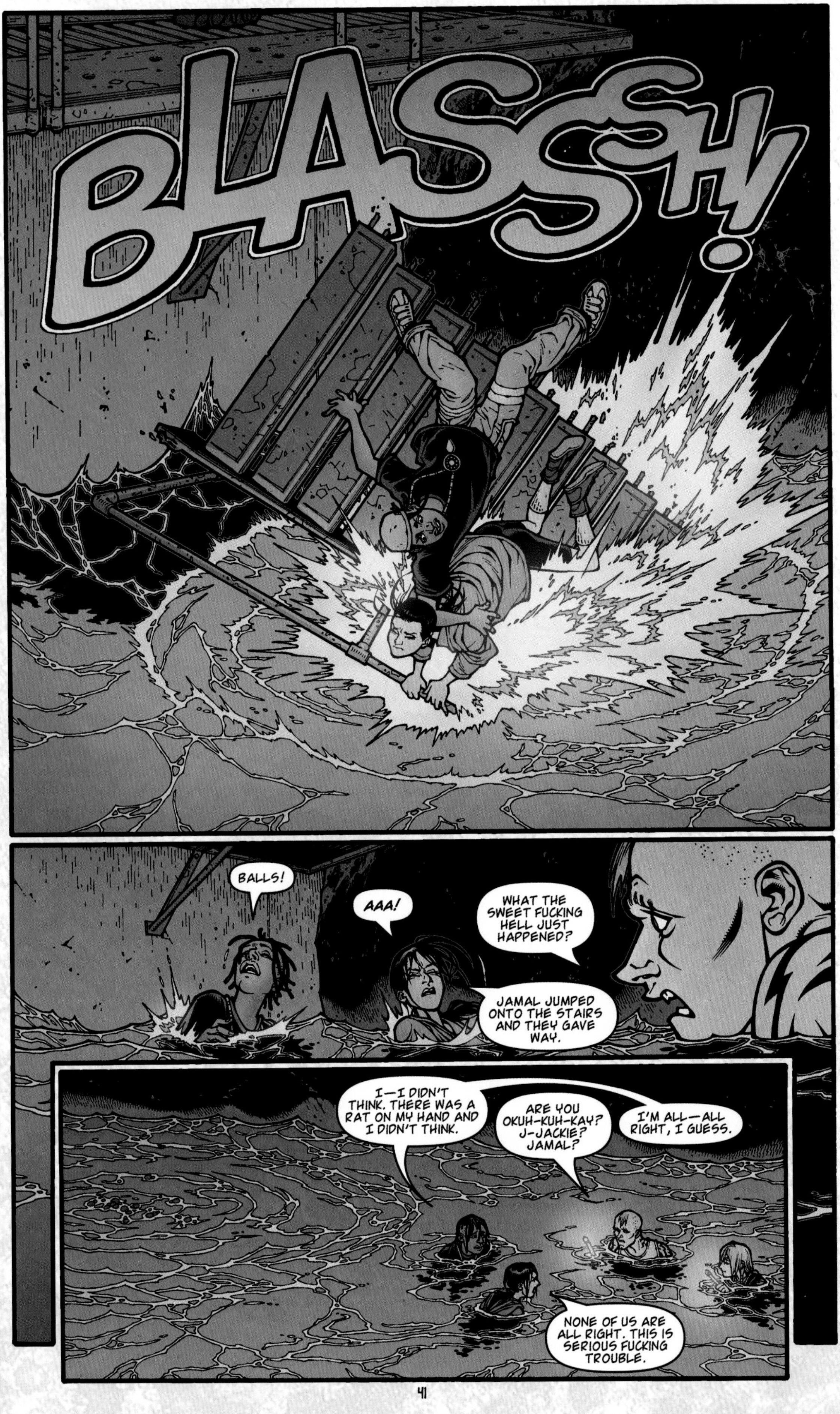
BLASSSH!
BALLS!
AAA!
WHAT THE SWEET FUCKING HELL JUST HAPPENED?
JAMAL JUMPED ONTO THE STAIRS AND THEY GAVE WAY.
I—I DIDN'T THINK. THERE WAS A RAT ON MY HAND AND I DIDN'T THINK.
ARE YOU OKUH-KUH-KAY? J-JACKIE? JAMAL?
I'M ALL—ALL RIGHT, I GUESS.
NONE OF US ARE ALL RIGHT. THIS IS SERIOUS FUCKING TROUBLE.

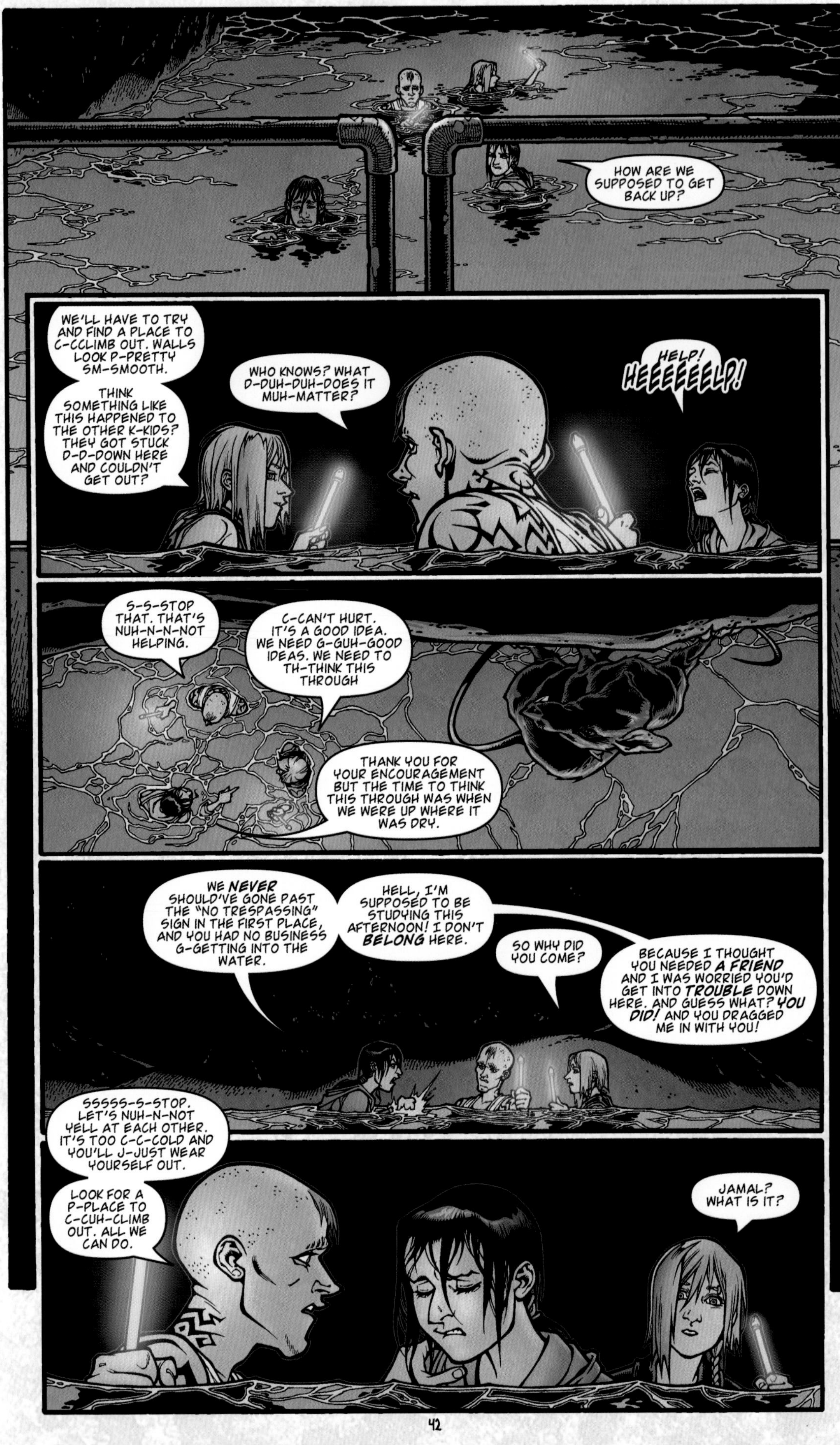
HOW ARE WE SUPPOSED TO GET BACK UP?
WE'LL HAVE TO TRY AND FIND A PLACE TO C-CCLIMB OUT. WALLS LOOK P-PRETTY SM-SMOOTH.
THINK SOMETHING LIKE THIS HAPPENED TO THE OTHER K-KIDS? THEY GOT STUCK D-D-DOWN HERE AND COULDN'T GET OUT?
WHO KNOWS? WHAT D-DUH-DUH-DOES IT MUH-MATTER?
HELP! HEEEEEELP!
S-S-STOP THAT. THAT'S NUH-N-N-NOT HELPING.
C-CAN'T HURT. IT'S A GOOD IDEA. WE NEED G-GUH-GOOD IDEAS. WE NEED TO TH-THINK THIS THROUGH
THANK YOU FOR YOUR ENCOURAGEMENT BUT THE TIME TO THINK THIS THROUGH WAS WHEN WE WERE UP WHERE IT WAS DRY.
WE NEVER SHOULD'VE GONE PAST THE "NO TRESPASSING" SIGN IN THE FIRST PLACE, AND YOU HAD NO BUSINESS G-GETTING INTO THE WATER.
HELL, I'M SUPPOSED TO BE STUDYING THIS AFTERNOON! I DON'T BELONG HERE.
SO WHY DID YOU COME?
BECAUSE I THOUGHT YOU NEEDED A FRIEND AND I WAS WORRIED YOU'D GET INTO TROUBLE DOWN HERE. AND GUESS WHAT? YOU DID! AND YOU DRAGGED ME IN WITH YOU!
SSSSS-S-STOP. LET'S NUH-N-NOT YELL AT EACH OTHER. IT'S TOO C-C-COLD AND YOU'LL J-JUST WEAR YOURSELF OUT.
LOOK FOR A P-PLACE TO C-CUH-CLIMB OUT. ALL WE CAN DO.
JAMAL? WHAT IS IT?

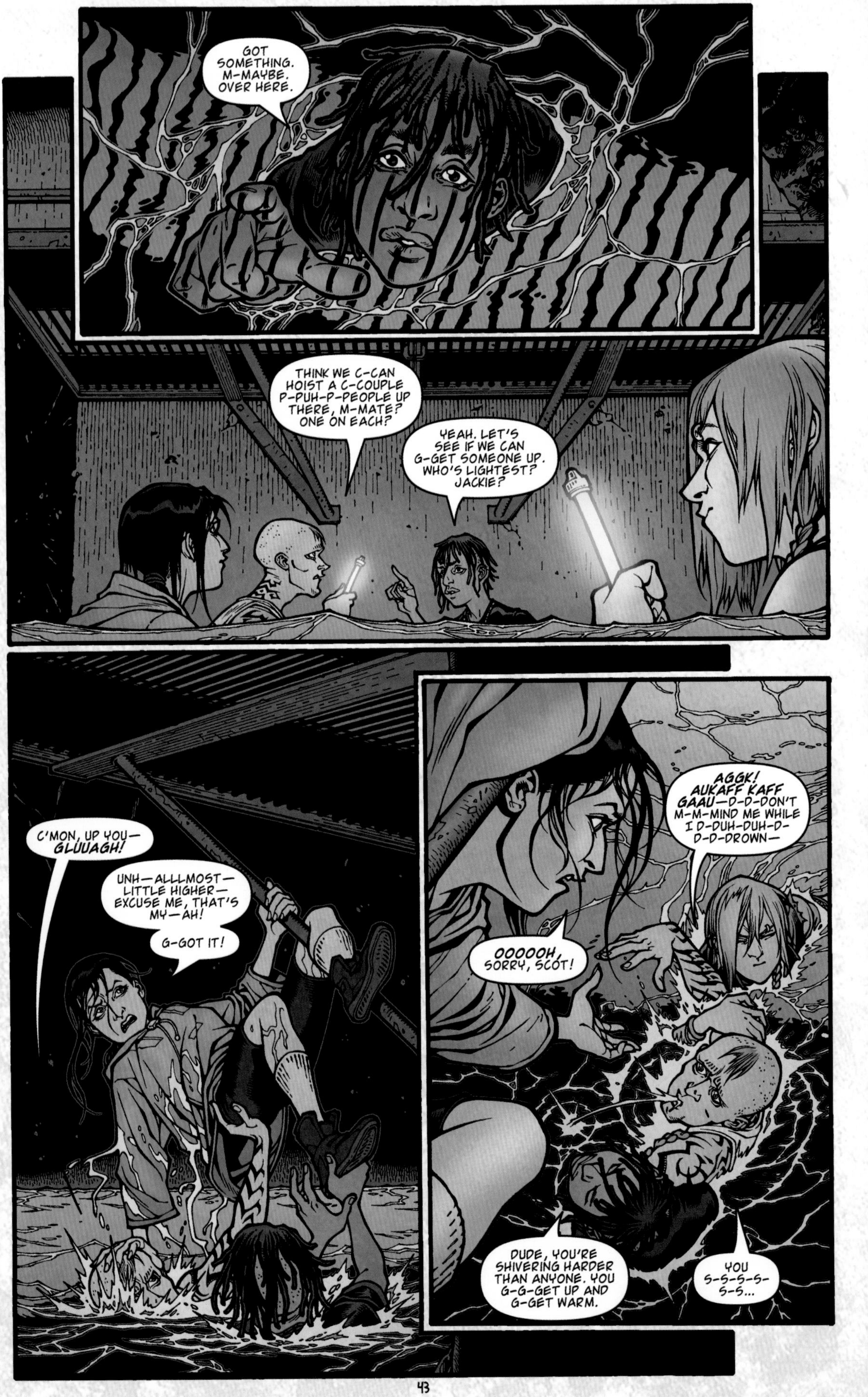
GOT SOMETHING. M-MAYBE. OVER HERE.
THINK WE C-CAN HOIST A C-COUPLE P-PUH-P-PEOPLE UP THERE, M-MATE? ONE ON EACH?
YEAH. LET'S SEE IF WE CAN G-GET SOMEONE UP. WHO'S LIGHTEST? JACKIE?
C'MON, UP YOU— GLUUAGH!
UNH—ALLLMOST—LITTLE HIGHER—EXCUSE ME, THAT'S MY—AH!
G-GOT IT!
AGGK! AUKAFF KAFF GAAU—D-D-DON'T M-M-MIND ME WHILE I D-DUH-DUH-D-D-D-DROWN—
OOOOOH, SORRY, SCOT!
DUDE, YOU'RE SHIVERING HARDER THAN ANYONE. YOU G-G-GET UP AND G-GET WARM.
YOU S-S-S-S-S-S...

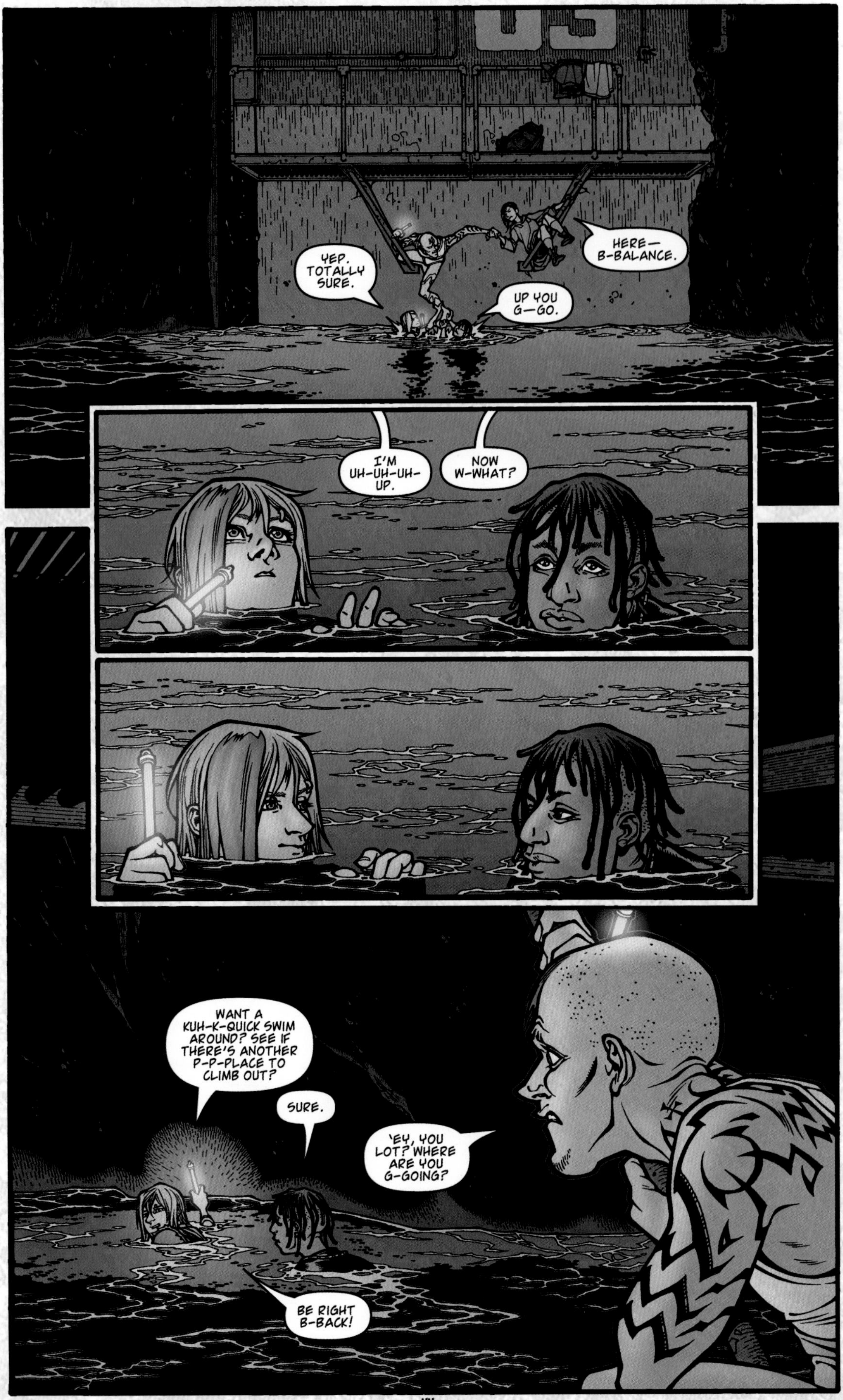
HERE—
B-BALANCE.
YEP.
TOTALLY
SURE.
UP YOU
G—GO.
I'M
UH-UH-UH-
UP.
NOW
W-WHAT?
WANT A
KUH-K-QUICK SWIM
AROUND? SEE IF
THERE'S ANOTHER
P-P-PLACE TO
CLIMB OUT?
SURE.
'EY, YOU
LOT? WHERE
ARE YOU
G-GOING?
BE RIGHT
B-BACK!

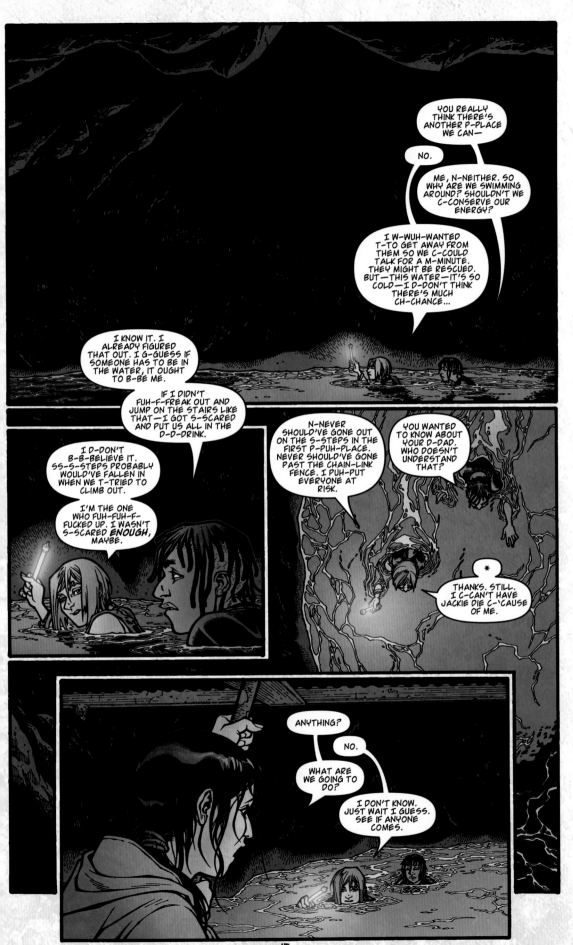

YOU REALLY THINK THERE'S ANOTHER P-PLACE WE CAN—

NO.

ME, N-NEITHER. SO WHY ARE WE SWIMMING AROUND? SHOULDN'T WE C-CONSERVE OUR ENERGY?

I W-WUH-WANTED T-TO GET AWAY FROM THEM SO WE C-COULD TALK FOR A M-MINUTE. THEY MIGHT BE RESCUED. BUT—THIS WATER—IT'S SO COLD—I D-DON'T THINK THERE'S MUCH CH-CHANCE...

I KNOW IT. I ALREADY FIGURED THAT OUT. I G-GUESS IF SOMEONE HAS TO BE IN THE WATER, IT OUGHT TO B-BE ME.

IF I DIDN'T FUH-F-FREAK OUT AND JUMP ON THE STAIRS LIKE THAT—I GOT S-SCARED AND PUT US ALL IN THE D-D-DRINK.

I D-DON'T B-B-BELIEVE IT. SS-S-STEPS PROBABLY WOULD'VE FALLEN IN WHEN WE T-TRIED TO CLIMB OUT.

I'M THE ONE WHO FUH-FUH-F-FUCKED UP. I WASN'T S-SCARED ENOUGH, MAYBE.

N-NEVER SHOULD'VE GONE OUT ON THE S-STEPS IN THE FIRST P-PUH-PLACE. NEVER SHOULD'VE GONE PAST THE CHAIN-LINK FENCE. I PUH-PUT EVERYONE AT RISK.

YOU WANTED TO KNOW ABOUT YOUR D-DAD. WHO DOESN'T UNDERSTAND THAT?

*

THANKS. STILL. I C-CAN'T HAVE JACKIE DIE C-'CAUSE OF ME.

ANYTHING?

NO.

WHAT ARE WE GOING TO DO?

I DON'T KNOW. JUST WAIT I GUESS. SEE IF ANYONE COMES.

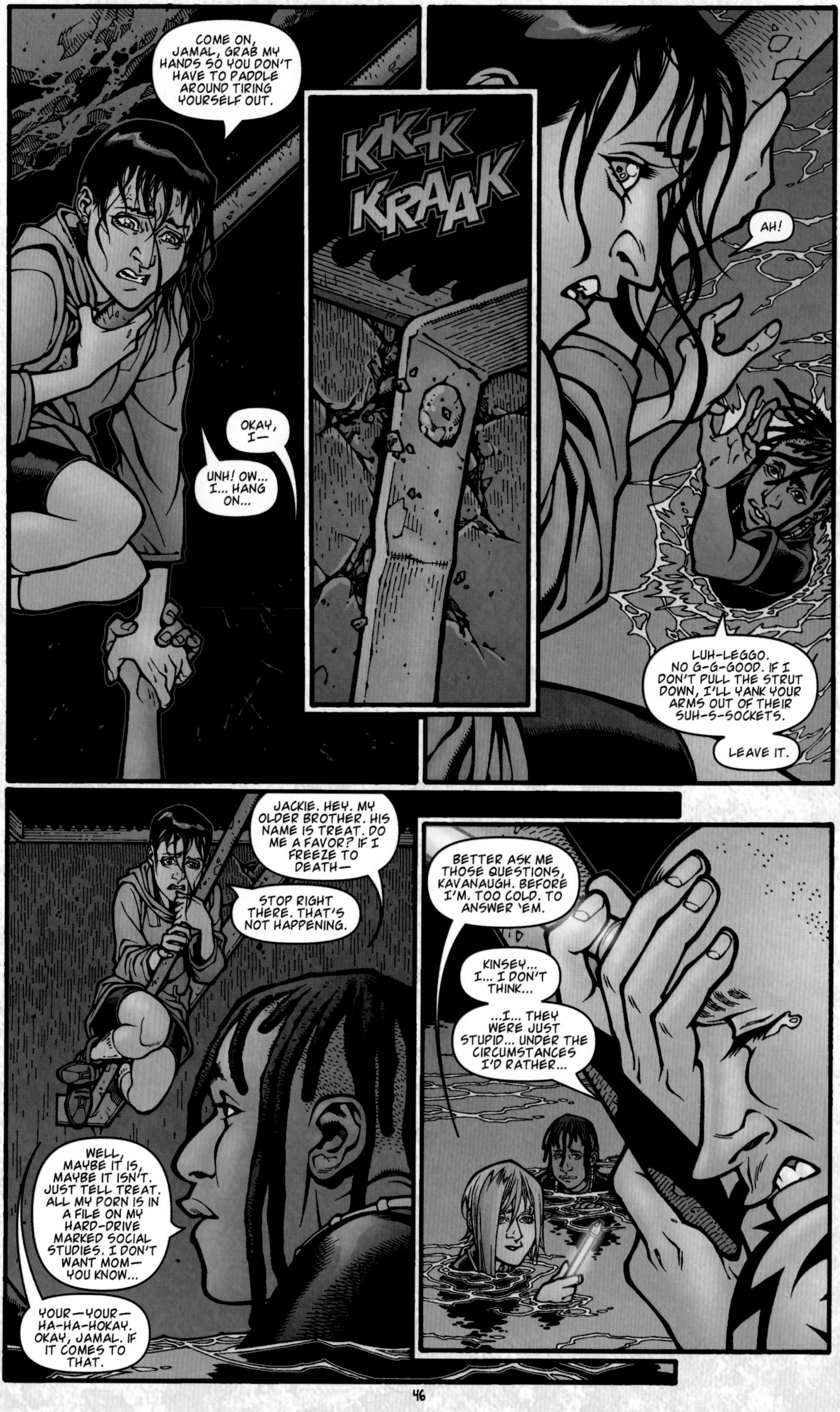
COME ON, JAMAL, GRAB MY HANDS SO YOU DON'T HAVE TO PADDLE AROUND TIRING YOURSELF OUT.
OKAY, I—
UNH! OW... I... HANG ON...
KK-K KRAAK
AH!
LUH-LEGGO. NO G-G-GOOD. IF I DON'T PULL THE STRUT DOWN, I'LL YANK YOUR ARMS OUT OF THEIR SUH-S-SOCKETS.
LEAVE IT.
JACKIE. HEY. MY OLDER BROTHER. HIS NAME IS TREAT. DO ME A FAVOR? IF I FREEZE TO DEATH—
STOP RIGHT THERE. THAT'S NOT HAPPENING.
WELL, MAYBE IT IS, MAYBE IT ISN'T. JUST TELL TREAT. ALL MY PORN IS IN A FILE ON MY HARD-DRIVE MARKED SOCIAL STUDIES. I DON'T WANT MOM— YOU KNOW...
YOUR—YOUR— HA-HA-HOKAY. OKAY, JAMAL. IF IT COMES TO THAT.
BETTER ASK ME THOSE QUESTIONS, KAVANAUGH. BEFORE I'M. TOO COLD. TO ANSWER 'EM.
KINSEY... I... DON'T THINK...
...I... THEY WERE JUST STUPID... UNDER THE CIRCUMSTANCES I'D RATHER...

F-FUCK HIM. I'LL TAKE HIS QUESTIONS IF HE DOESN'T WANT 'EM.

WHAT'S THE BEST THING YOU REMEMBER ABOUT YOUR D-DAD?

HIM READING TO ME. WHEN I WAS LITTLE. WE HAD A B-BLANKET, A SPECIAL READING BLANKET. IT SMELLED LIKE HIM. LIKE—FALL. AUTUMN. FUH-F-FOOTBALL. WHATEVER. LIKE THINGS ENDING.

MY D-DAD AND I BUILT A BARN. FOR HIS BROTHER. IT WAS LIKE THE BEST SUMMER EVER. I'D B-BUILD THAT BARN IN MY SLEEP SOMETIMES, ME AND HIM AND MY OLDER BROTHER.

IS YOUR DAD—?

HE GOT IT IN AFGHANISTAN.

I'M SO. SO. SORRY.

HEY. FEELING IS MUTUAL.

N-NEXT?

WELL, FIRST OF ALL... I LIKE YOU AND EVERYTHING... I MEAN, I DON'T *LIKE* YOU, LIKE YOU, BUT YOU KNOW...

SCOT IS THE ONE WITH THE C-CRUSH AND I IN NO WAY, SHAPE, OR FORM W-WANT TO STEP ON HIS T-TOES...

RIGHT. BROS B-BEFORE HOS. GOT IT. GUH-G-GET TO THE P-POINT BEFORE I DROWN PLEASE.

I'M GOING TO BE SEVENTEEN IN FOUR MONTHS AND MOST GUYS MY AGE HAVE G-GIRLFRIENDS—

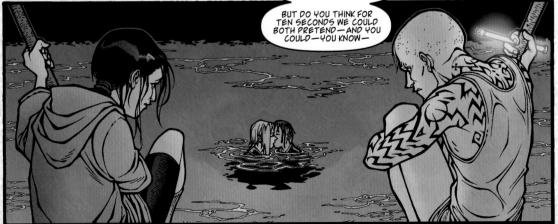

BUT DO YOU THINK FOR TEN SECONDS WE COULD BOTH PRETEND—AND YOU COULD—YOU KNOW—

I SAW THAT, MATE. WE'LL HAVE WORDS ABOUT THIS ONE LATER.
YEAH. LATER.
WAS IT—
NICE ONE. TOTAL MOVIE STAR KISS.
HEY. I JUST NUH-NOTICED. YOUR VOICE ISN'T SH-SHAKING SO HARD.
YOURS, NEITHER. YOU THINK. THAT'S. A GOOD THING?
PROBABLY NOT.
MAYBE YOU BETTER... GET TO... THAT LAST... QUESTION...
ARE YOU SCARED—TO DIE?
NO. NOT REALLY.
WHY?
THAT'S FOUR QUESTIONS. SORRY, JAMAL.
STAY UP. KINSEY. STAY UP.
WE CAN'T JUST SIT HERE AND WATCH THEM DROWN.
I SAW A TV SHOW WHERE SOMEONE MADE A LIFE PRESERVER OUT OF A PAIR OF JEANS.
YOU'RE WEARING BVDS AND I'M IN SHORTS. WE NEED TO GET THEM UP OUT OF THE WATER. UP HERE. SOMEHOW.
ARE YOU DAFT, WOMAN? THERE'S NO ROOM AND THESE STRUTS CAN BARELY HOLD OUR WEIGHT. WE'D PULL THEM DOWN AND THE CATWALK, TOO.
PULL THEM DOWN.

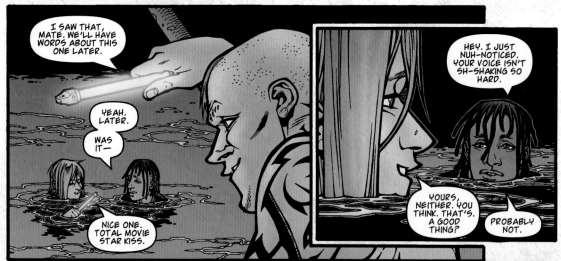

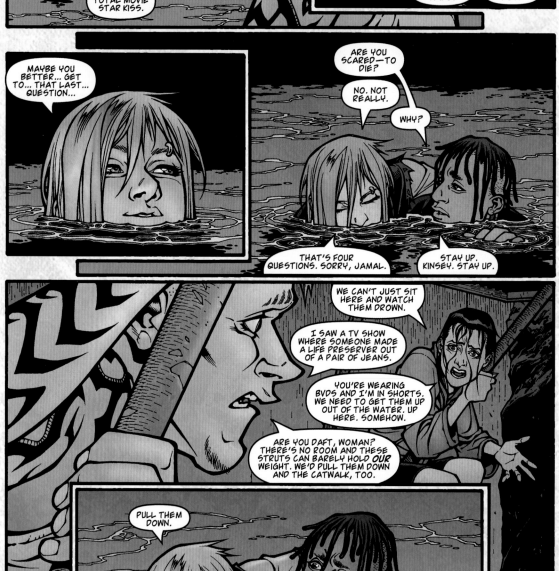

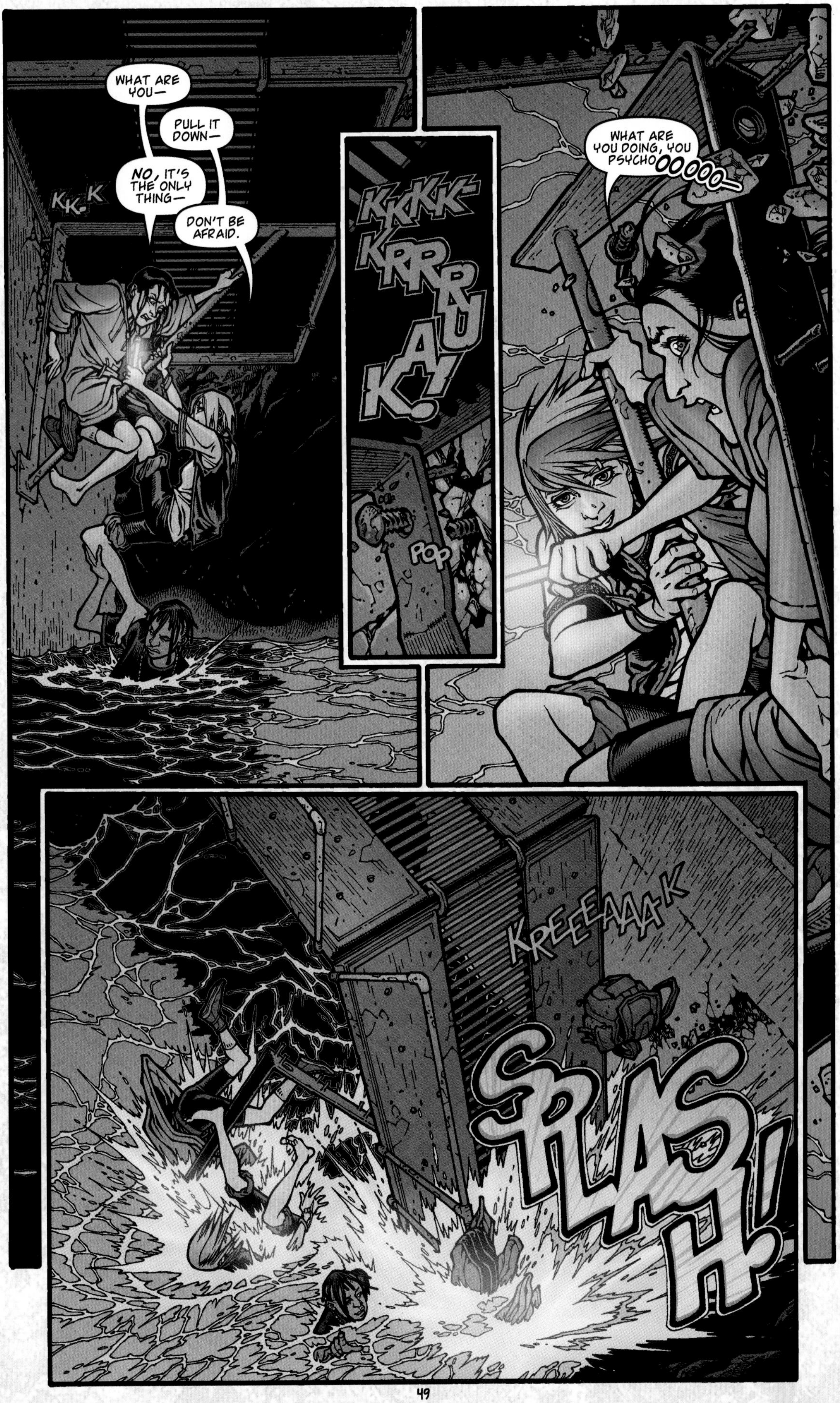

WHAT ARE YOU—
PULL IT DOWN—
NO, IT'S THE ONLY THING—
DON'T BE AFRAID.
KK-K
KKKK-KRRRAUK!
POP
WHAT ARE YOU DOING, YOU PSYCHOOOOOO—
KREEEAAAK
SPLASH!

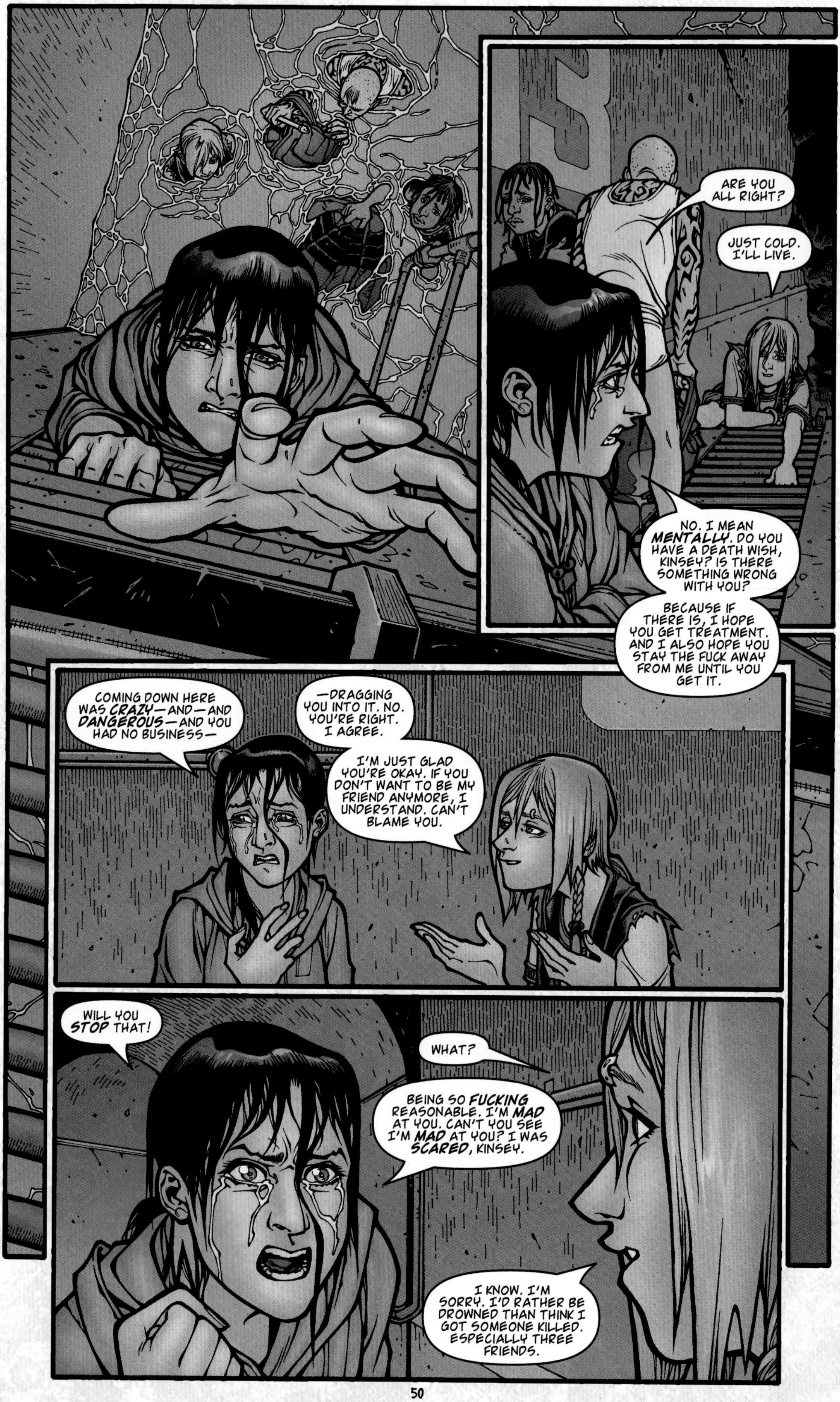
ARE YOU ALL RIGHT?
JUST COLD. I'LL LIVE.
NO. I MEAN MENTALLY. DO YOU HAVE A DEATH WISH, KINSEY? IS THERE SOMETHING WRONG WITH YOU?
BECAUSE IF THERE IS, I HOPE YOU GET TREATMENT. AND I ALSO HOPE YOU STAY THE FUCK AWAY FROM ME UNTIL YOU GET IT.
COMING DOWN HERE WAS CRAZY—AND—AND DANGEROUS—AND YOU HAD NO BUSINESS—
—DRAGGING YOU INTO IT. NO. YOU'RE RIGHT. I AGREE.
I'M JUST GLAD YOU'RE OKAY. IF YOU DON'T WANT TO BE MY FRIEND ANYMORE, I UNDERSTAND. CAN'T BLAME YOU.
WILL YOU STOP THAT!
WHAT?
BEING SO FUCKING REASONABLE. I'M MAD AT YOU. CAN'T YOU SEE I'M MAD AT YOU? I WAS SCARED, KINSEY.
I KNOW. I'M SORRY. I'D RATHER BE DROWNED THAN THINK I GOT SOMEONE KILLED. ESPECIALLY THREE FRIENDS.

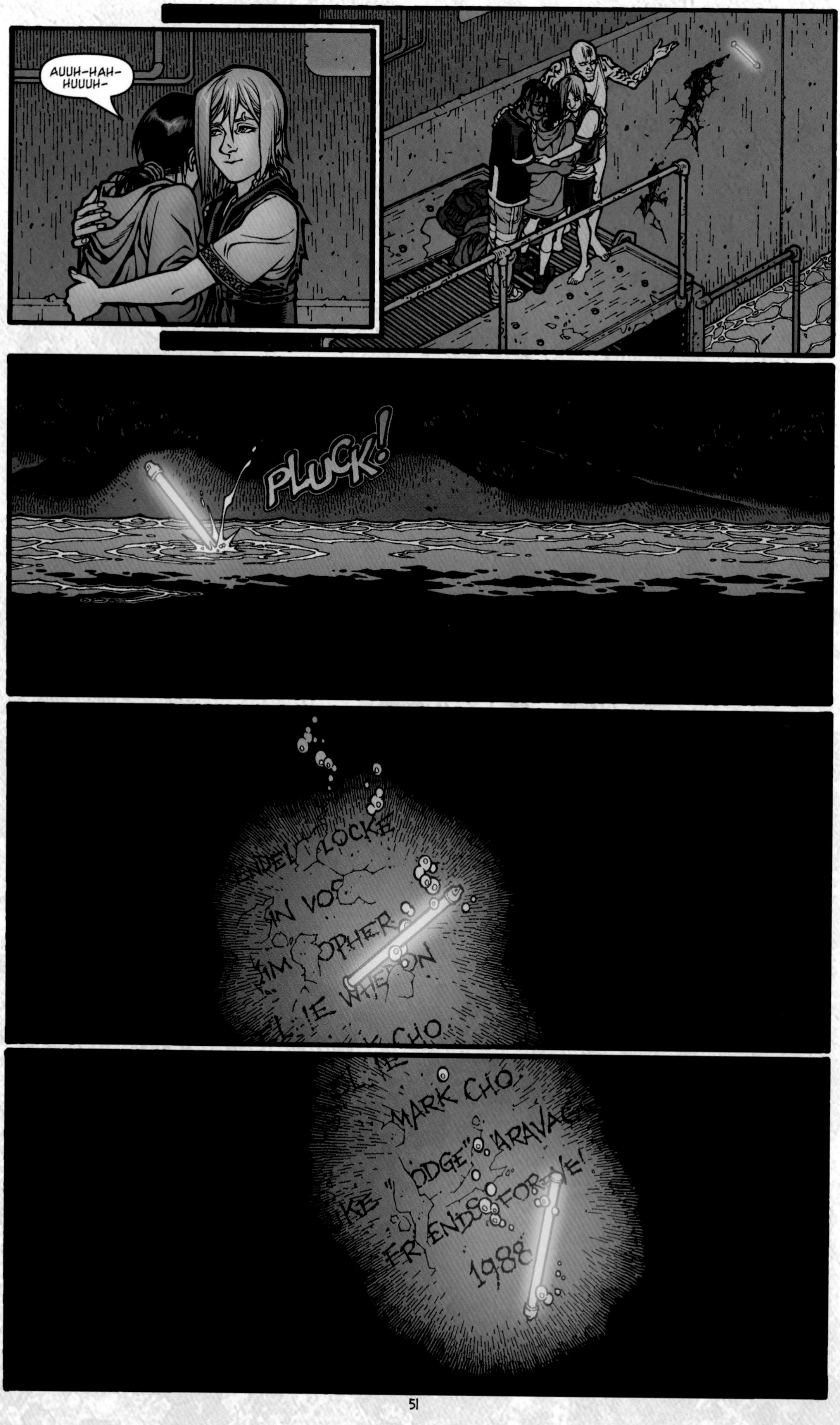
AUUH-HAH-HUUUH-
PLUCK!
LOCKE
CHO
MARK CHO
1988

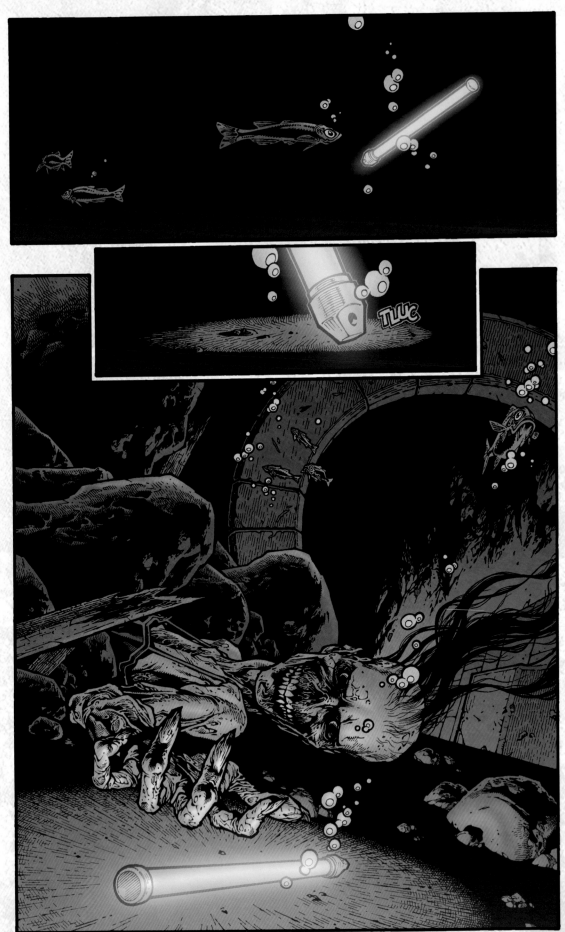

TLUC

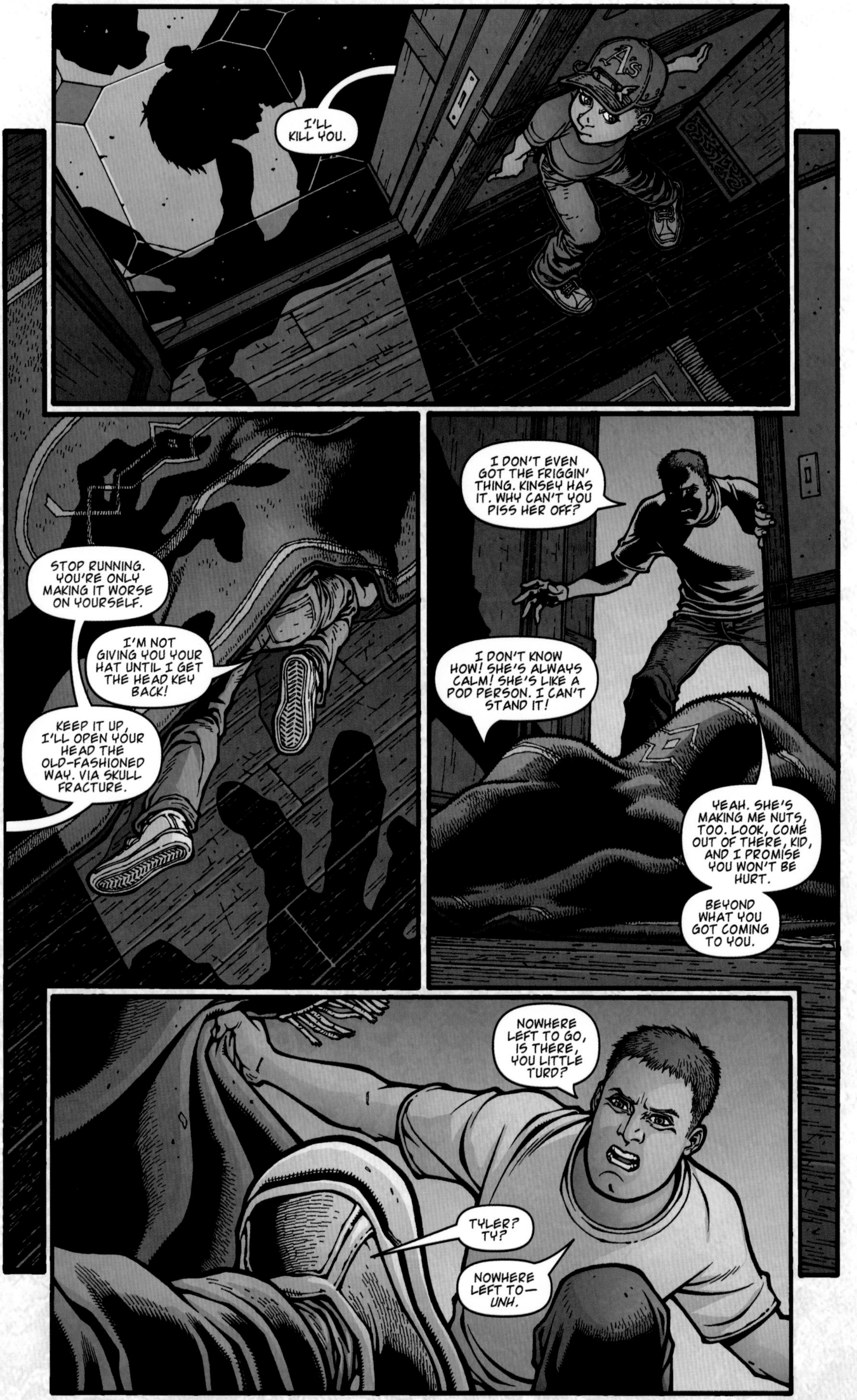
I'LL KILL YOU.
STOP RUNNING. YOU'RE ONLY MAKING IT WORSE ON YOURSELF.
I'M NOT GIVING YOU YOUR HAT UNTIL I GET THE HEAD KEY BACK!
KEEP IT UP, I'LL OPEN YOUR HEAD THE OLD-FASHIONED WAY. VIA SKULL FRACTURE.
I DON'T EVEN GOT THE FRIGGIN' THING. KINSEY HAS IT. WHY CAN'T YOU PISS HER OFF?
I DON'T KNOW HOW! SHE'S ALWAYS CALM! SHE'S LIKE A POD PERSON. I CAN'T STAND IT!
YEAH. SHE'S MAKING ME NUTS, TOO. LOOK, COME OUT OF THERE, KID, AND I PROMISE YOU WON'T BE HURT.
BEYOND WHAT YOU GOT COMING TO YOU.
NOWHERE LEFT TO GO, IS THERE, YOU LITTLE TURD?
TYLER? TY?
NOWHERE LEFT TO— UNH.

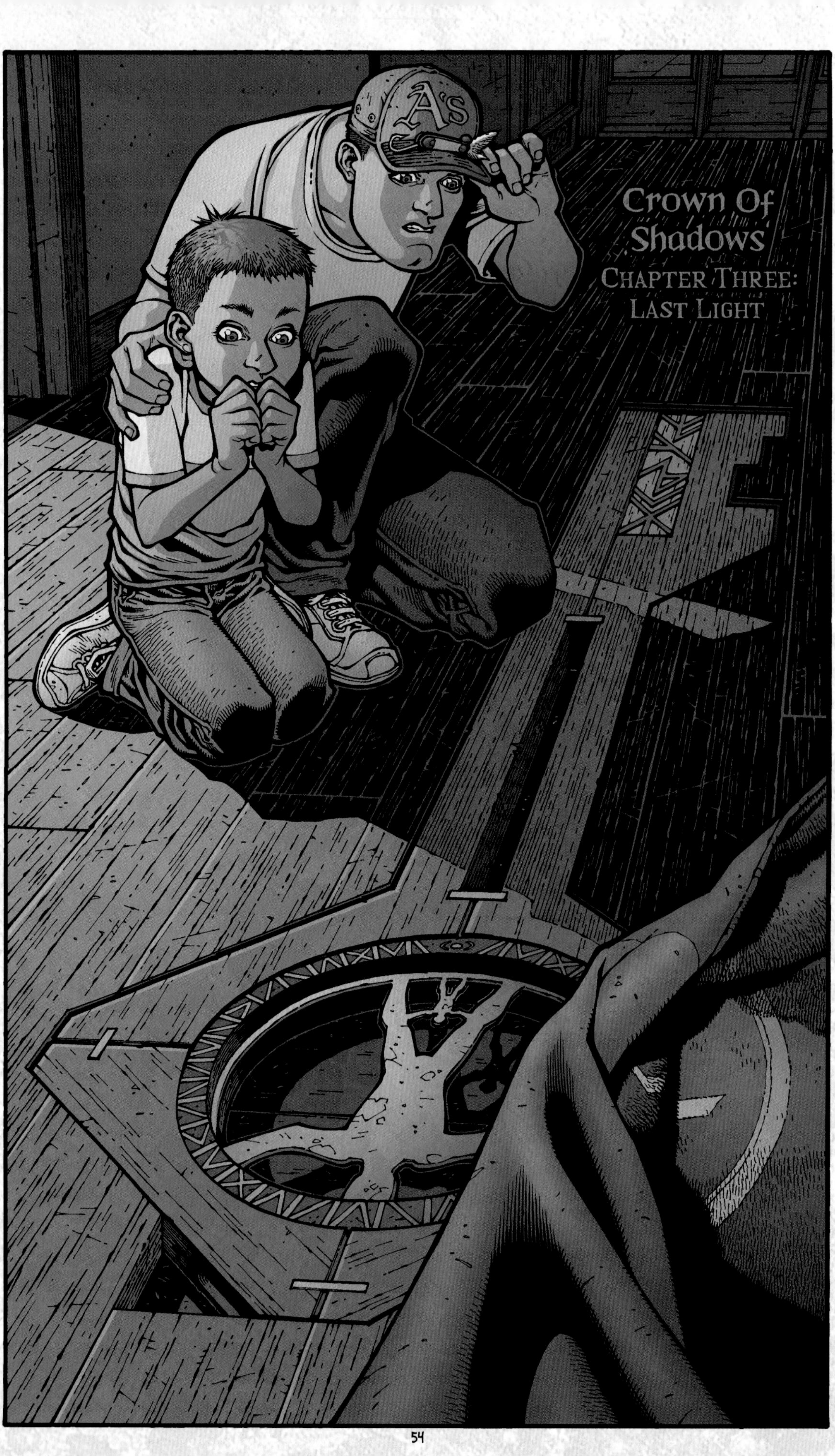

A'S
Crown Of Shadows
Chapter Three: Last Light

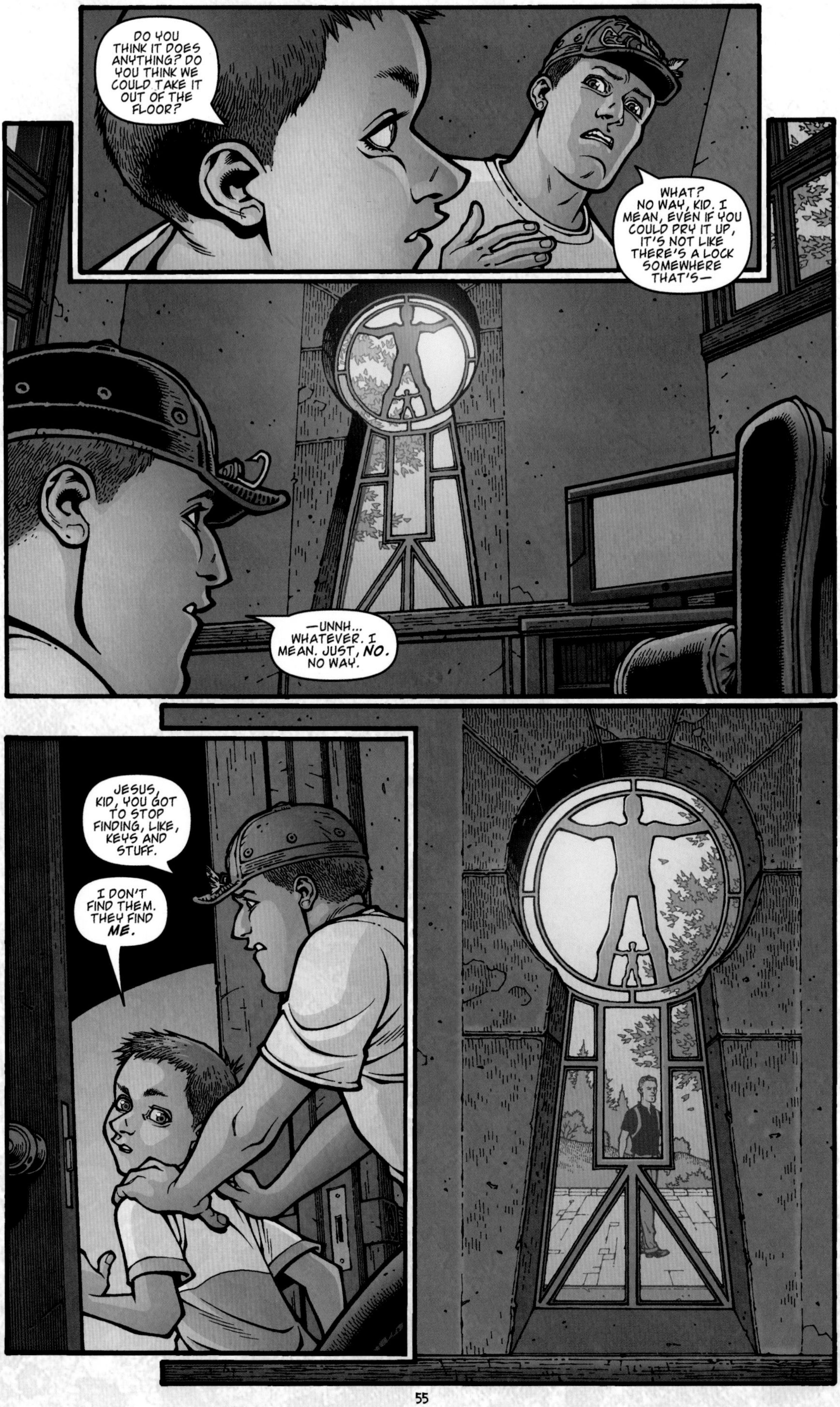
DO YOU THINK IT DOES ANYTHING? DO YOU THINK WE COULD TAKE IT OUT OF THE FLOOR?
WHAT? NO WAY, KID. I MEAN, EVEN IF YOU COULD PRY IT UP, IT'S NOT LIKE THERE'S A LOCK SOMEWHERE THAT'S—
—UNNH... WHATEVER. I MEAN. JUST, NO. NO WAY.
JESUS, KID, YOU GOT TO STOP FINDING, LIKE, KEYS AND STUFF.
I DON'T FIND THEM. THEY FIND ME.

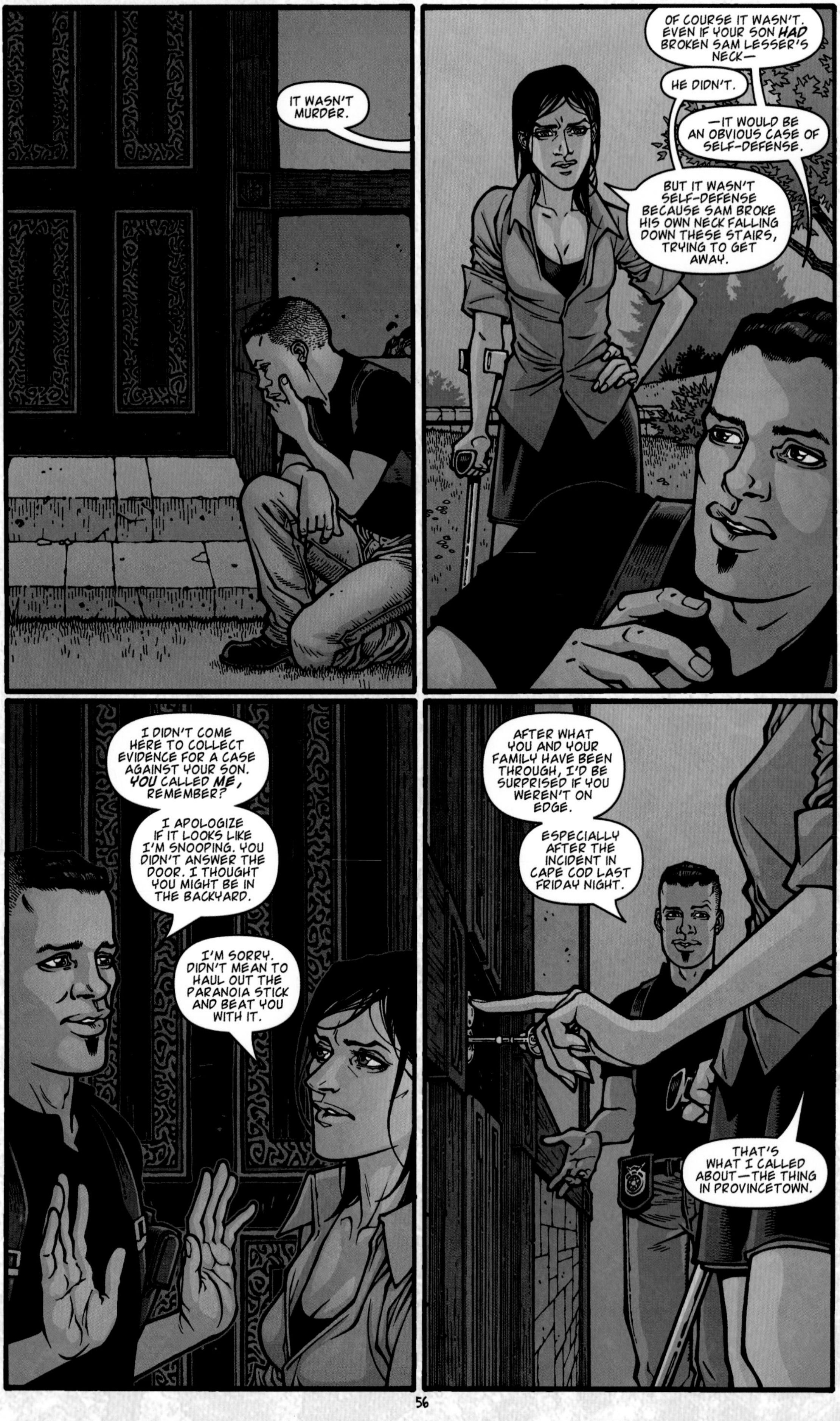
IT WASN'T MURDER.
OF COURSE IT WASN'T. EVEN IF YOUR SON HAD BROKEN SAM LESSER'S NECK—
HE DIDN'T.
—IT WOULD BE AN OBVIOUS CASE OF SELF-DEFENSE.
BUT IT WASN'T SELF-DEFENSE BECAUSE SAM BROKE HIS OWN NECK FALLING DOWN THESE STAIRS, TRYING TO GET AWAY.
I DIDN'T COME HERE TO COLLECT EVIDENCE FOR A CASE AGAINST YOUR SON. YOU CALLED ME, REMEMBER?
I APOLOGIZE IF IT LOOKS LIKE I'M SNOOPING. YOU DIDN'T ANSWER THE DOOR. I THOUGHT YOU MIGHT BE IN THE BACKYARD.
I'M SORRY. DIDN'T MEAN TO HAUL OUT THE PARANOIA STICK AND BEAT YOU WITH IT.
AFTER WHAT YOU AND YOUR FAMILY HAVE BEEN THROUGH, I'D BE SURPRISED IF YOU WEREN'T ON EDGE.
ESPECIALLY AFTER THE INCIDENT IN CAPE COD LAST FRIDAY NIGHT.
THAT'S WHAT I CALLED ABOUT—THE THING IN PROVINCETOWN.

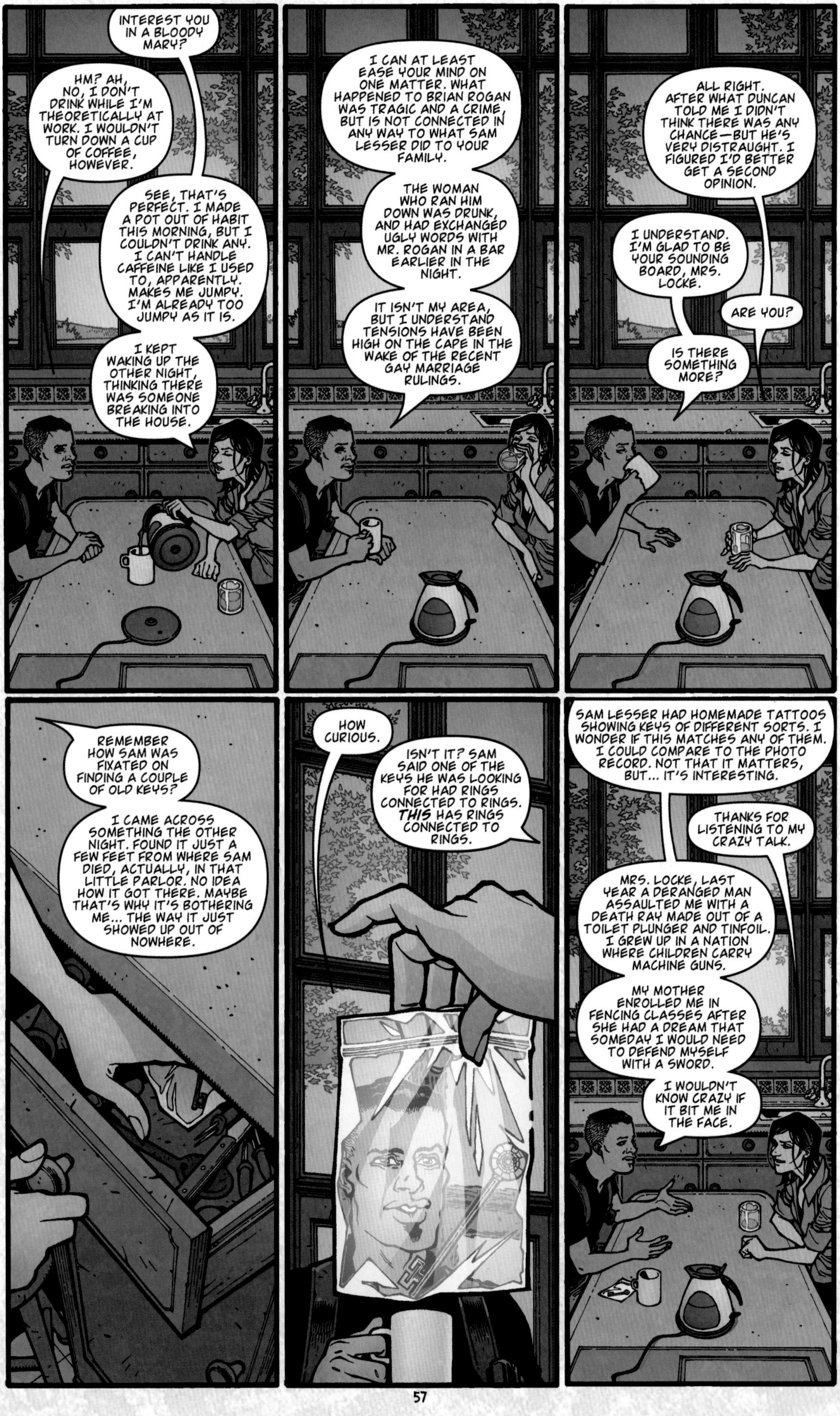

INTEREST YOU IN A BLOODY MARY?
HM? AH, NO, I DON'T DRINK WHILE I'M THEORETICALLY AT WORK. I WOULDN'T TURN DOWN A CUP OF COFFEE, HOWEVER.
SEE, THAT'S PERFECT. I MADE A POT OUT OF HABIT THIS MORNING, BUT I COULDN'T DRINK ANY. I CAN'T HANDLE CAFFEINE LIKE I USED TO, APPARENTLY. MAKES ME JUMPY. I'M ALREADY TOO JUMPY AS IT IS.
I KEPT WAKING UP THE OTHER NIGHT, THINKING THERE WAS SOMEONE BREAKING INTO THE HOUSE.
I CAN AT LEAST EASE YOUR MIND ON ONE MATTER. WHAT HAPPENED TO BRIAN ROGAN WAS TRAGIC AND A CRIME, BUT IS NOT CONNECTED IN ANY WAY TO WHAT SAM LESSER DID TO YOUR FAMILY.
THE WOMAN WHO RAN HIM DOWN WAS DRUNK, AND HAD EXCHANGED UGLY WORDS WITH MR. ROGAN IN A BAR EARLIER IN THE NIGHT.
IT ISN'T MY AREA, BUT I UNDERSTAND TENSIONS HAVE BEEN HIGH ON THE CAPE IN THE WAKE OF THE RECENT GAY MARRIAGE RULINGS.
ALL RIGHT. AFTER WHAT DUNCAN TOLD ME I DIDN'T THINK THERE WAS ANY CHANCE—BUT HE'S VERY DISTRAUGHT. I FIGURED I'D BETTER GET A SECOND OPINION.
I UNDERSTAND. I'M GLAD TO BE YOUR SOUNDING BOARD, MRS. LOCKE.
IS THERE SOMETHING MORE?
ARE YOU?
REMEMBER HOW SAM WAS FIXATED ON FINDING A COUPLE OF OLD KEYS?
I CAME ACROSS SOMETHING THE OTHER NIGHT. FOUND IT JUST A FEW FEET FROM WHERE SAM DIED, ACTUALLY, IN THAT LITTLE PARLOR. NO IDEA HOW IT GOT THERE. MAYBE THAT'S WHY IT'S BOTHERING ME... THE WAY IT JUST SHOWED UP OUT OF NOWHERE.
HOW CURIOUS.
ISN'T IT? SAM SAID ONE OF THE KEYS HE WAS LOOKING FOR HAD RINGS CONNECTED TO RINGS. *THIS* HAS RINGS CONNECTED TO RINGS.
SAM LESSER HAD HOMEMADE TATTOOS SHOWING KEYS OF DIFFERENT SORTS. I WONDER IF THIS MATCHES ANY OF THEM. I COULD COMPARE TO THE PHOTO RECORD. NOT THAT IT MATTERS, BUT... IT'S INTERESTING.
THANKS FOR LISTENING TO MY CRAZY TALK.
MRS. LOCKE, LAST YEAR A DERANGED MAN ASSAULTED ME WITH A DEATH RAY MADE OUT OF A TOILET PLUNGER AND TINFOIL. I GREW UP IN A NATION WHERE CHILDREN CARRY MACHINE GUNS.
MY MOTHER ENROLLED ME IN FENCING CLASSES AFTER SHE HAD A DREAM THAT SOMEDAY I WOULD NEED TO DEFEND MYSELF WITH A SWORD.
I WOULDN'T KNOW CRAZY IF IT BIT ME IN THE FACE.

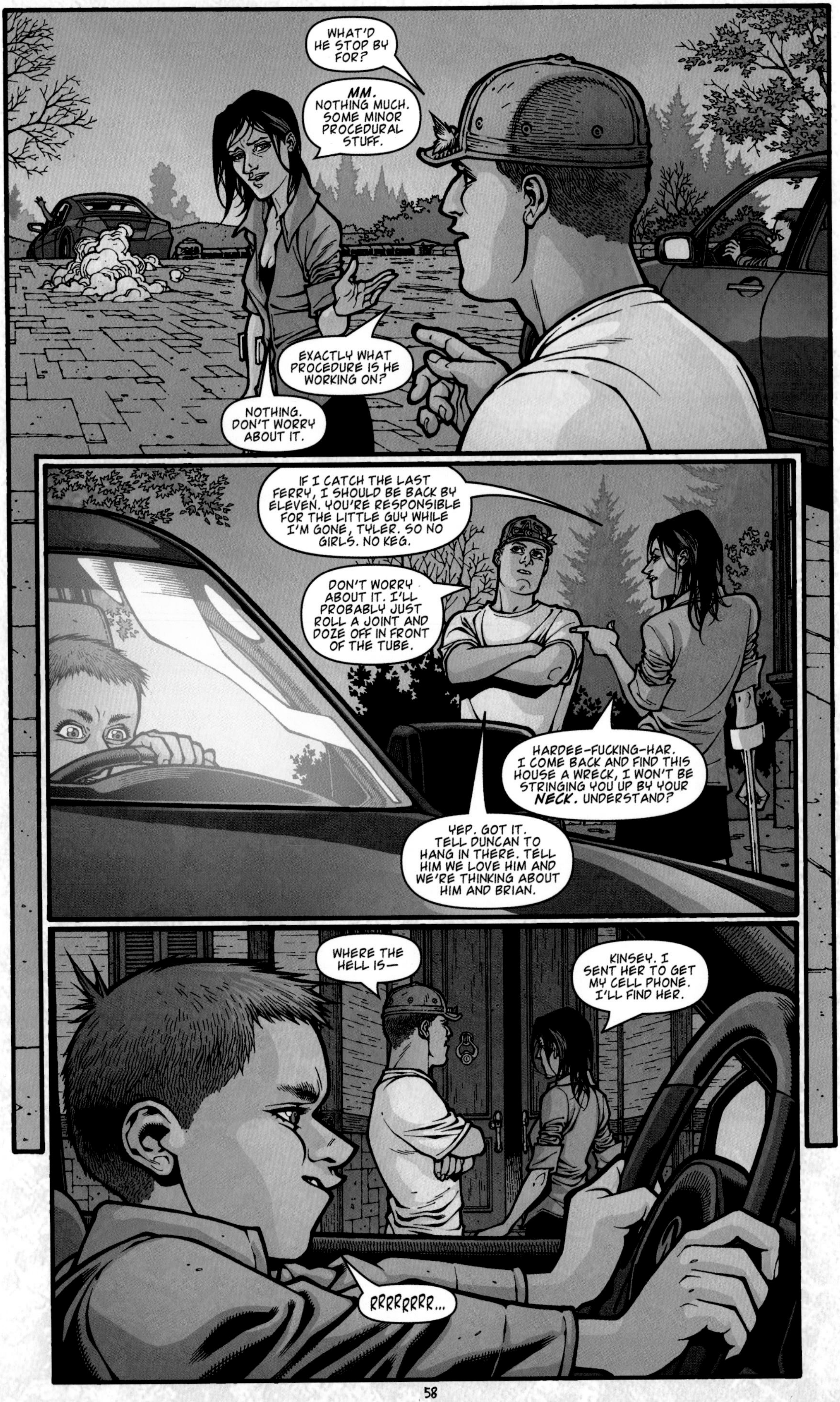
WHAT'D HE STOP BY FOR?
MM. NOTHING MUCH. SOME MINOR PROCEDURAL STUFF.
EXACTLY WHAT PROCEDURE IS HE WORKING ON?
NOTHING. DON'T WORRY ABOUT IT.
IF I CATCH THE LAST FERRY, I SHOULD BE BACK BY ELEVEN. YOU'RE RESPONSIBLE FOR THE LITTLE GUY WHILE I'M GONE, TYLER. SO NO GIRLS. NO KEG.
DON'T WORRY ABOUT IT. I'LL PROBABLY JUST ROLL A JOINT AND DOZE OFF IN FRONT OF THE TUBE.
HARDEE-FUCKING-HAR. I COME BACK AND FIND THIS HOUSE A WRECK, I WON'T BE STRINGING YOU UP BY YOUR NECK. UNDERSTAND?
YEP. GOT IT. TELL DUNCAN TO HANG IN THERE. TELL HIM WE LOVE HIM AND WE'RE THINKING ABOUT HIM AND BRIAN.
WHERE THE HELL IS—
KINSEY. I SENT HER TO GET MY CELL PHONE. I'LL FIND HER.
RRRRRRRR...

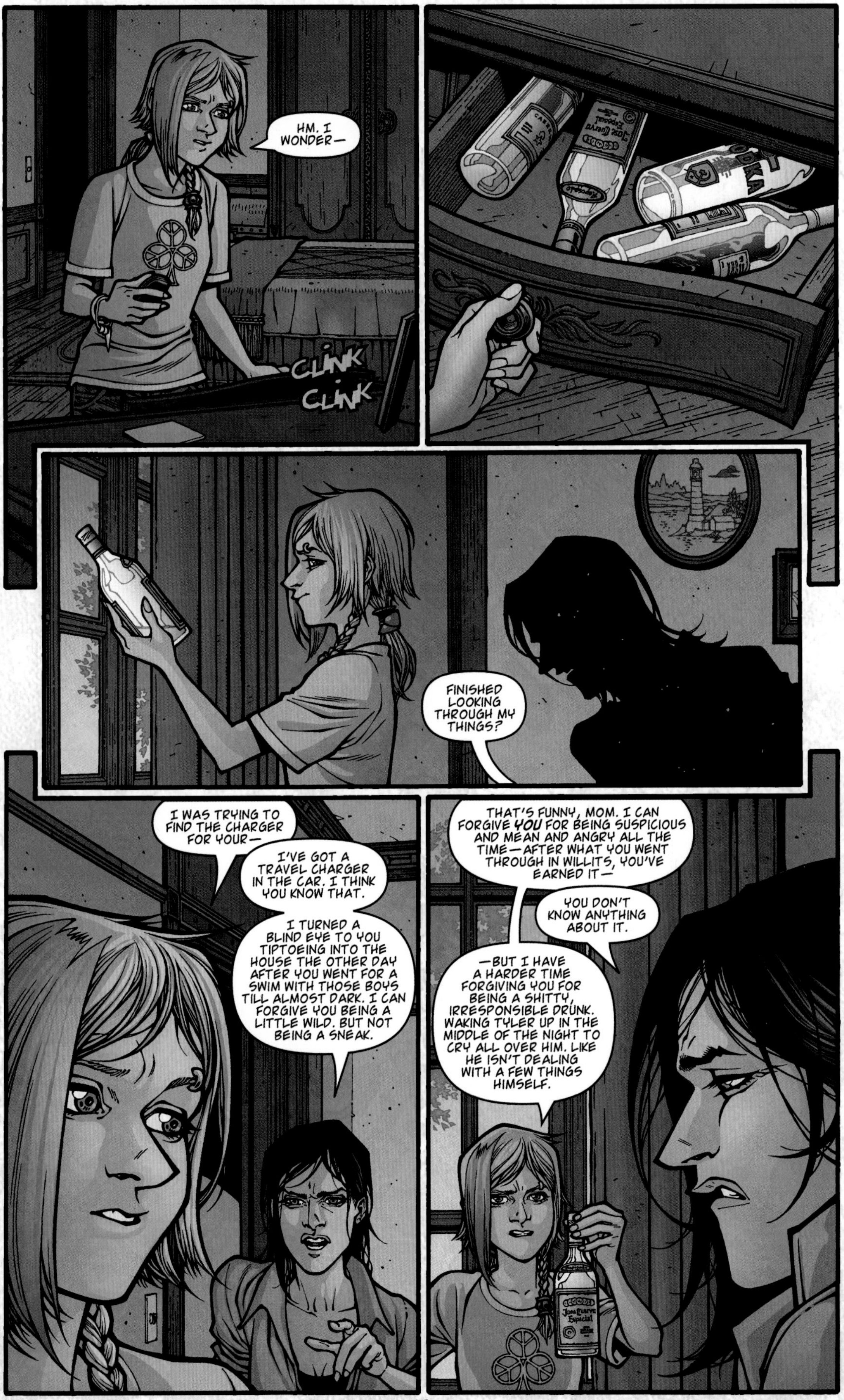
HM. I WONDER—
CLINK
CLINK
FINISHED LOOKING THROUGH MY THINGS?
I WAS TRYING TO FIND THE CHARGER FOR YOUR—
I'VE GOT A TRAVEL CHARGER IN THE CAR. I THINK YOU KNOW THAT.
I TURNED A BLIND EYE TO YOU TIPTOEING INTO THE HOUSE THE OTHER DAY AFTER YOU WENT FOR A SWIM WITH THOSE BOYS TILL ALMOST DARK. I CAN FORGIVE YOU BEING A LITTLE WILD. BUT NOT BEING A SNEAK.
THAT'S FUNNY, MOM. I CAN FORGIVE *YOU* FOR BEING SUSPICIOUS AND MEAN AND ANGRY ALL THE TIME—AFTER WHAT YOU WENT THROUGH IN WILLITS, YOU'VE EARNED IT—
YOU DON'T KNOW ANYTHING ABOUT IT.
—BUT I HAVE A HARDER TIME FORGIVING YOU FOR BEING A SHITTY, IRRESPONSIBLE DRUNK. WAKING TYLER UP IN THE MIDDLE OF THE NIGHT TO CRY ALL OVER HIM. LIKE HE ISN'T DEALING WITH A FEW THINGS HIMSELF.

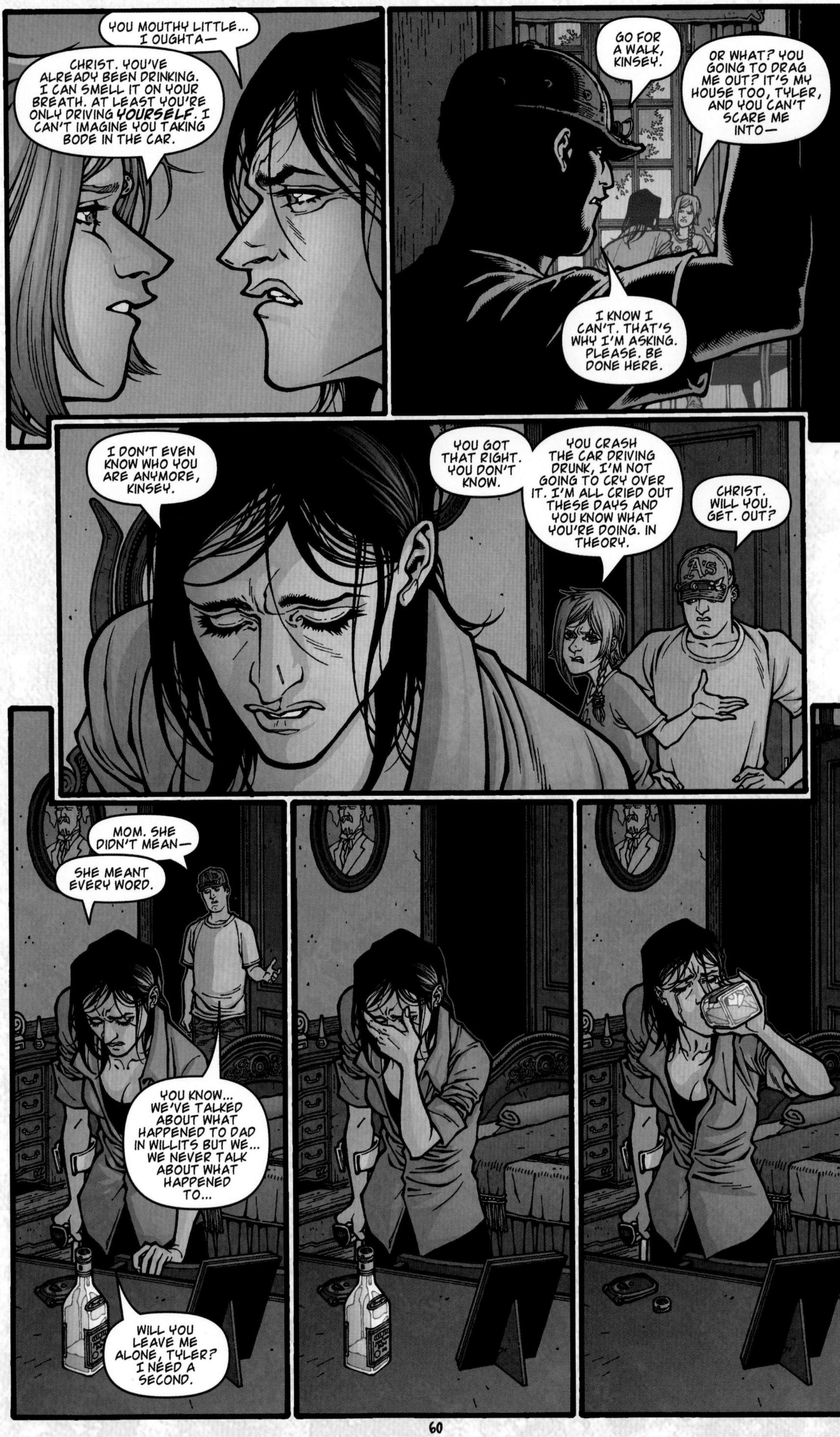
YOU MOUTHY LITTLE... I OUGHTA—
CHRIST. YOU'VE ALREADY BEEN DRINKING. I CAN SMELL IT ON YOUR BREATH. AT LEAST YOU'RE ONLY DRIVING YOURSELF. I CAN'T IMAGINE YOU TAKING BODE IN THE CAR.
GO FOR A WALK, KINSEY.
OR WHAT? YOU GOING TO DRAG ME OUT? IT'S MY HOUSE TOO, TYLER, AND YOU CAN'T SCARE ME INTO—
I KNOW I CAN'T. THAT'S WHY I'M ASKING. PLEASE. BE DONE HERE.
I DON'T EVEN KNOW WHO YOU ARE ANYMORE, KINSEY.
YOU GOT THAT RIGHT. YOU DON'T KNOW.
YOU CRASH THE CAR DRIVING DRUNK, I'M NOT GOING TO CRY OVER IT. I'M ALL CRIED OUT THESE DAYS AND YOU KNOW WHAT YOU'RE DOING. IN THEORY.
CHRIST. WILL YOU. GET. OUT?
MOM. SHE DIDN'T MEAN—
SHE MEANT EVERY WORD.
YOU KNOW... WE'VE TALKED ABOUT WHAT HAPPENED TO DAD IN WILLITS BUT WE... WE NEVER TALK ABOUT WHAT HAPPENED TO...
WILL YOU LEAVE ME ALONE, TYLER? I NEED A SECOND.

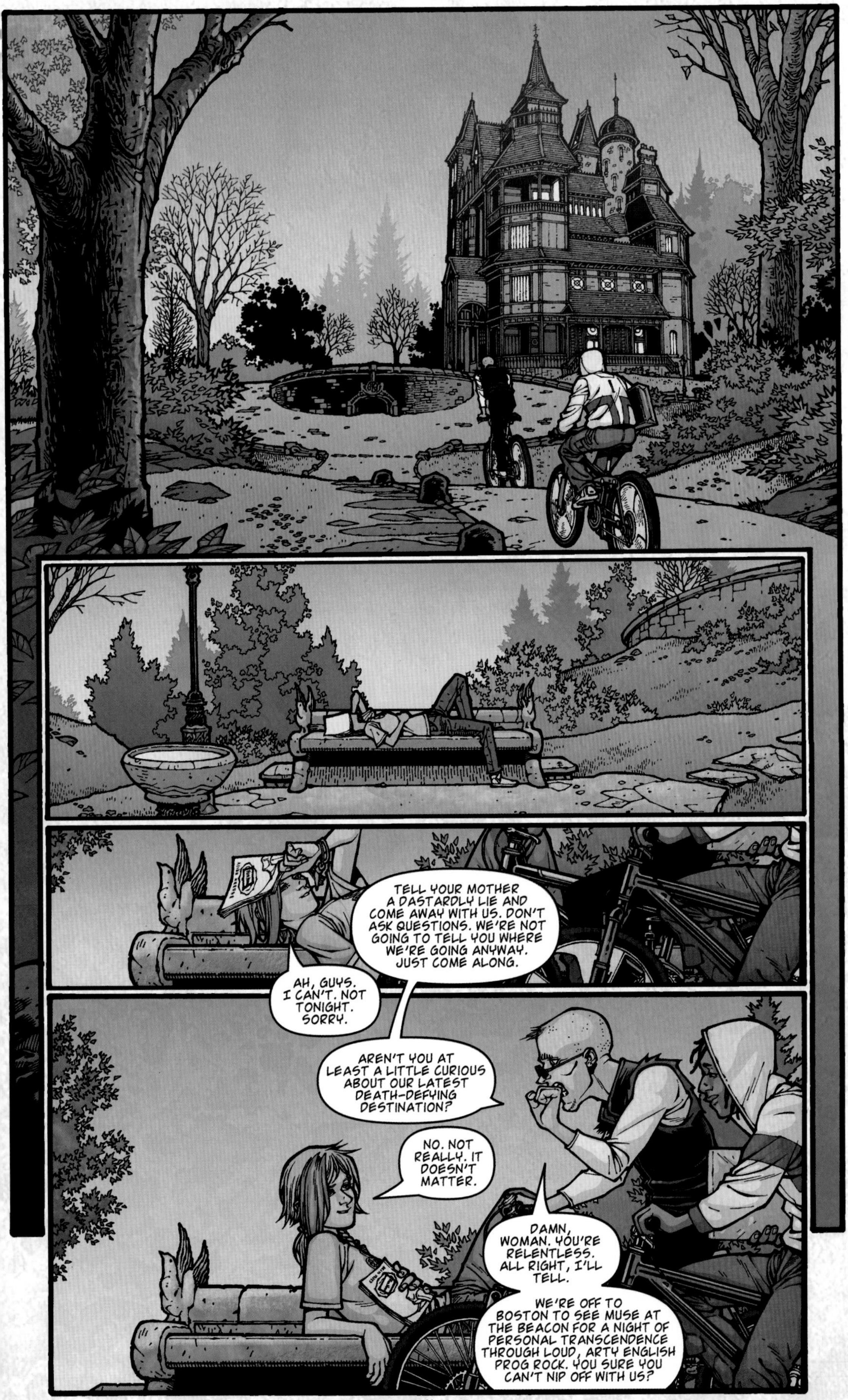
TELL YOUR MOTHER A DASTARDLY LIE AND COME AWAY WITH US. DON'T ASK QUESTIONS. WE'RE NOT GOING TO TELL YOU WHERE WE'RE GOING ANYWAY. JUST COME ALONG.
AH, GUYS. I CAN'T. NOT TONIGHT. SORRY.
AREN'T YOU AT LEAST A LITTLE CURIOUS ABOUT OUR LATEST DEATH-DEFYING DESTINATION?
NO. NOT REALLY. IT DOESN'T MATTER.
DAMN, WOMAN. YOU'RE RELENTLESS. ALL RIGHT, I'LL TELL.
WE'RE OFF TO BOSTON TO SEE MUSE AT THE BEACON FOR A NIGHT OF PERSONAL TRANSCENDENCE THROUGH LOUD, ARTY ENGLISH PROG ROCK. YOU SURE YOU CAN'T NIP OFF WITH US?

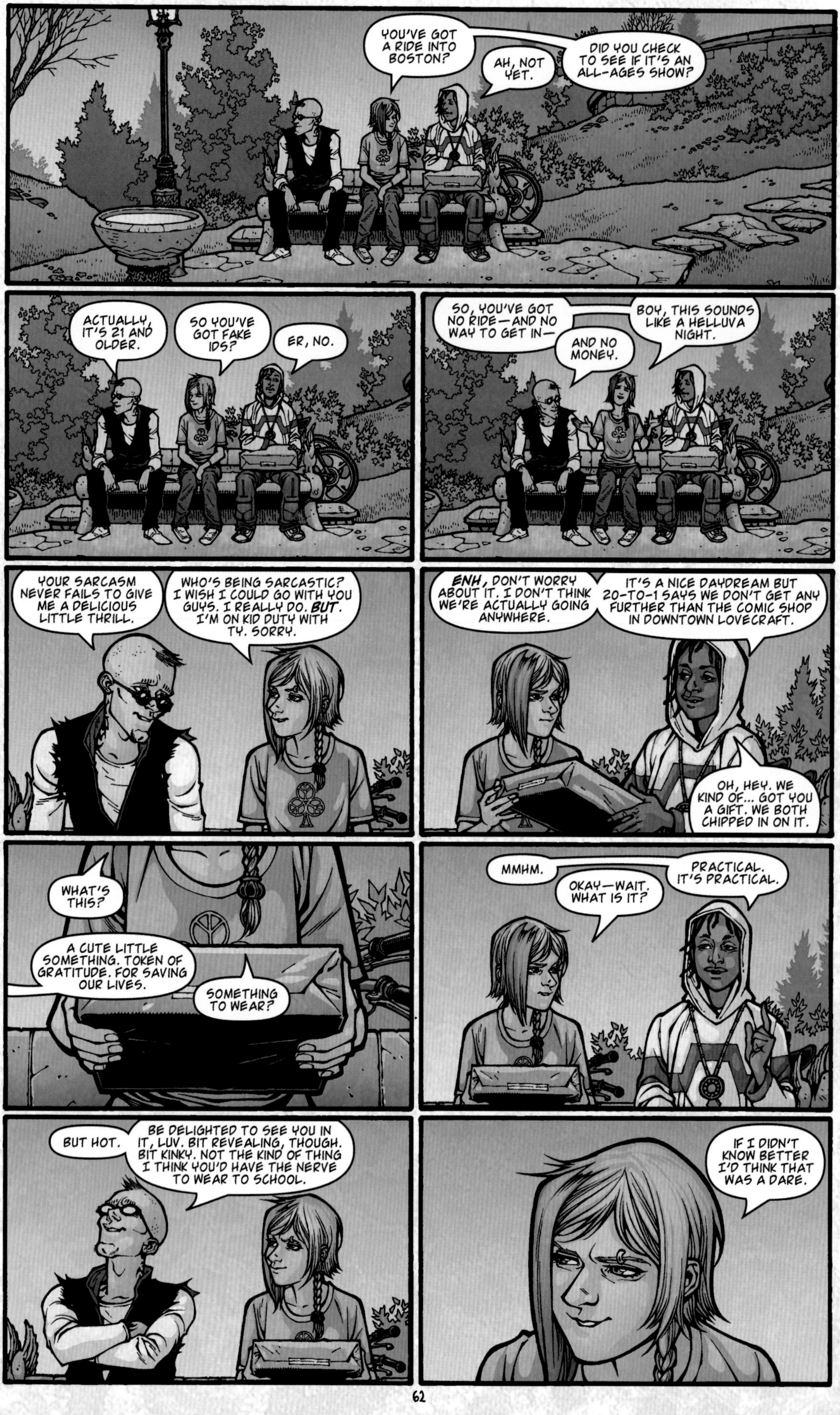
YOU'VE GOT A RIDE INTO BOSTON?
AH, NOT YET.
DID YOU CHECK TO SEE IF IT'S AN ALL-AGES SHOW?
ACTUALLY, IT'S 21 AND OLDER.
SO YOU'VE GOT FAKE IDS?
ER, NO.
SO, YOU'VE GOT NO RIDE—AND NO WAY TO GET IN—
AND NO MONEY.
BOY, THIS SOUNDS LIKE A HELLUVA NIGHT.
YOUR SARCASM NEVER FAILS TO GIVE ME A DELICIOUS LITTLE THRILL.
WHO'S BEING SARCASTIC? I WISH I COULD GO WITH YOU GUYS. I REALLY DO. BUT. I'M ON KID DUTY WITH TY. SORRY.
ENH, DON'T WORRY ABOUT IT. I DON'T THINK WE'RE ACTUALLY GOING ANYWHERE.
IT'S A NICE DAYDREAM BUT 20-TO-1 SAYS WE DON'T GET ANY FURTHER THAN THE COMIC SHOP IN DOWNTOWN LOVECRAFT.
OH, HEY. WE KIND OF... GOT YOU A GIFT. WE BOTH CHIPPED IN ON IT.
WHAT'S THIS?
A CUTE LITTLE SOMETHING. TOKEN OF GRATITUDE. FOR SAVING OUR LIVES.
SOMETHING TO WEAR?
MMHM.
OKAY—WAIT. WHAT IS IT?
PRACTICAL. IT'S PRACTICAL.
BUT HOT.
BE DELIGHTED TO SEE YOU IN IT, LUV. BIT REVEALING, THOUGH. BIT KINKY. NOT THE KIND OF THING I THINK YOU'D HAVE THE NERVE TO WEAR TO SCHOOL.
IF I DIDN'T KNOW BETTER I'D THINK THAT WAS A DARE.

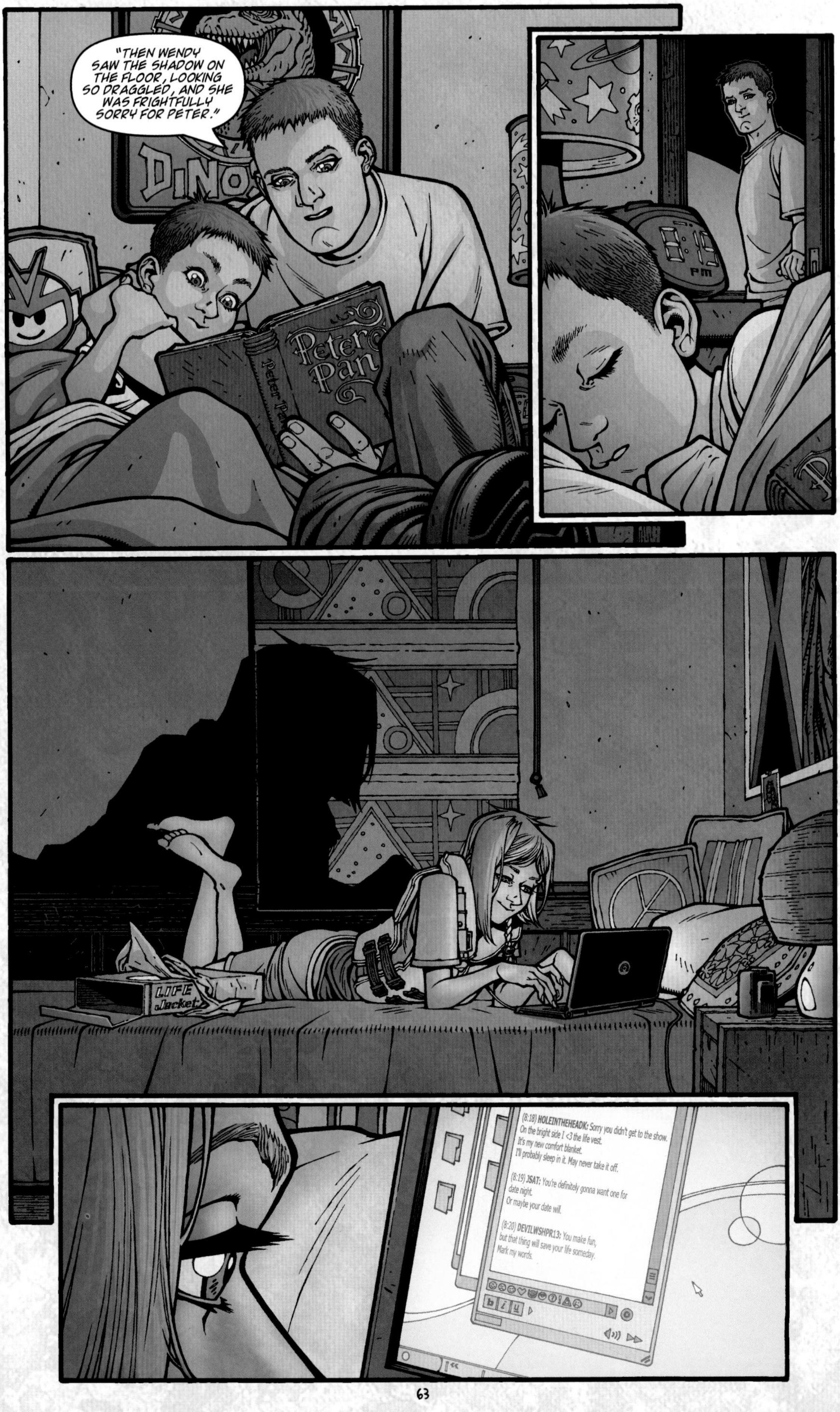
"THEN WENDY SAW THE SHADOW ON THE FLOOR, LOOKING SO DRAGGLED, AND SHE WAS FRIGHTFULLY SORRY FOR PETER."
Peter Pan
LIFE Jacket
(8:18) HOLEINTHEHEADK: Sorry you didn't get to the show.
On the bright side I <3 the life vest.
It's my new comfort blanket.
I'll probably sleep in it. May never take it off.
(8:19) JSAT: You're definitely gonna want one for date night.
Or maybe your date will.
(8:20) DEVILWSHPR13: You make fun,
but that thing will save your life someday.
Mark my words.

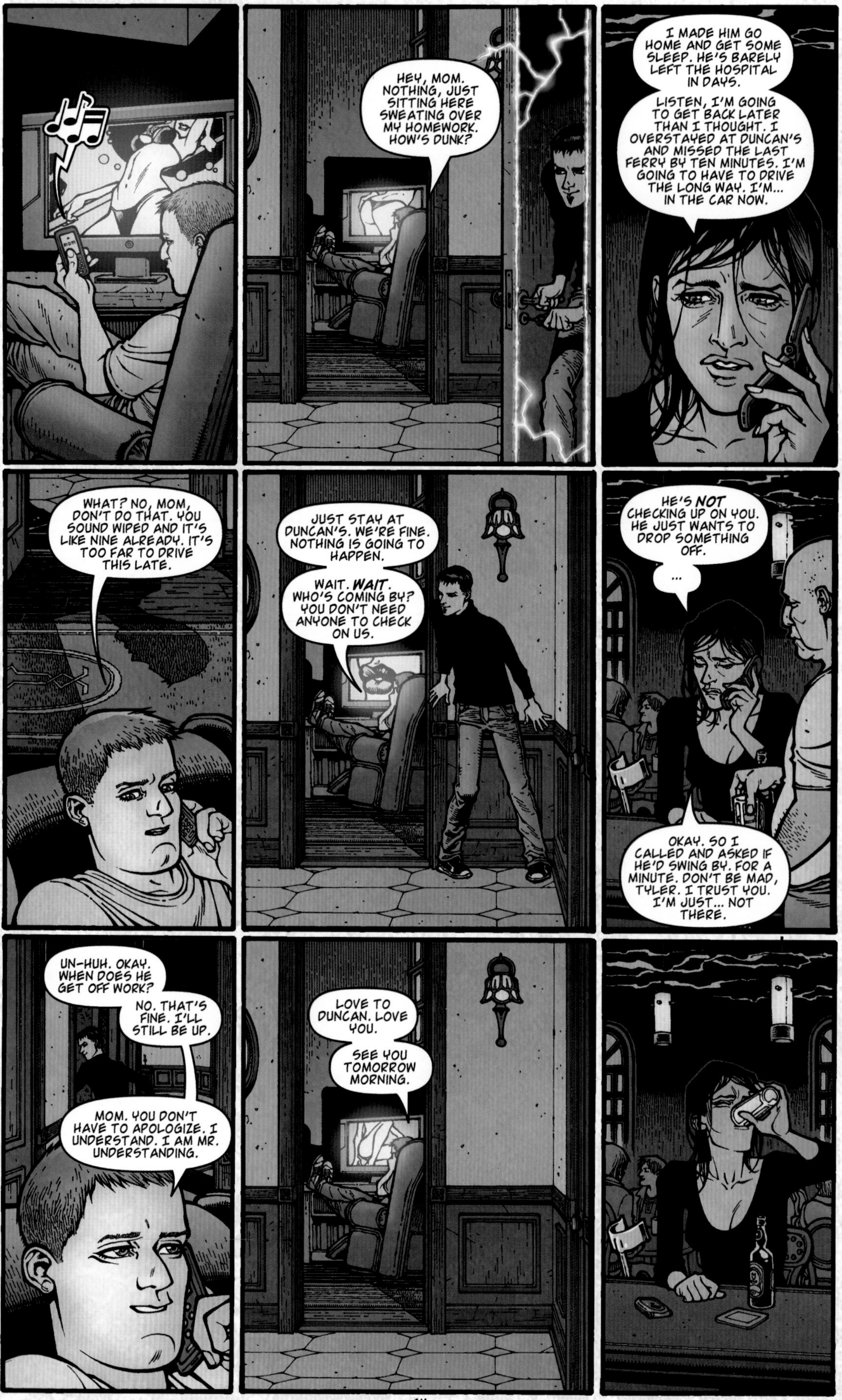
HEY, MOM. NOTHING, JUST SITTING HERE SWEATING OVER MY HOMEWORK. HOW'S DUNK?
I MADE HIM GO HOME AND GET SOME SLEEP. HE'S BARELY LEFT THE HOSPITAL IN DAYS.
LISTEN, I'M GOING TO GET BACK LATER THAN I THOUGHT. I OVERSTAYED AT DUNCAN'S AND MISSED THE LAST FERRY BY TEN MINUTES. I'M GOING TO HAVE TO DRIVE THE LONG WAY. I'M... IN THE CAR NOW.
WHAT? NO, MOM, DON'T DO THAT. YOU SOUND WIPED AND IT'S LIKE NINE ALREADY. IT'S TOO FAR TO DRIVE THIS LATE.
JUST STAY AT DUNCAN'S. WE'RE FINE. NOTHING IS GOING TO HAPPEN.
WAIT. WAIT. WHO'S COMING BY? YOU DON'T NEED ANYONE TO CHECK ON US.
HE'S NOT CHECKING UP ON YOU. HE JUST WANTS TO DROP SOMETHING OFF.
...
OKAY. SO I CALLED AND ASKED IF HE'D SWING BY. FOR A MINUTE. DON'T BE MAD, TYLER. I TRUST YOU. I'M JUST... NOT THERE.
UN-HUH. OKAY. WHEN DOES HE GET OFF WORK?
NO. THAT'S FINE. I'LL STILL BE UP.
MOM. YOU DON'T HAVE TO APOLOGIZE. I UNDERSTAND. I AM MR. UNDERSTANDING.
LOVE TO DUNCAN. LOVE YOU.
SEE YOU TOMORROW MORNING.

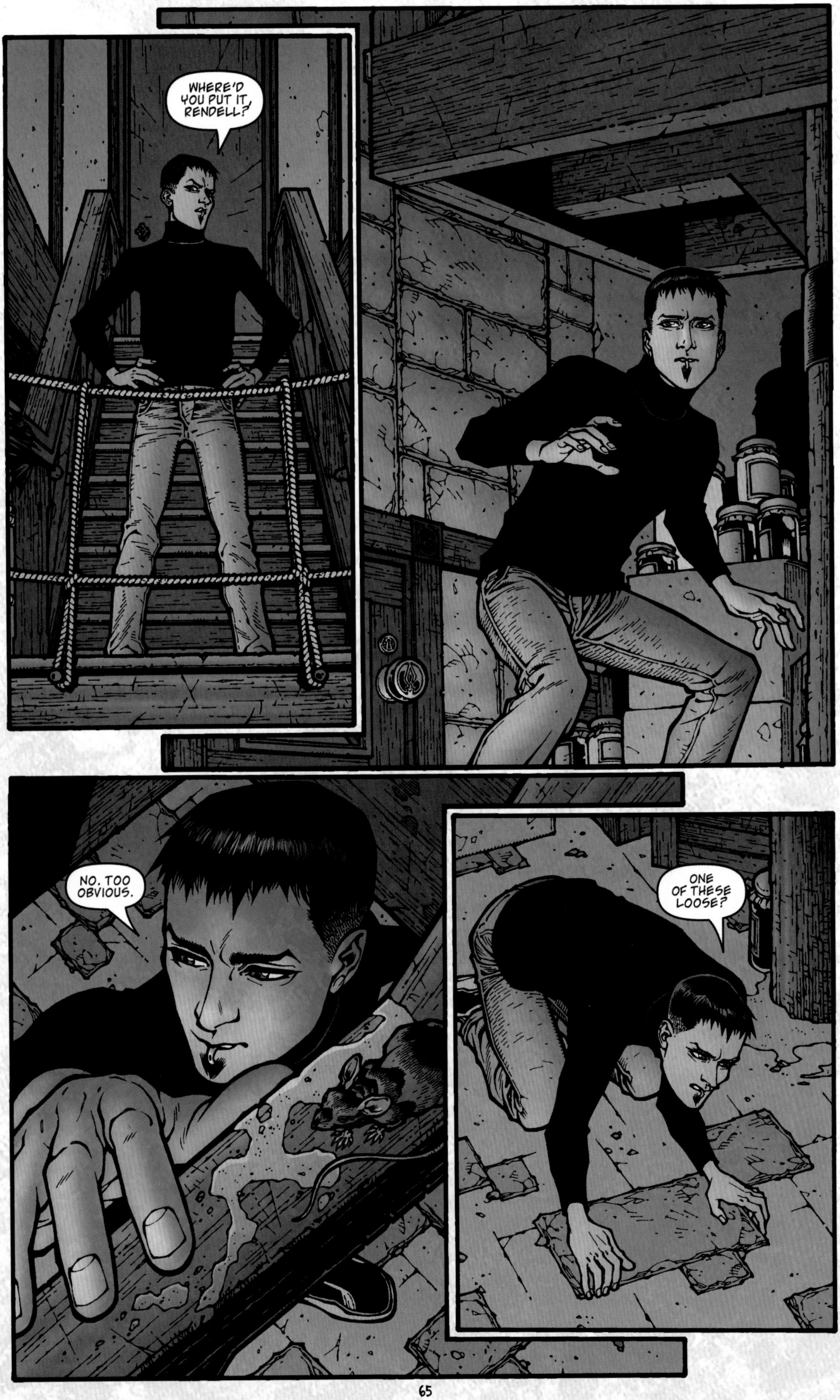
WHERE'D YOU PUT IT, RENDELL?
NO. TOO OBVIOUS.
ONE OF THESE LOOSE?

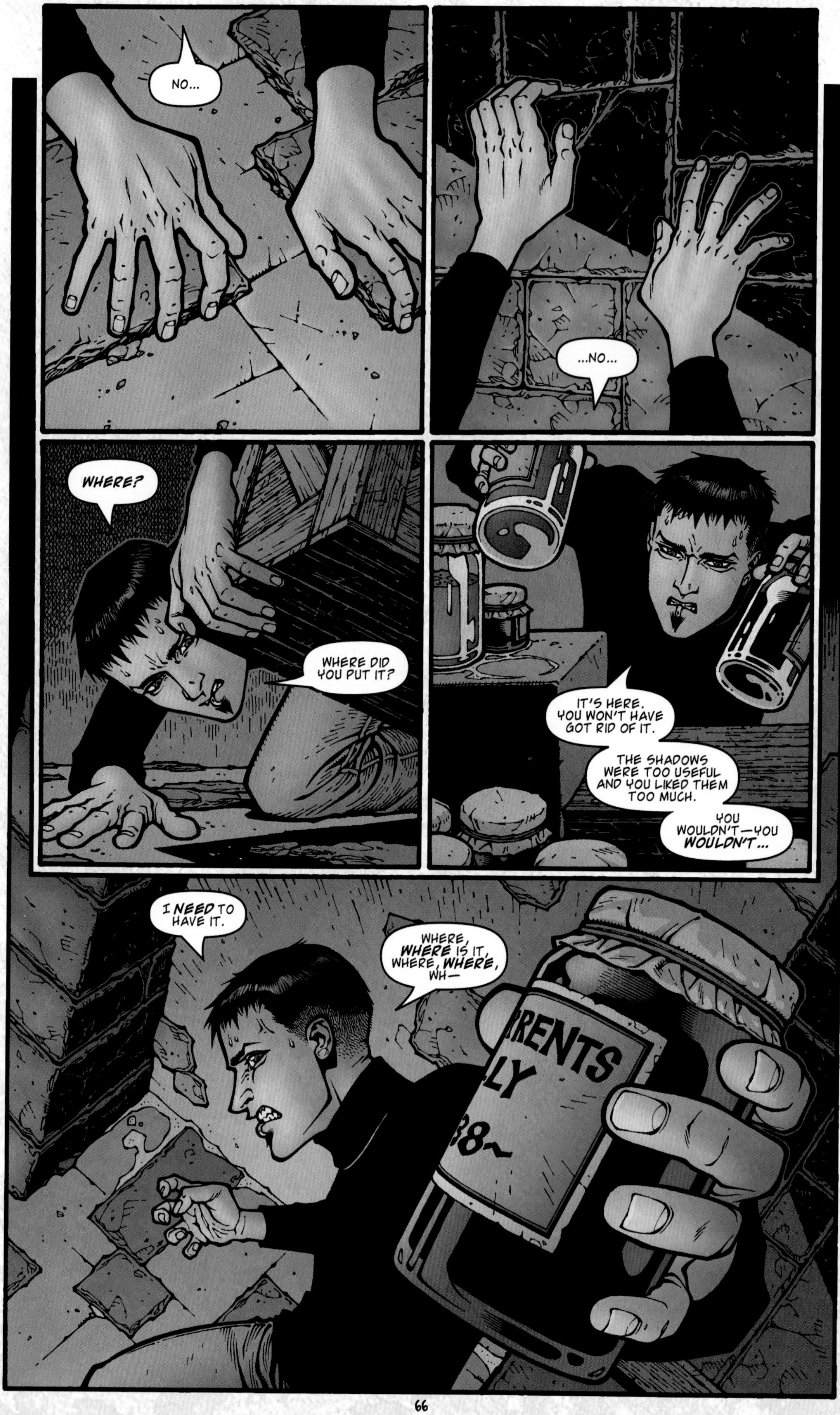
NO...
...NO...
WHERE?
WHERE DID YOU PUT IT?
IT'S HERE. YOU WON'T HAVE GOT RID OF IT.
THE SHADOWS WERE TOO USEFUL AND YOU LIKED THEM TOO MUCH.
YOU WOULDN'T—YOU ***WOULDN'T...***
I ***NEED*** TO HAVE IT.
WHERE, ***WHERE*** IS IT, WHERE, ***WHERE,*** WH—

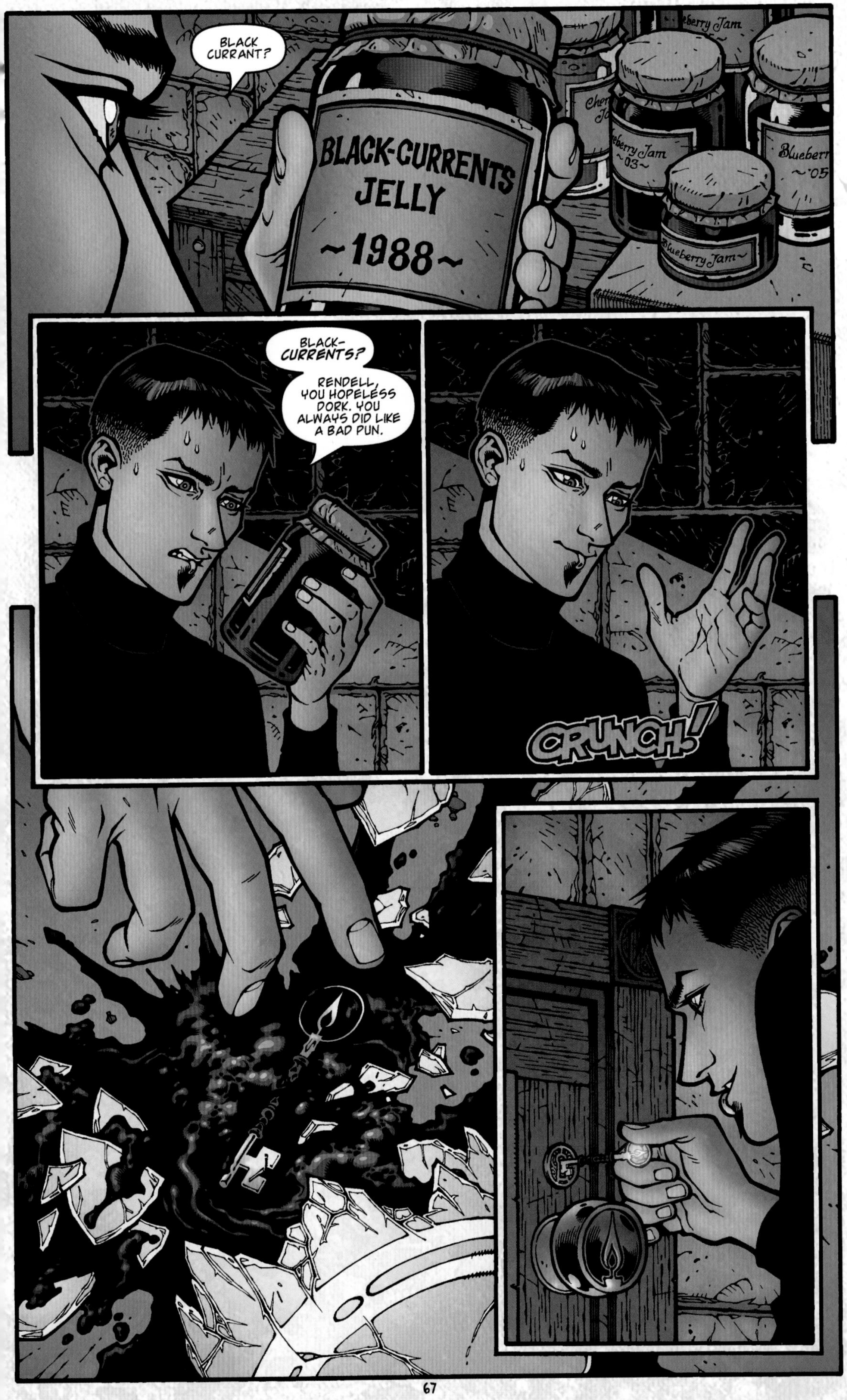

BLACK CURRANT?
BLACK-CURRENTS JELLY ~1988~
Blueberry Jam
Blueberry Jam ~03~
Blueberry ~05
Blueberry Jam
BLACK-CURRENTS?
RENDELL, YOU HOPELESS DORK. YOU ALWAYS DID LIKE A BAD PUN.
CRUNCH!

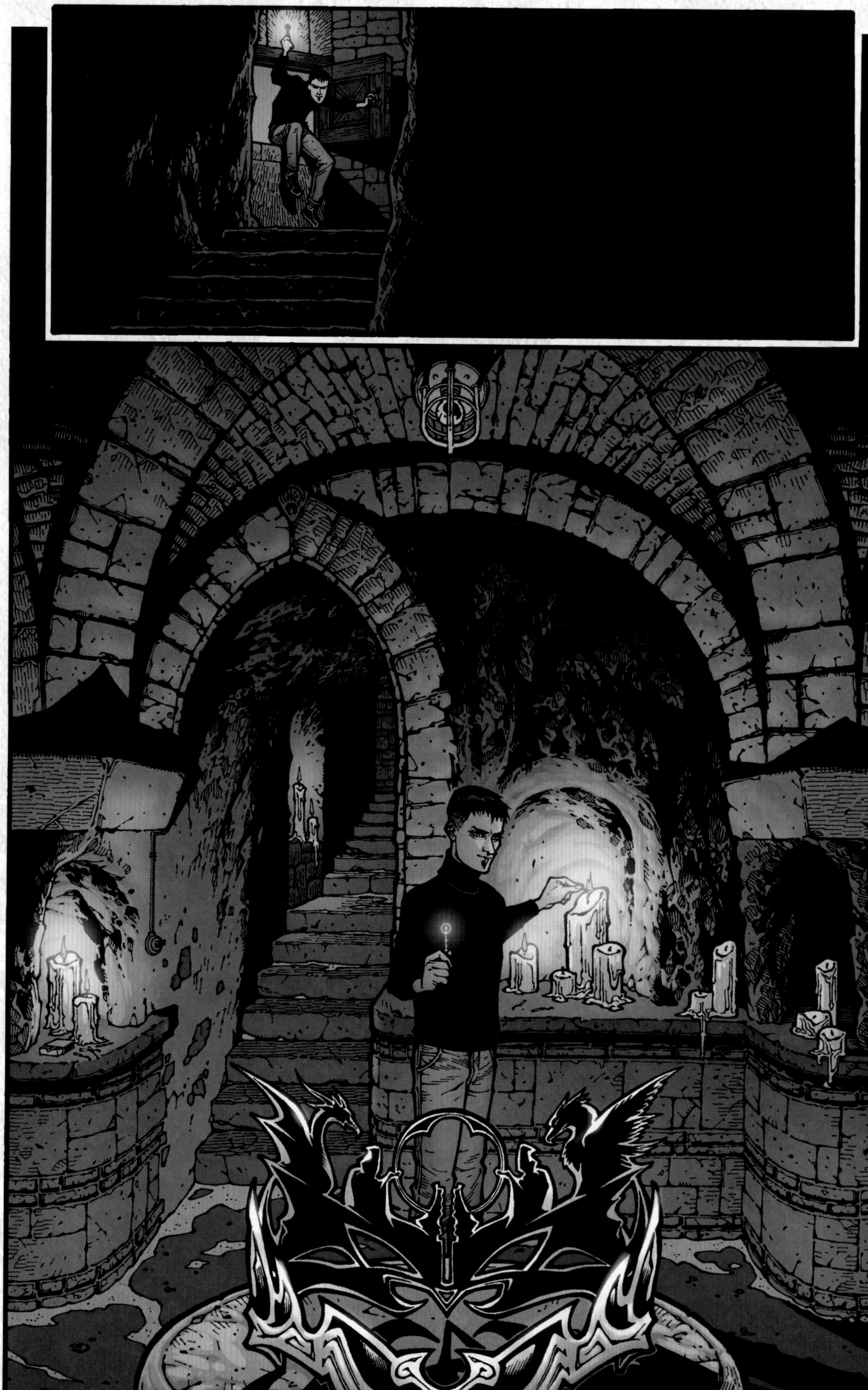

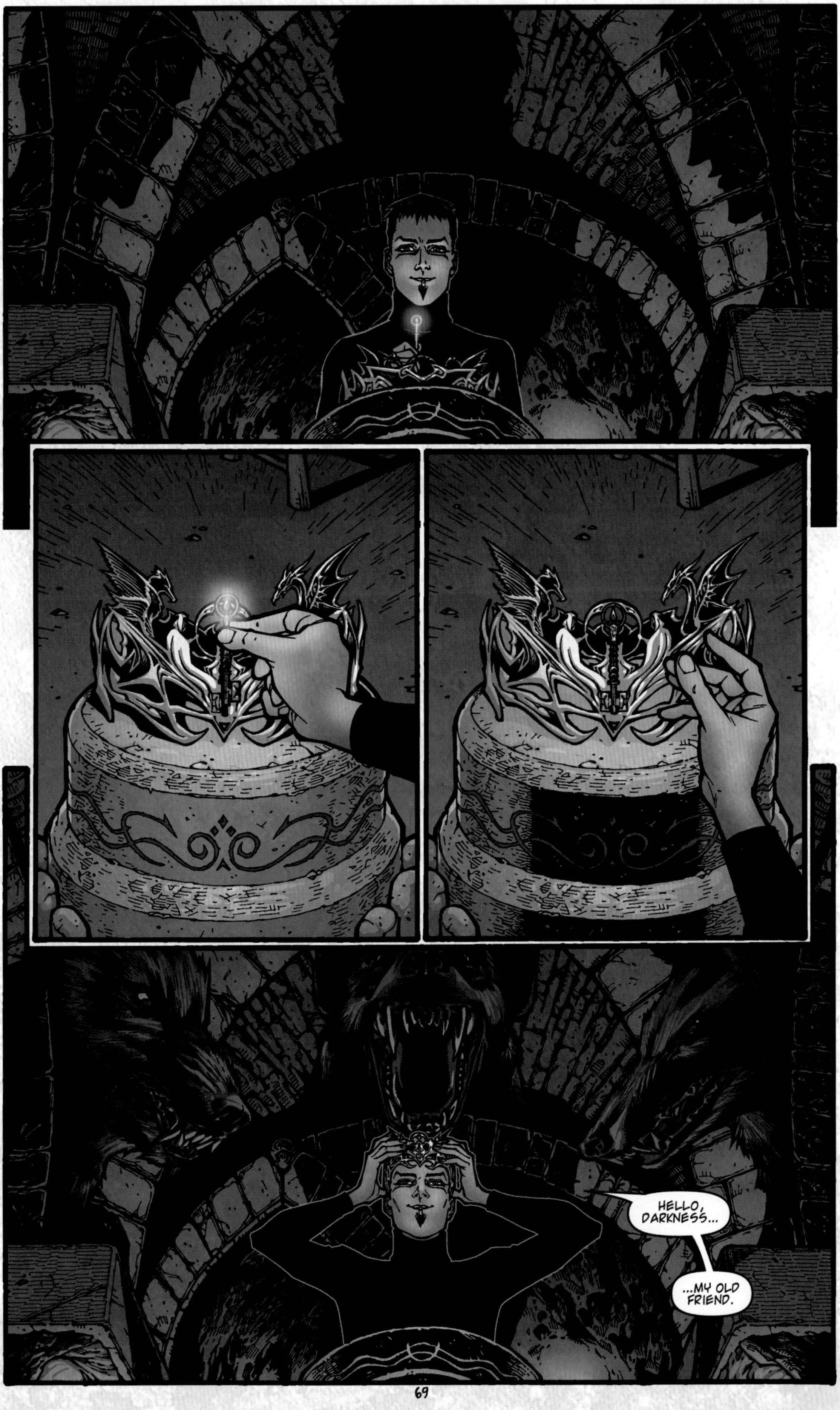
HELLO, DARKNESS...
...MY OLD FRIEND.

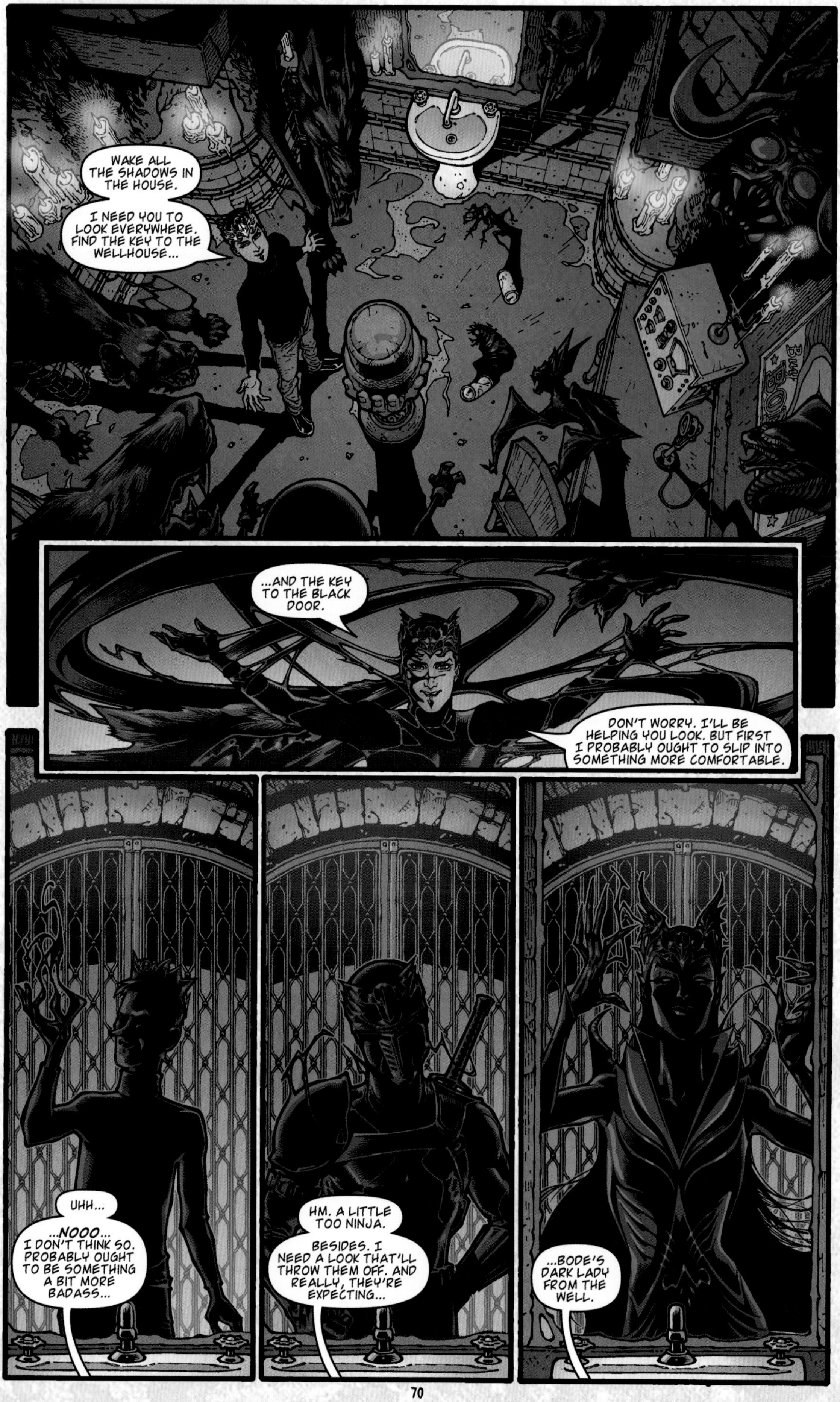
WAKE ALL THE SHADOWS IN THE HOUSE.
I NEED YOU TO LOOK EVERYWHERE. FIND THE KEY TO THE WELLHOUSE...
...AND THE KEY TO THE BLACK DOOR.
DON'T WORRY. I'LL BE HELPING YOU LOOK. BUT FIRST I PROBABLY OUGHT TO SLIP INTO SOMETHING MORE COMFORTABLE.
UHH...
...NOOO... I DON'T THINK SO. PROBABLY OUGHT TO BE SOMETHING A BIT MORE BADASS...
HM. A LITTLE TOO NINJA.
BESIDES. I NEED A LOOK THAT'LL THROW THEM OFF. AND REALLY, THEY'RE EXPECTING...
...BODE'S DARK LADY FROM THE WELL.

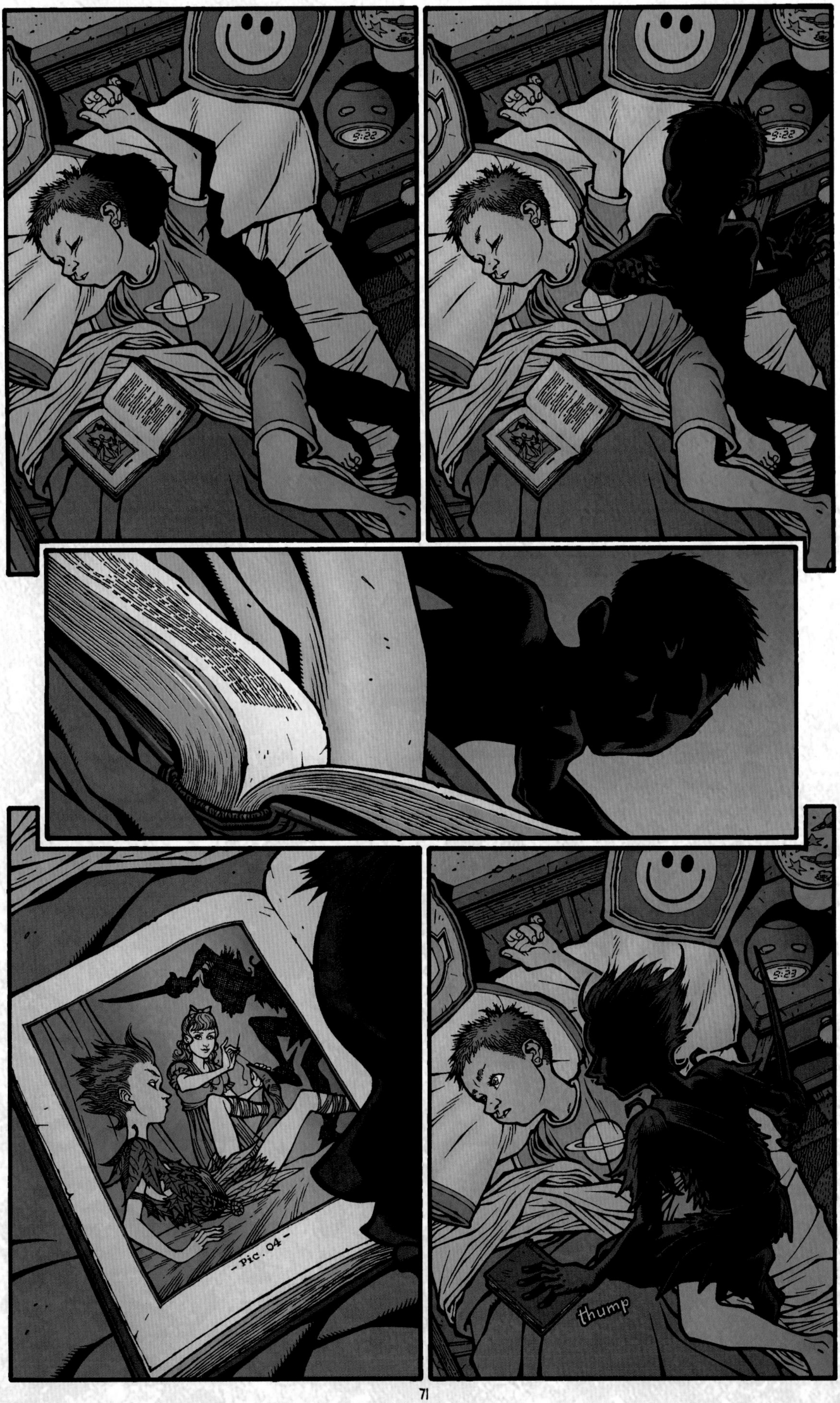

5:22
5:22
- Pic. 04 -
5:23
thump

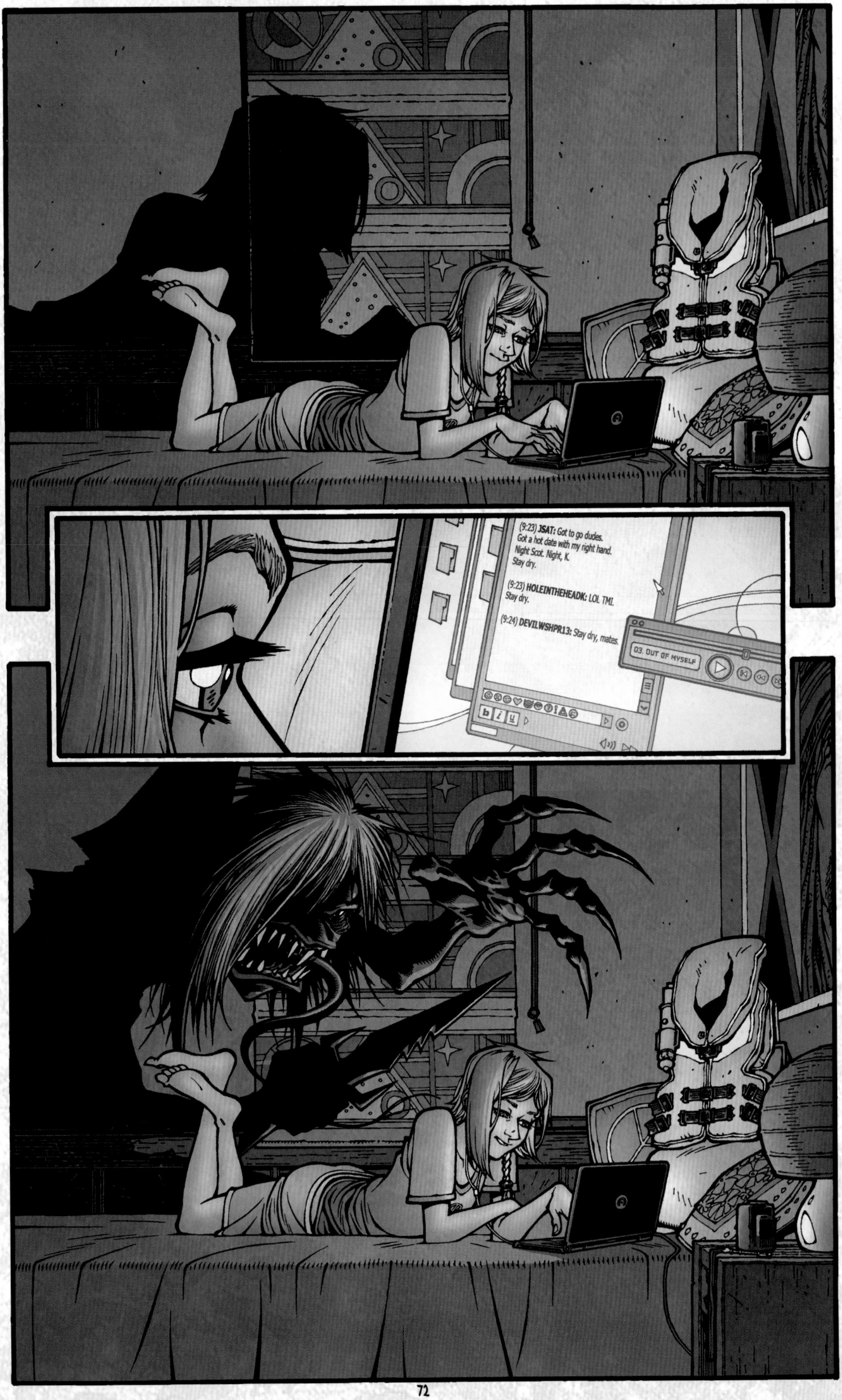

(9:23) JSAT: Got to go dudes.
Got a hot date with my right hand.
Night Scot. Night, K.
Stay dry.
(9:23) HOLEINTHEHEADK: LOL TMI.
Stay dry.
(9:24) DEVILWSHPR13: Stay dry, mates.
03. OUT OF MYSELF

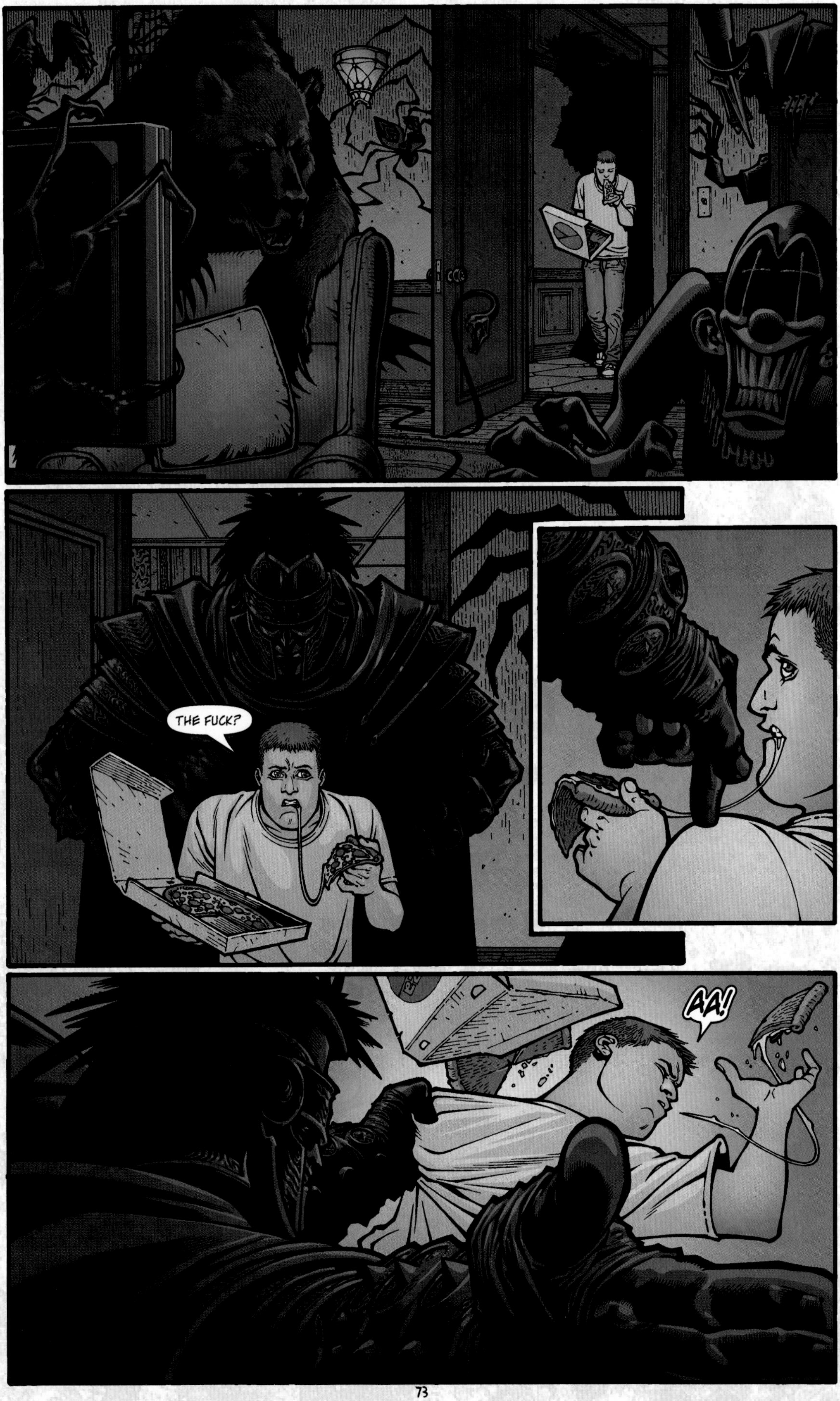

THE FUCK?
AA!

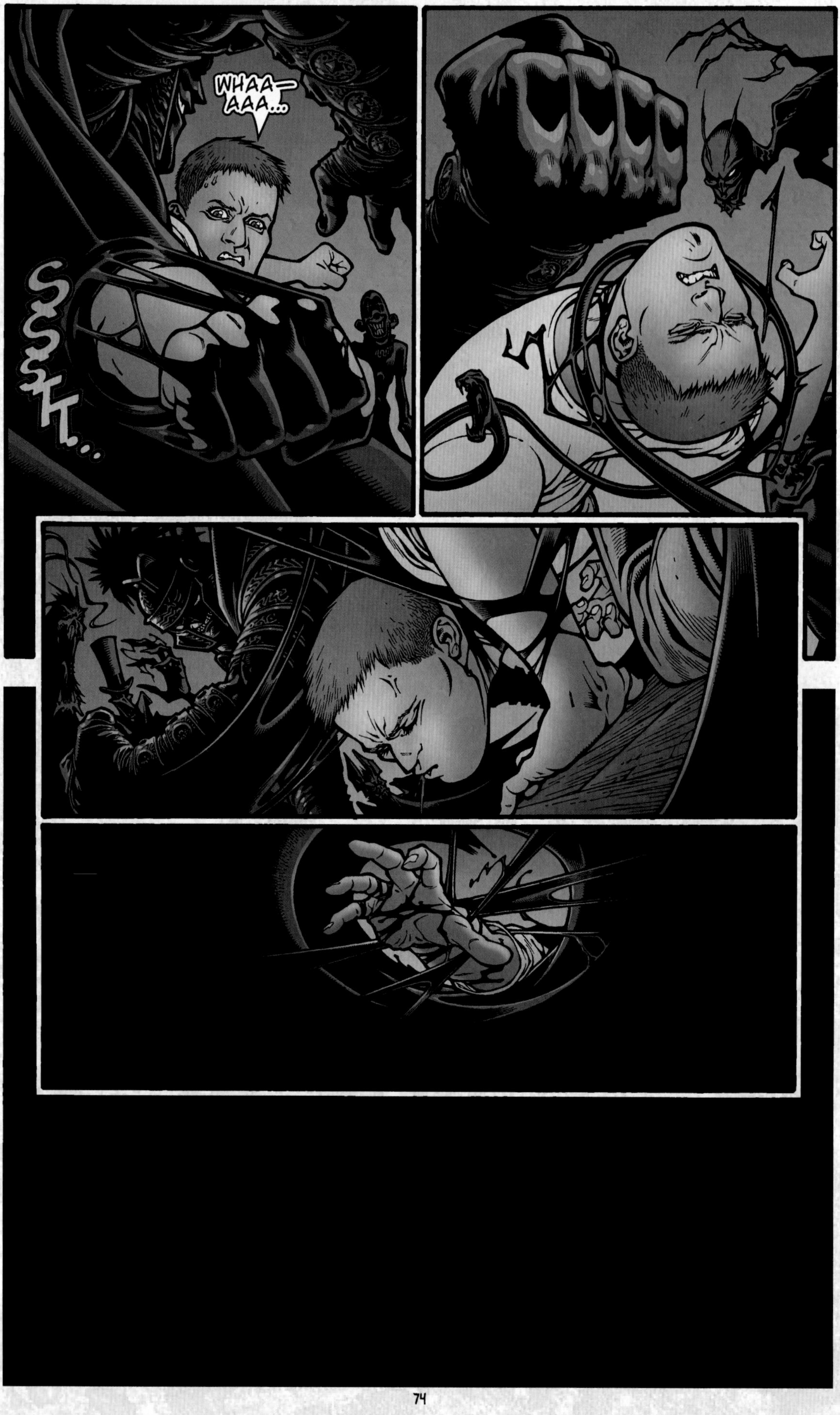
WHAA—
AAA...
SSSKK...

Crown Of Shadows

Chapter Four: Shadow Play

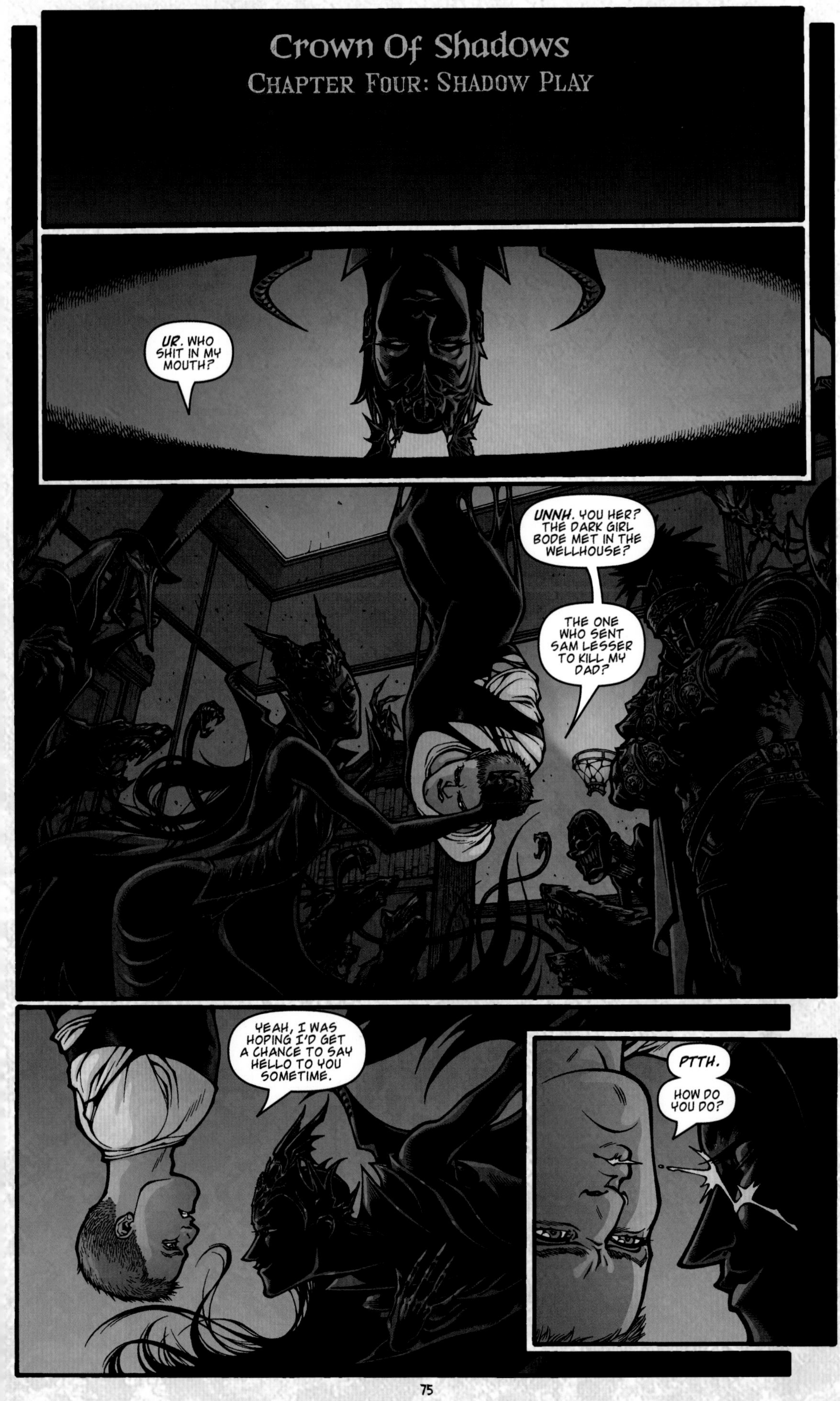
UR. WHO SHIT IN MY MOUTH?
UNNH. YOU HER? THE DARK GIRL BODE MET IN THE WELLHOUSE?
THE ONE WHO SENT SAM LESSER TO KILL MY DAD?
YEAH, I WAS HOPING I'D GET A CHANCE TO SAY HELLO TO YOU SOMETIME.
PTTH.
HOW DO YOU DO?

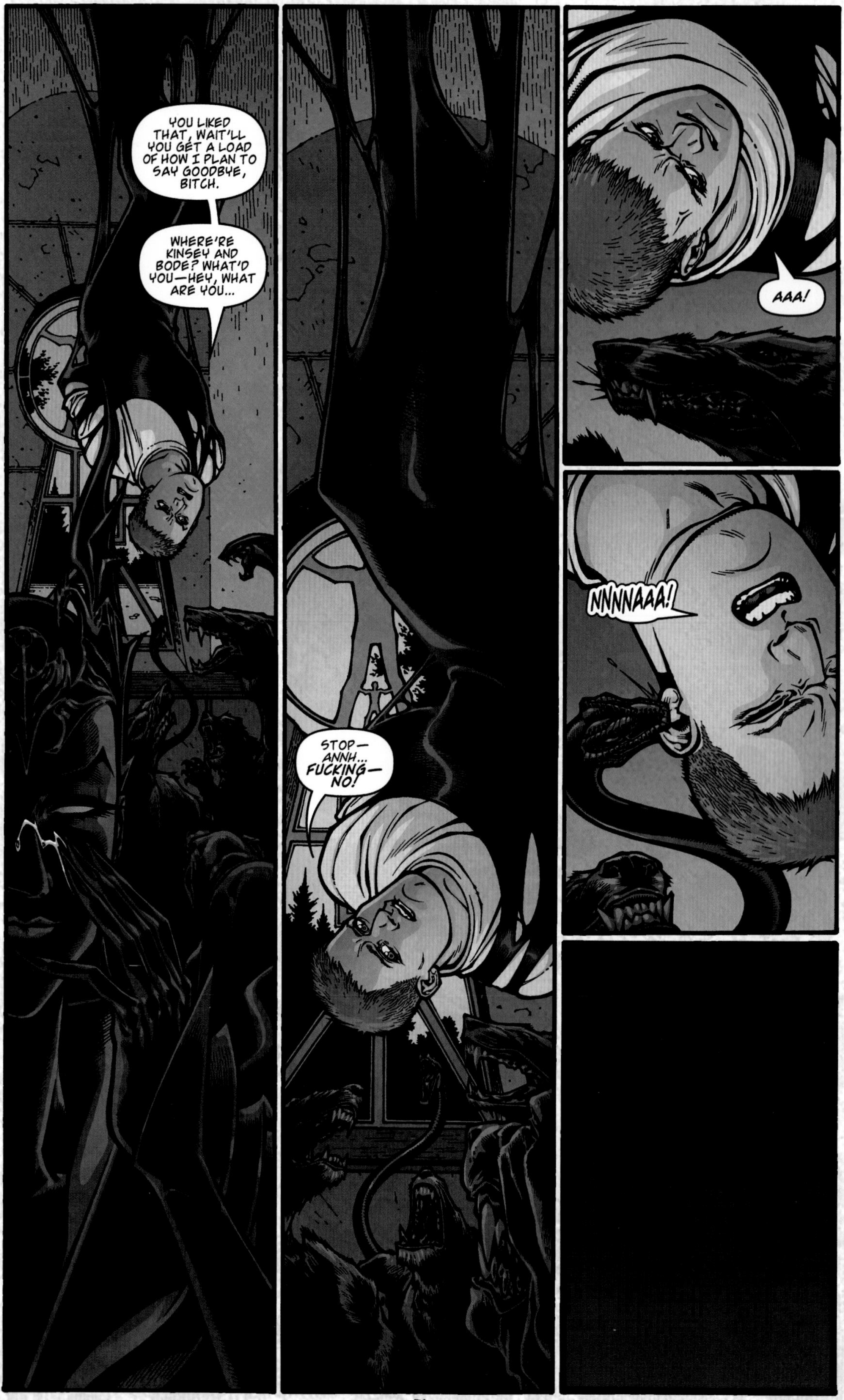
YOU LIKED THAT, WAIT'LL YOU GET A LOAD OF HOW I PLAN TO SAY GOODBYE, BITCH.
WHERE'RE KINSEY AND BODE? WHAT'D YOU—HEY, WHAT ARE YOU...
STOP— ANNH... FUCKING— NO!
AAA!
NNNNAAA!

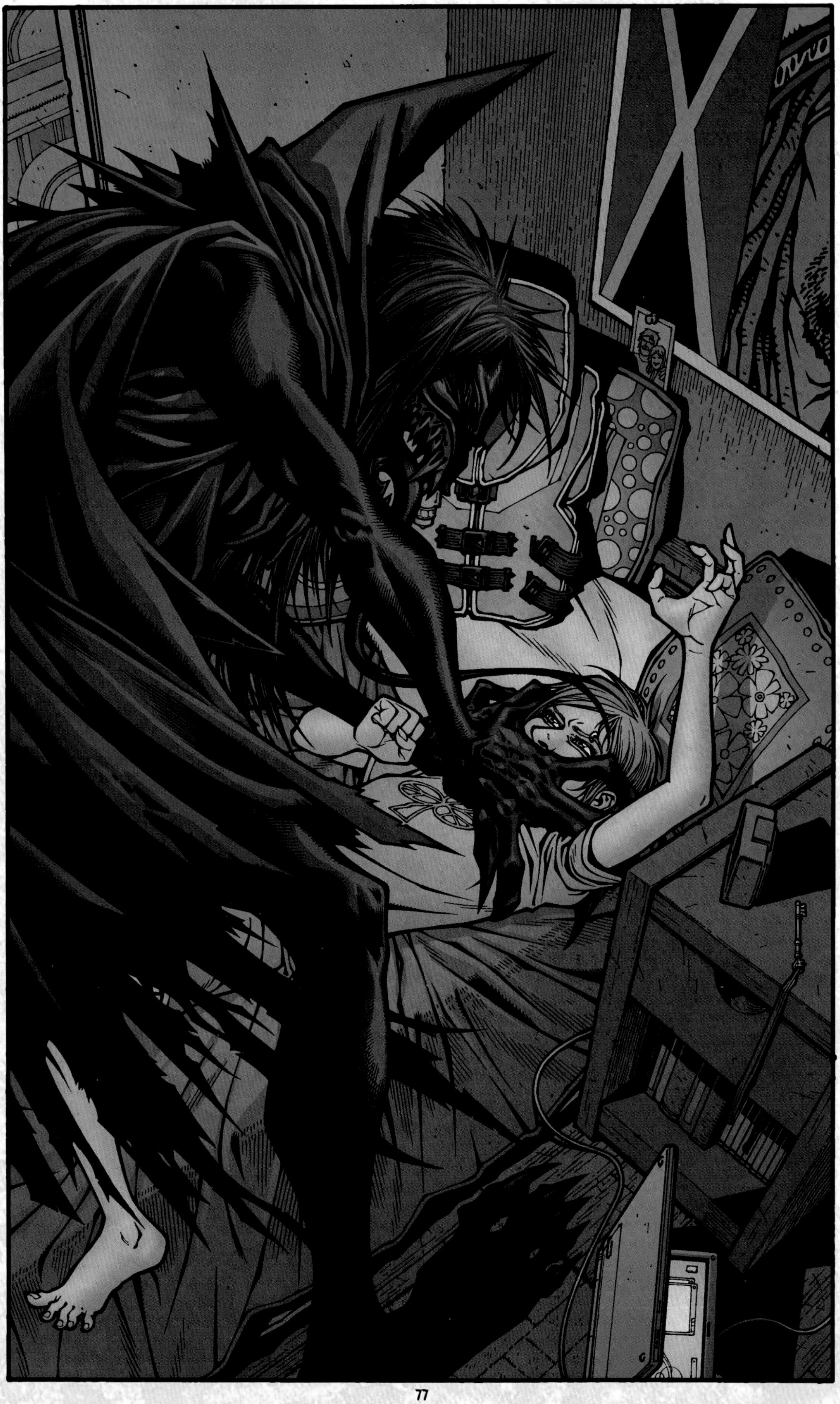

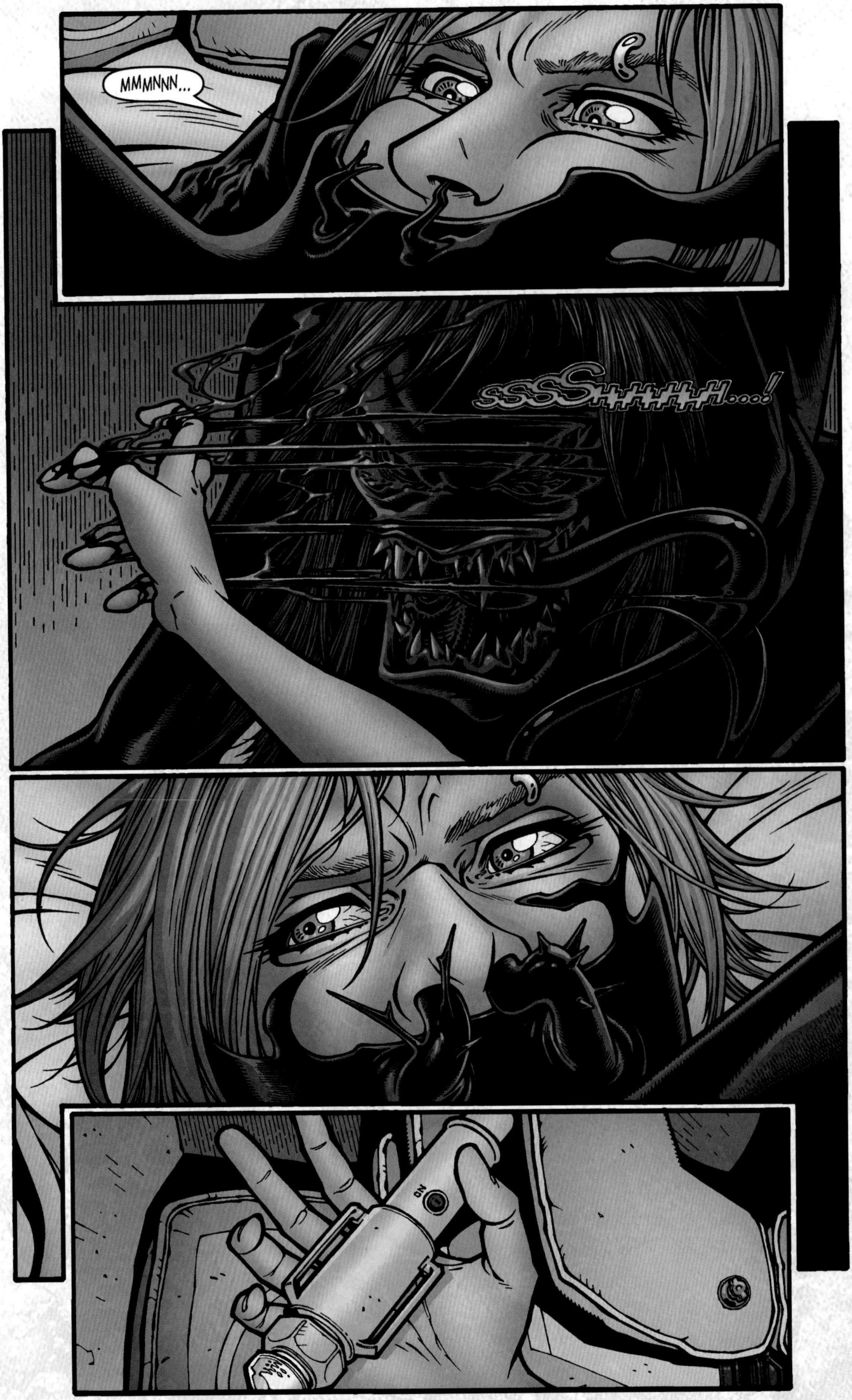
MMMNNN...
sssSHHHHHH...!
ON

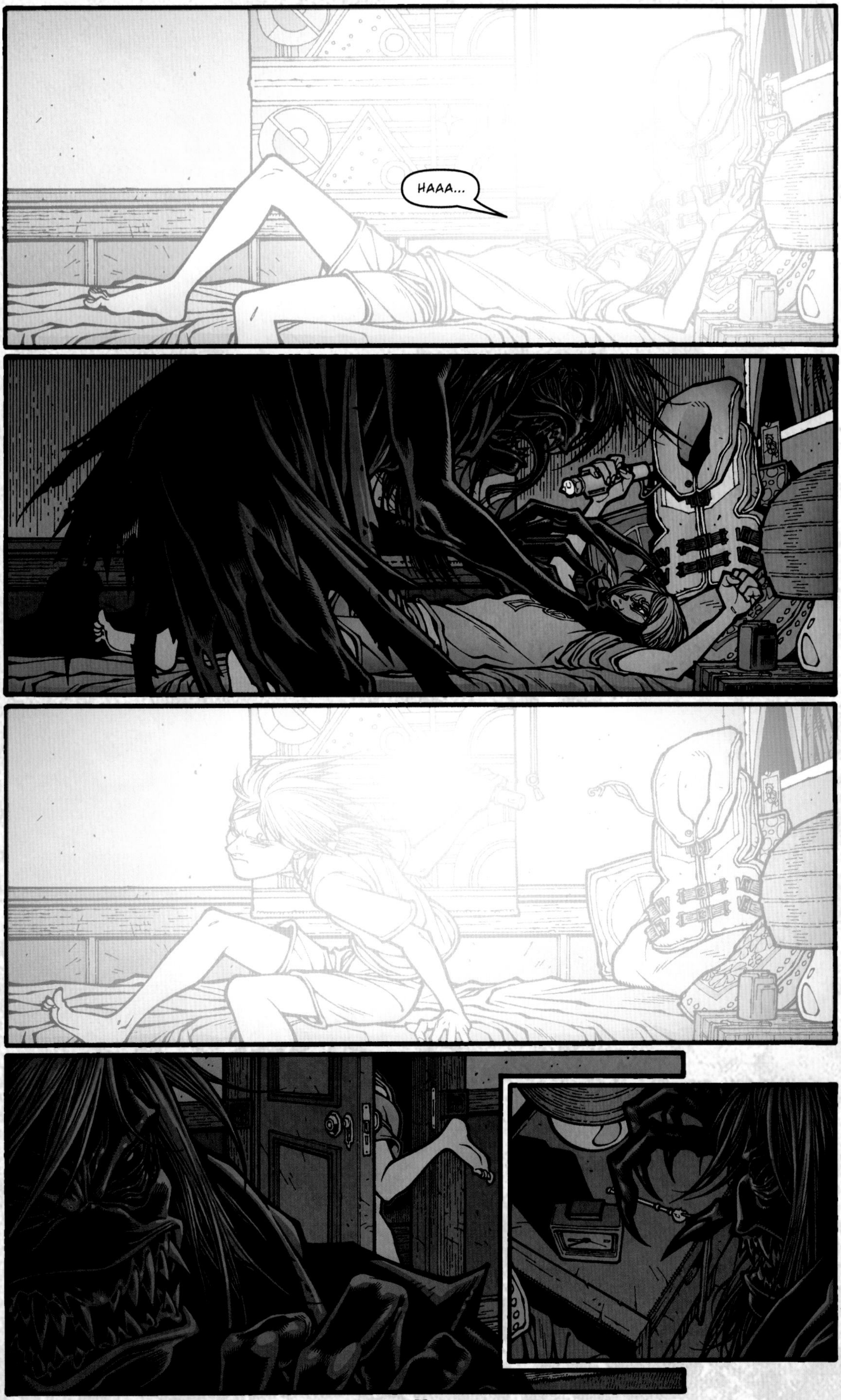
HAAA...

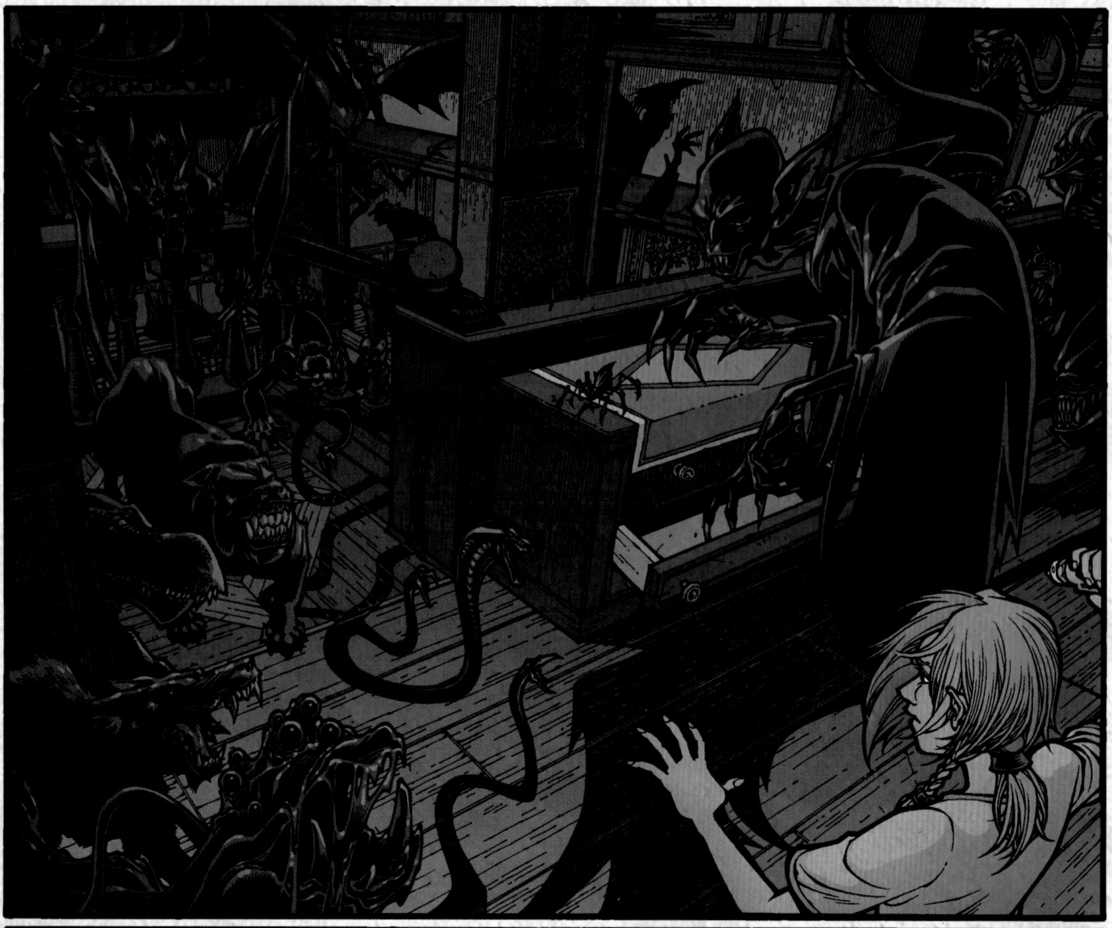

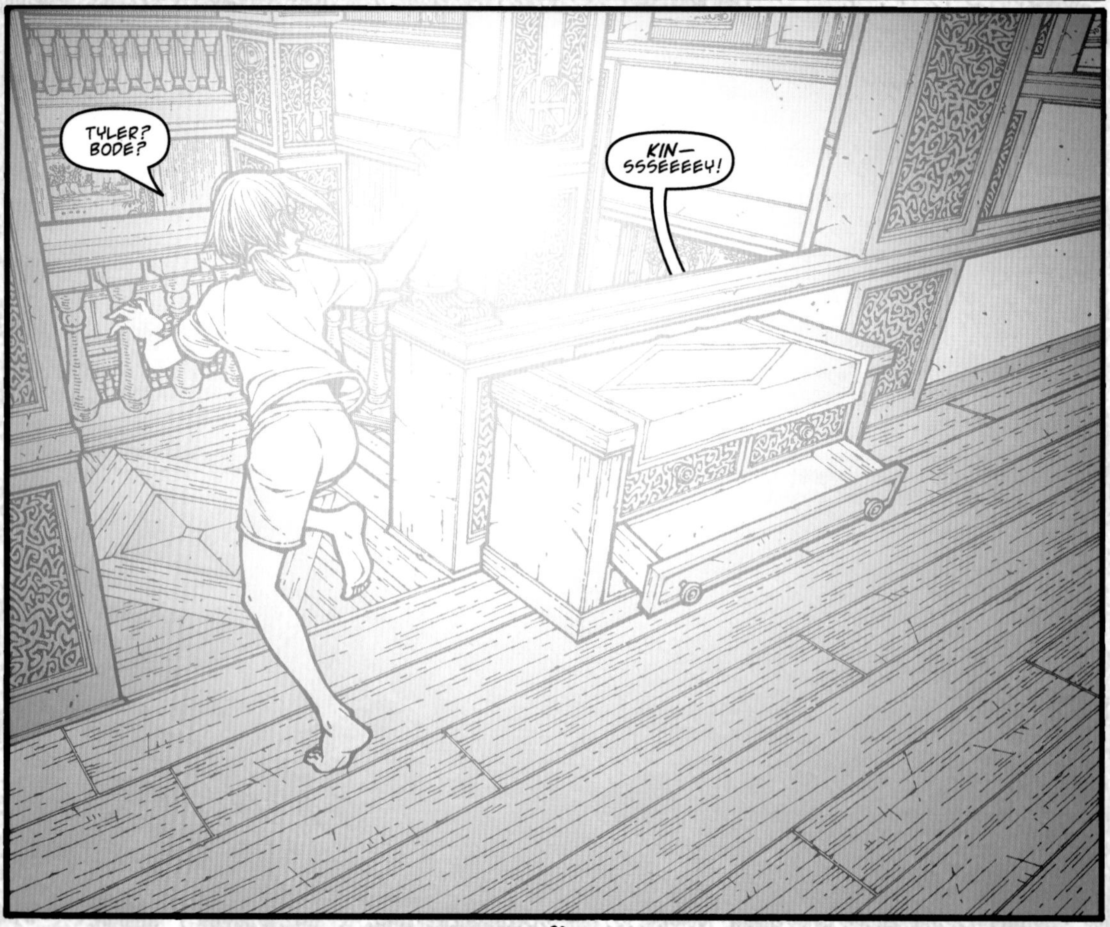
TYLER?
BODE?
KIN—
SSSEEEEEY!

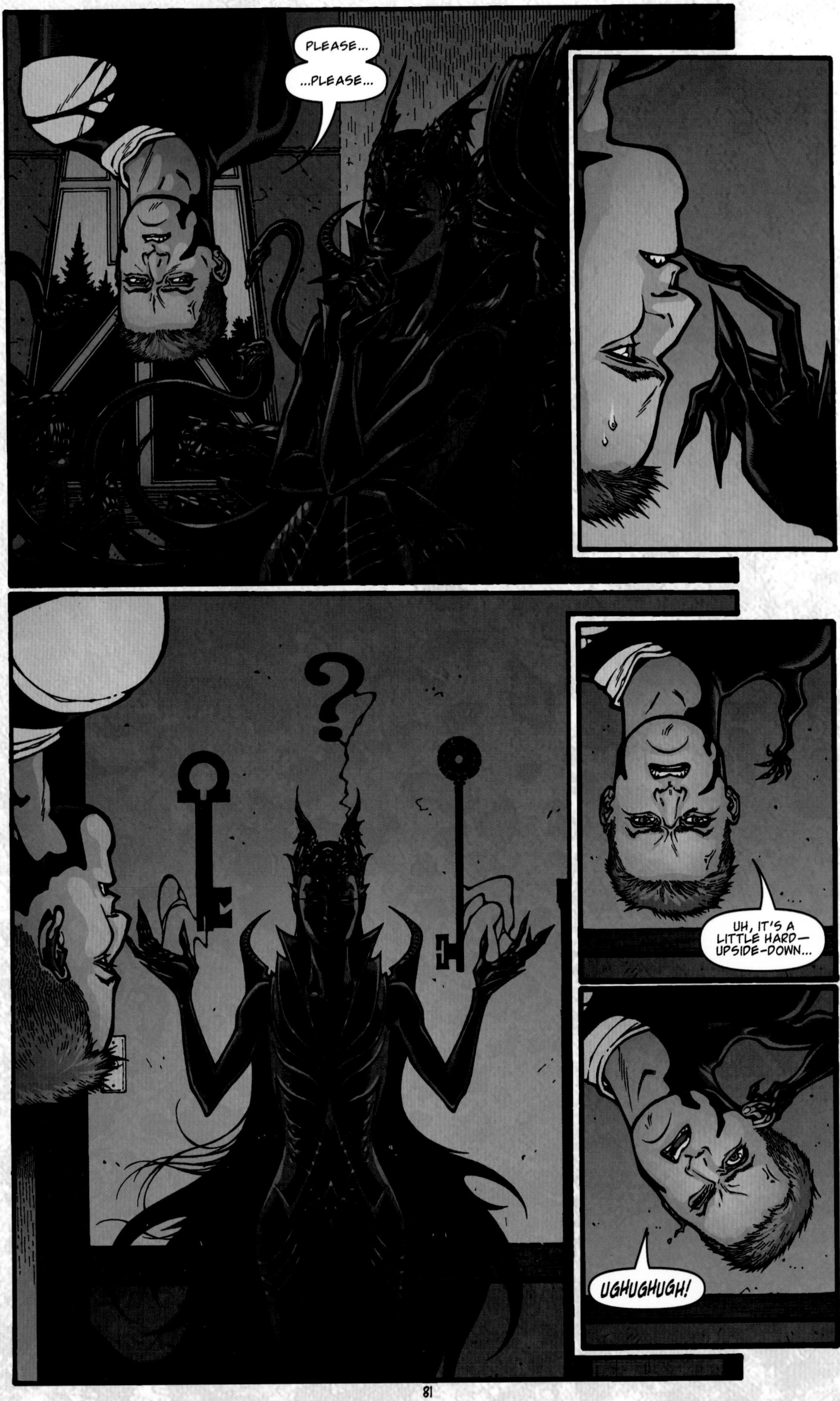
PLEASE...
...PLEASE...
UH, IT'S A LITTLE HARD—UPSIDE-DOWN...
UGHUGHUGH!

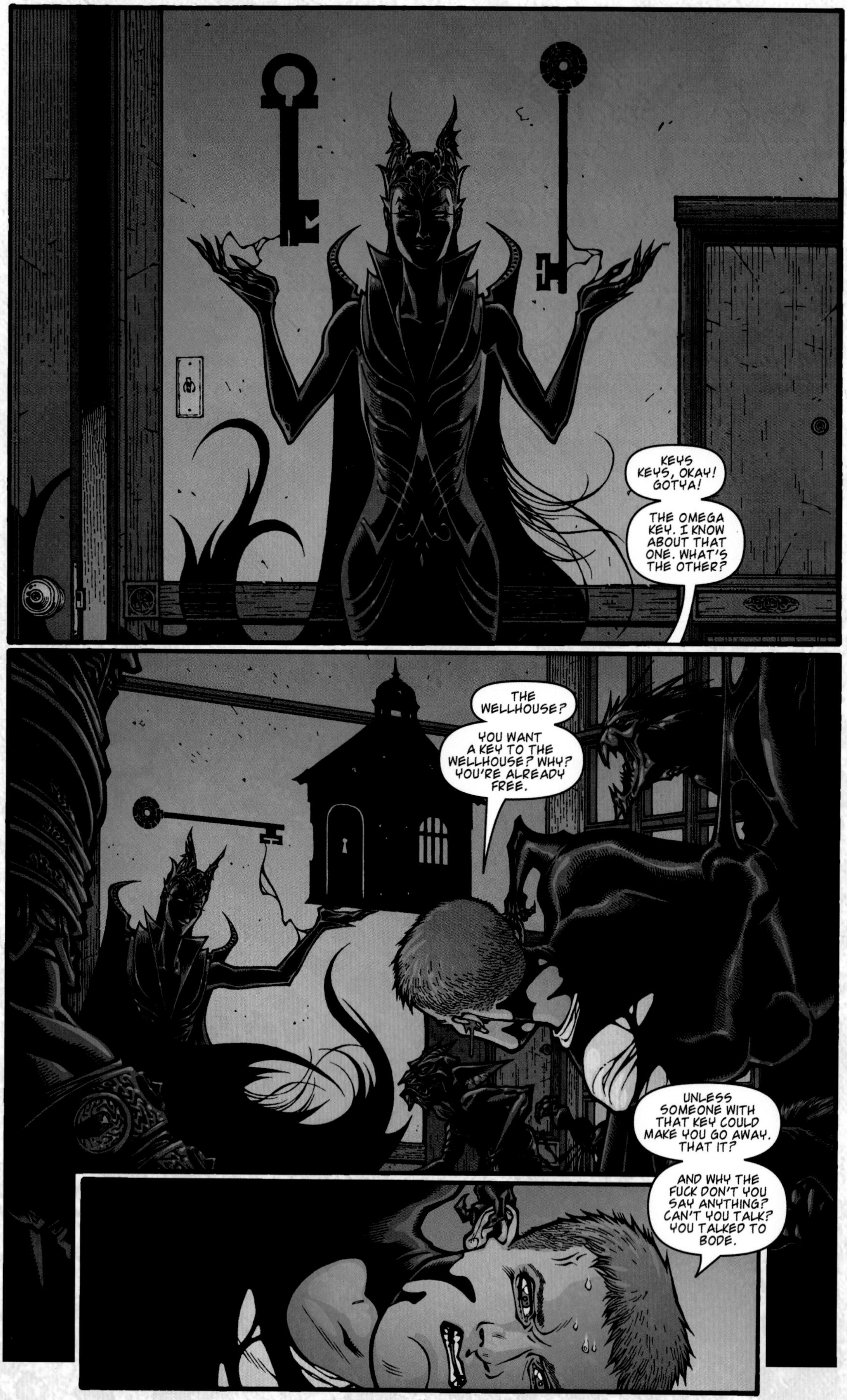
KEYS KEYS, OKAY! GOTYA!
THE OMEGA KEY. I KNOW ABOUT THAT ONE. WHAT'S THE OTHER?
THE WELLHOUSE?
YOU WANT A KEY TO THE WELLHOUSE? WHY? YOU'RE ALREADY FREE.
UNLESS SOMEONE WITH THAT KEY COULD MAKE YOU GO AWAY. THAT IT?
AND WHY THE FUCK DON'T YOU SAY ANYTHING? CAN'T YOU TALK? YOU TALKED TO BODE.

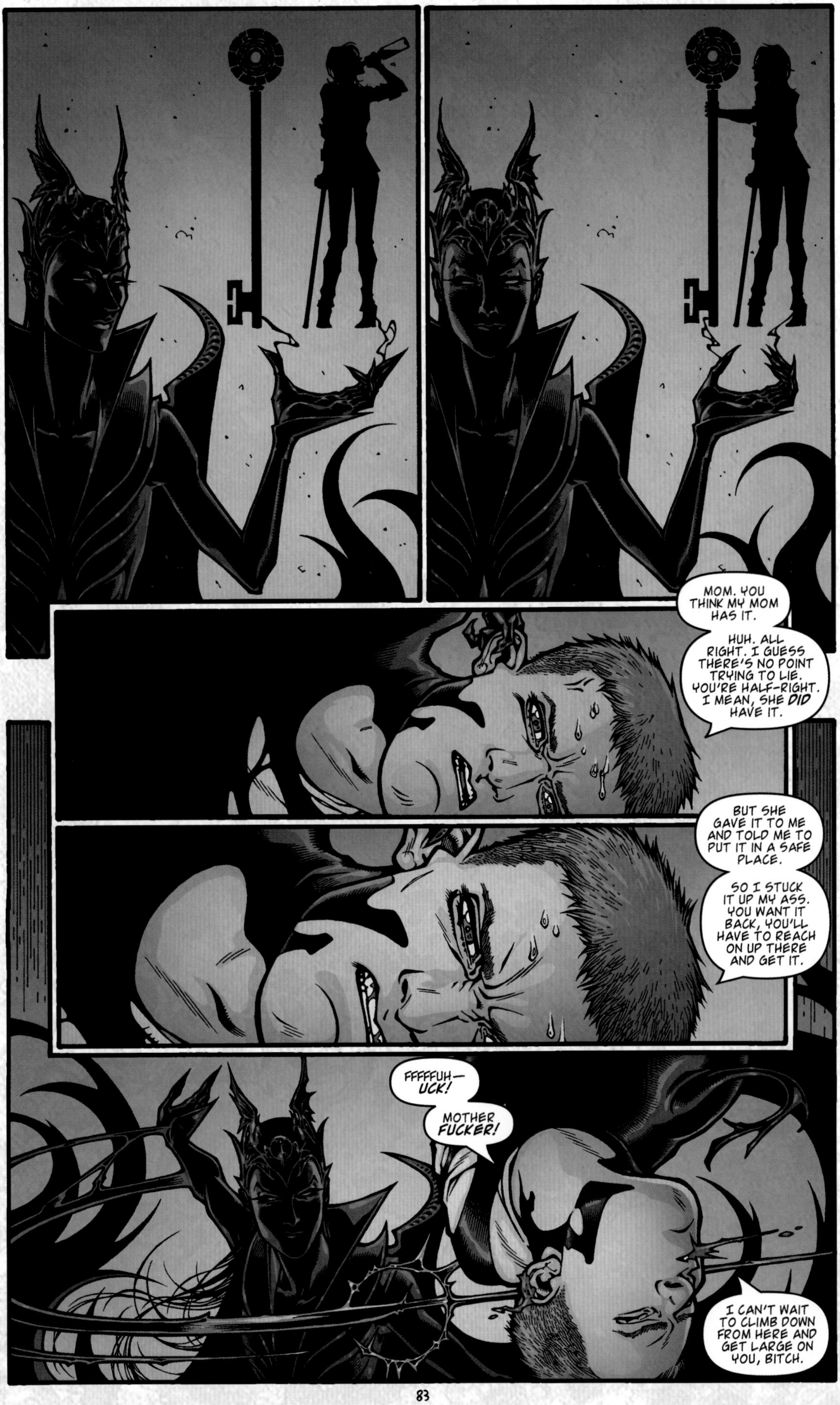

MOM. YOU THINK MY MOM HAS IT.
HUH. ALL RIGHT. I GUESS THERE'S NO POINT TRYING TO LIE. YOU'RE HALF-RIGHT. I MEAN, SHE *DID* HAVE IT.
BUT SHE GAVE IT TO ME AND TOLD ME TO PUT IT IN A SAFE PLACE.
SO I STUCK IT UP MY ASS. YOU WANT IT BACK, YOU'LL HAVE TO REACH ON UP THERE AND GET IT.
FFFFFUH— *UCK!*
MOTHER *FUCKER!*
I CAN'T WAIT TO CLIMB DOWN FROM HERE AND GET LARGE ON YOU, BITCH.

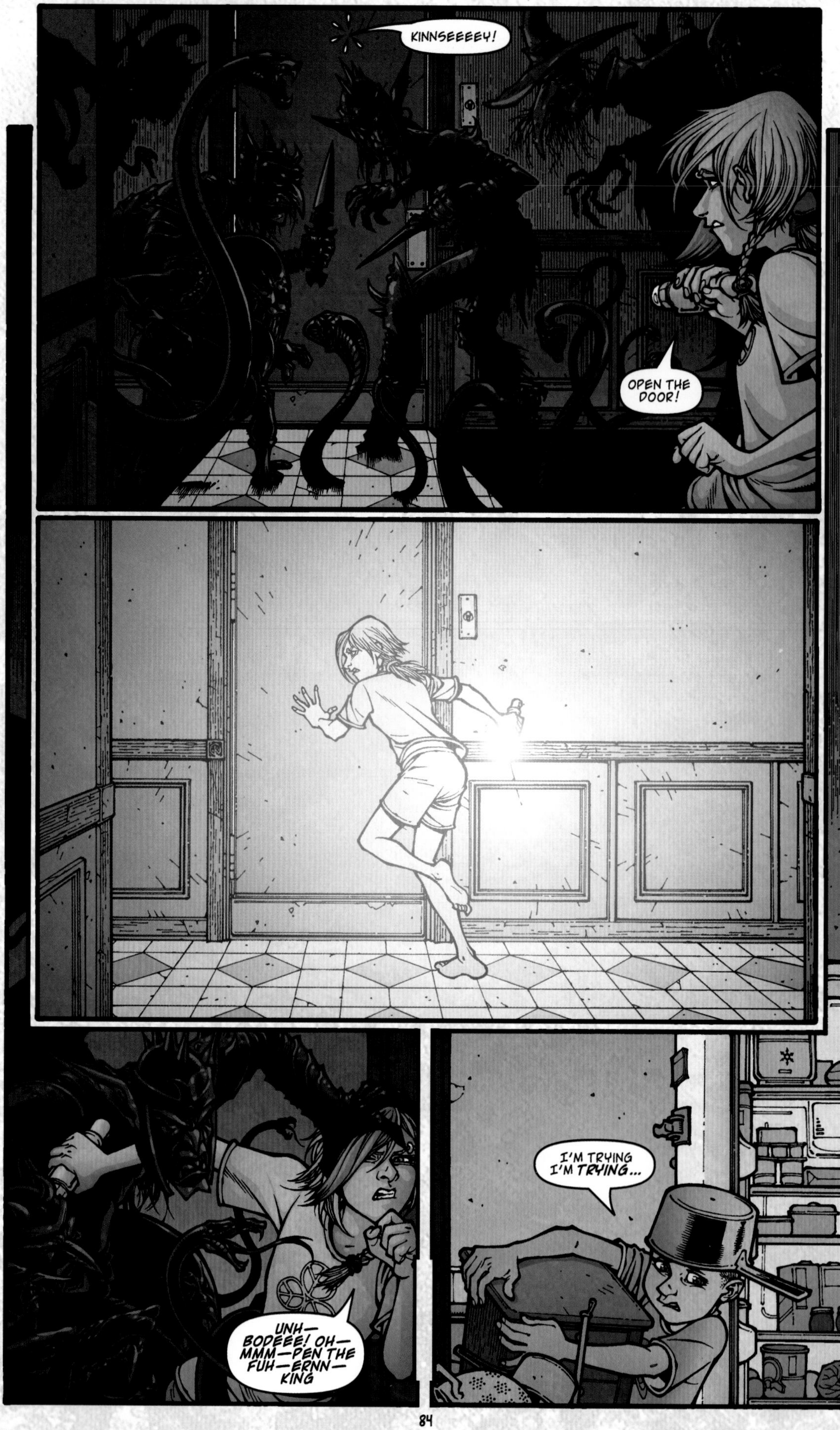
KINNSEEEEY!
OPEN THE DOOR!
UNH— BODEEE! OH— MMM—PEN THE FUH—ERNN— KING
I'M TRYING I'M TRYING...

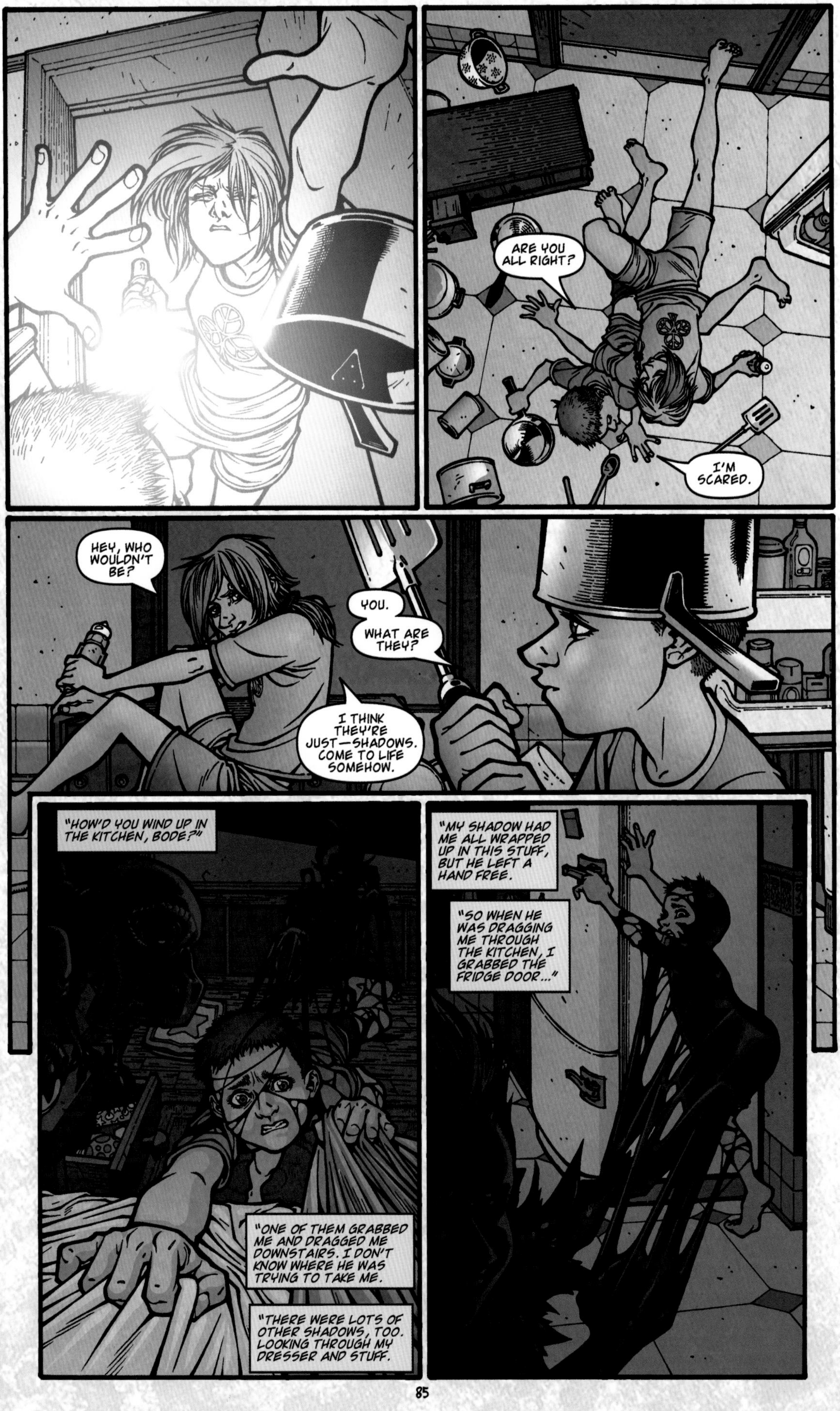

ARE YOU ALL RIGHT?
I'M SCARED.
HEY, WHO WOULDN'T BE?
YOU.
WHAT ARE THEY?
I THINK THEY'RE JUST—SHADOWS. COME TO LIFE SOMEHOW.
"HOW'D YOU WIND UP IN THE KITCHEN, BODE?"
"ONE OF THEM GRABBED ME AND DRAGGED ME DOWNSTAIRS. I DON'T KNOW WHERE HE WAS TRYING TO TAKE ME.
"THERE WERE LOTS OF OTHER SHADOWS, TOO. LOOKING THROUGH MY DRESSER AND STUFF.
"MY SHADOW HAD ME ALL WRAPPED UP IN THIS STUFF, BUT HE LEFT A HAND FREE.
"SO WHEN HE WAS DRAGGING ME THROUGH THE KITCHEN, I GRABBED THE FRIDGE DOOR..."

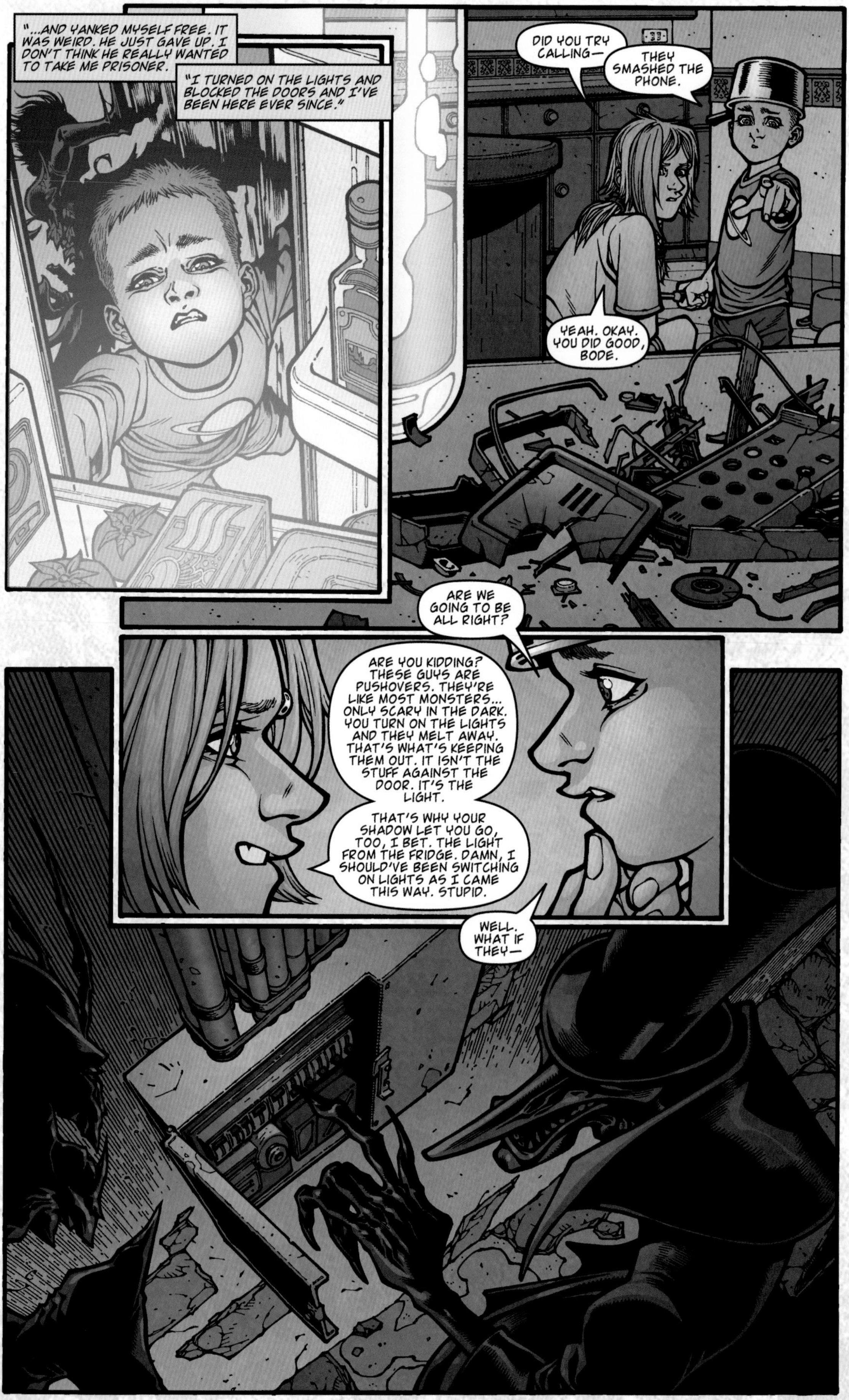

"...AND YANKED MYSELF FREE. IT WAS WEIRD. HE JUST GAVE UP. I DON'T THINK HE REALLY WANTED TO TAKE ME PRISONER.
"I TURNED ON THE LIGHTS AND BLOCKED THE DOORS AND I'VE BEEN HERE EVER SINCE."
DID YOU TRY CALLING—
THEY SMASHED THE PHONE.
YEAH. OKAY. YOU DID GOOD, BODE.
ARE WE GOING TO BE ALL RIGHT?
ARE YOU KIDDING? THESE GUYS ARE PUSHOVERS. THEY'RE LIKE MOST MONSTERS... ONLY SCARY IN THE DARK. YOU TURN ON THE LIGHTS AND THEY MELT AWAY. THAT'S WHAT'S KEEPING THEM OUT. IT ISN'T THE STUFF AGAINST THE DOOR. IT'S THE LIGHT.
THAT'S WHY YOUR SHADOW LET YOU GO, TOO, I BET. THE LIGHT FROM THE FRIDGE. DAMN, I SHOULD'VE BEEN SWITCHING ON LIGHTS AS I CAME THIS WAY. STUPID.
WELL. WHAT IF THEY—

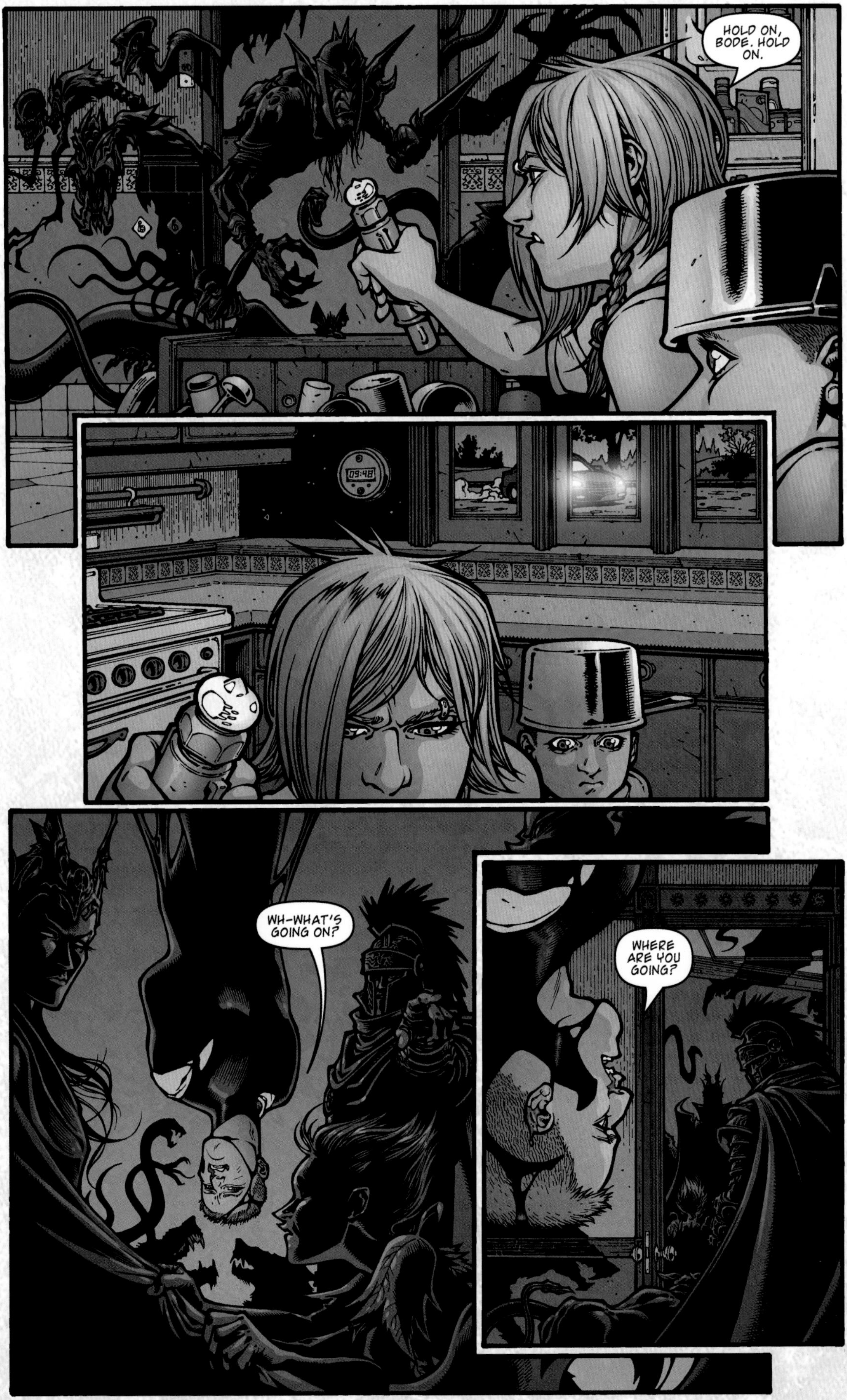

HOLD ON, BODE. HOLD ON.
WH-WHAT'S GOING ON?
WHERE ARE YOU GOING?

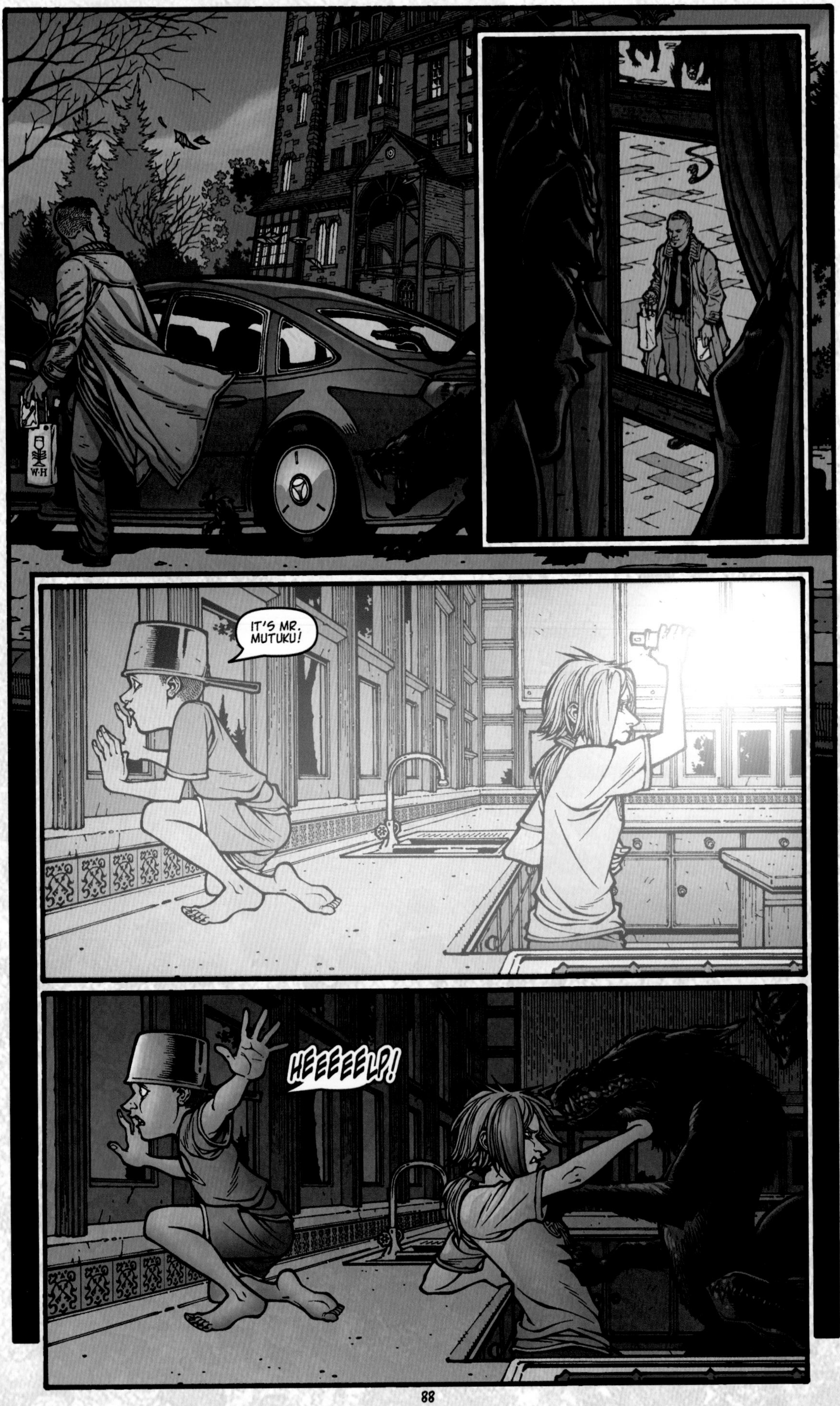
W-H
IT'S MR. MUTUKU!
HEEEEELP!

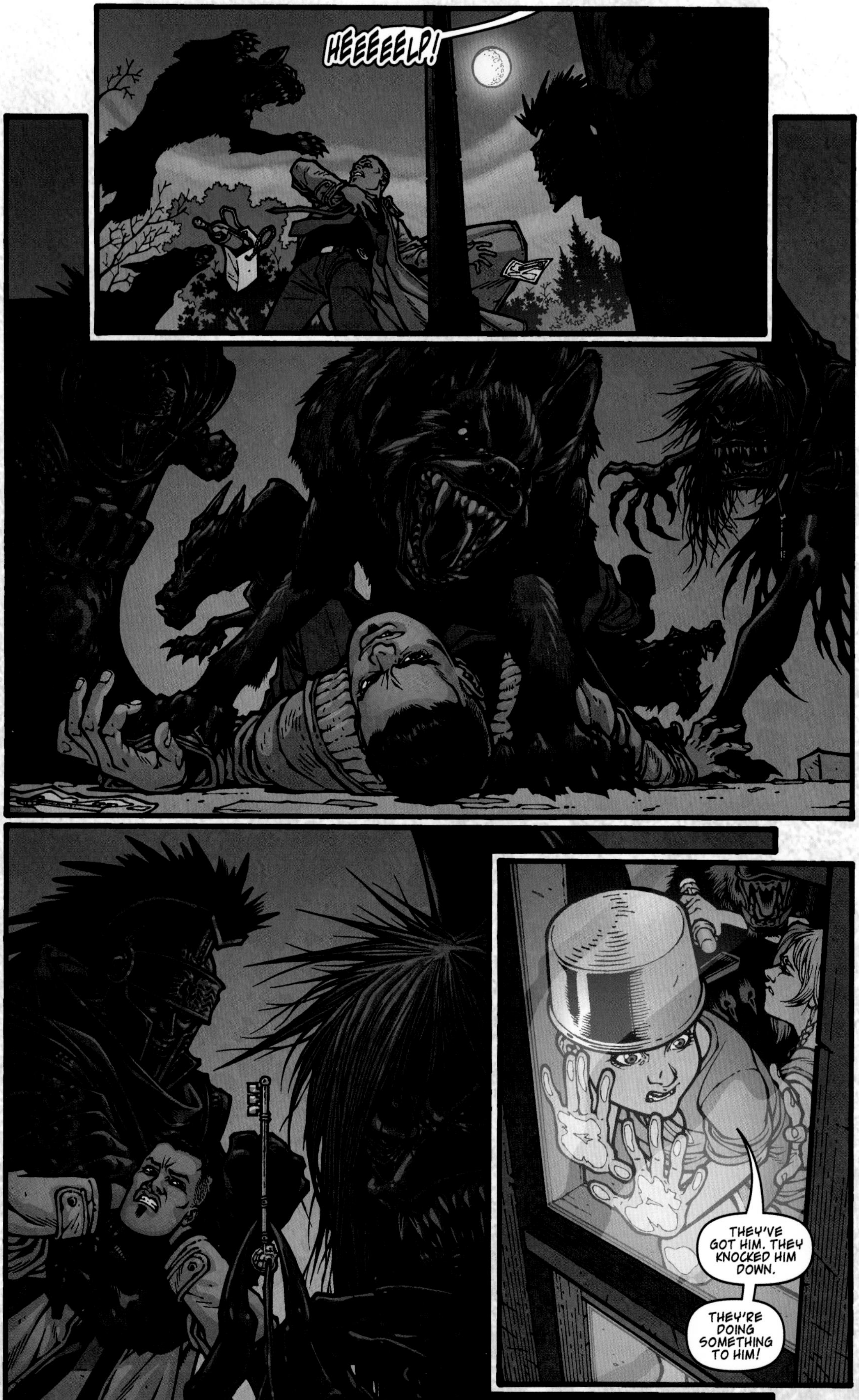
HEEEEELP!
THEY'VE GOT HIM. THEY KNOCKED HIM DOWN.
THEY'RE DOING SOMETHING TO HIM!

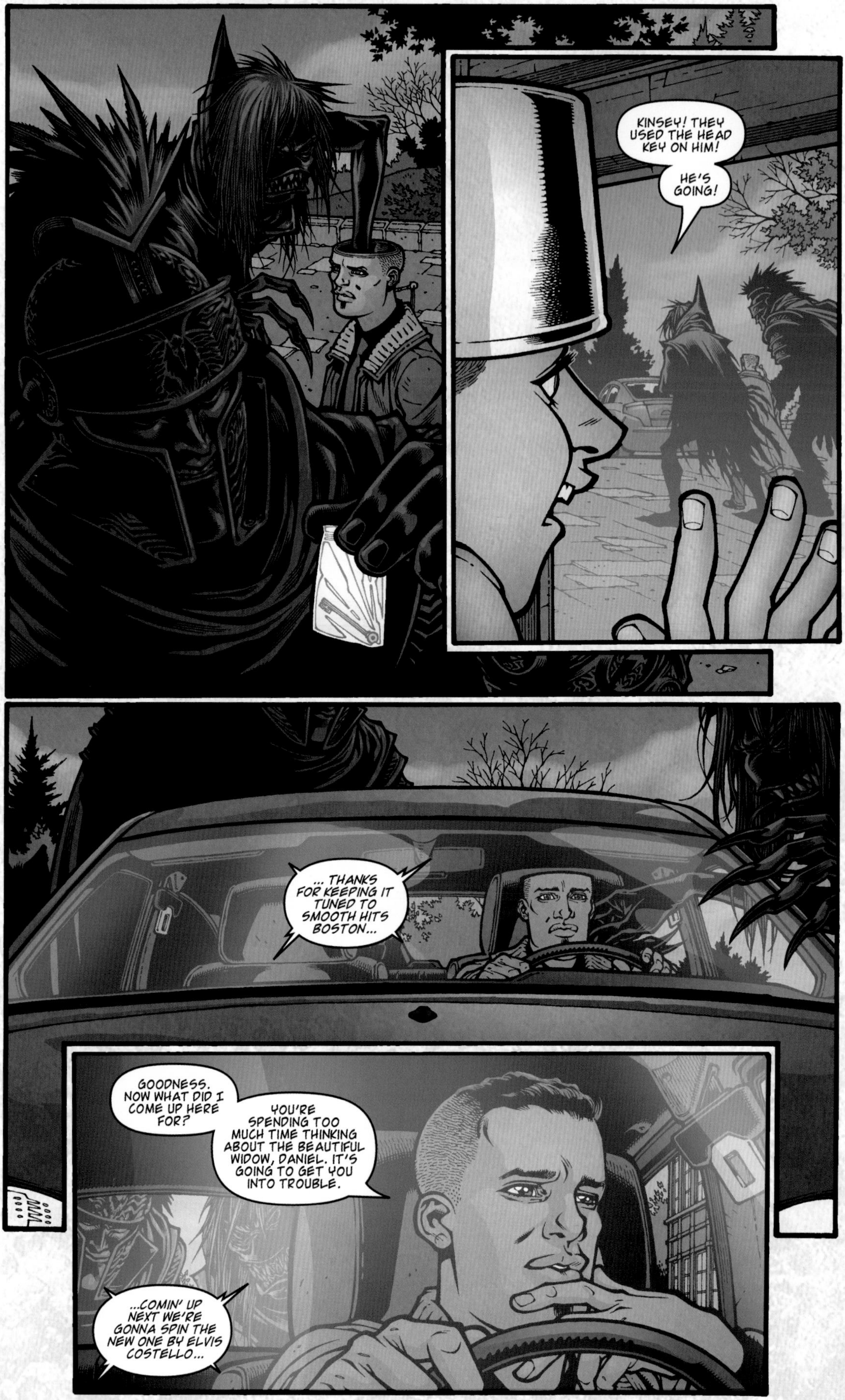
KINSEY! THEY USED THE HEAD KEY ON HIM!
HE'S GOING!
... THANKS FOR KEEPING IT TUNED TO SMOOTH HITS BOSTON...
GOODNESS. NOW WHAT DID I COME UP HERE FOR?
YOU'RE SPENDING TOO MUCH TIME THINKING ABOUT THE BEAUTIFUL WIDOW, DANIEL. IT'S GOING TO GET YOU INTO TROUBLE.
...COMIN' UP NEXT WE'RE GONNA SPIN THE NEW ONE BY ELVIS COSTELLO...

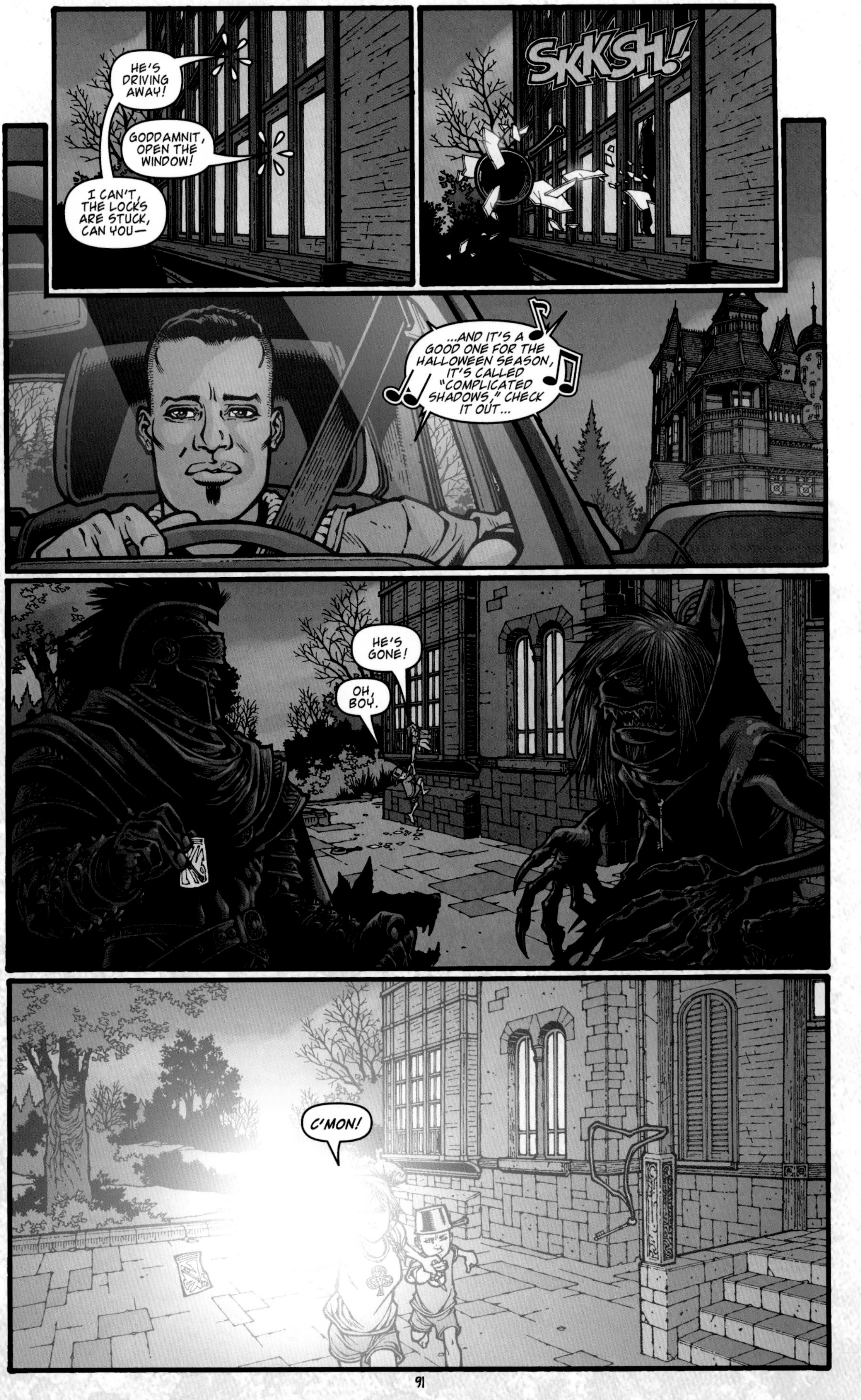
HE'S DRIVING AWAY!
GODDAMNIT, OPEN THE WINDOW!
I CAN'T, THE LOCKS ARE STUCK, CAN YOU—
SKKSH!
...AND IT'S A GOOD ONE FOR THE HALLOWEEN SEASON, IT'S CALLED "COMPLICATED SHADOWS," CHECK IT OUT...
HE'S GONE!
OH, BOY.
C'MON!

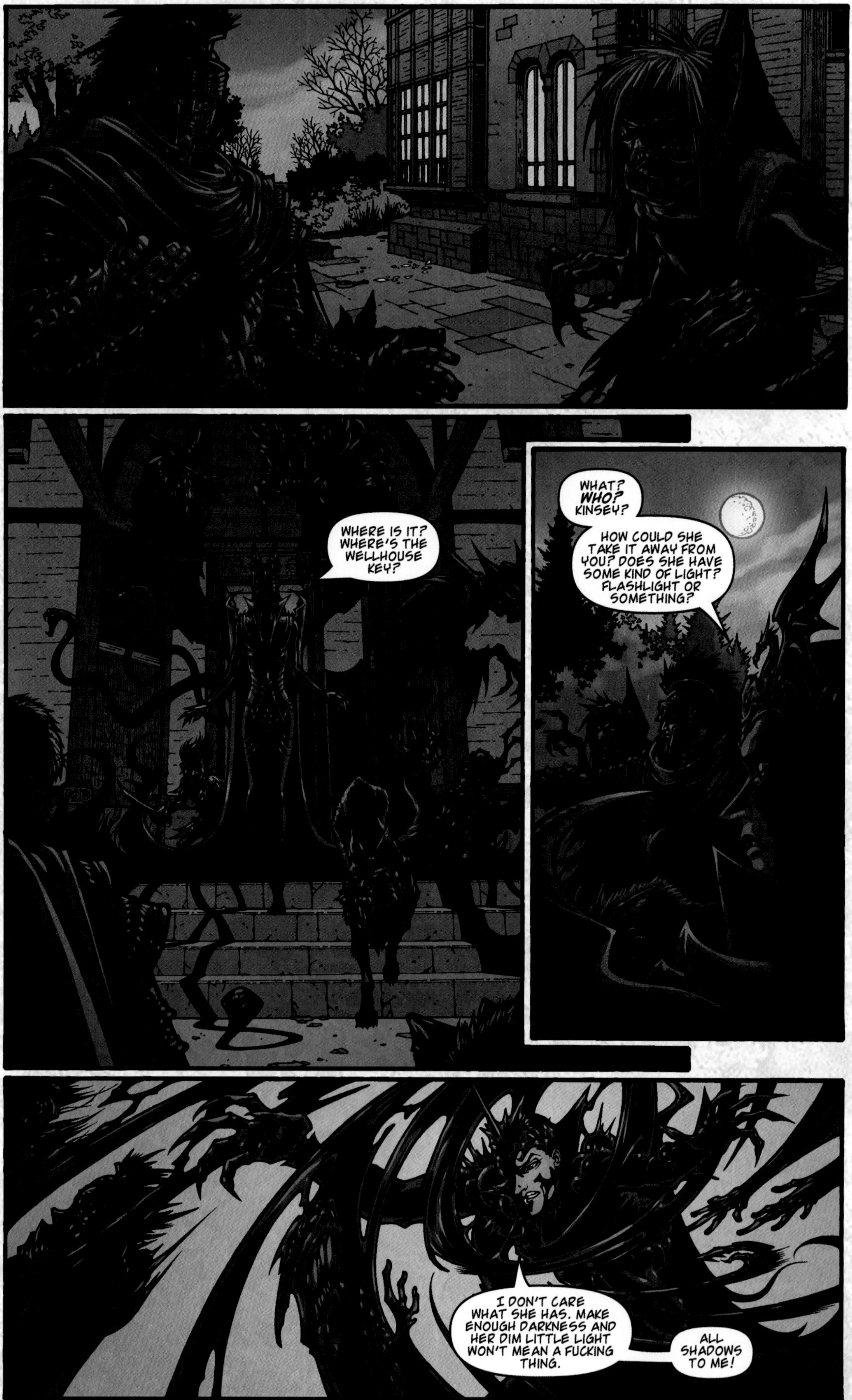
WHERE IS IT? WHERE'S THE WELLHOUSE KEY?
WHAT? WHO? KINSEY?
HOW COULD SHE TAKE IT AWAY FROM YOU? DOES SHE HAVE SOME KIND OF LIGHT? FLASHLIGHT OR SOMETHING?
I DON'T CARE WHAT SHE HAS. MAKE ENOUGH DARKNESS AND HER DIM LITTLE LIGHT WON'T MEAN A FUCKING THING.
ALL SHADOWS TO ME!

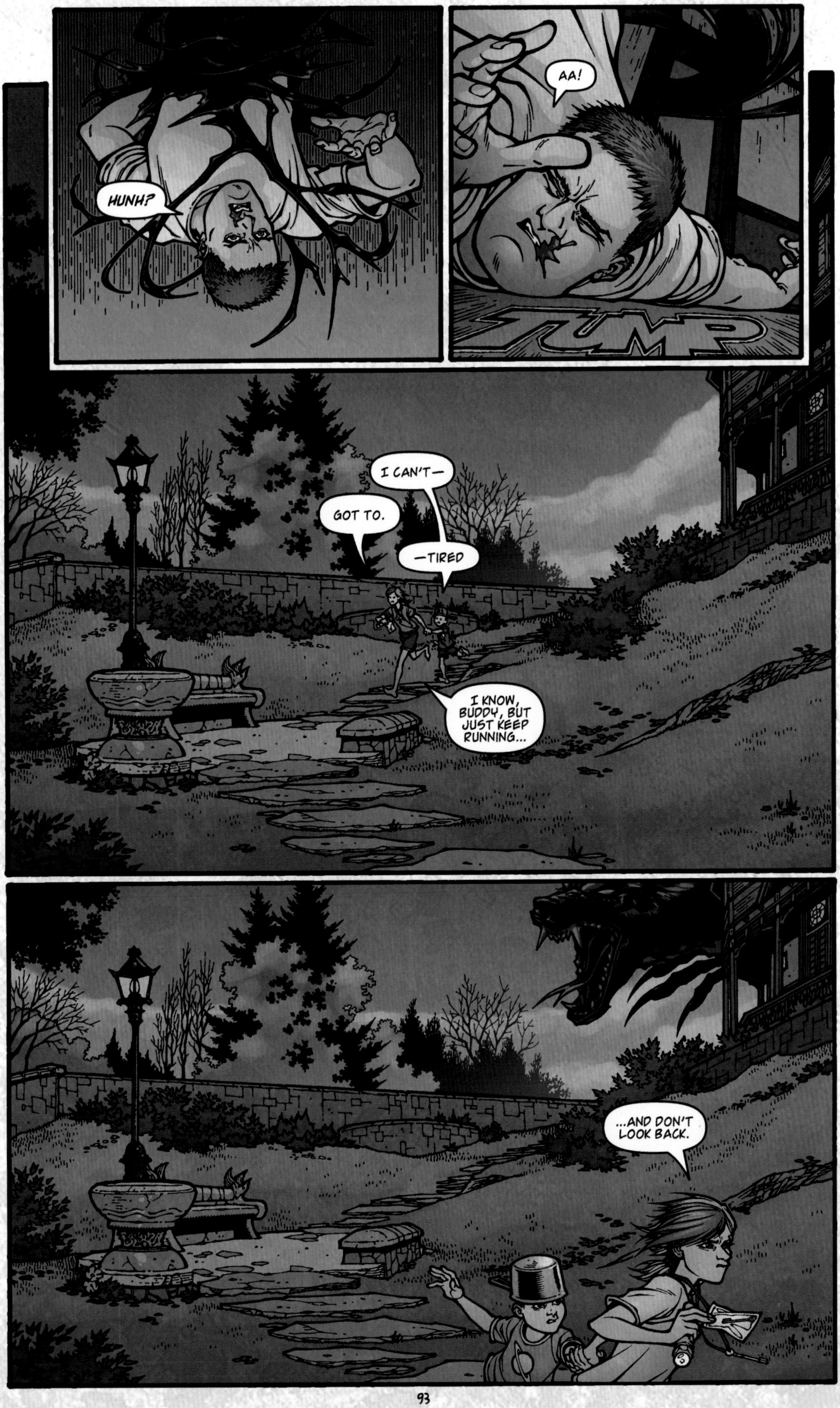
HUNH?
AA!
TUMP
I CAN'T—
GOT TO.
—TIRED
I KNOW, BUDDY, BUT JUST KEEP RUNNING...
...AND DON'T LOOK BACK.

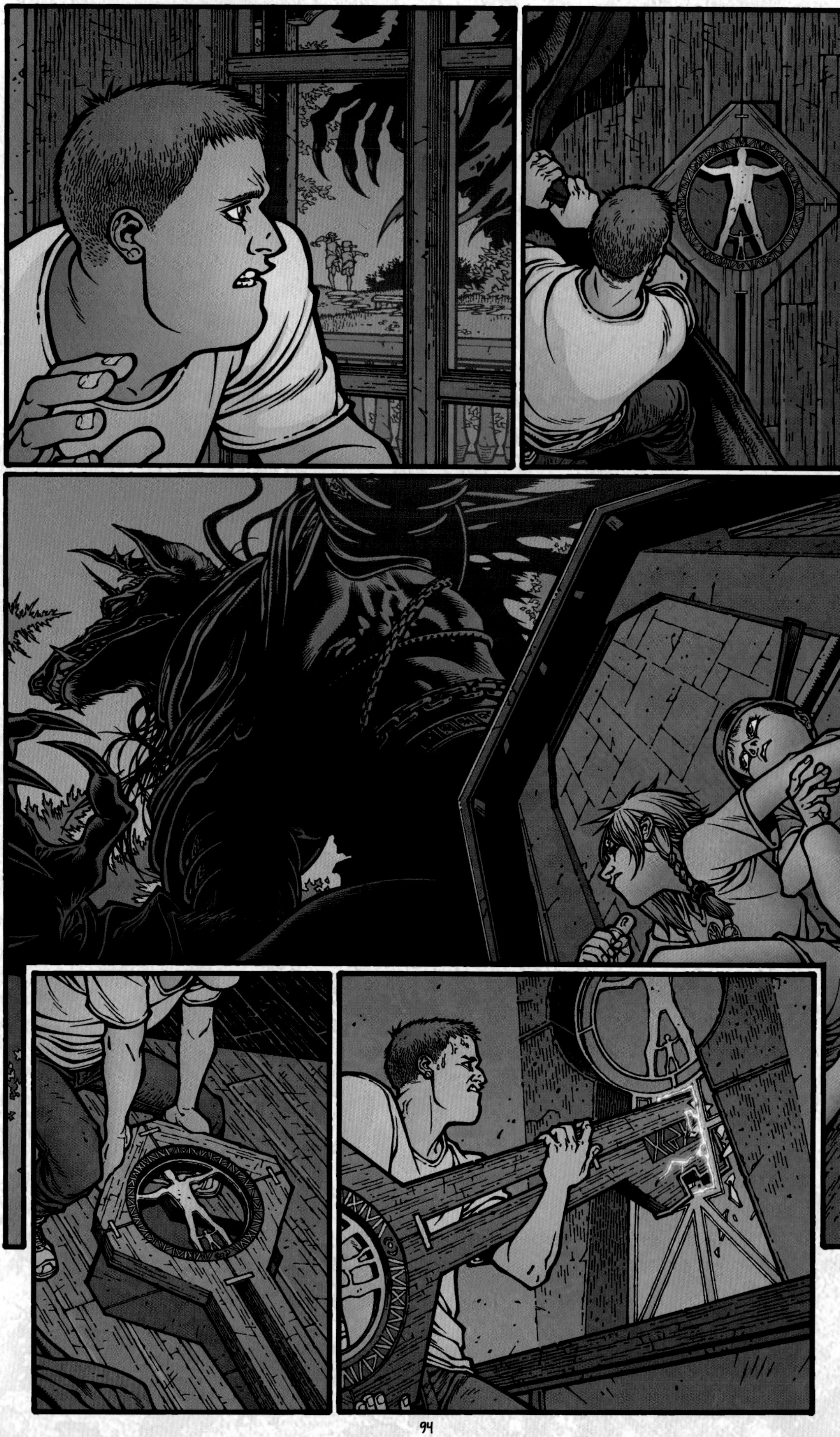

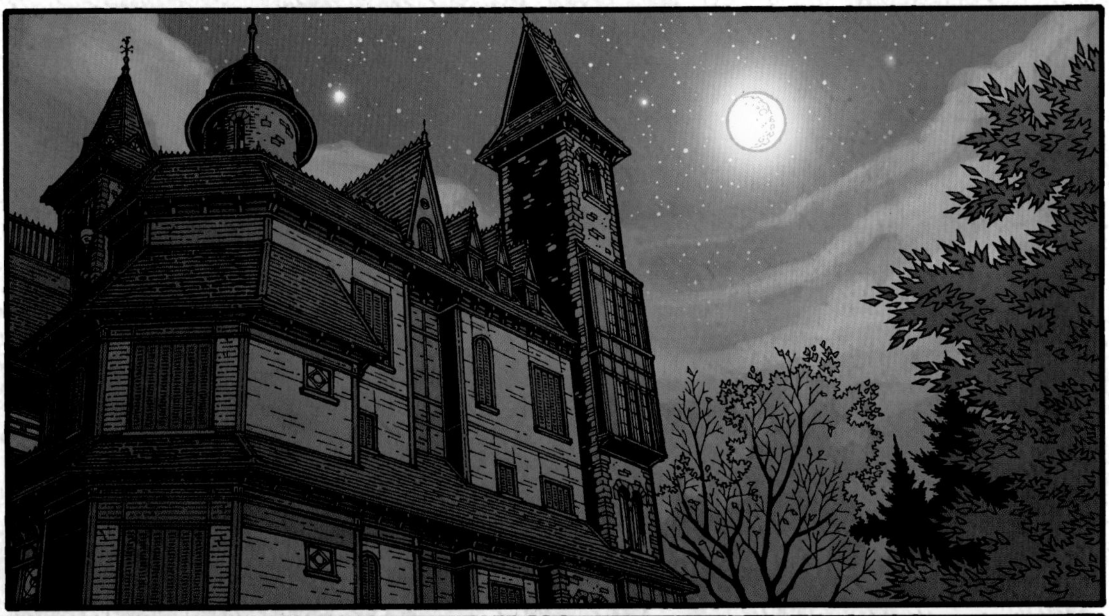

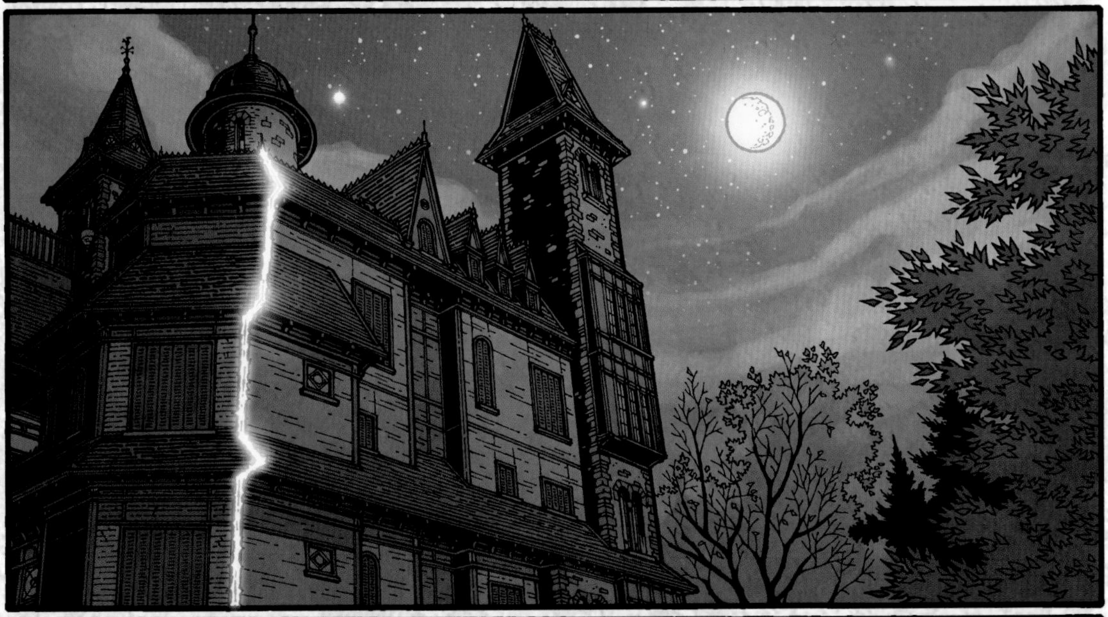

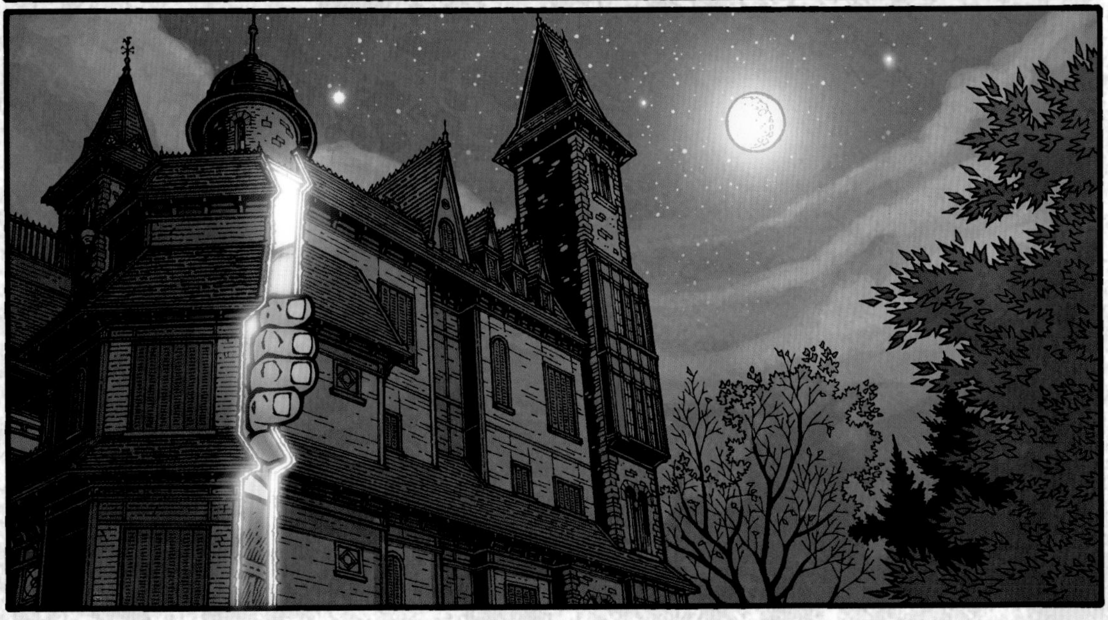

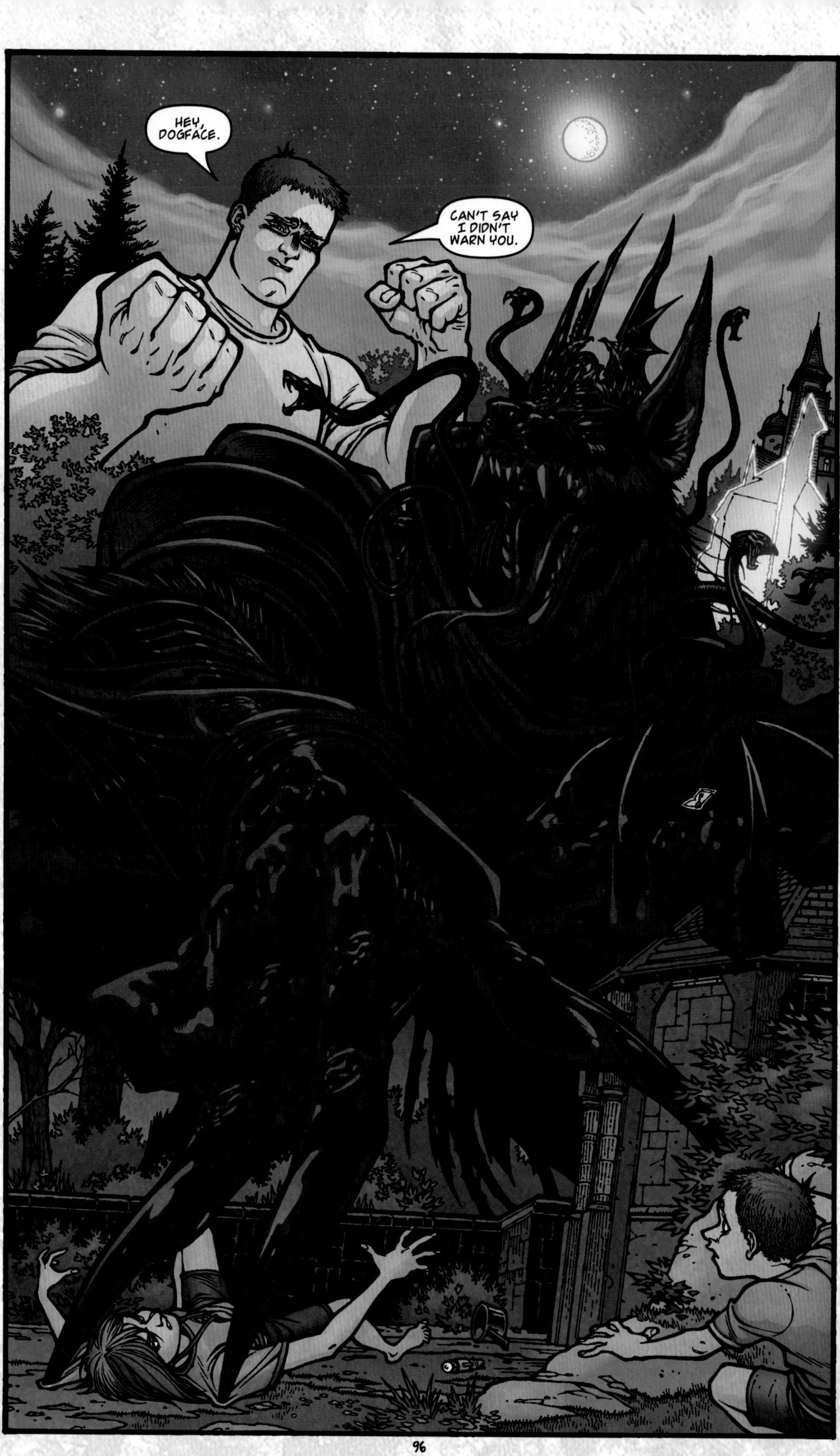
HEY, DOGFACE.
CAN'T SAY I DIDN'T WARN YOU.

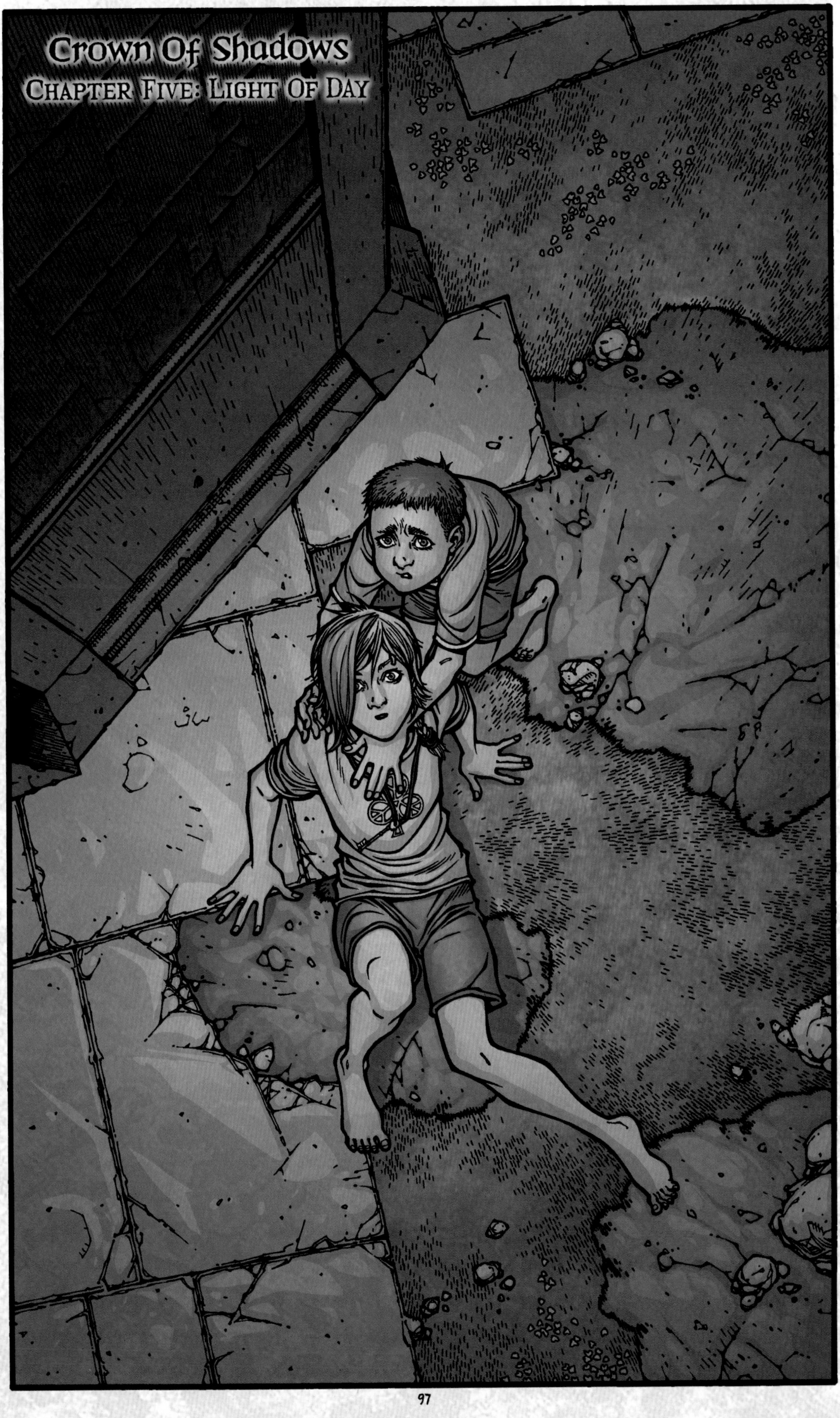
Crown Of Shadows
Chapter Five: Light Of Day

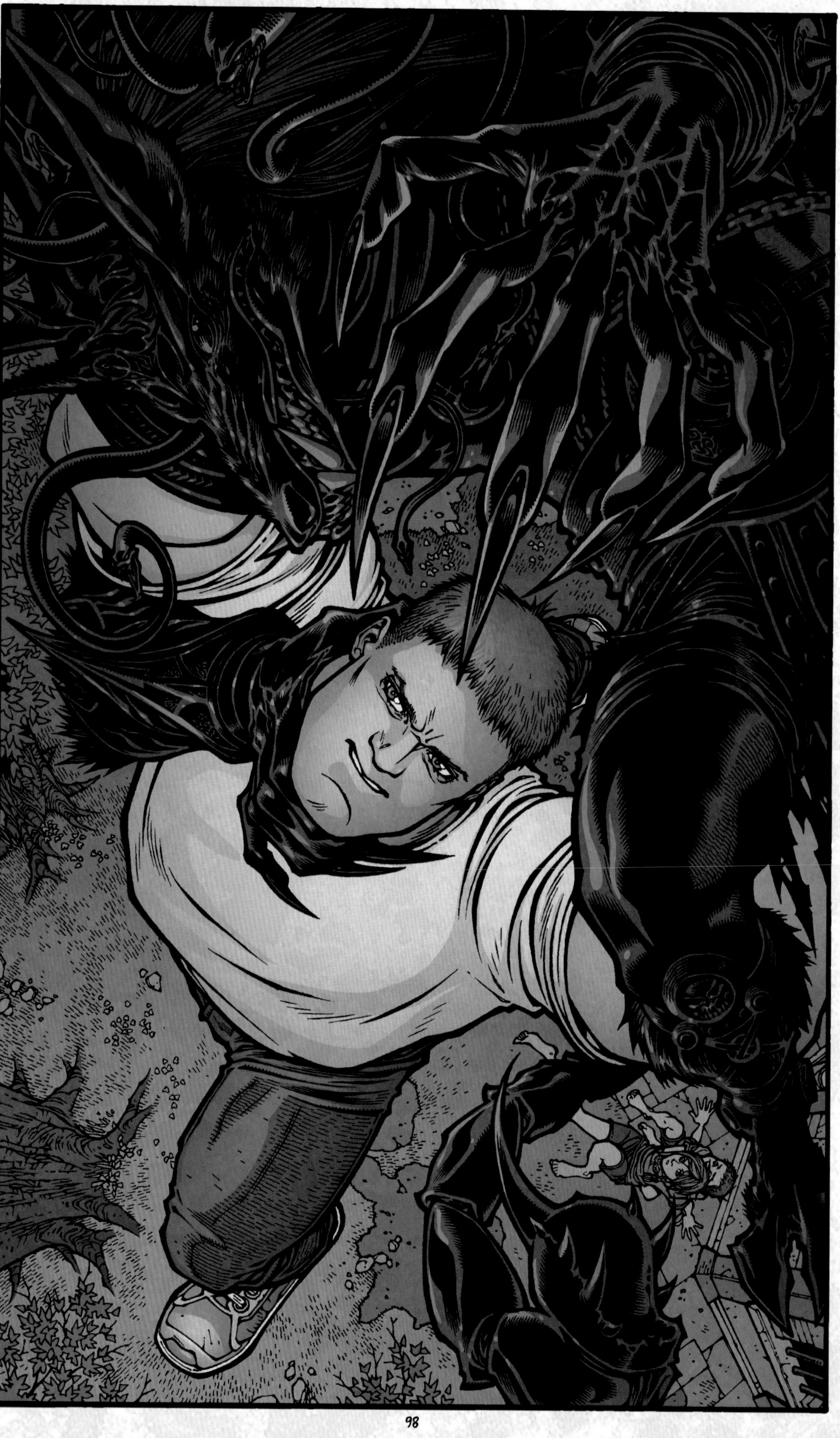

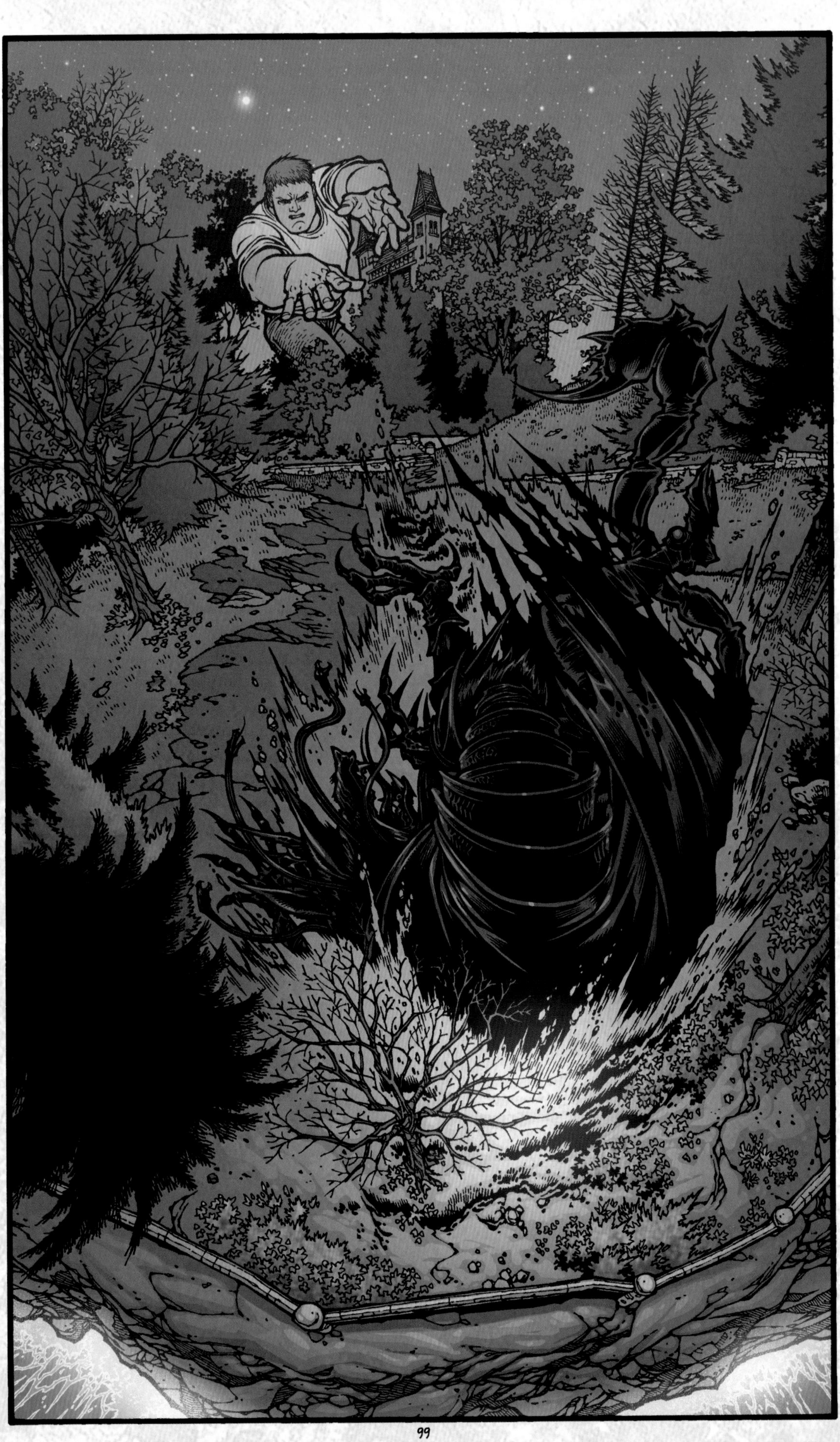

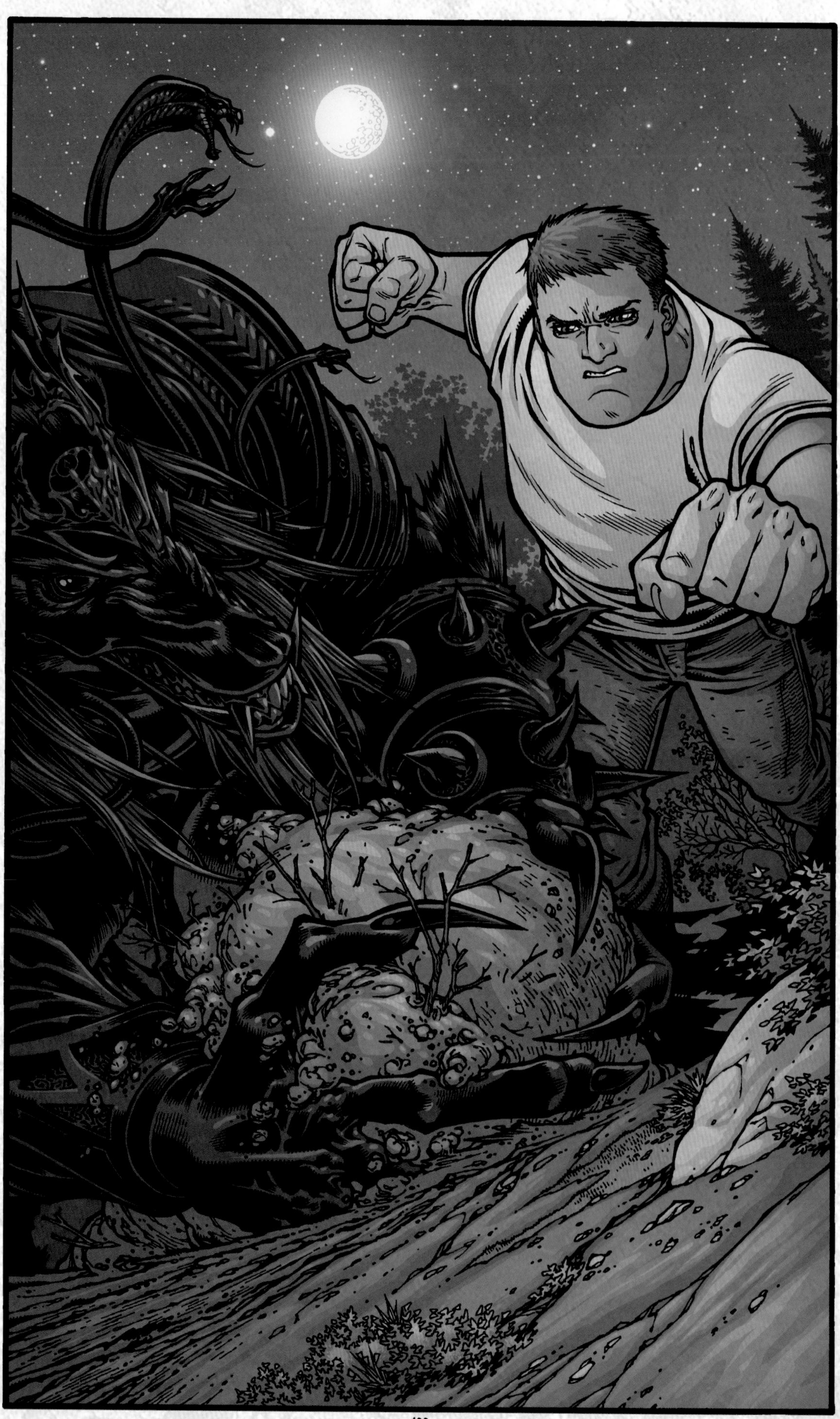

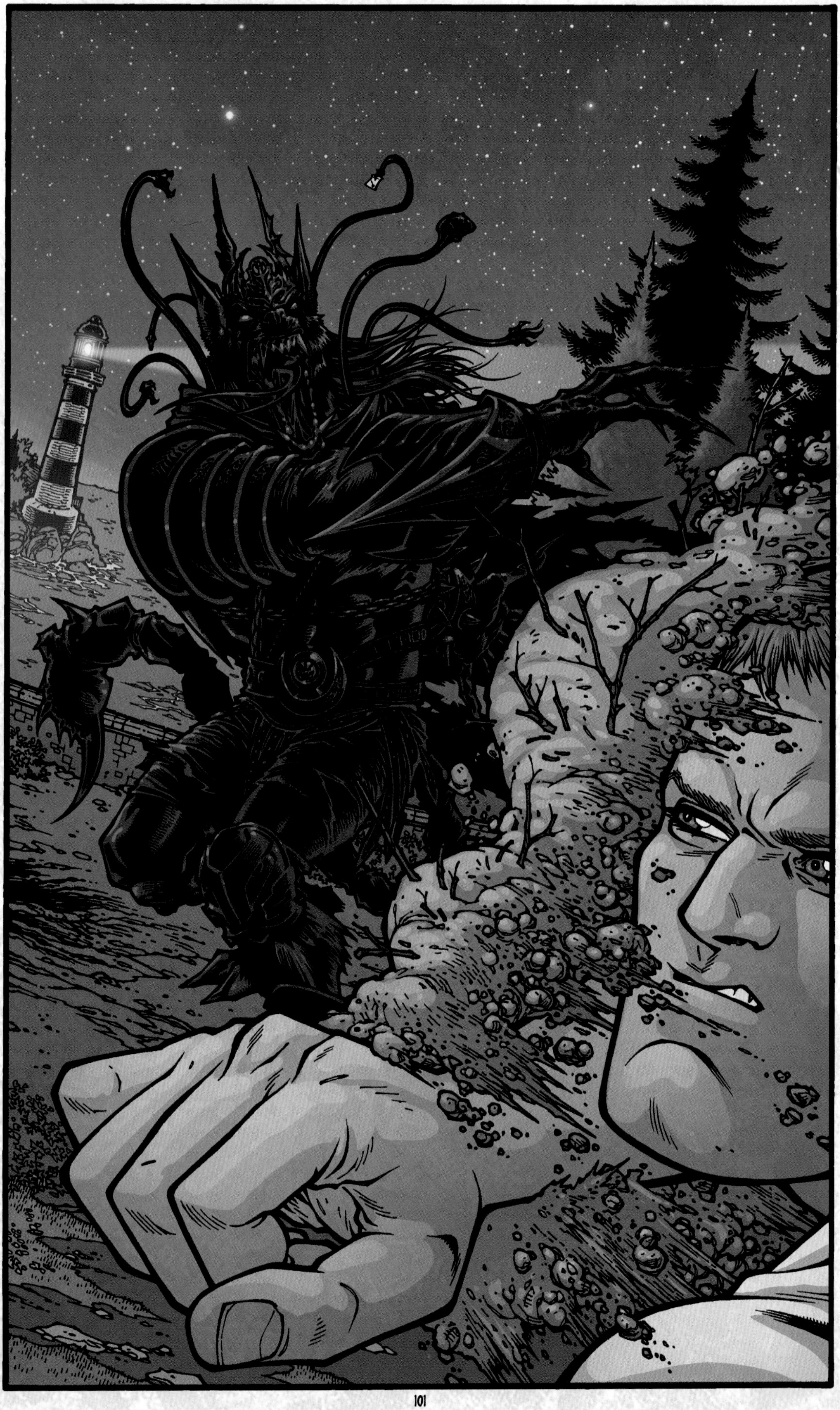

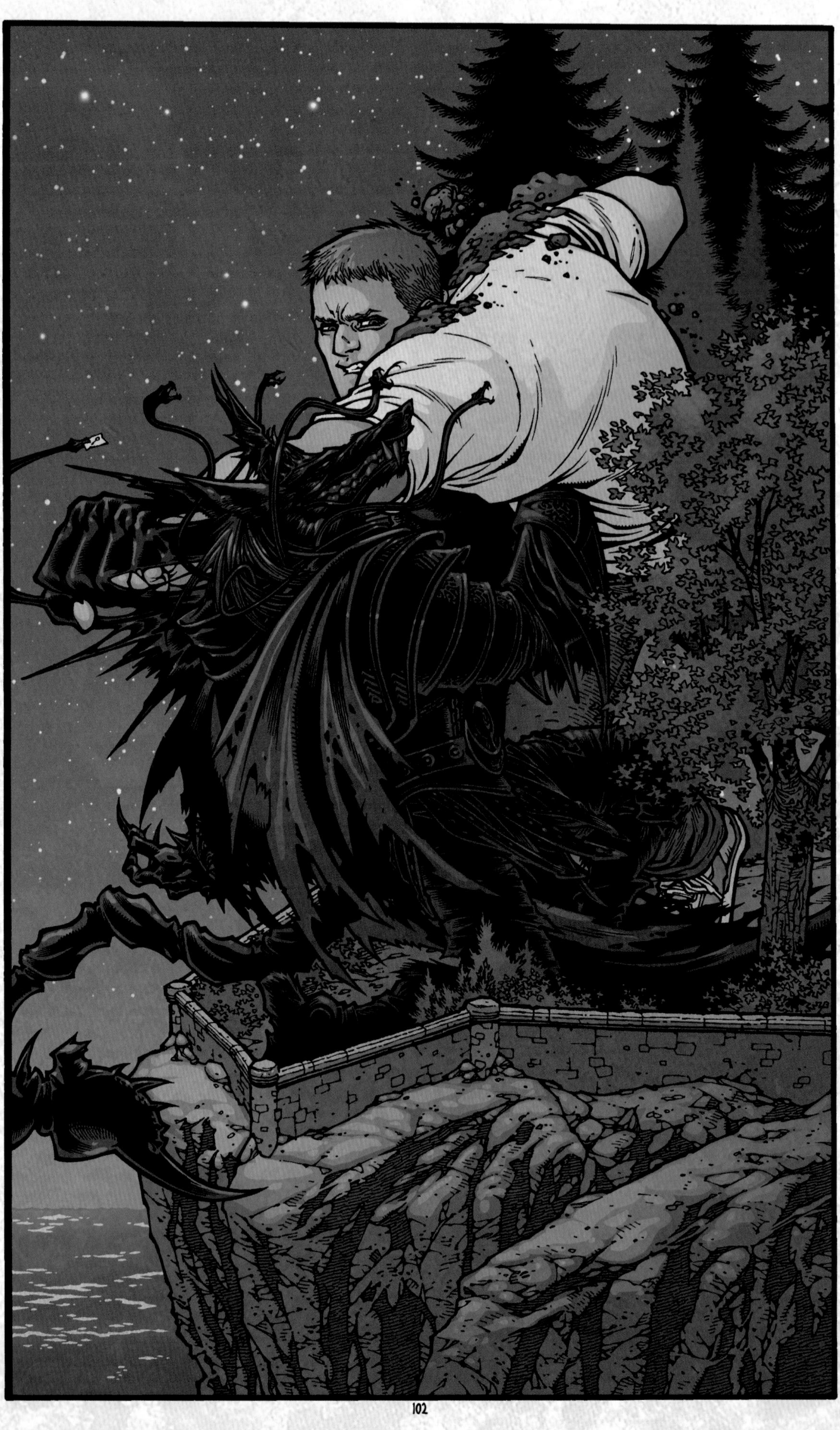

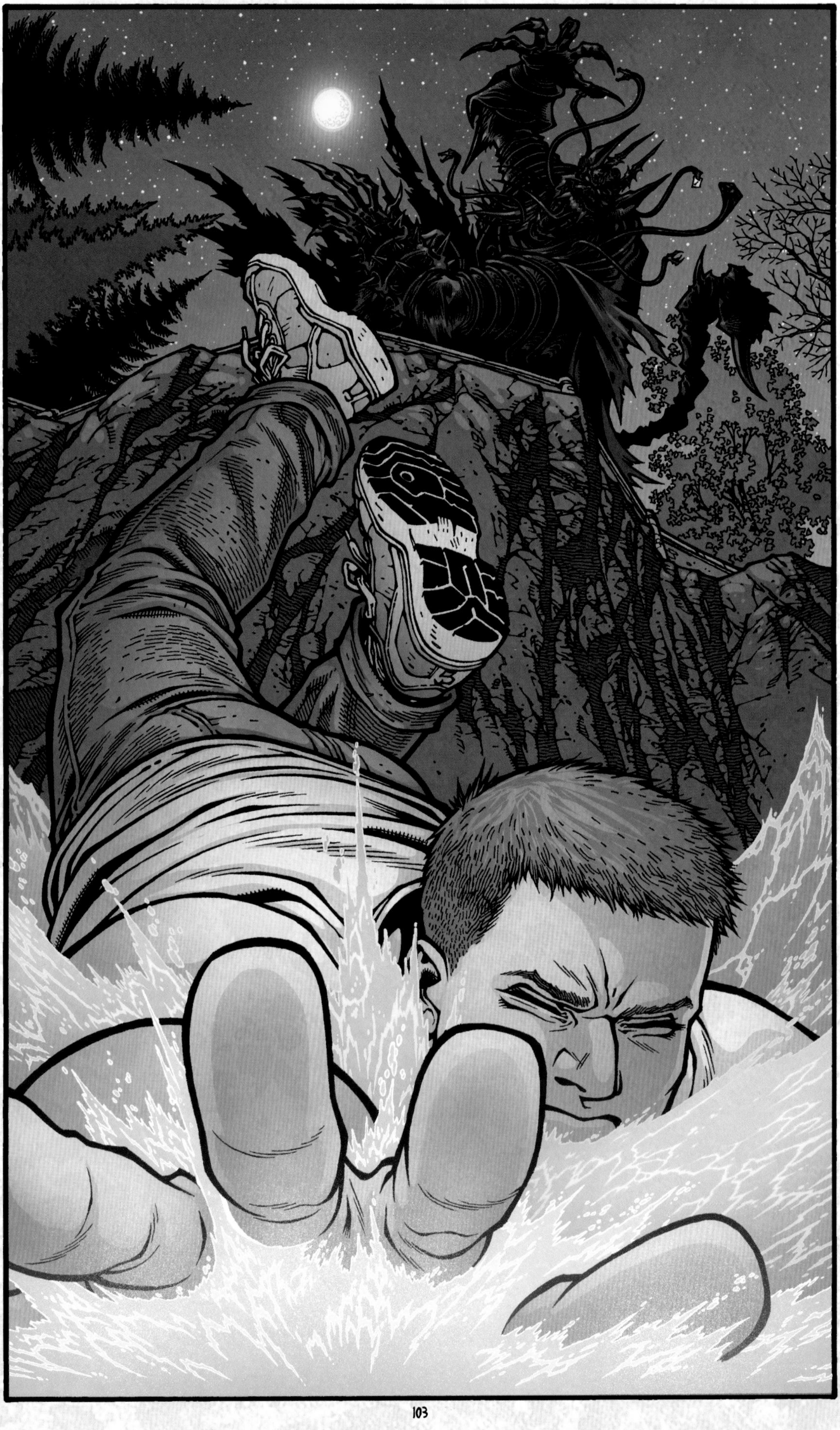

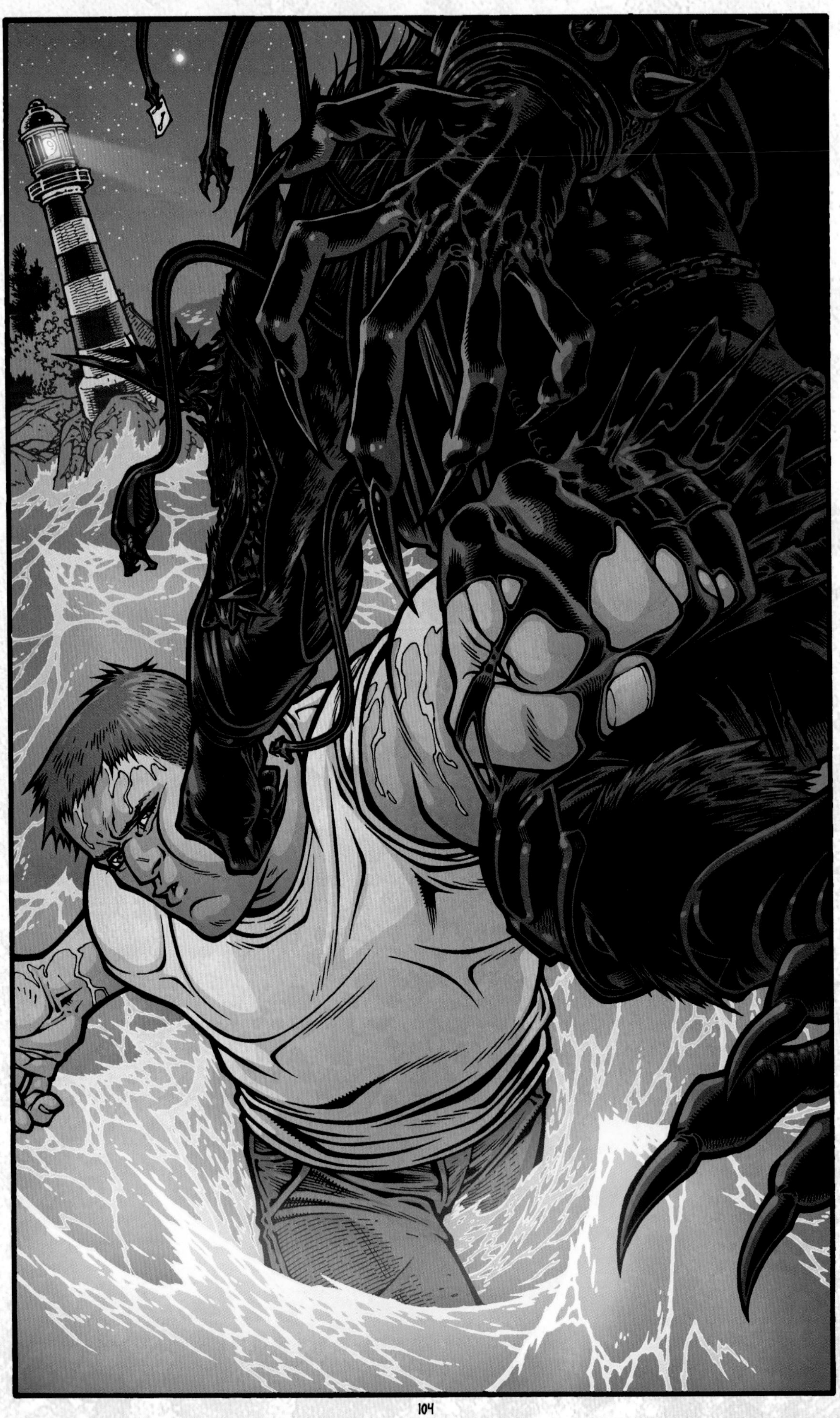

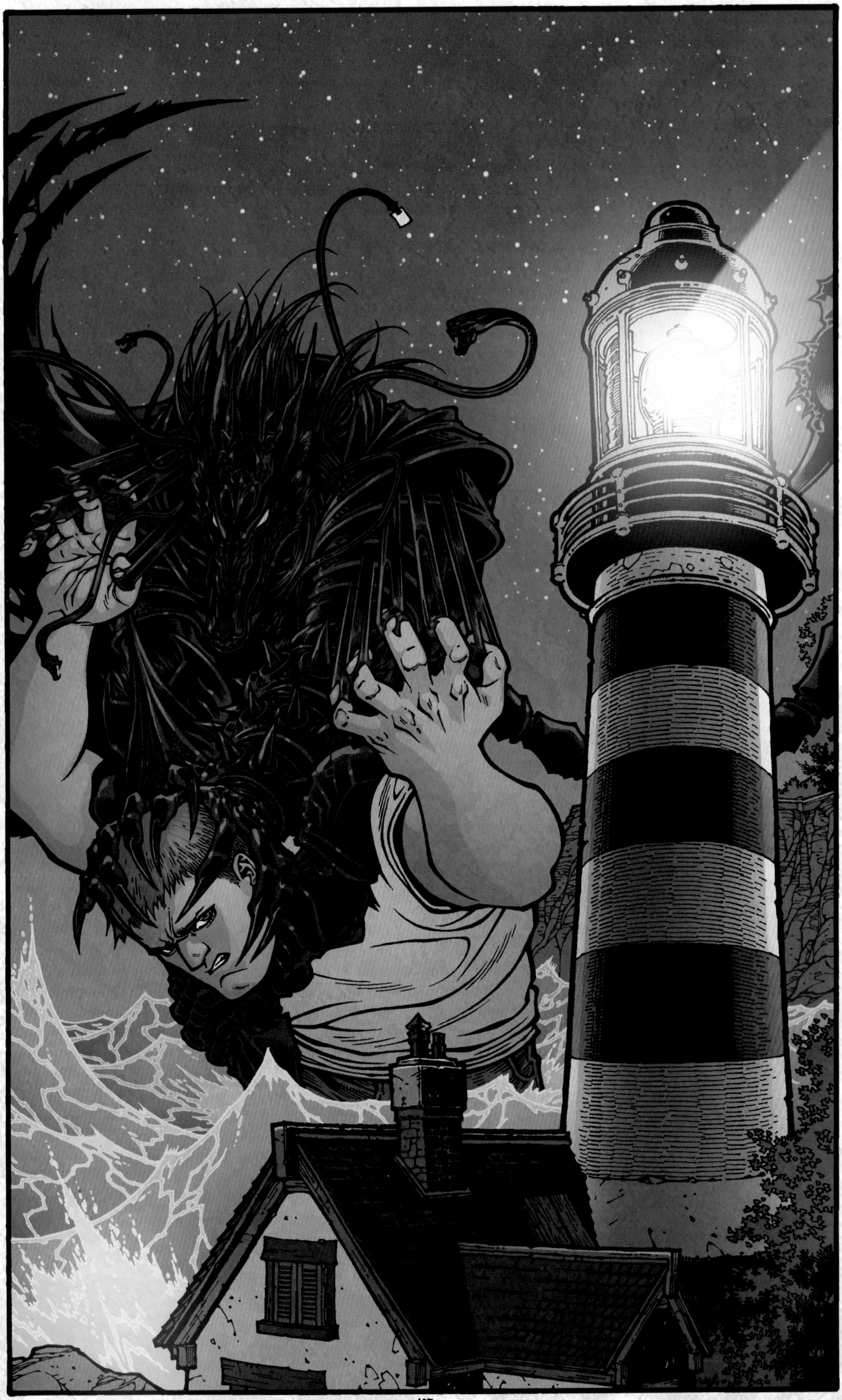

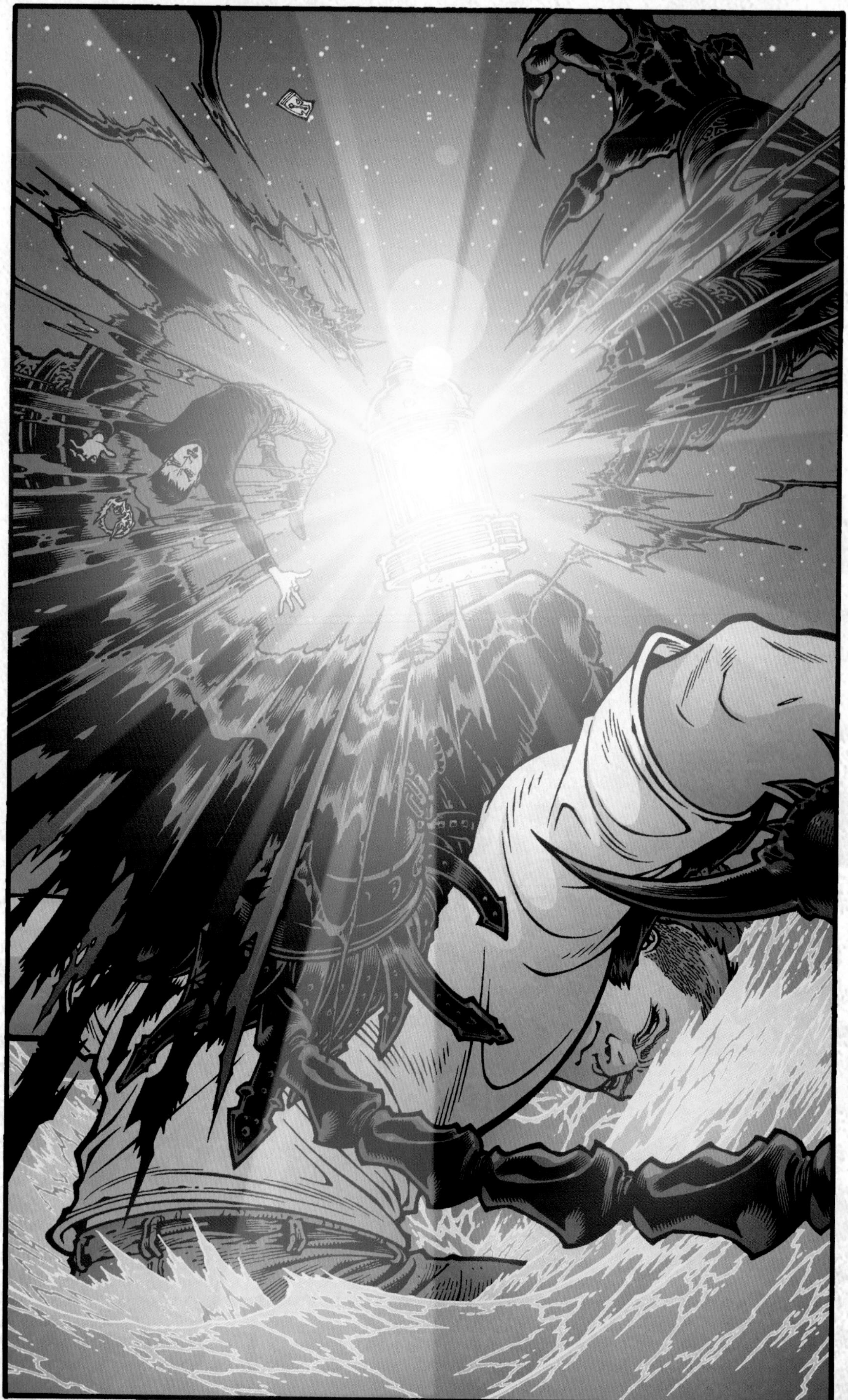

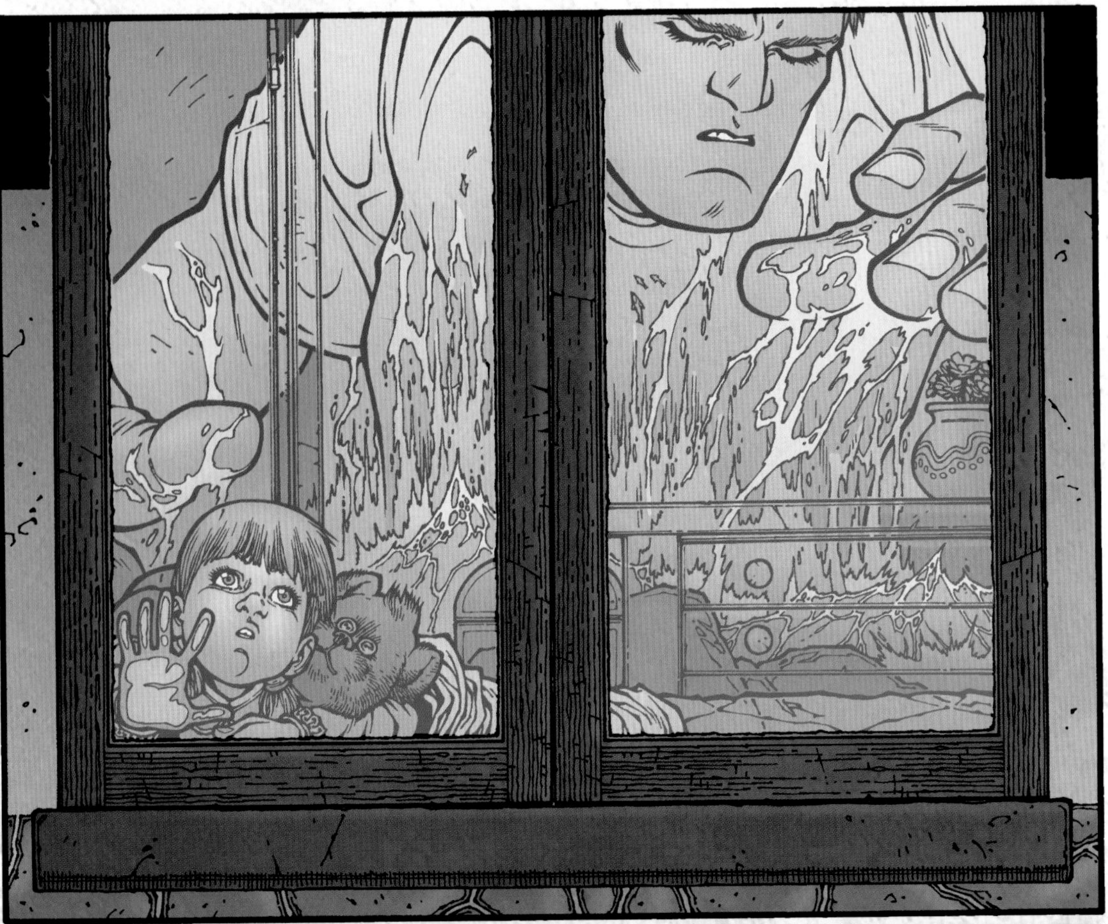

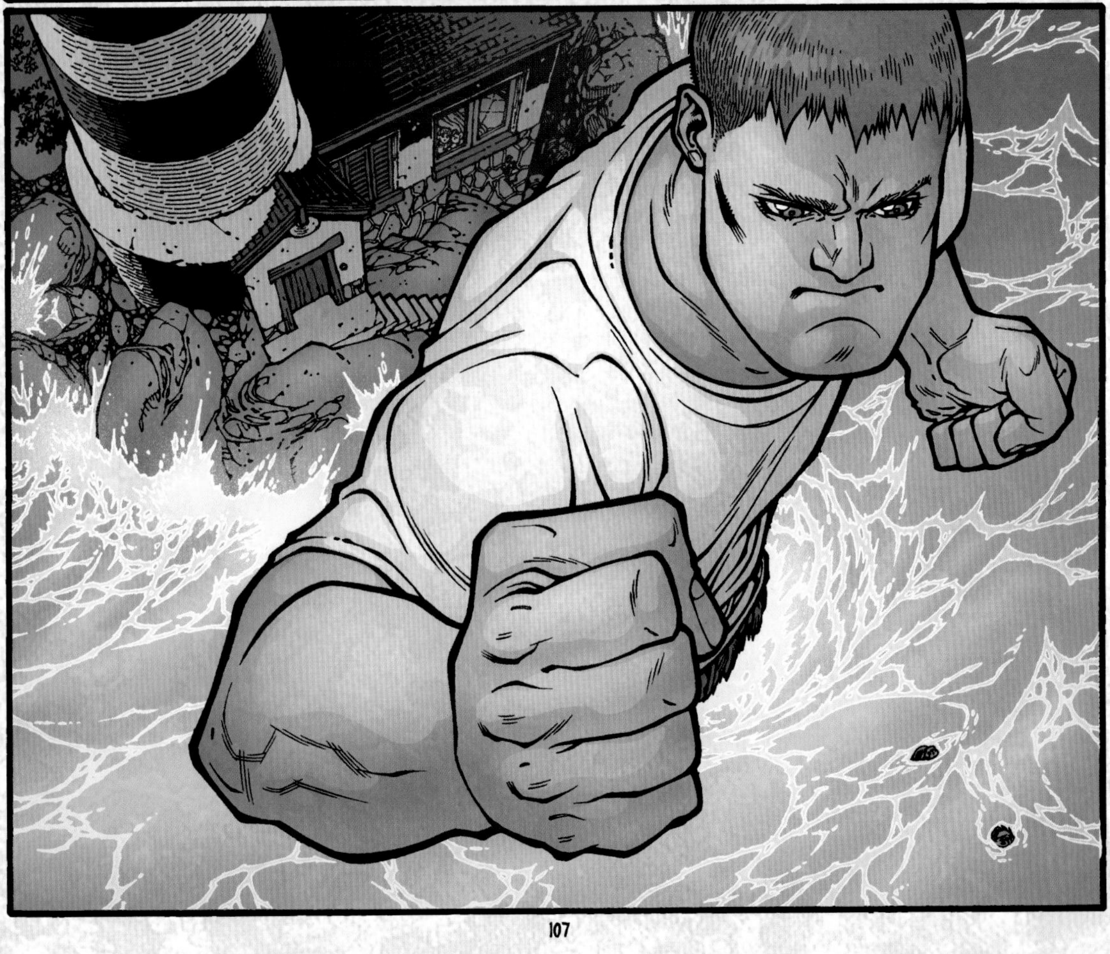

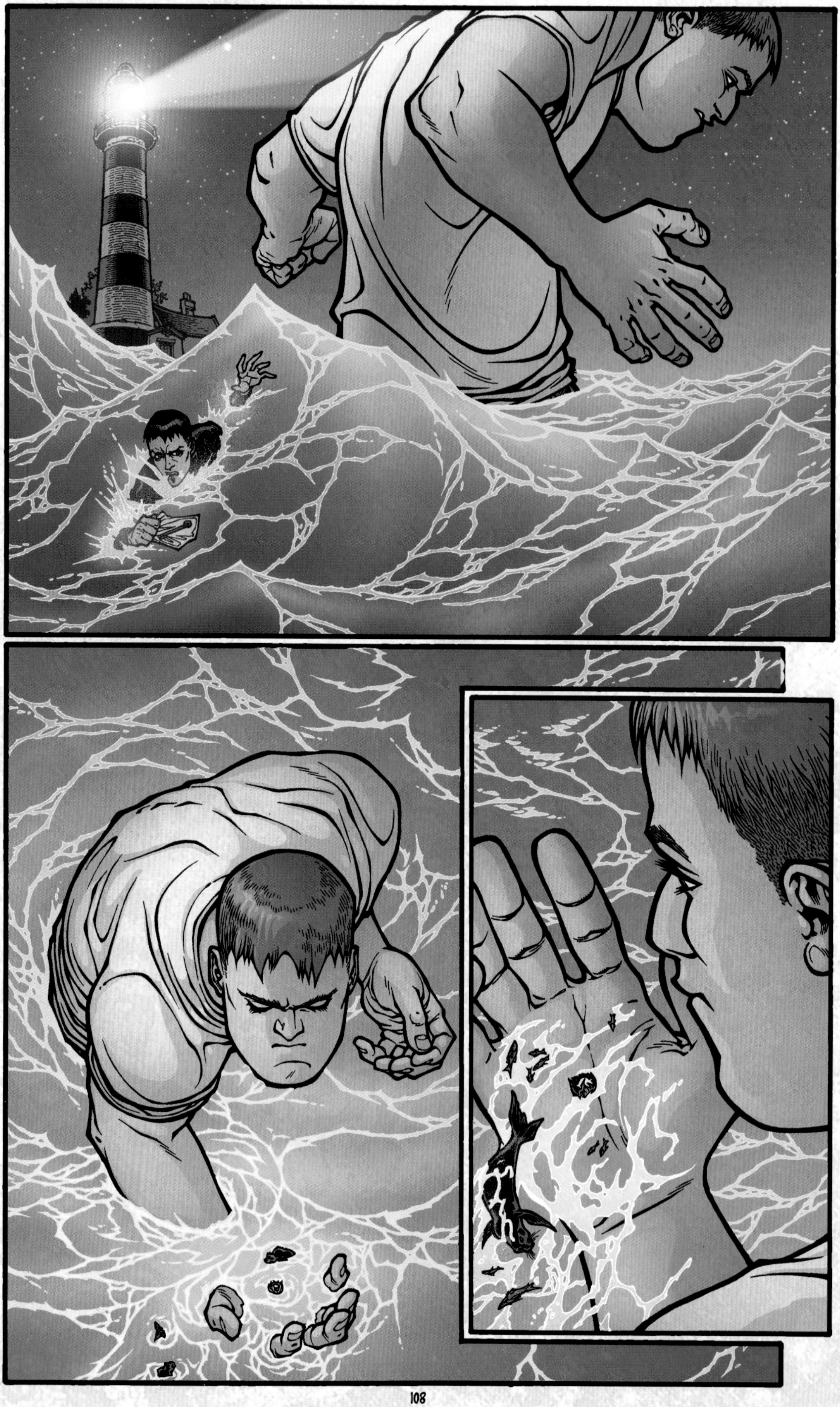

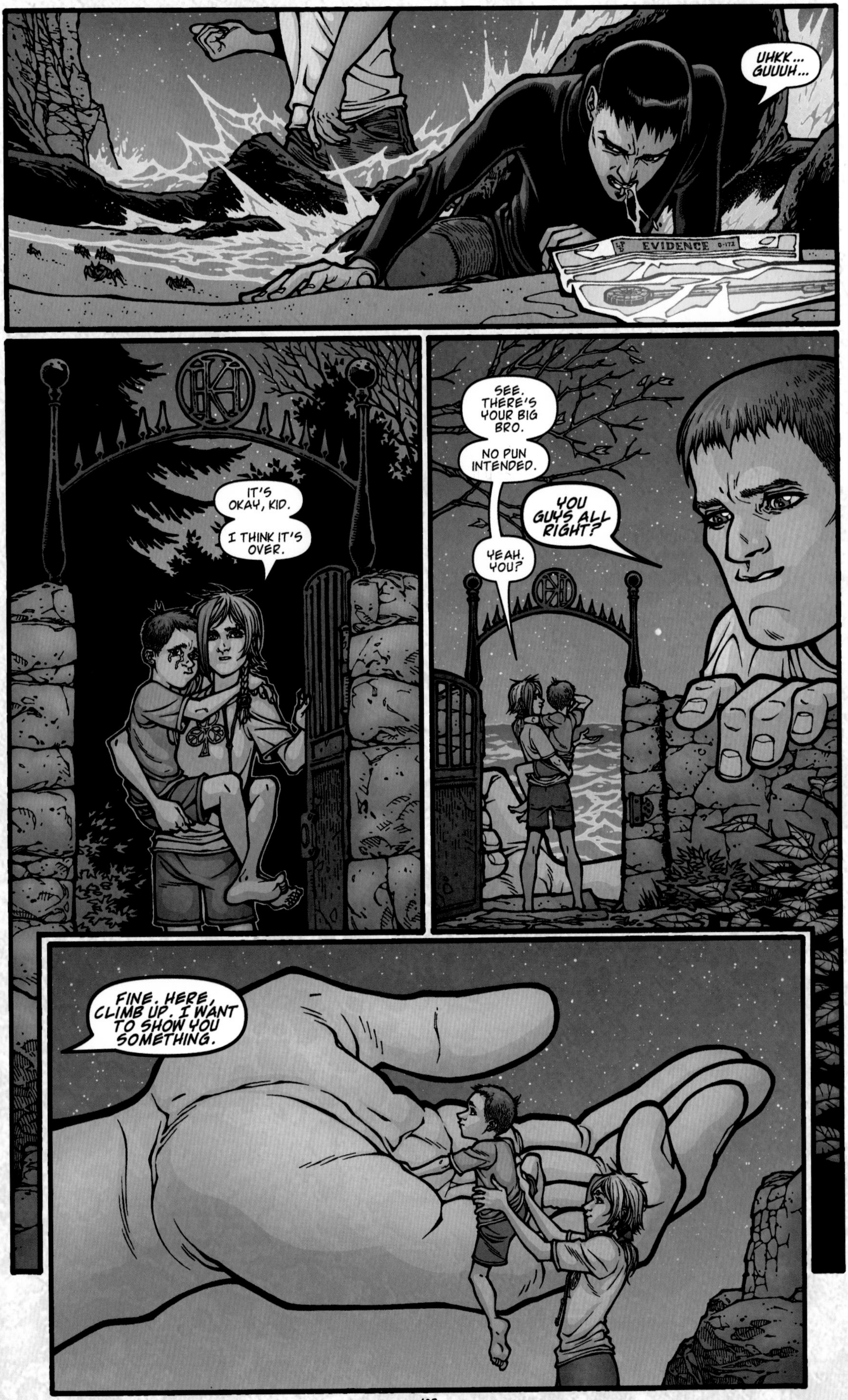

UHKK... GUUUH...
EVIDENCE
IT'S OKAY, KID.
I THINK IT'S OVER.
SEE. THERE'S YOUR BIG BRO.
NO PUN INTENDED.
YOU GUYS ALL RIGHT?
YEAH. YOU?
FINE. HERE, CLIMB UP. I WANT TO SHOW YOU SOMETHING.

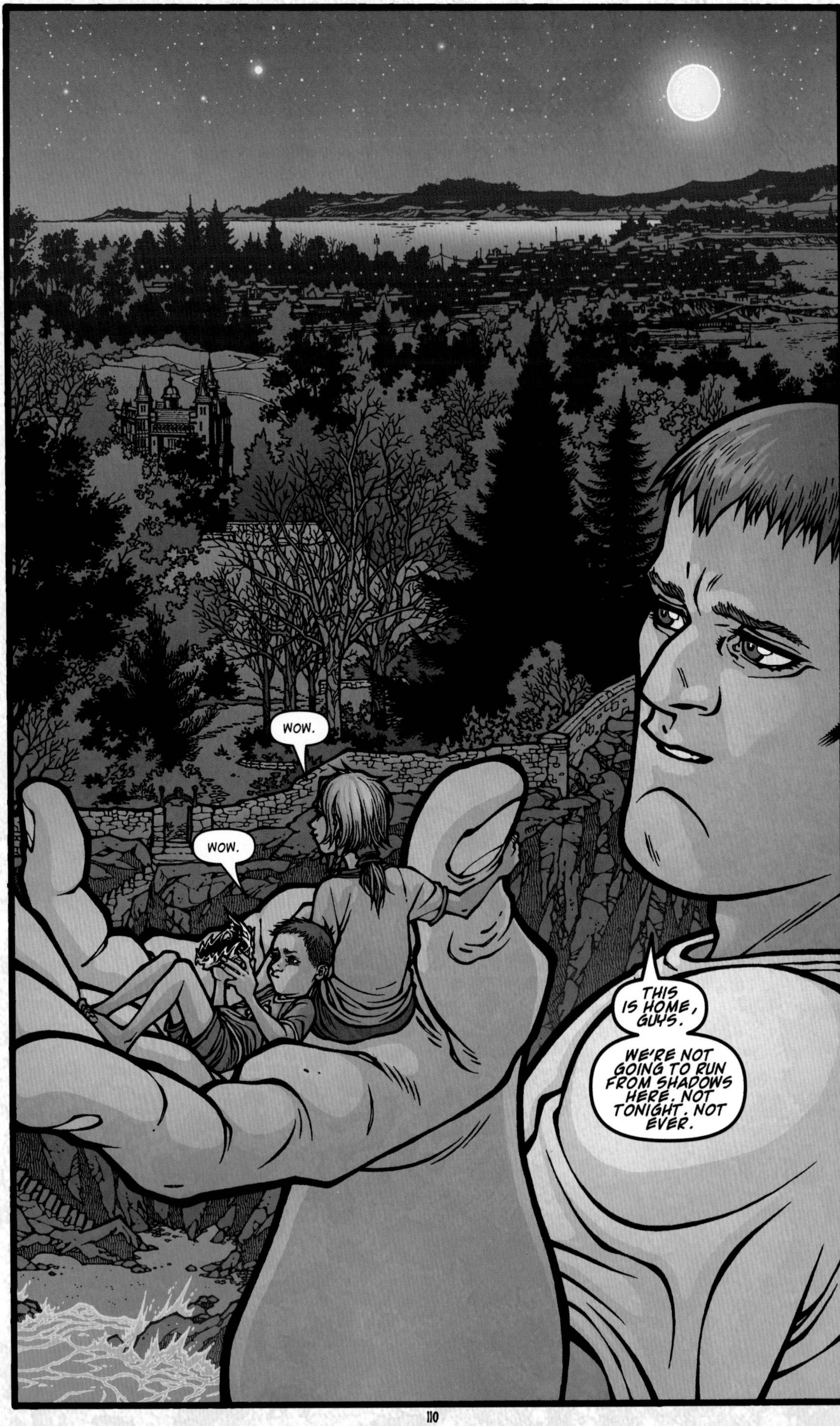
WOW.
WOW.
THIS IS HOME, GUYS.
WE'RE NOT GOING TO RUN FROM SHADOWS HERE. NOT TONIGHT. NOT EVER.

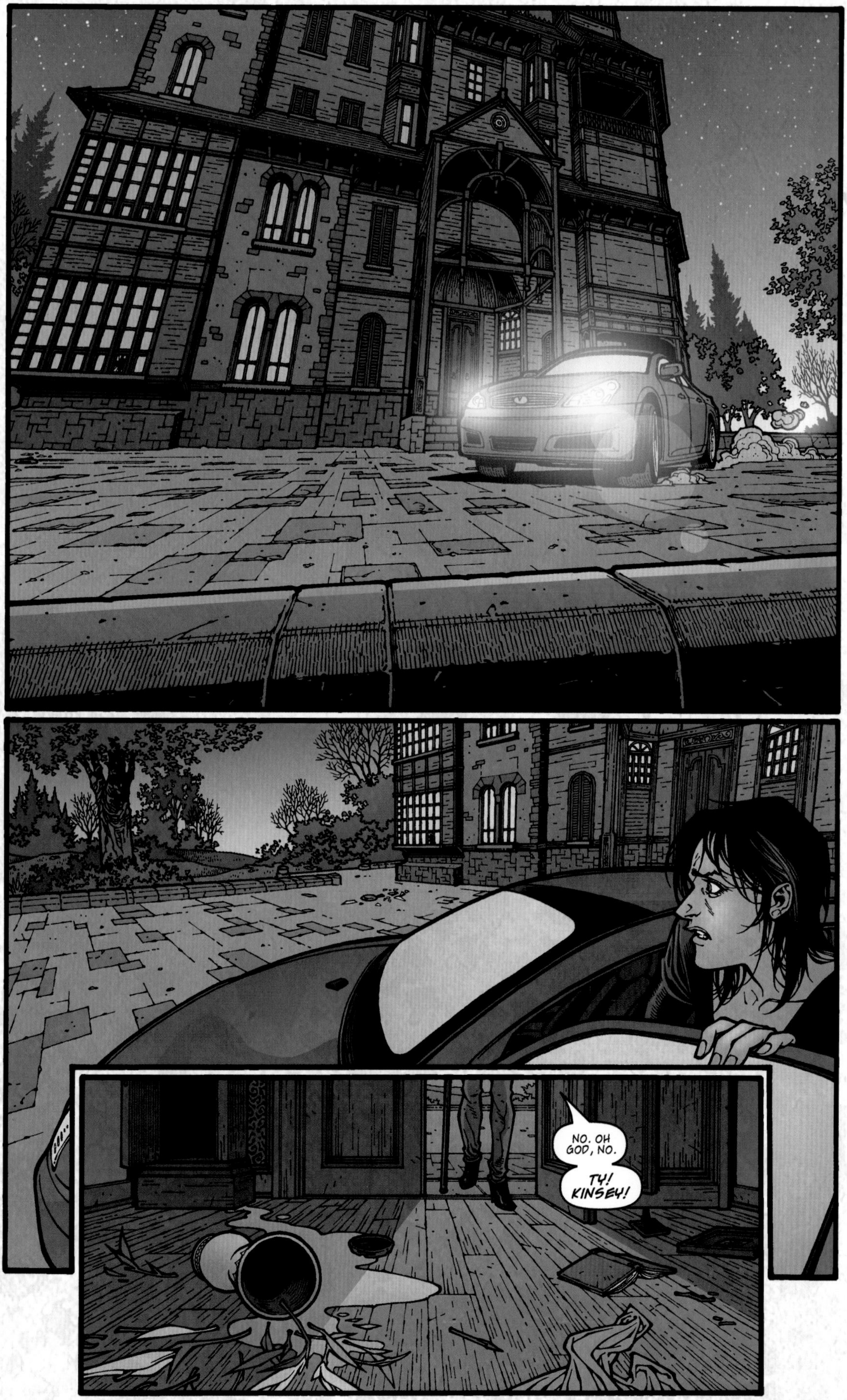
NO. OH GOD, NO.
TY! KINSEY!

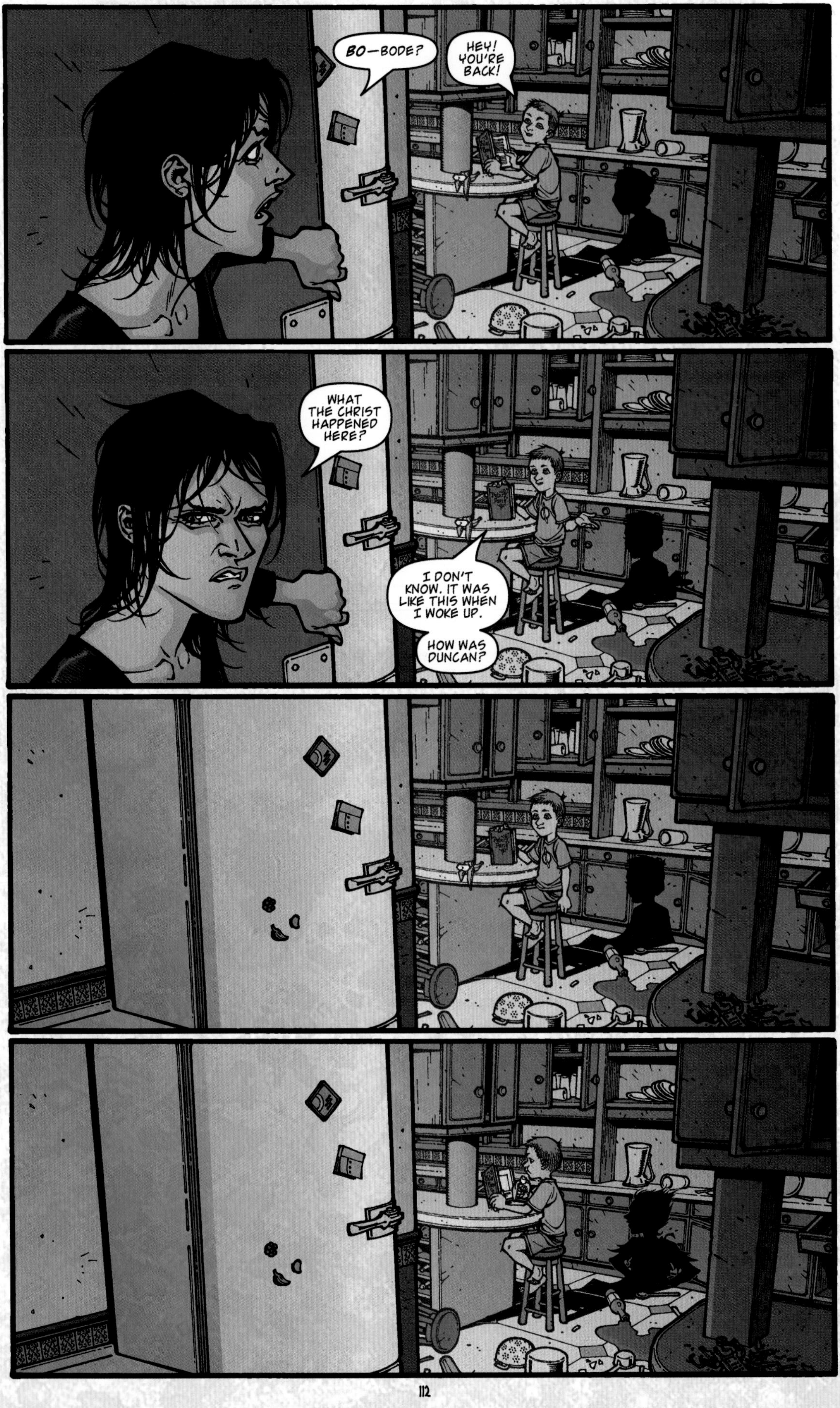
BO—BODE?
HEY! YOU'RE BACK!
WHAT THE CHRIST HAPPENED HERE?
I DON'T KNOW. IT WAS LIKE THIS WHEN I WOKE UP.
HOW WAS DUNCAN?

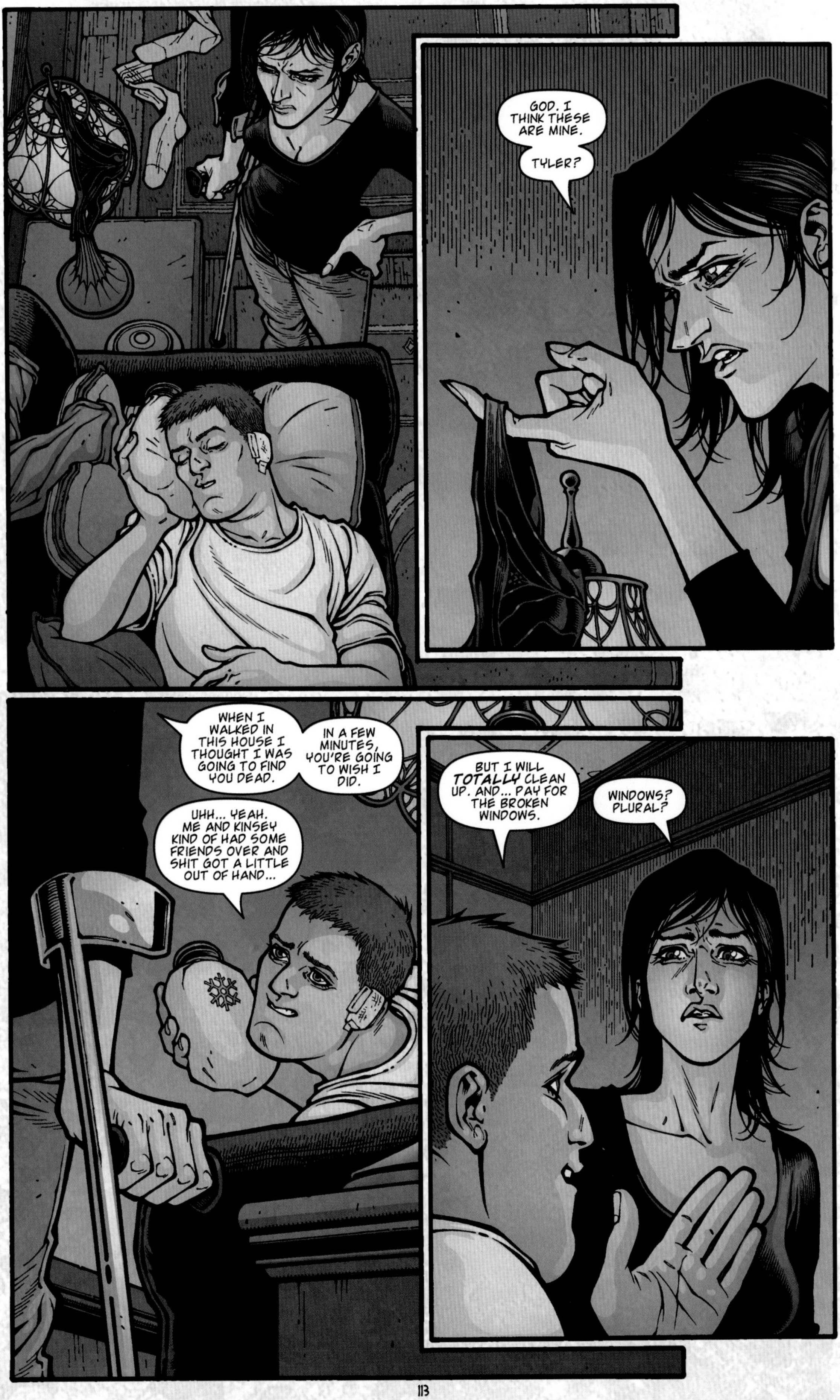

GOD. I THINK THESE ARE MINE.
TYLER?
WHEN I WALKED IN THIS HOUSE I THOUGHT I WAS GOING TO FIND YOU DEAD.
IN A FEW MINUTES, YOU'RE GOING TO WISH I DID.
UHH... YEAH. ME AND KINSEY KIND OF HAD SOME FRIENDS OVER AND SHIT GOT A LITTLE OUT OF HAND...
BUT I WILL TOTALLY CLEAN UP. AND... PAY FOR THE BROKEN WINDOWS.
WINDOWS? PLURAL?

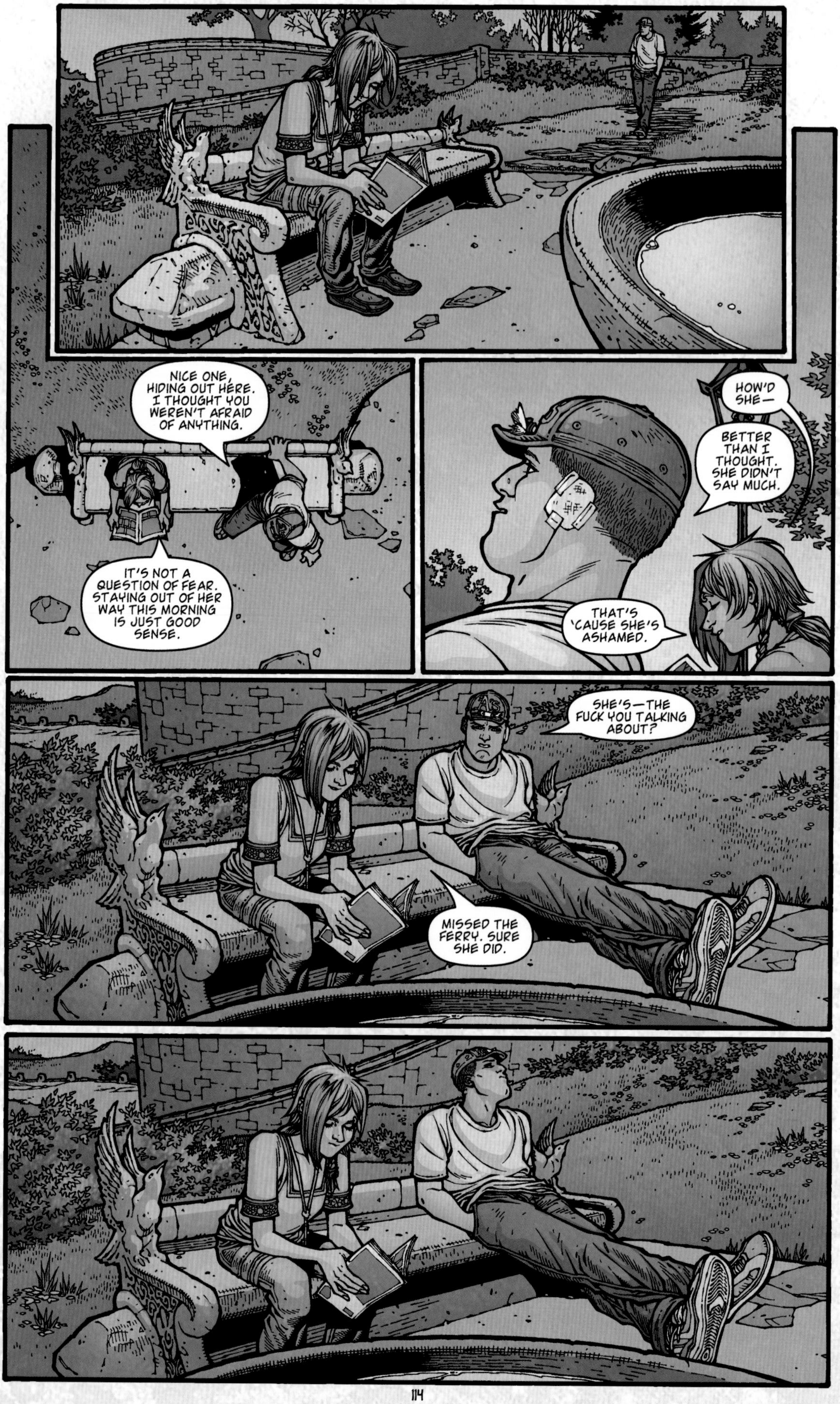
NICE ONE, HIDING OUT HERE. I THOUGHT YOU WEREN'T AFRAID OF ANYTHING.
IT'S NOT A QUESTION OF FEAR. STAYING OUT OF HER WAY THIS MORNING IS JUST GOOD SENSE.
HOW'D SHE—
BETTER THAN I THOUGHT. SHE DIDN'T SAY MUCH.
THAT'S 'CAUSE SHE'S ASHAMED.
SHE'S—THE FUCK YOU TALKING ABOUT?
MISSED THE FERRY. SURE SHE DID.

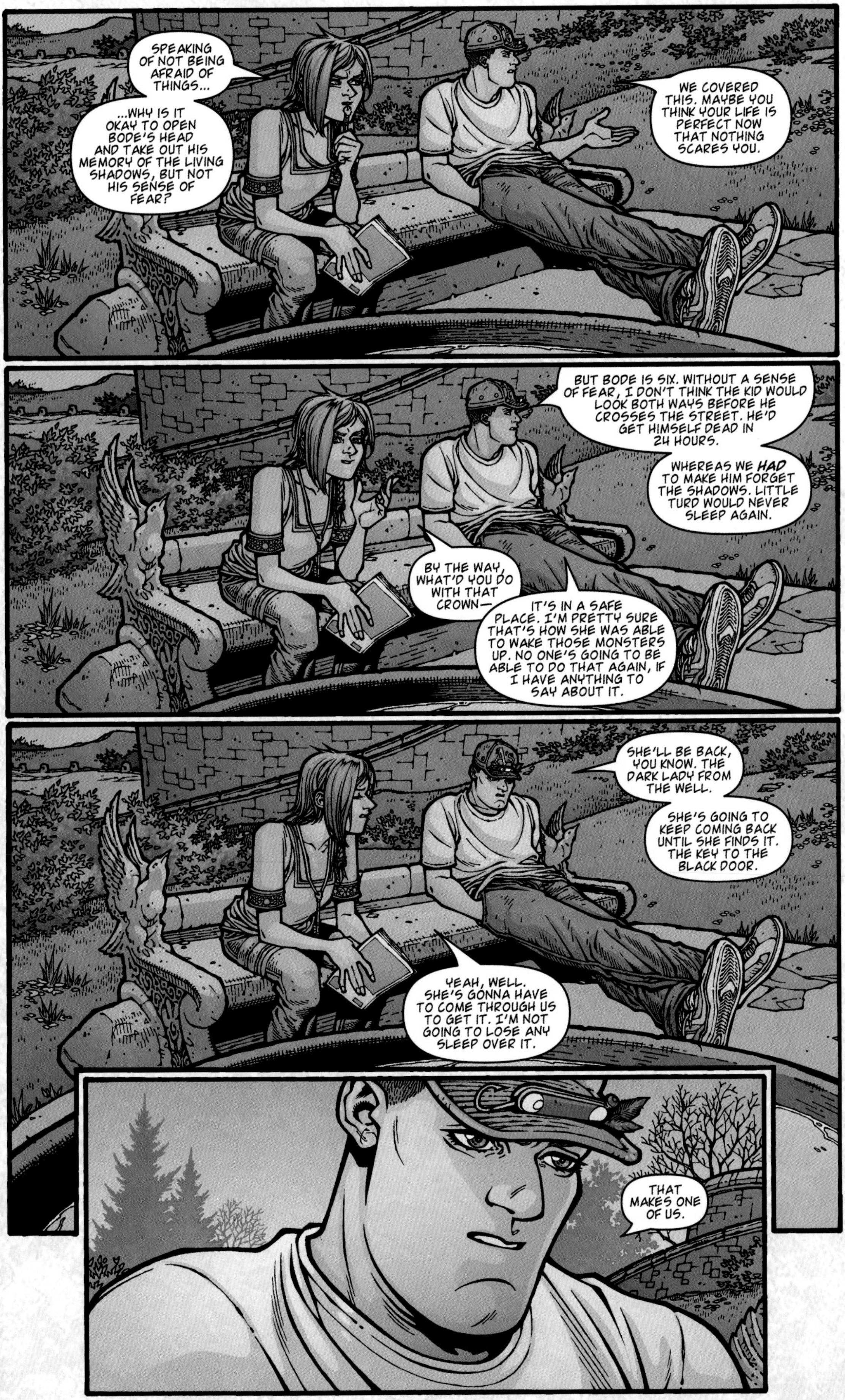
SPEAKING OF NOT BEING AFRAID OF THINGS...
...WHY IS IT OKAY TO OPEN BODE'S HEAD AND TAKE OUT HIS MEMORY OF THE LIVING SHADOWS, BUT NOT HIS SENSE OF FEAR?
WE COVERED THIS. MAYBE YOU THINK YOUR LIFE IS PERFECT NOW THAT NOTHING SCARES YOU.
BUT BODE IS SIX. WITHOUT A SENSE OF FEAR, I DON'T THINK THE KID WOULD LOOK BOTH WAYS BEFORE HE CROSSES THE STREET. HE'D GET HIMSELF DEAD IN 24 HOURS.
WHEREAS WE *HAD* TO MAKE HIM FORGET THE SHADOWS. LITTLE TURD WOULD NEVER SLEEP AGAIN.
BY THE WAY, WHAT'D YOU DO WITH THAT CROWN—
IT'S IN A SAFE PLACE. I'M PRETTY SURE THAT'S HOW SHE WAS ABLE TO WAKE THOSE MONSTERS UP. NO ONE'S GOING TO BE ABLE TO DO THAT AGAIN, IF I HAVE ANYTHING TO SAY ABOUT IT.
SHE'LL BE BACK, YOU KNOW. THE DARK LADY FROM THE WELL.
SHE'S GOING TO KEEP COMING BACK UNTIL SHE FINDS IT. THE KEY TO THE BLACK DOOR.
YEAH, WELL. SHE'S GONNA HAVE TO COME THROUGH US TO GET IT. I'M NOT GOING TO LOSE ANY SLEEP OVER IT.
THAT MAKES ONE OF US.

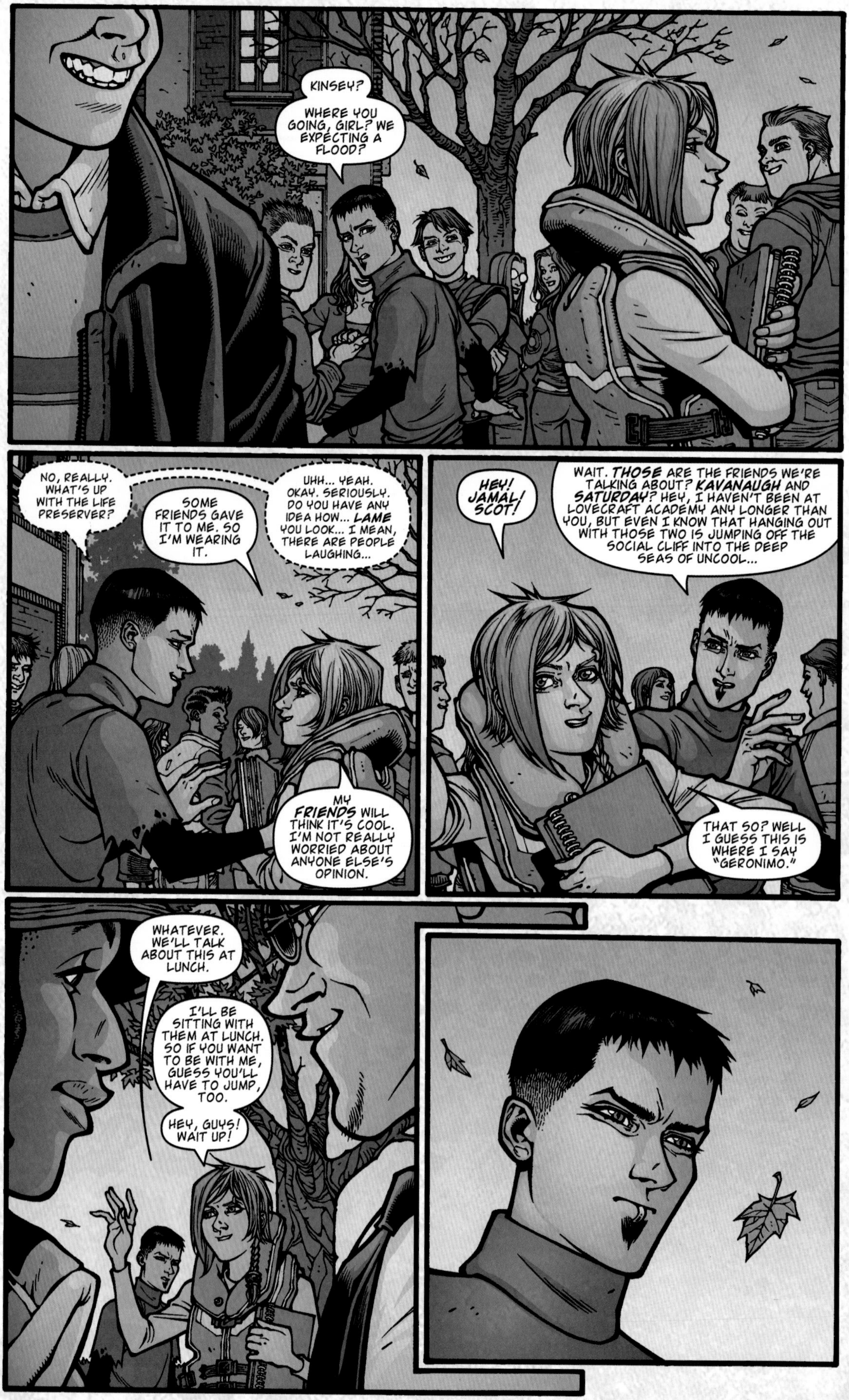
KINSEY?
WHERE YOU GOING, GIRL? WE EXPECTING A FLOOD?
NO, REALLY. WHAT'S UP WITH THE LIFE PRESERVER?
SOME FRIENDS GAVE IT TO ME. SO I'M WEARING IT.
UHH... YEAH. OKAY. SERIOUSLY. DO YOU HAVE ANY IDEA HOW... LAME YOU LOOK... I MEAN, THERE ARE PEOPLE LAUGHING...
MY FRIENDS WILL THINK IT'S COOL. I'M NOT REALLY WORRIED ABOUT ANYONE ELSE'S OPINION.
HEY! JAMAL! SCOT!
WAIT. THOSE ARE THE FRIENDS WE'RE TALKING ABOUT? KAVANAUGH AND SATURDAY? HEY, I HAVEN'T BEEN AT LOVECRAFT ACADEMY ANY LONGER THAN YOU, BUT EVEN I KNOW THAT HANGING OUT WITH THOSE TWO IS JUMPING OFF THE SOCIAL CLIFF INTO THE DEEP SEAS OF UNCOOL...
THAT SO? WELL I GUESS THIS IS WHERE I SAY "GERONIMO."
WHATEVER. WE'LL TALK ABOUT THIS AT LUNCH.
I'LL BE SITTING WITH THEM AT LUNCH. SO IF YOU WANT TO BE WITH ME, GUESS YOU'LL HAVE TO JUMP, TOO.
HEY, GUYS! WAIT UP!

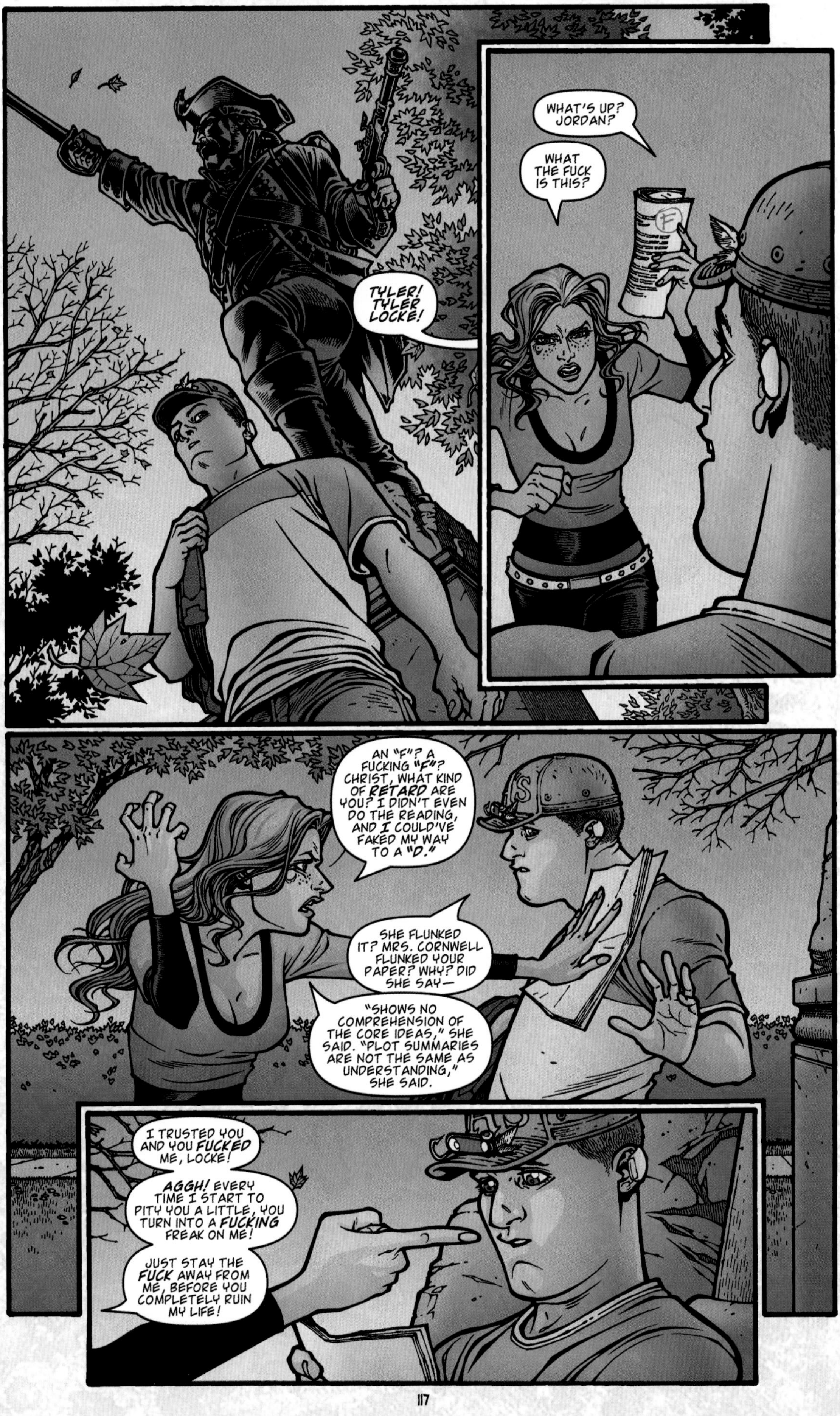
TYLER! TYLER LOCKE!
WHAT'S UP? JORDAN?
WHAT THE FUCK IS THIS?
AN "F"? A FUCKING "F"? CHRIST, WHAT KIND OF RETARD ARE YOU? I DIDN'T EVEN DO THE READING, AND I COULD'VE FAKED MY WAY TO A "D."
SHE FLUNKED IT? MRS. CORNWELL FLUNKED YOUR PAPER? WHY? DID SHE SAY—
"SHOWS NO COMPREHENSION OF THE CORE IDEAS," SHE SAID. "PLOT SUMMARIES ARE NOT THE SAME AS UNDERSTANDING," SHE SAID.
I TRUSTED YOU AND YOU FUCKED ME, LOCKE!
AGGH! EVERY TIME I START TO PITY YOU A LITTLE, YOU TURN INTO A FUCKING FREAK ON ME!
JUST STAY THE FUCK AWAY FROM ME, BEFORE YOU COMPLETELY RUIN MY LIFE!

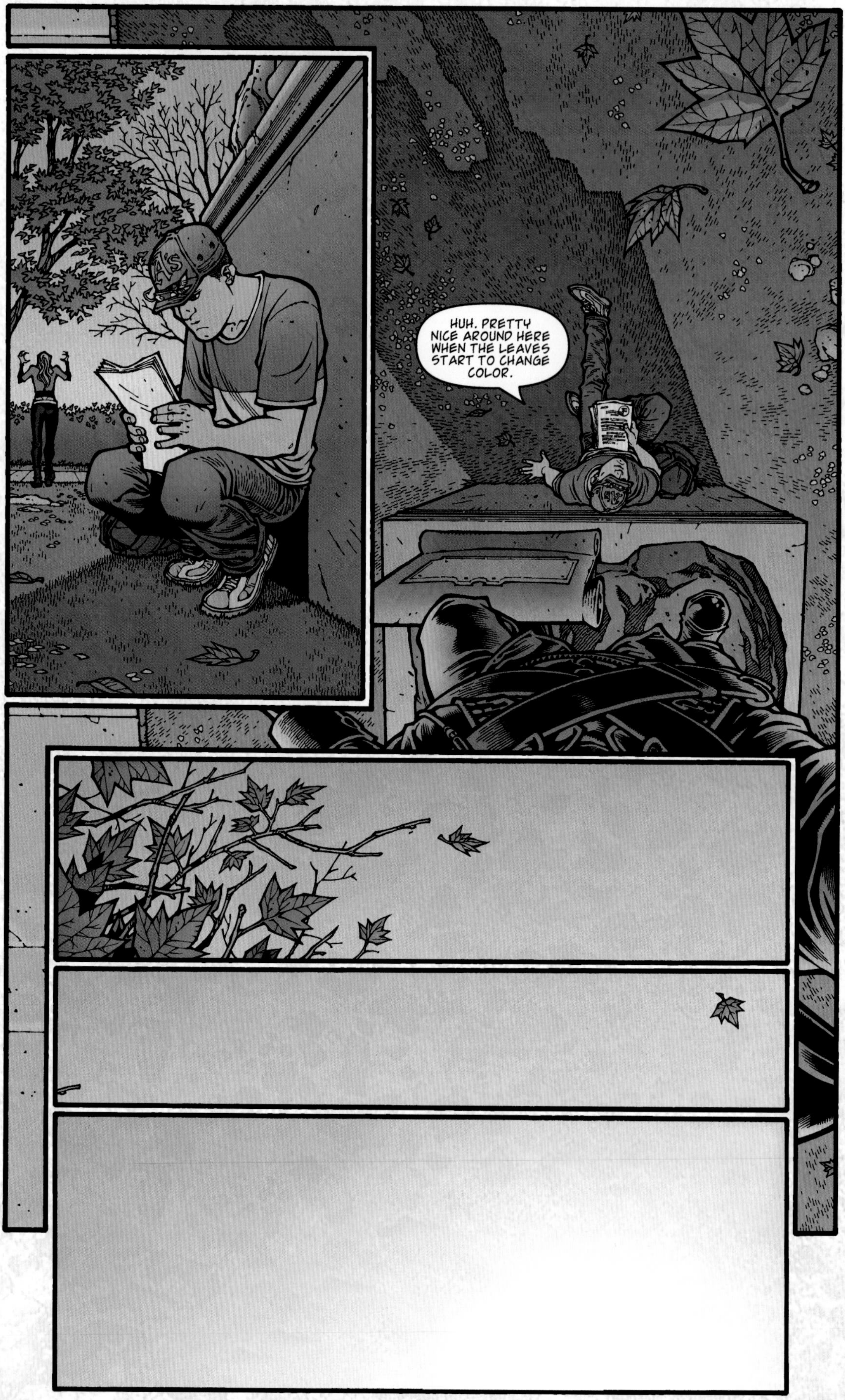
HUH. PRETTY NICE AROUND HERE WHEN THE LEAVES START TO CHANGE COLOR.

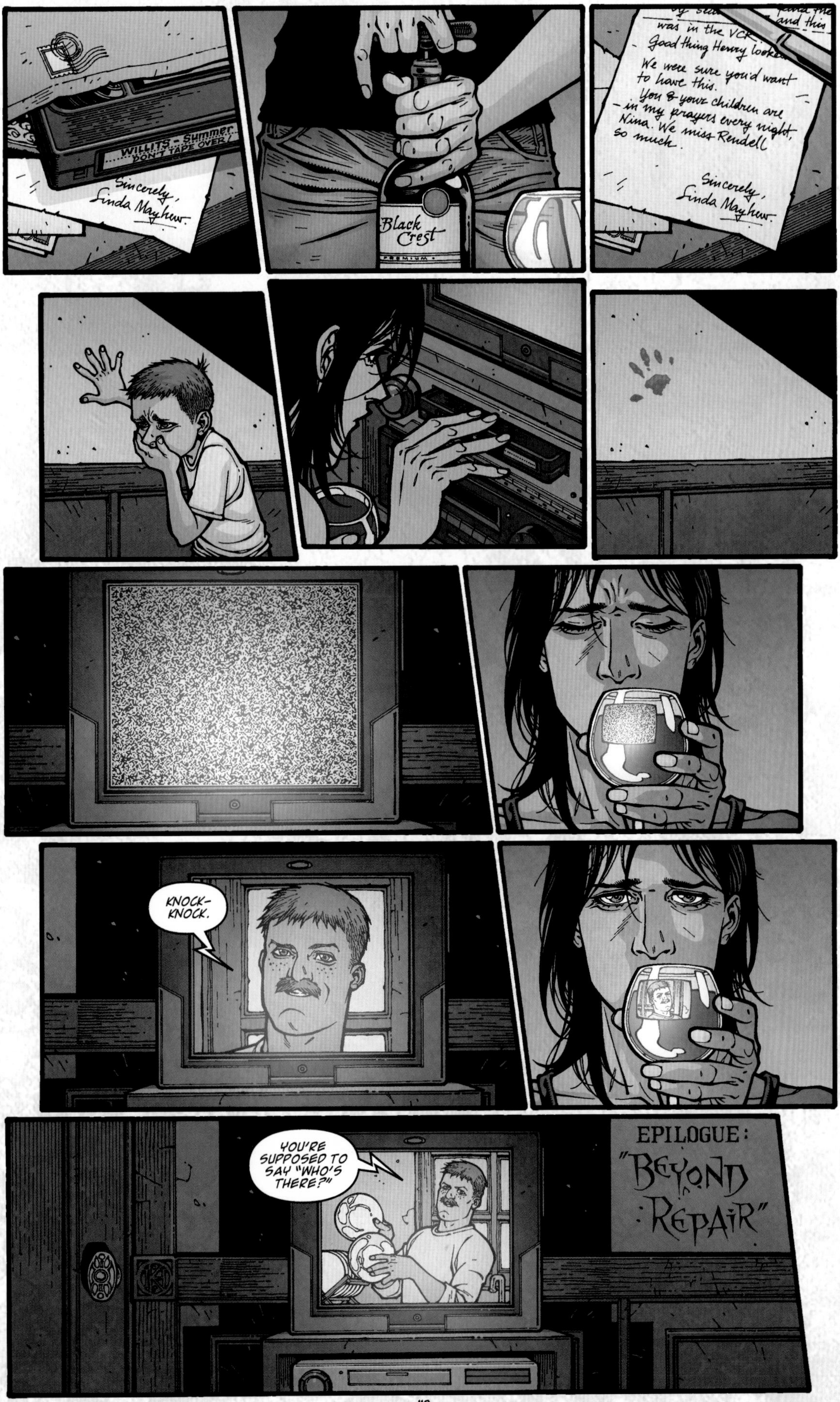
WILLITS - Summer
DON'T TAPE OVER
Sincerely,
Linda Mayhew.
Black Crest
PREMIUM
was in the VCR
Good thing Henry looked
We were sure you'd want to have this.
You & your children are in my prayers every night, Nina. We miss Rendell so much.
Sincerely,
Linda Mayhew.
KNOCK-KNOCK.
YOU'RE SUPPOSED TO SAY "WHO'S THERE?"
EPILOGUE:
"BEYOND REPAIR"

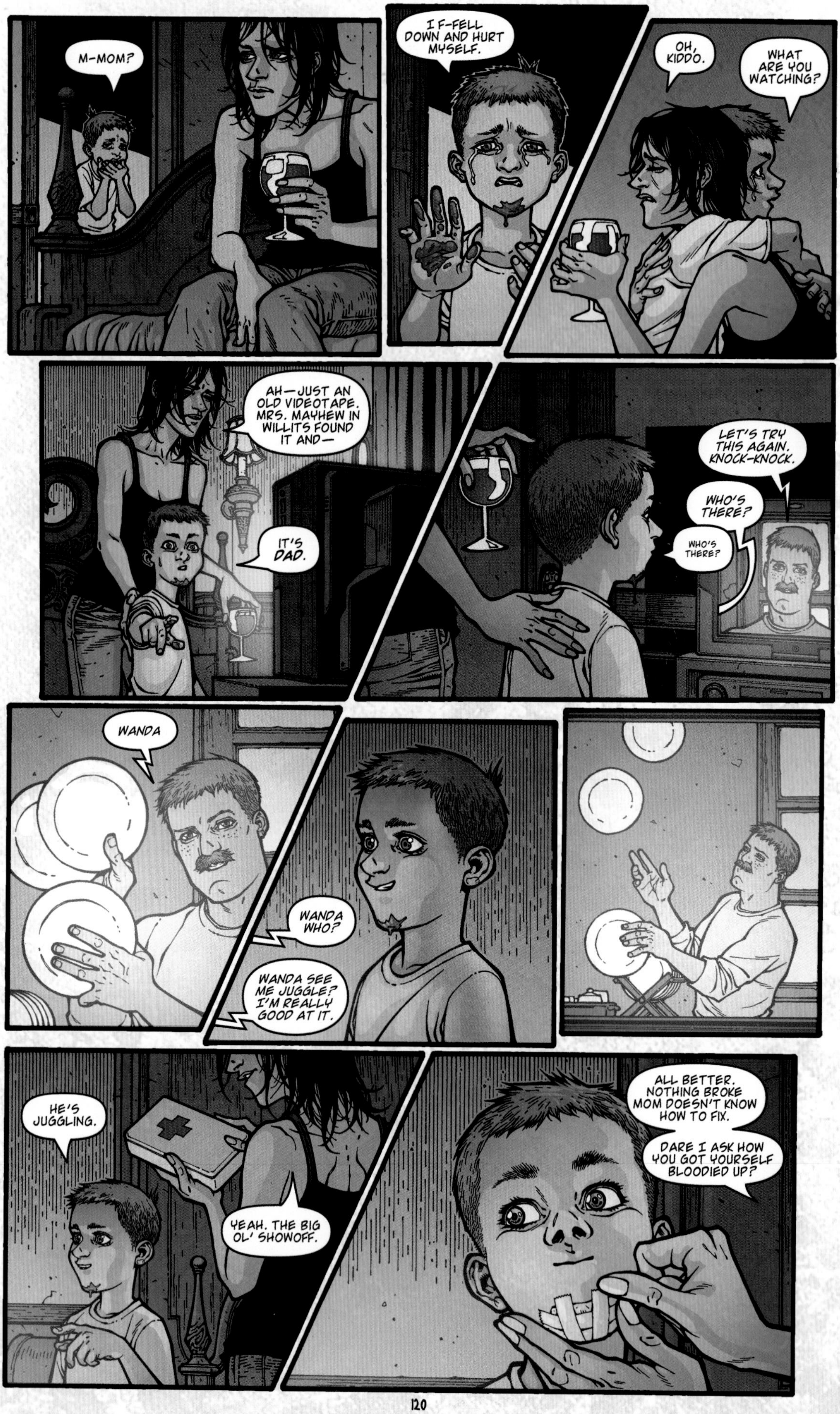
M-MOM?
I F-FELL DOWN AND HURT MYSELF.
OH, KIDDO.
WHAT ARE YOU WATCHING?
AH—JUST AN OLD VIDEOTAPE. MRS. MAYHEW IN WILLITS FOUND IT AND—
IT'S DAD.
LET'S TRY THIS AGAIN. KNOCK-KNOCK.
WHO'S THERE?
WHO'S THERE?
WANDA
WANDA WHO?
WANDA SEE ME JUGGLE? I'M REALLY GOOD AT IT.
HE'S JUGGLING.
YEAH. THE BIG OL' SHOWOFF.
ALL BETTER. NOTHING BROKE MOM DOESN'T KNOW HOW TO FIX.
DARE I ASK HOW YOU GOT YOURSELF BLOODIED UP?

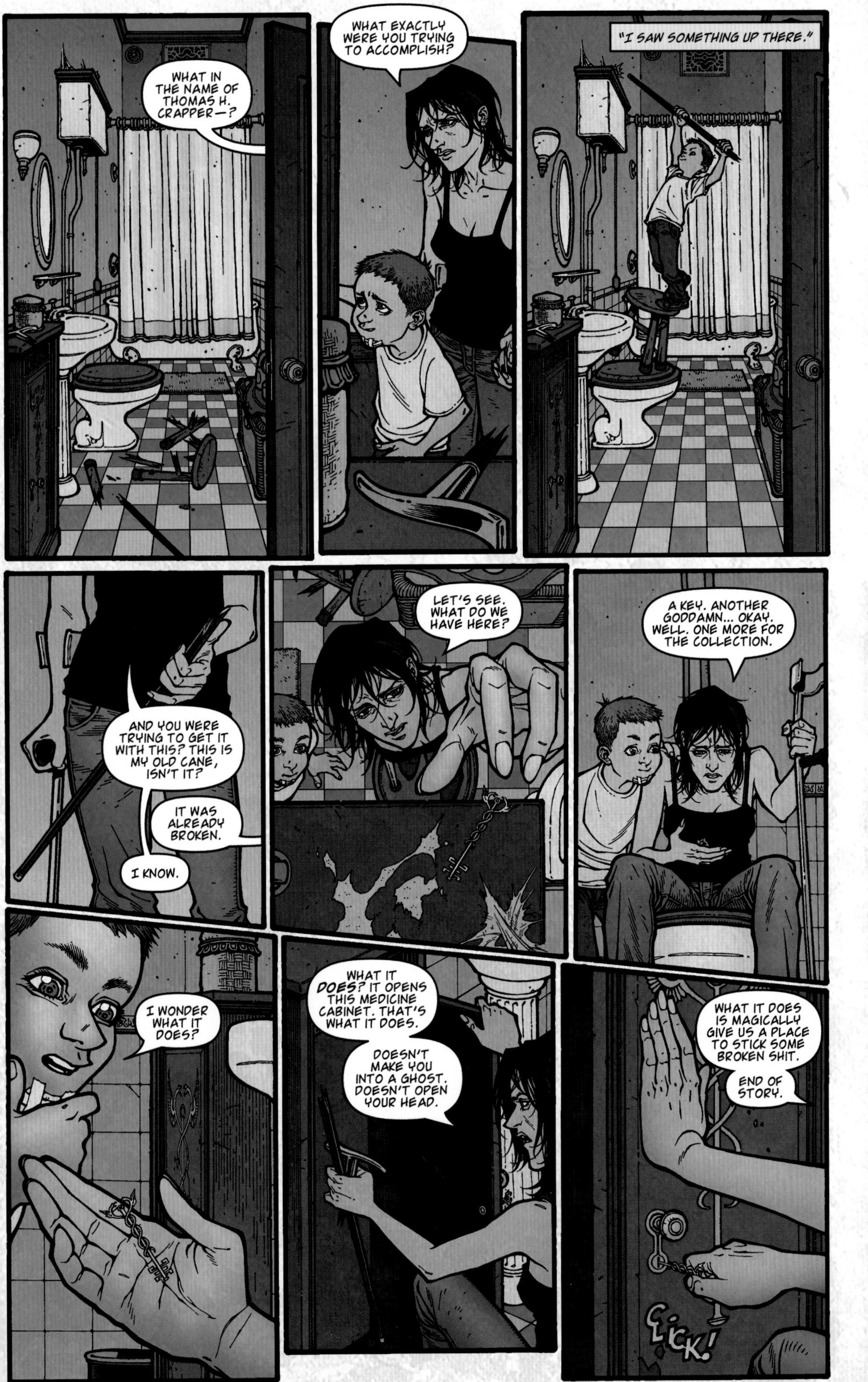
WHAT IN THE NAME OF THOMAS H. CRAPPER—?
WHAT EXACTLY WERE YOU TRYING TO ACCOMPLISH?
"I SAW SOMETHING UP THERE."
AND YOU WERE TRYING TO GET IT WITH THIS? THIS IS MY OLD CANE, ISN'T IT?
IT WAS ALREADY BROKEN.
I KNOW.
LET'S SEE. WHAT DO WE HAVE HERE?
A KEY. ANOTHER GODDAMN... OKAY. WELL. ONE MORE FOR THE COLLECTION.
I WONDER WHAT IT DOES?
WHAT IT DOES? IT OPENS THIS MEDICINE CABINET. THAT'S WHAT IT DOES.
DOESN'T MAKE YOU INTO A GHOST. DOESN'T OPEN YOUR HEAD.
WHAT IT DOES IS MAGICALLY GIVE US A PLACE TO STICK SOME BROKEN SHIT.
END OF STORY.
CLICK!

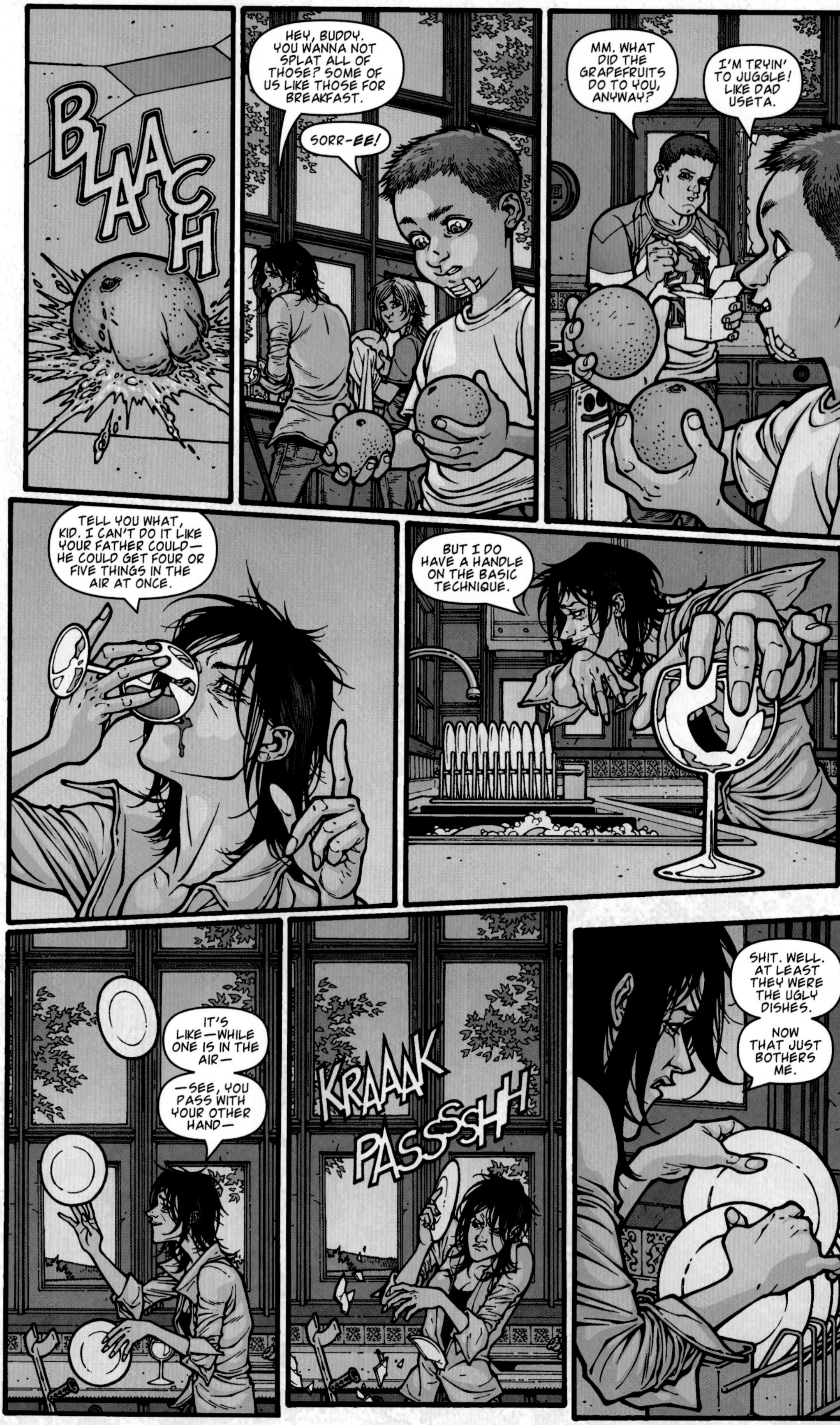
BLAACH
HEY, BUDDY. YOU WANNA NOT SPLAT ALL OF THOSE? SOME OF US LIKE THOSE FOR BREAKFAST.
SORR-EE!
MM. WHAT DID THE GRAPEFRUITS DO TO YOU, ANYWAY?
I'M TRYIN' TO JUGGLE! LIKE DAD USETA.
TELL YOU WHAT, KID. I CAN'T DO IT LIKE YOUR FATHER COULD—HE COULD GET FOUR OR FIVE THINGS IN THE AIR AT ONCE.
BUT I DO HAVE A HANDLE ON THE BASIC TECHNIQUE.
IT'S LIKE—WHILE ONE IS IN THE AIR—
—SEE, YOU PASS WITH YOUR OTHER HAND—
KRAAAK
PASSSSHH
SHIT. WELL. AT LEAST THEY WERE THE UGLY DISHES.
NOW THAT JUST BOTHERS ME.

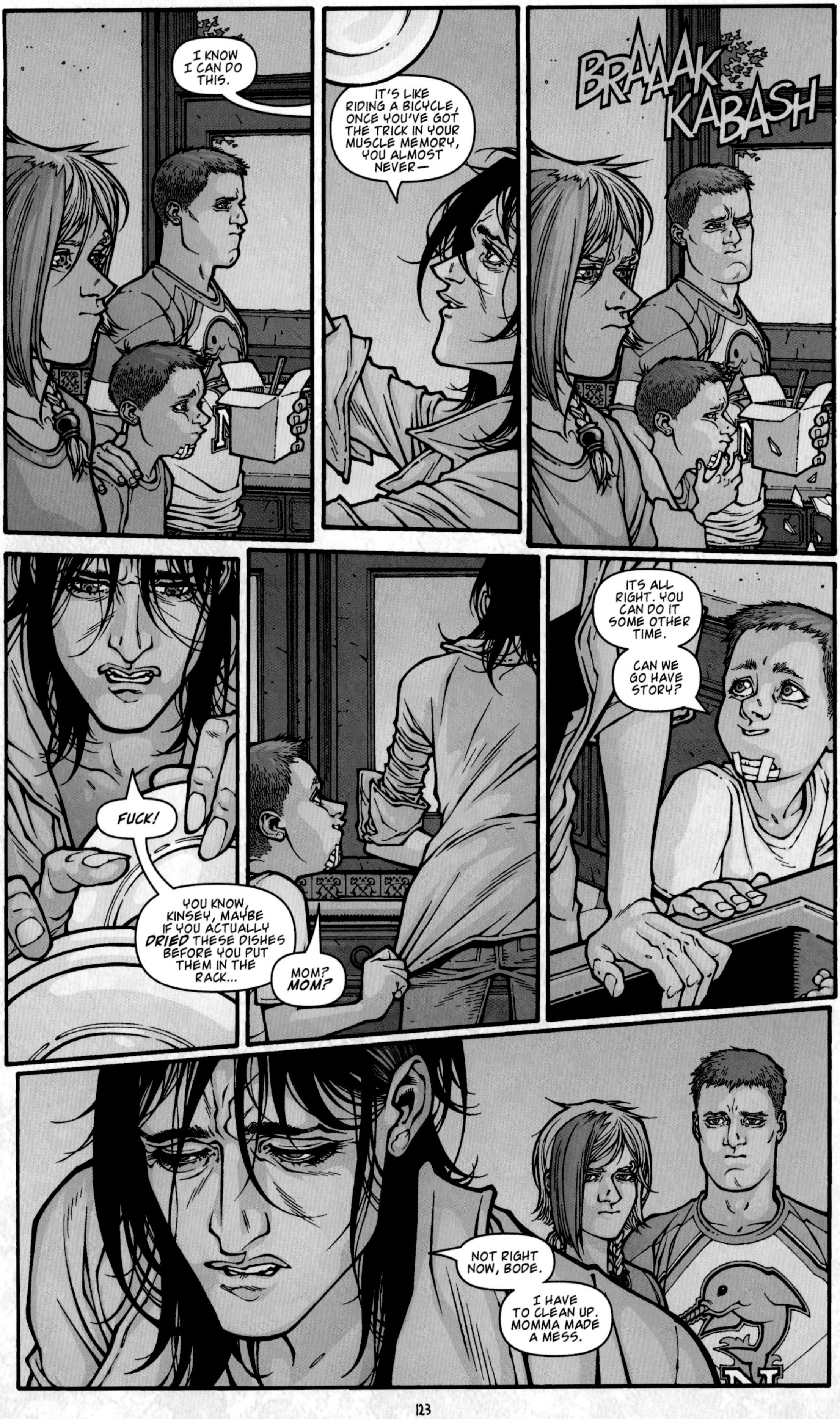
I KNOW I CAN DO THIS.
IT'S LIKE RIDING A BICYCLE, ONCE YOU'VE GOT THE TRICK IN YOUR MUSCLE MEMORY, YOU ALMOST NEVER—
BRAAAK KABASH
FUCK!
YOU KNOW, KINSEY, MAYBE IF YOU ACTUALLY DRIED THESE DISHES BEFORE YOU PUT THEM IN THE RACK...
MOM? MOM?
ITS ALL RIGHT. YOU CAN DO IT SOME OTHER TIME.
CAN WE GO HAVE STORY?
NOT RIGHT NOW, BODE.
I HAVE TO CLEAN UP. MOMMA MADE A MESS.

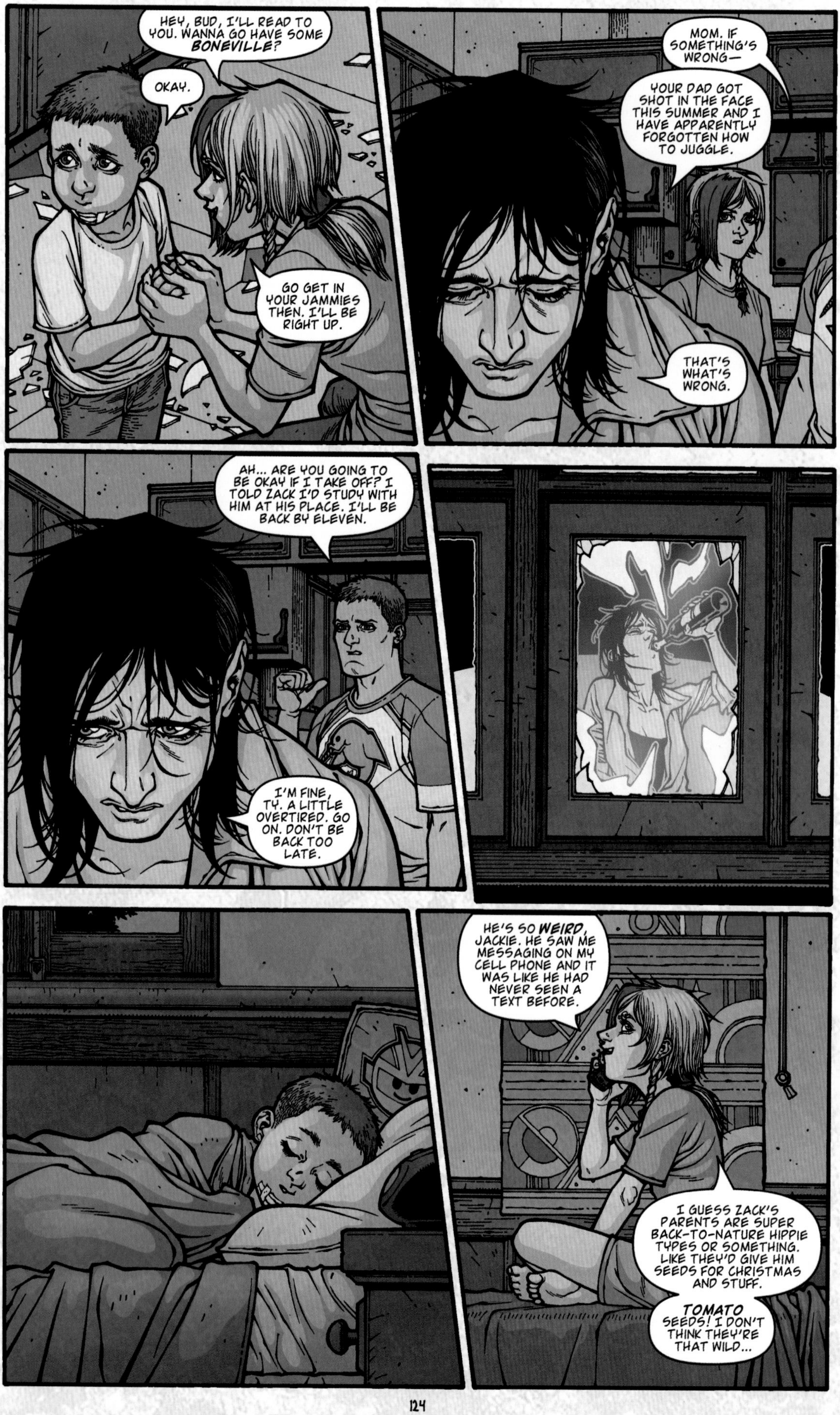

HEY, BUD, I'LL READ TO YOU. WANNA GO HAVE SOME *BONEVILLE*?
OKAY.
GO GET IN YOUR JAMMIES THEN. I'LL BE RIGHT UP.
MOM. IF SOMETHING'S WRONG—
YOUR DAD GOT SHOT IN THE FACE THIS SUMMER AND I HAVE APPARENTLY FORGOTTEN HOW TO JUGGLE.
THAT'S WHAT'S WRONG.
AH... ARE YOU GOING TO BE OKAY IF I TAKE OFF? I TOLD ZACK I'D STUDY WITH HIM AT HIS PLACE. I'LL BE BACK BY ELEVEN.
I'M FINE, TY. A LITTLE OVERTIRED. GO ON. DON'T BE BACK TOO LATE.
HE'S SO *WEIRD*, JACKIE. HE SAW ME MESSAGING ON MY CELL PHONE AND IT WAS LIKE HE HAD NEVER SEEN A TEXT BEFORE.
I GUESS ZACK'S PARENTS ARE SUPER BACK-TO-NATURE HIPPIE TYPES OR SOMETHING. LIKE THEY'D GIVE HIM SEEDS FOR CHRISTMAS AND STUFF.
TOMATO SEEDS! I DON'T THINK THEY'RE THAT WILD...

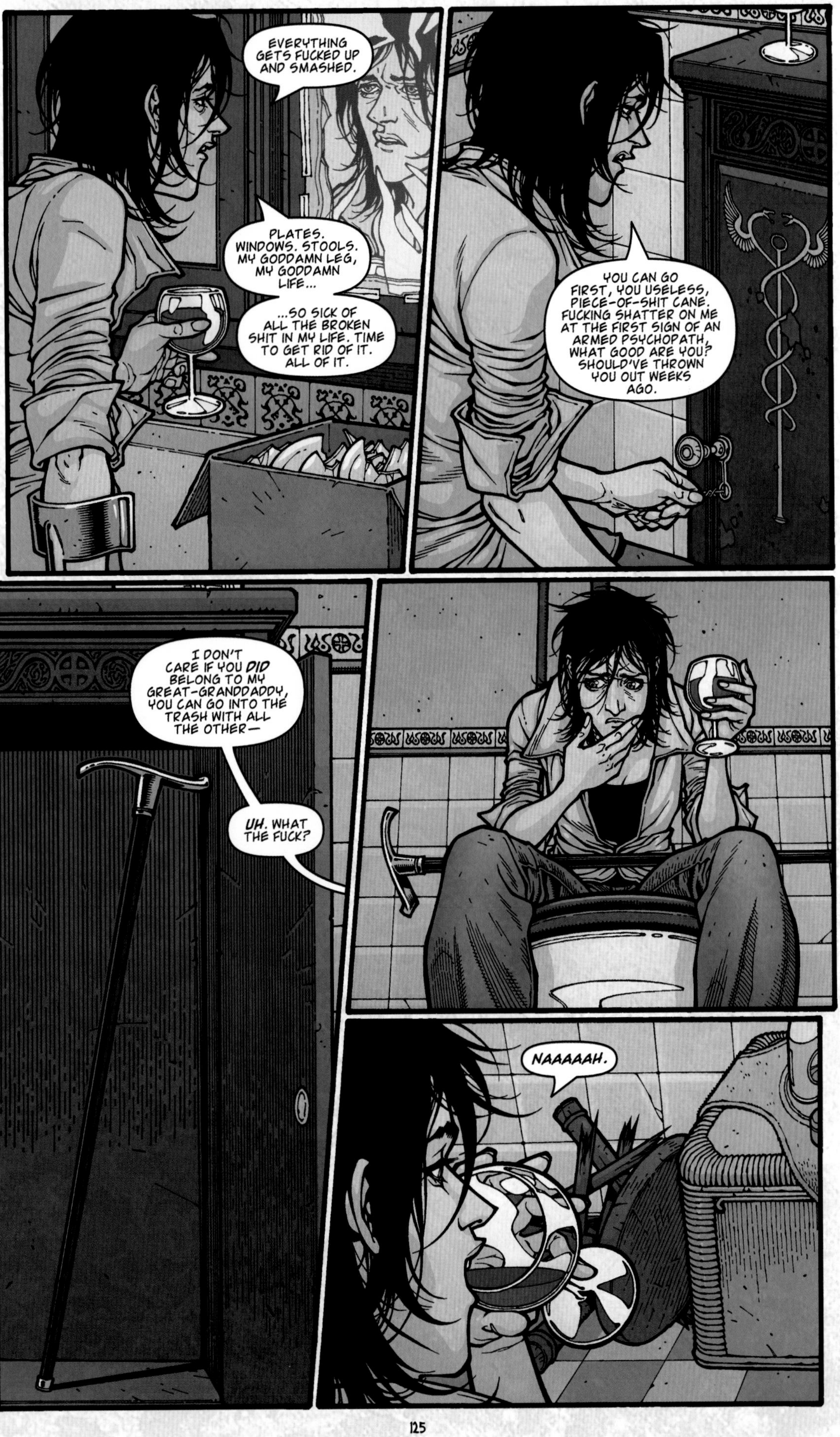
EVERYTHING GETS FUCKED UP AND SMASHED.
PLATES. WINDOWS. STOOLS. MY GODDAMN LEG, MY GODDAMN LIFE...
...SO SICK OF ALL THE BROKEN SHIT IN MY LIFE. TIME TO GET RID OF IT. ALL OF IT.
YOU CAN GO FIRST, YOU USELESS, PIECE-OF-SHIT CANE. FUCKING SHATTER ON ME AT THE FIRST SIGN OF AN ARMED PSYCHOPATH, WHAT GOOD ARE YOU? SHOULD'VE THROWN YOU OUT WEEKS AGO.
I DON'T CARE IF YOU *DID* BELONG TO MY GREAT-GRANDDADDY, YOU CAN GO INTO THE TRASH WITH ALL THE OTHER—
UH. WHAT THE FUCK?
NAAAAAH.

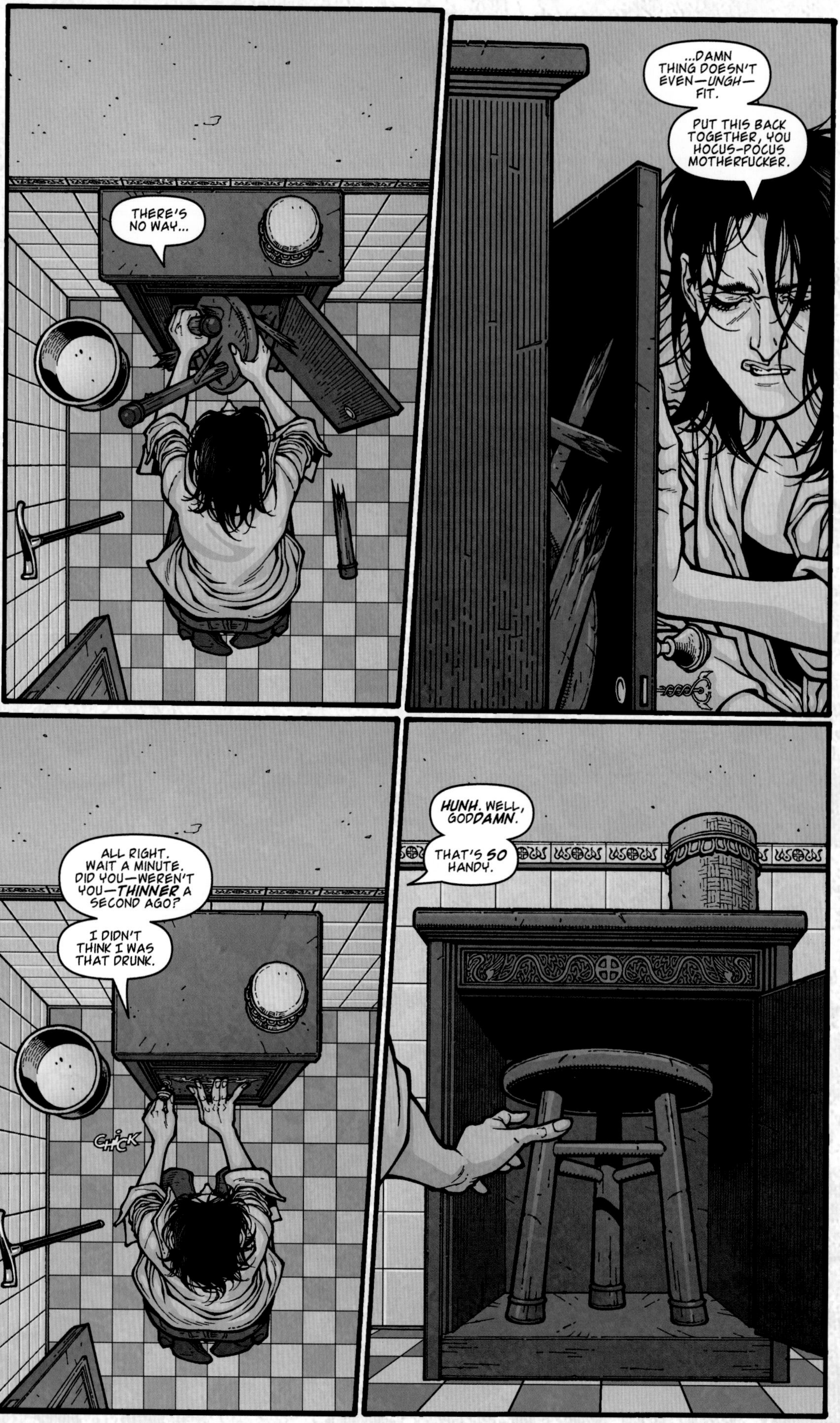
THERE'S NO WAY...
...DAMN THING DOESN'T EVEN—UNGH—FIT.
PUT THIS BACK TOGETHER, YOU HOCUS-POCUS MOTHERFUCKER.
ALL RIGHT. WAIT A MINUTE. DID YOU—WEREN'T YOU—THINNER A SECOND AGO?
I DIDN'T THINK I WAS THAT DRUNK.
CHICK
HUNH. WELL, GODDAMN.
THAT'S SO HANDY.

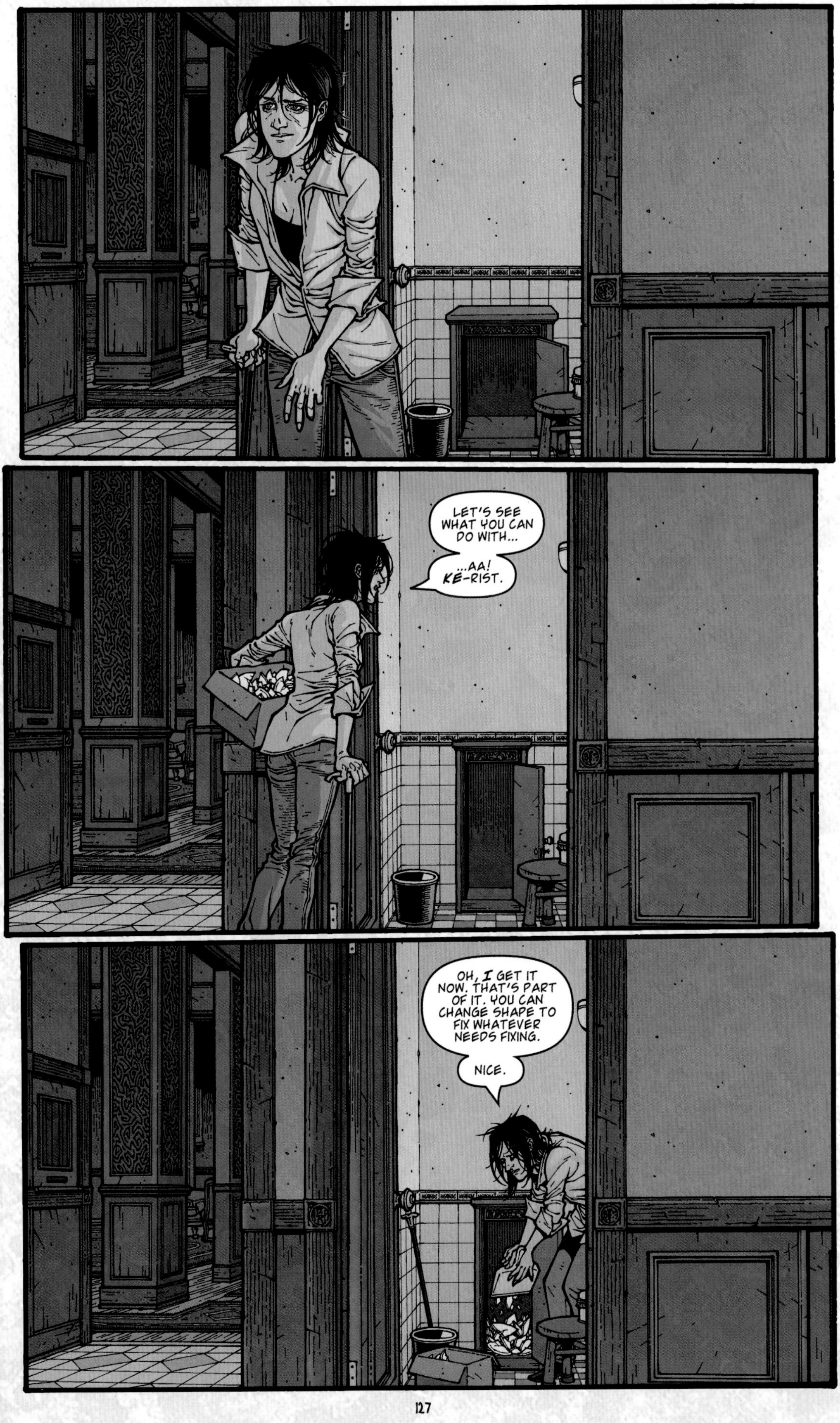
LET'S SEE WHAT YOU CAN DO WITH...
...AA! KE-RIST.
OH, I GET IT NOW. THAT'S PART OF IT. YOU CAN CHANGE SHAPE TO FIX WHATEVER NEEDS FIXING.
NICE.

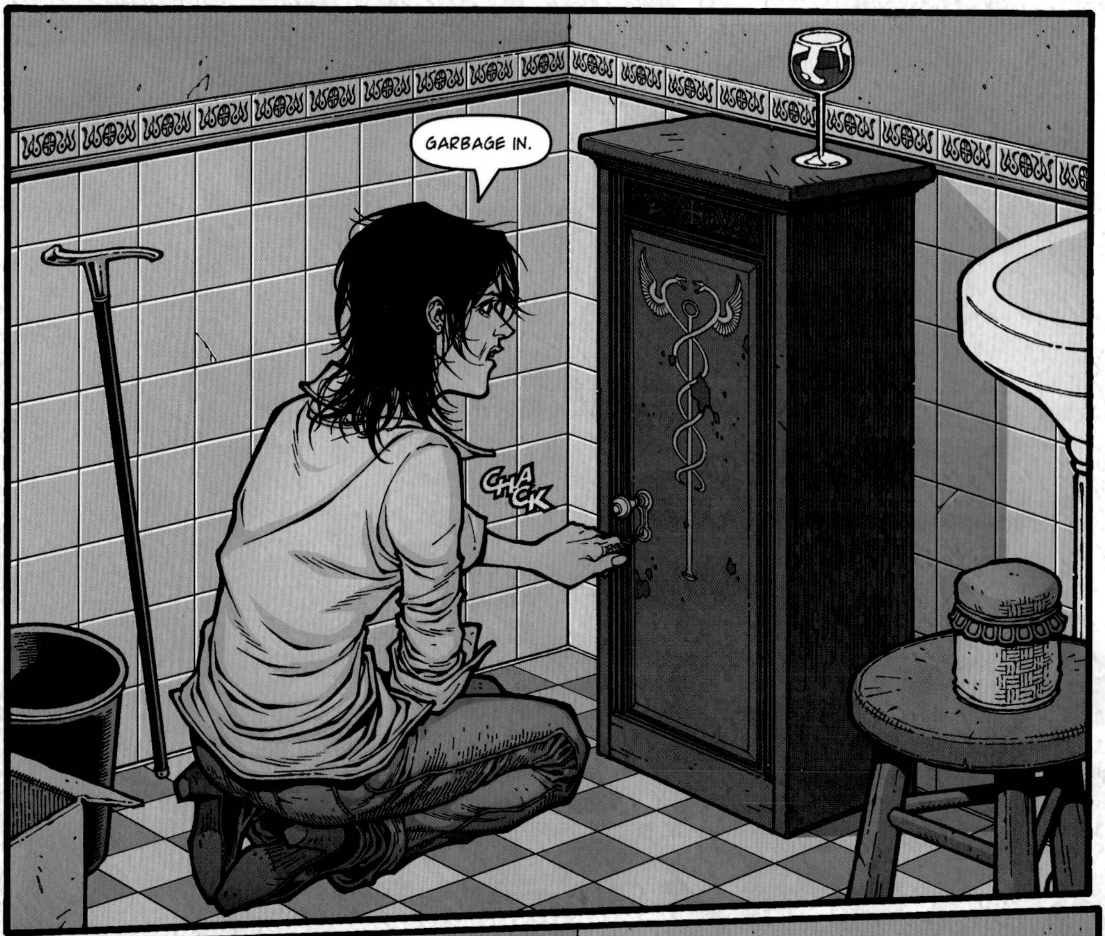
GARBAGE IN.
CHACK

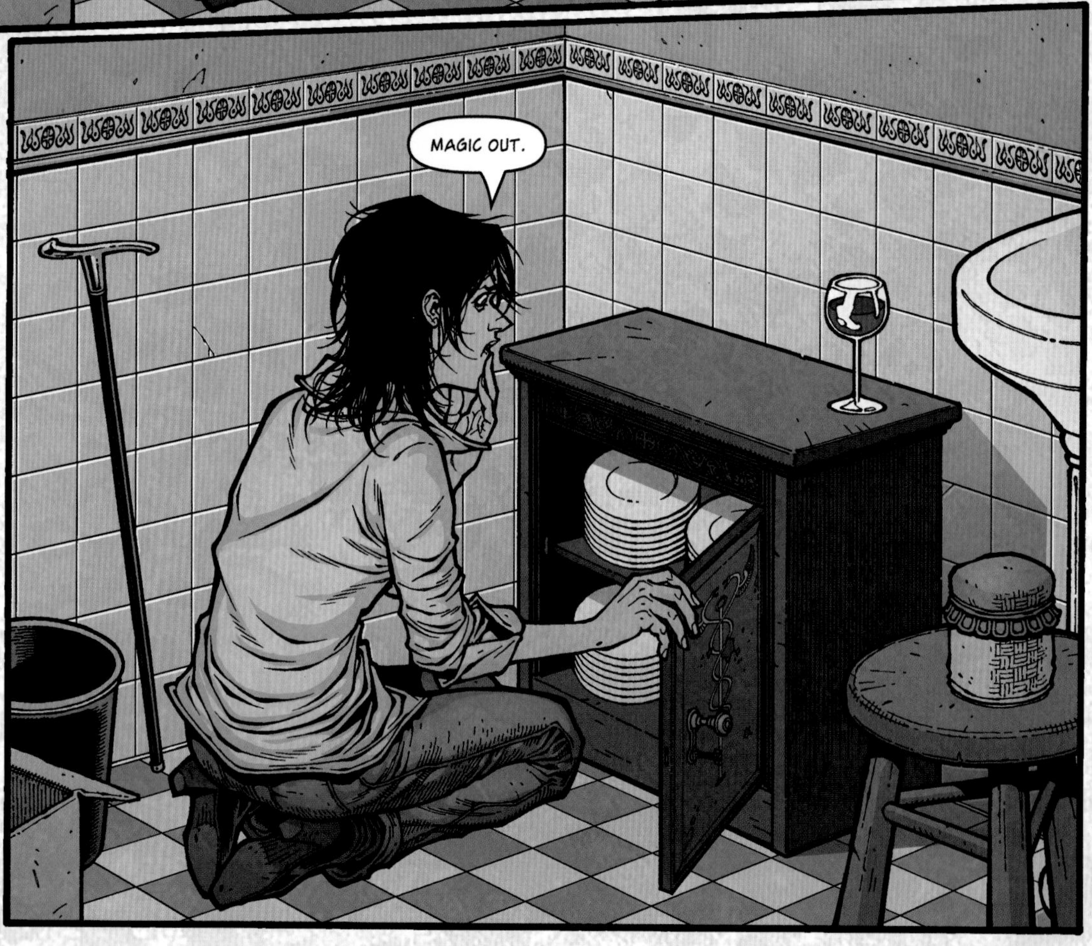
MAGIC OUT.

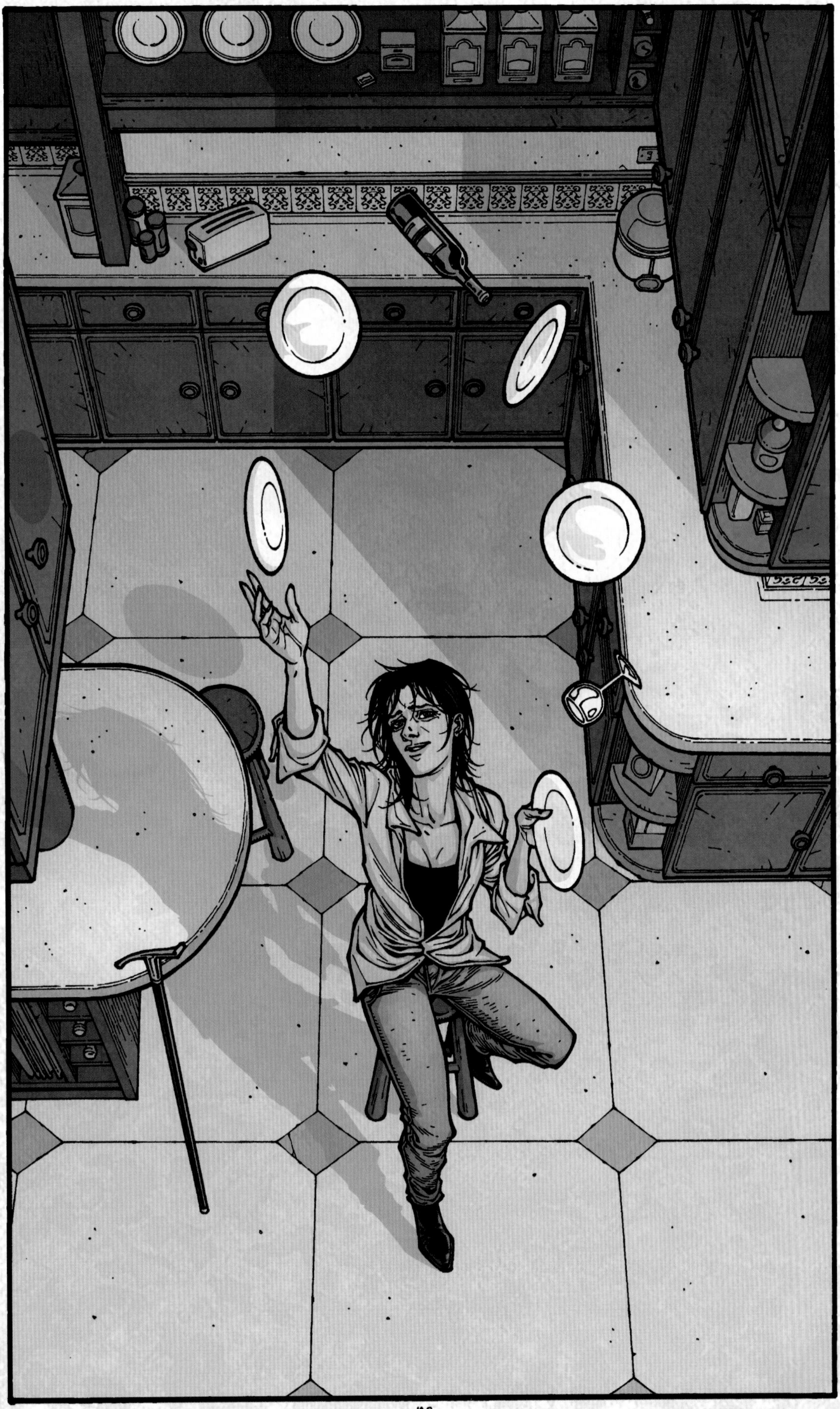

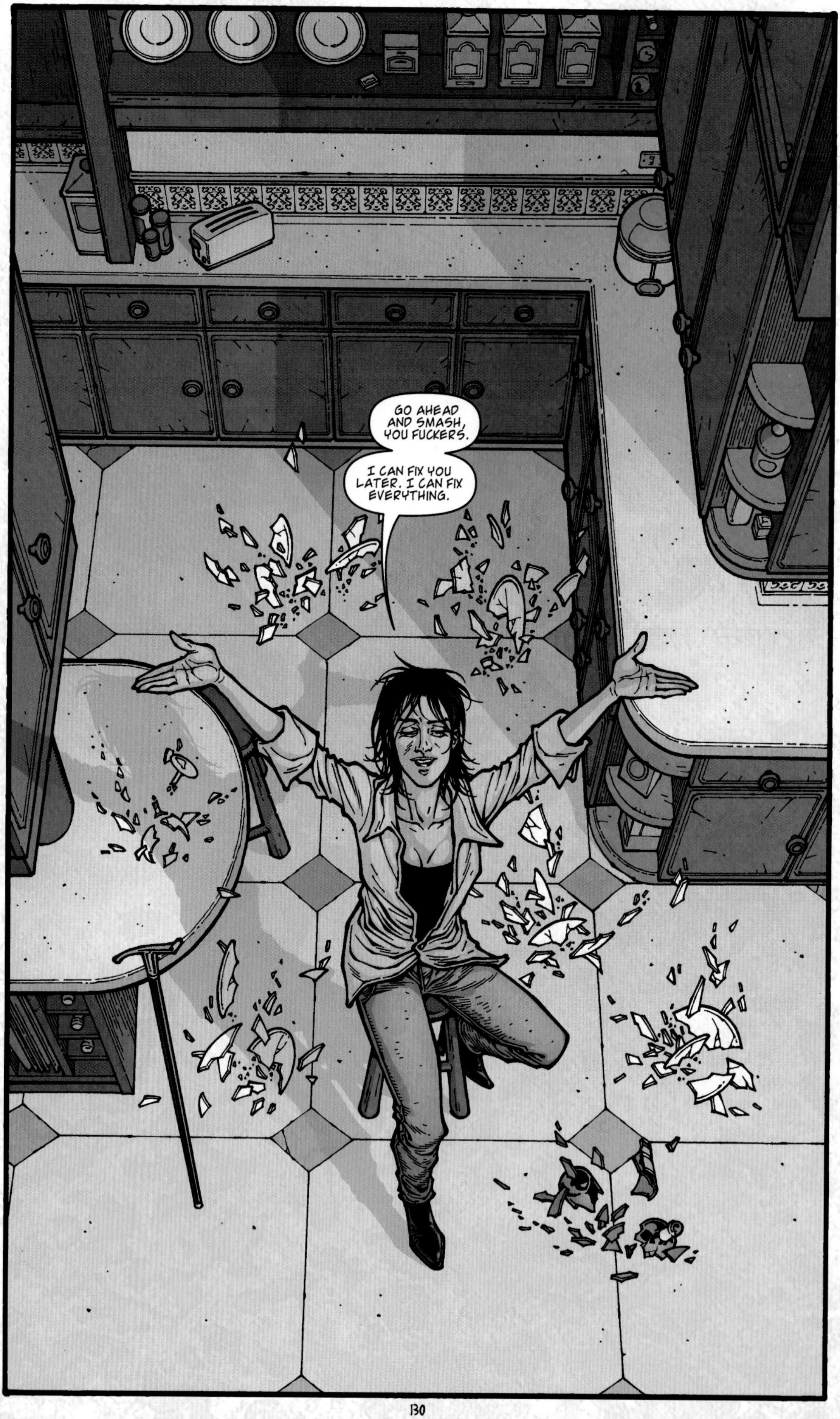
GO AHEAD AND SMASH, YOU FUCKERS.
I CAN FIX YOU LATER. I CAN FIX EVERYTHING.

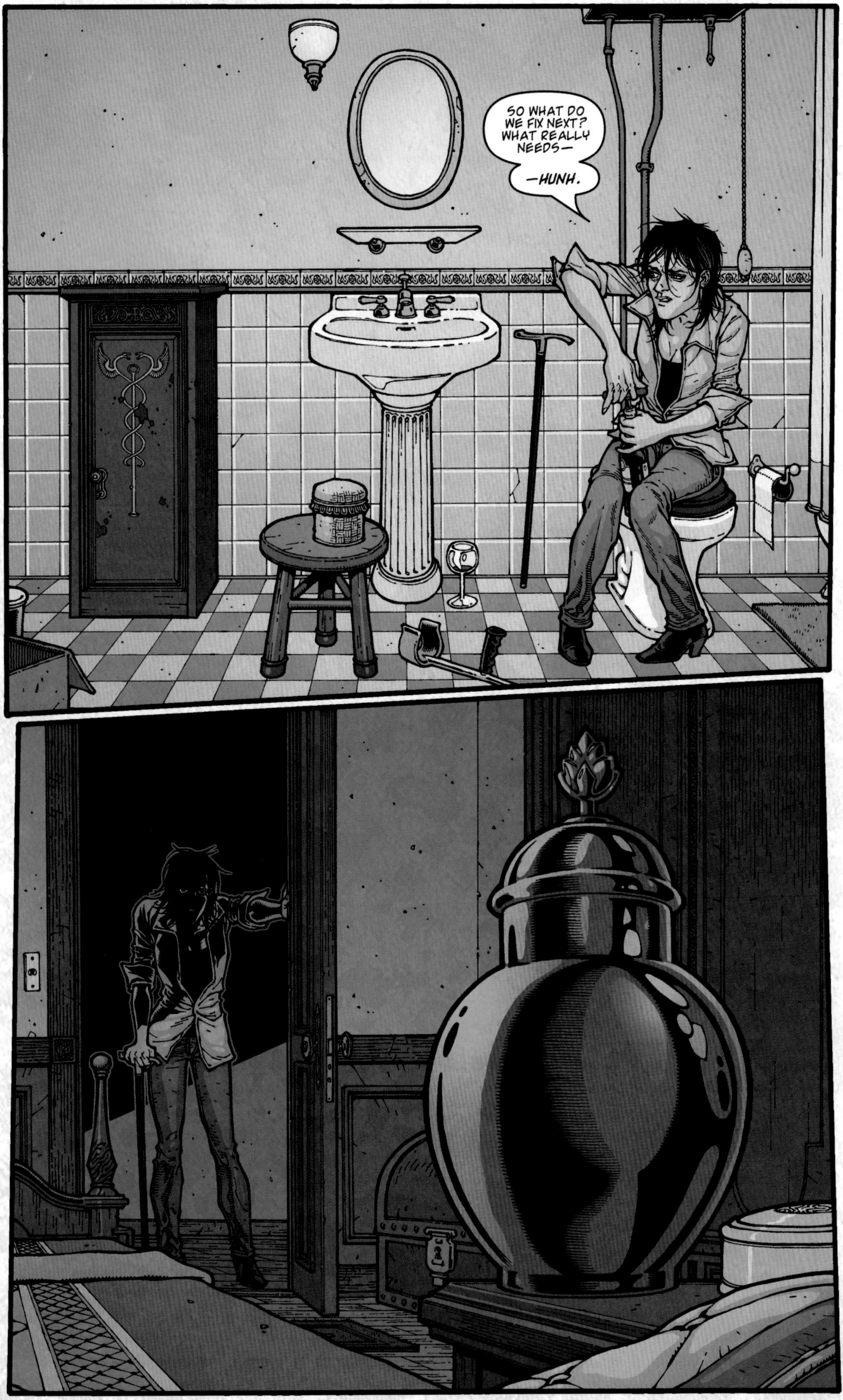
SO WHAT DO WE FIX NEXT? WHAT REALLY NEEDS—
—HUNH.

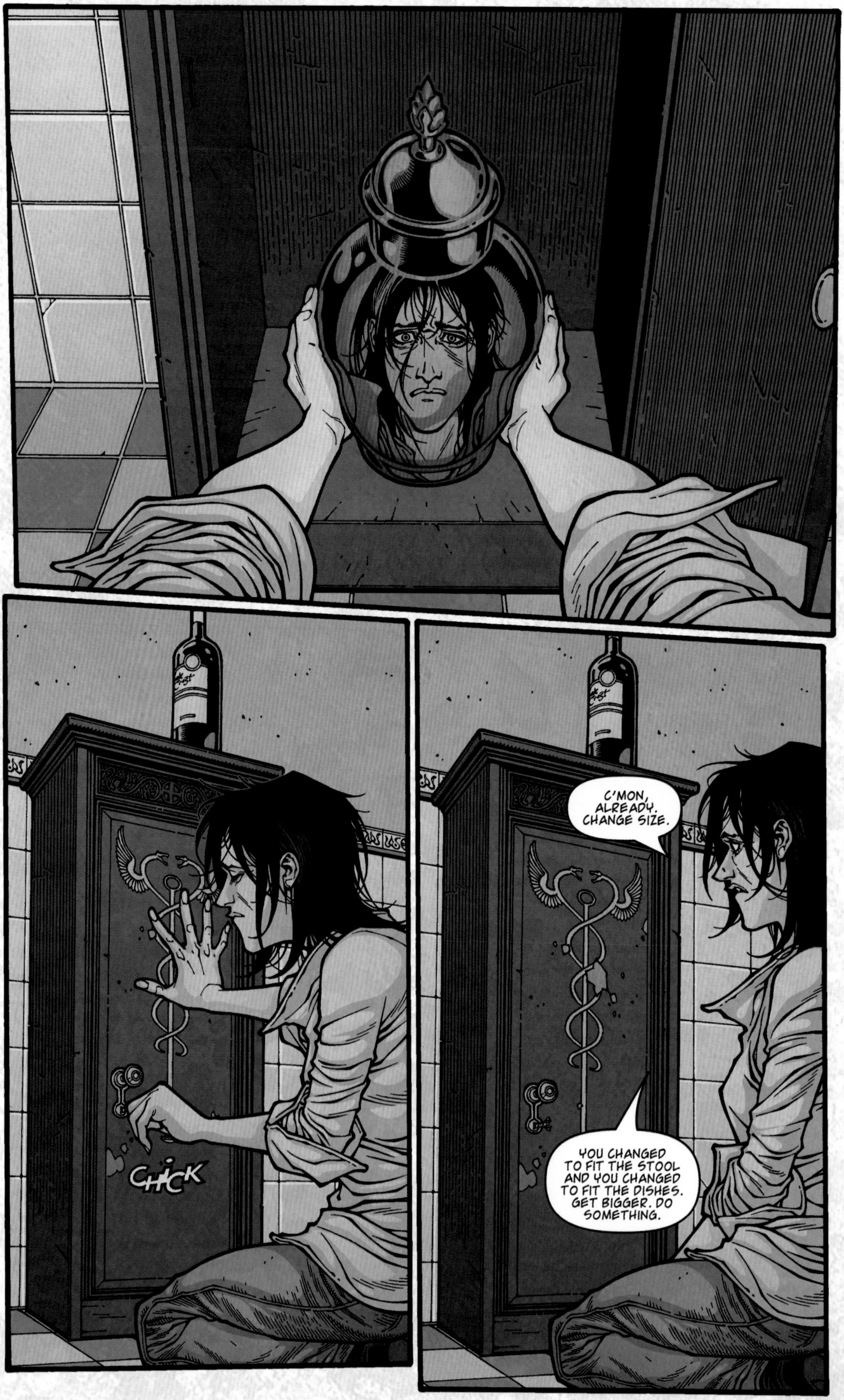
CHICK
C'MON, ALREADY. CHANGE SIZE.
YOU CHANGED TO FIT THE STOOL AND YOU CHANGED TO FIT THE DISHES. GET BIGGER. DO SOMETHING.

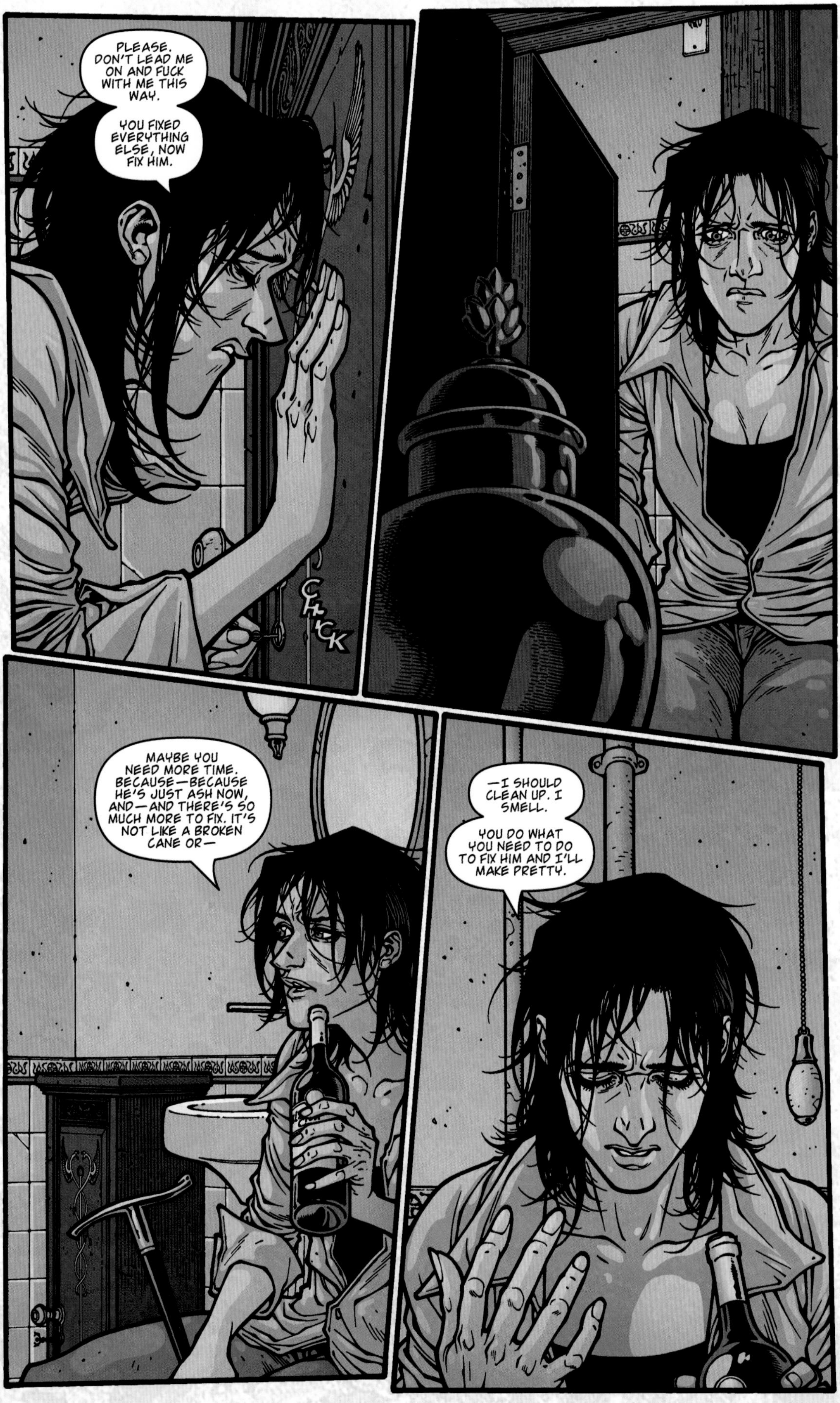
PLEASE. DON'T LEAD ME ON AND FUCK WITH ME THIS WAY.
YOU FIXED EVERYTHING ELSE, NOW FIX HIM.
CHICK
MAYBE YOU NEED MORE TIME. BECAUSE—BECAUSE HE'S JUST ASH NOW, AND—AND THERE'S SO MUCH MORE TO FIX. IT'S NOT LIKE A BROKEN CANE OR—
—I SHOULD CLEAN UP. I SMELL.
YOU DO WHAT YOU NEED TO DO TO FIX HIM AND I'LL MAKE PRETTY.

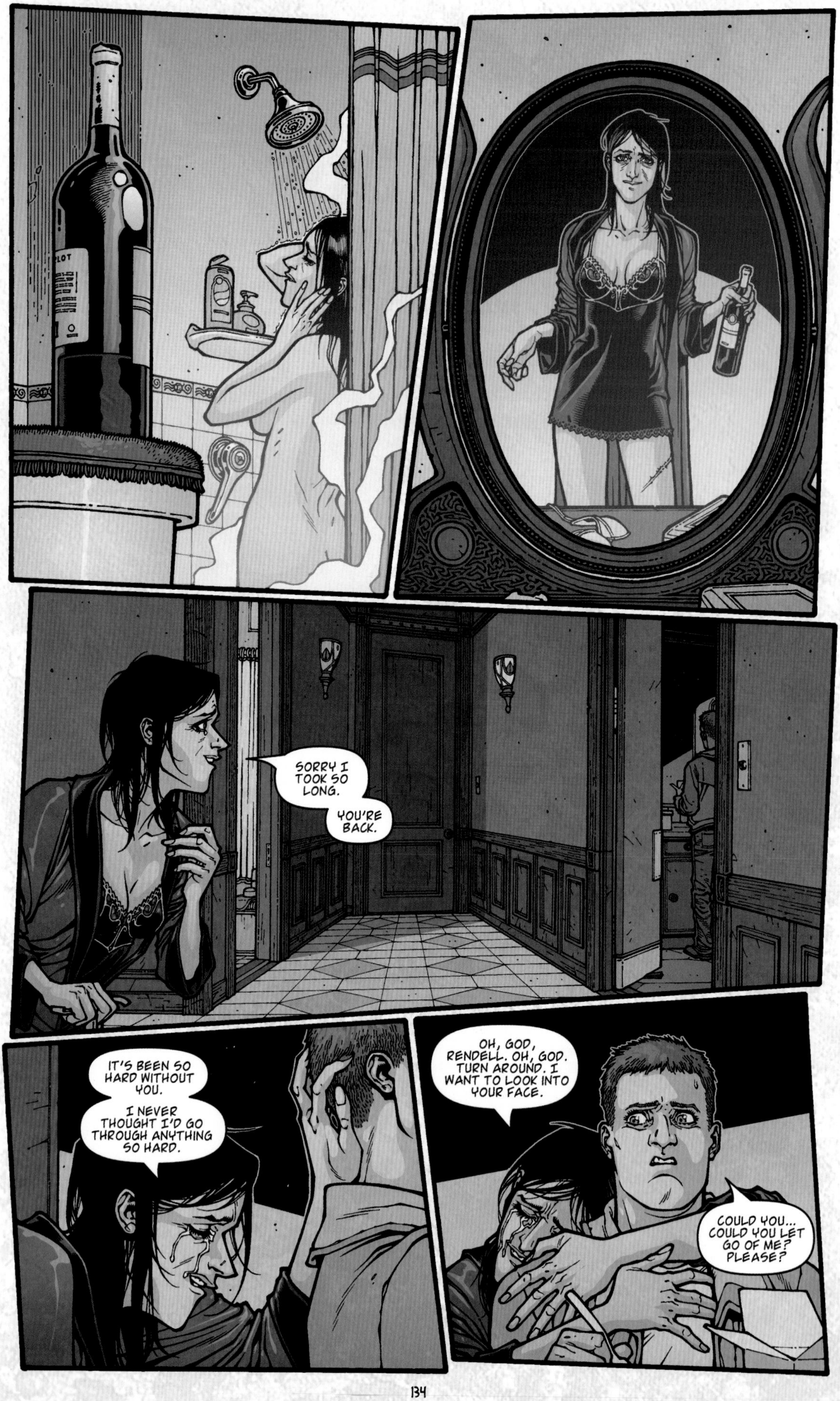
PLOT
SORRY I TOOK SO LONG.
YOU'RE BACK.
IT'S BEEN SO HARD WITHOUT YOU.
I NEVER THOUGHT I'D GO THROUGH ANYTHING SO HARD.
OH, GOD, RENDELL. OH, GOD. TURN AROUND. I WANT TO LOOK INTO YOUR FACE.
COULD YOU... COULD YOU LET GO OF ME? PLEASE?

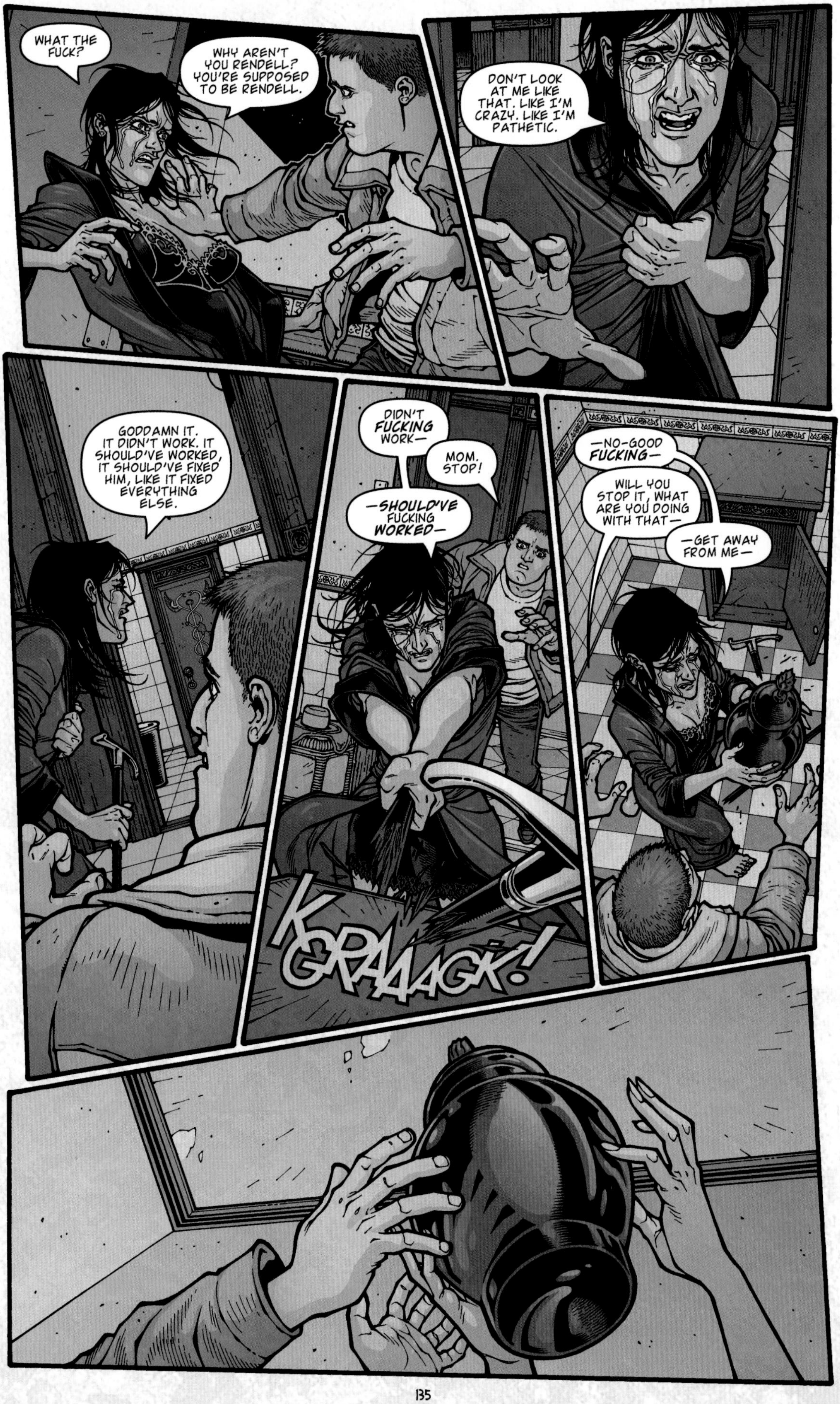
WHAT THE FUCK?
WHY AREN'T YOU RENDELL? YOU'RE SUPPOSED TO BE RENDELL.
DON'T LOOK AT ME LIKE THAT. LIKE I'M CRAZY. LIKE I'M PATHETIC.
GODDAMN IT. IT DIDN'T WORK. IT SHOULD'VE WORKED, IT SHOULD'VE FIXED HIM, LIKE IT FIXED EVERYTHING ELSE.
DIDN'T FUCKING WORK—
MOM. STOP!
—SHOULD'VE FUCKING WORKED—
KGRAAAGK!
—NO-GOOD FUCKING—
WILL YOU STOP IT, WHAT ARE YOU DOING WITH THAT—
—GET AWAY FROM ME—

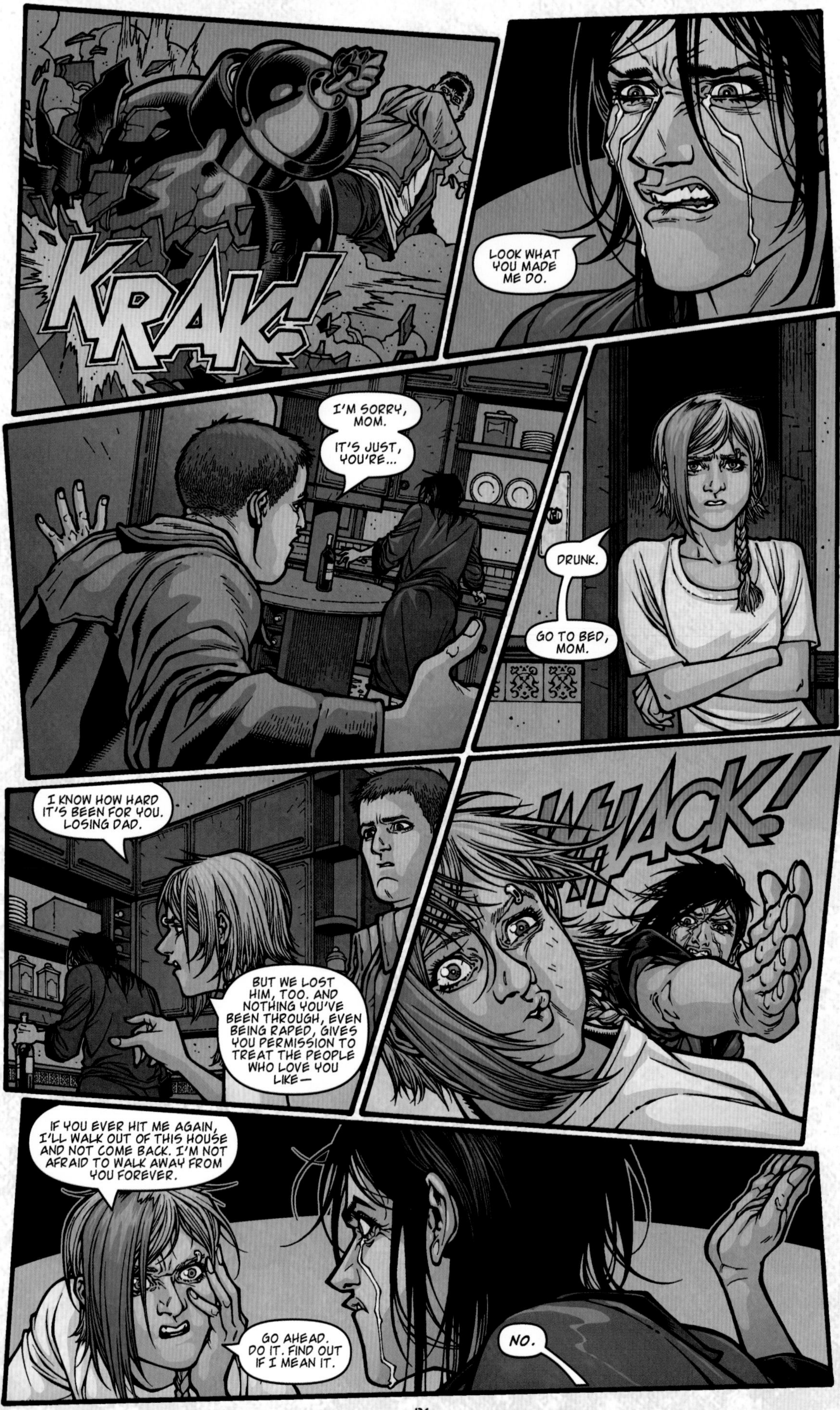
KRAK!
LOOK WHAT YOU MADE ME DO.
I'M SORRY, MOM.
IT'S JUST, YOU'RE...
DRUNK.
GO TO BED, MOM.
I KNOW HOW HARD IT'S BEEN FOR YOU. LOSING DAD.
BUT WE LOST HIM, TOO. AND NOTHING YOU'VE BEEN THROUGH, EVEN BEING RAPED, GIVES YOU PERMISSION TO TREAT THE PEOPLE WHO LOVE YOU LIKE—
WHACK!
IF YOU EVER HIT ME AGAIN, I'LL WALK OUT OF THIS HOUSE AND NOT COME BACK. I'M NOT AFRAID TO WALK AWAY FROM YOU FOREVER.
GO AHEAD. DO IT. FIND OUT IF I MEAN IT.
NO.

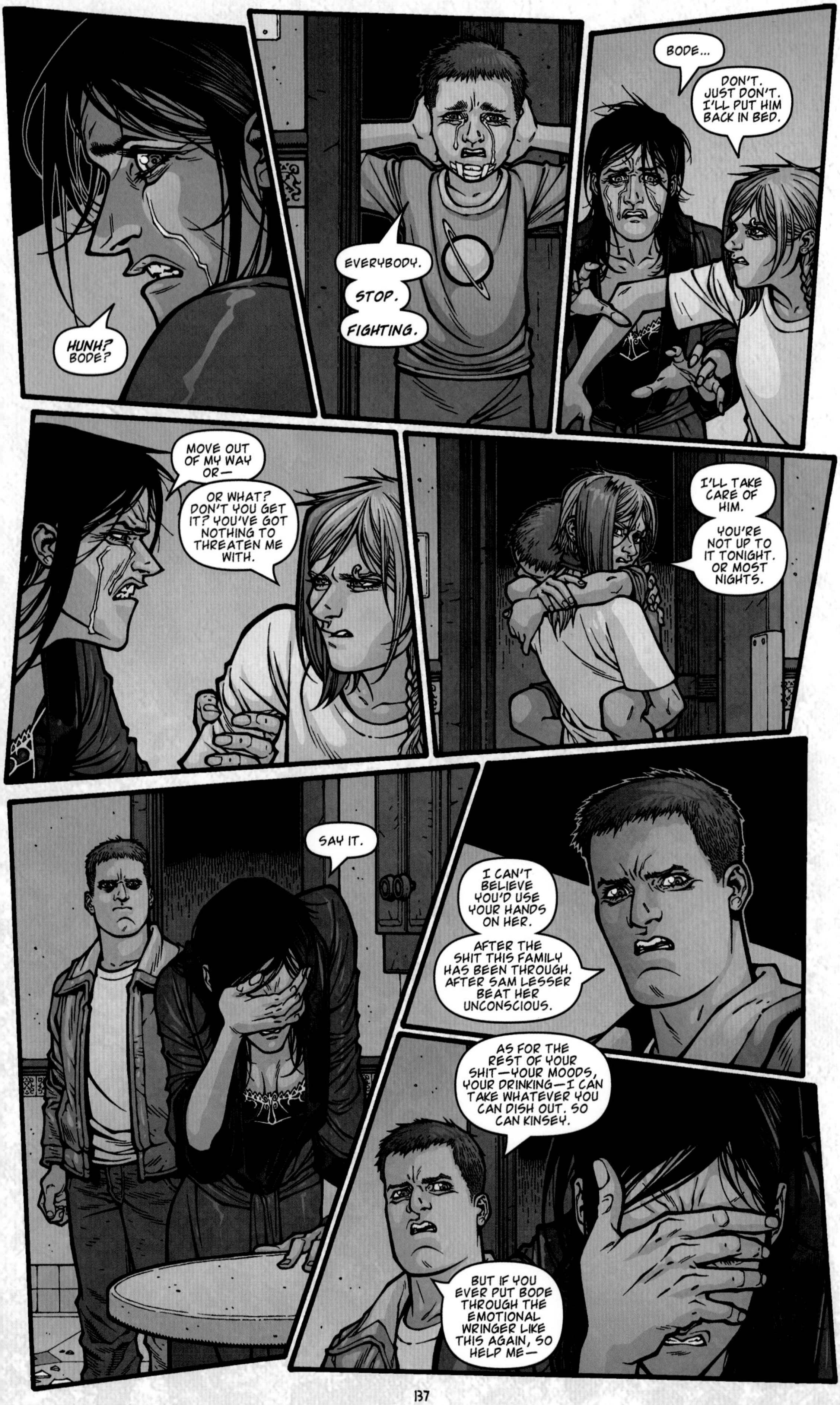
HUNH? BODE?
EVERYBODY.
STOP.
FIGHTING.
BODE...
DON'T. JUST DON'T. I'LL PUT HIM BACK IN BED.
MOVE OUT OF MY WAY OR—
OR WHAT? DON'T YOU GET IT? YOU'VE GOT NOTHING TO THREATEN ME WITH.
I'LL TAKE CARE OF HIM.
YOU'RE NOT UP TO IT TONIGHT. OR MOST NIGHTS.
SAY IT.
I CAN'T BELIEVE YOU'D USE YOUR HANDS ON HER.
AFTER THE SHIT THIS FAMILY HAS BEEN THROUGH. AFTER SAM LESSER BEAT HER UNCONSCIOUS.
AS FOR THE REST OF YOUR SHIT—YOUR MOODS, YOUR DRINKING—I CAN TAKE WHATEVER YOU CAN DISH OUT. SO CAN KINSEY.
BUT IF YOU EVER PUT BODE THROUGH THE EMOTIONAL WRINGER LIKE THIS AGAIN, SO HELP ME—

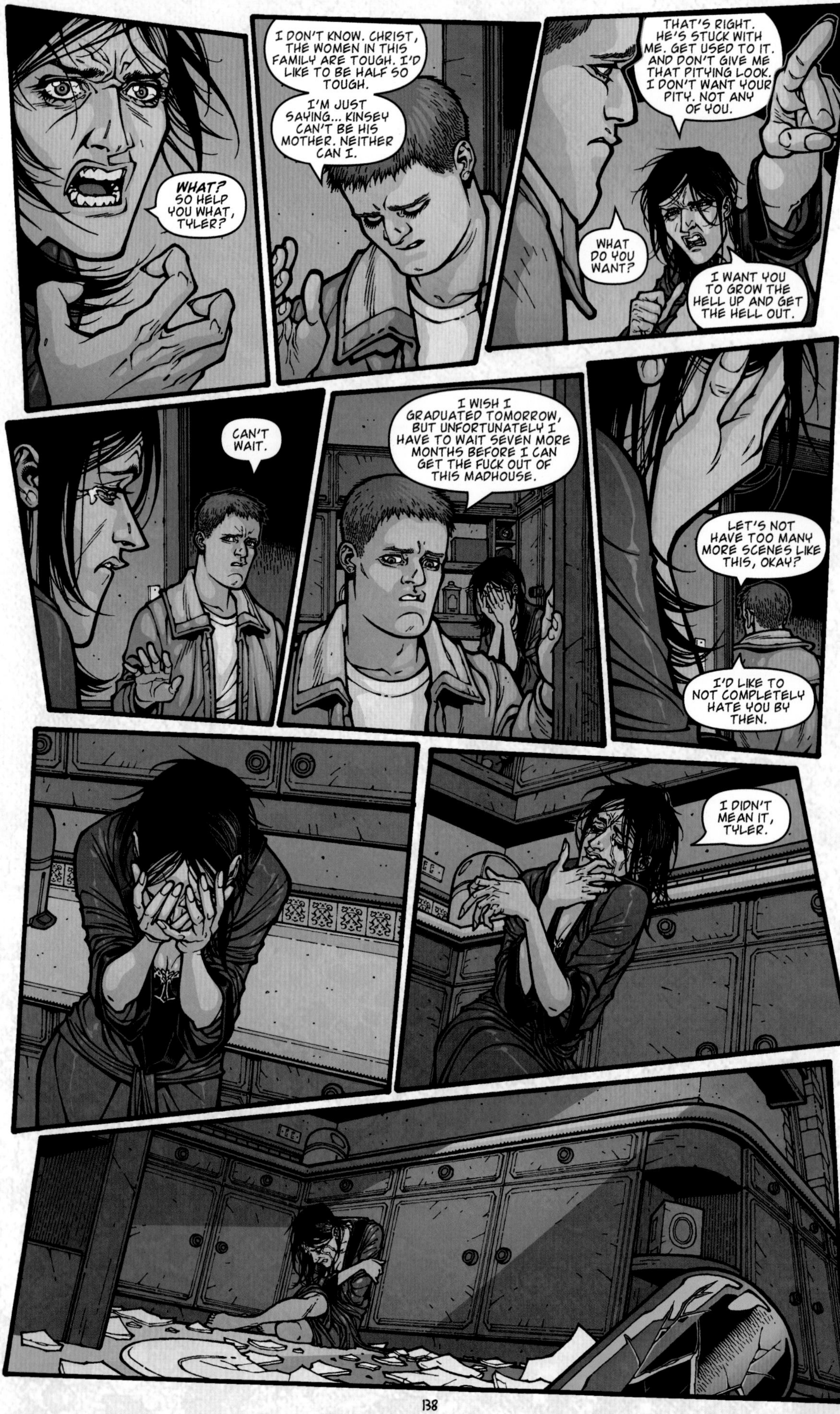
WHAT? SO HELP YOU WHAT, TYLER?
I DON'T KNOW. CHRIST, THE WOMEN IN THIS FAMILY ARE TOUGH. I'D LIKE TO BE HALF SO TOUGH.
I'M JUST SAYING... KINSEY CAN'T BE HIS MOTHER. NEITHER CAN I.
THAT'S RIGHT. HE'S STUCK WITH ME. GET USED TO IT. AND DON'T GIVE ME THAT PITYING LOOK. I DON'T WANT YOUR PITY. NOT ANY OF YOU.
WHAT DO YOU WANT?
I WANT YOU TO GROW THE HELL UP AND GET THE HELL OUT.
CAN'T WAIT.
I WISH I GRADUATED TOMORROW, BUT UNFORTUNATELY I HAVE TO WAIT SEVEN MORE MONTHS BEFORE I CAN GET THE FUCK OUT OF THIS MADHOUSE.
LET'S NOT HAVE TOO MANY MORE SCENES LIKE THIS, OKAY?
I'D LIKE TO NOT COMPLETELY HATE YOU BY THEN.
I DIDN'T MEAN IT, TYLER.

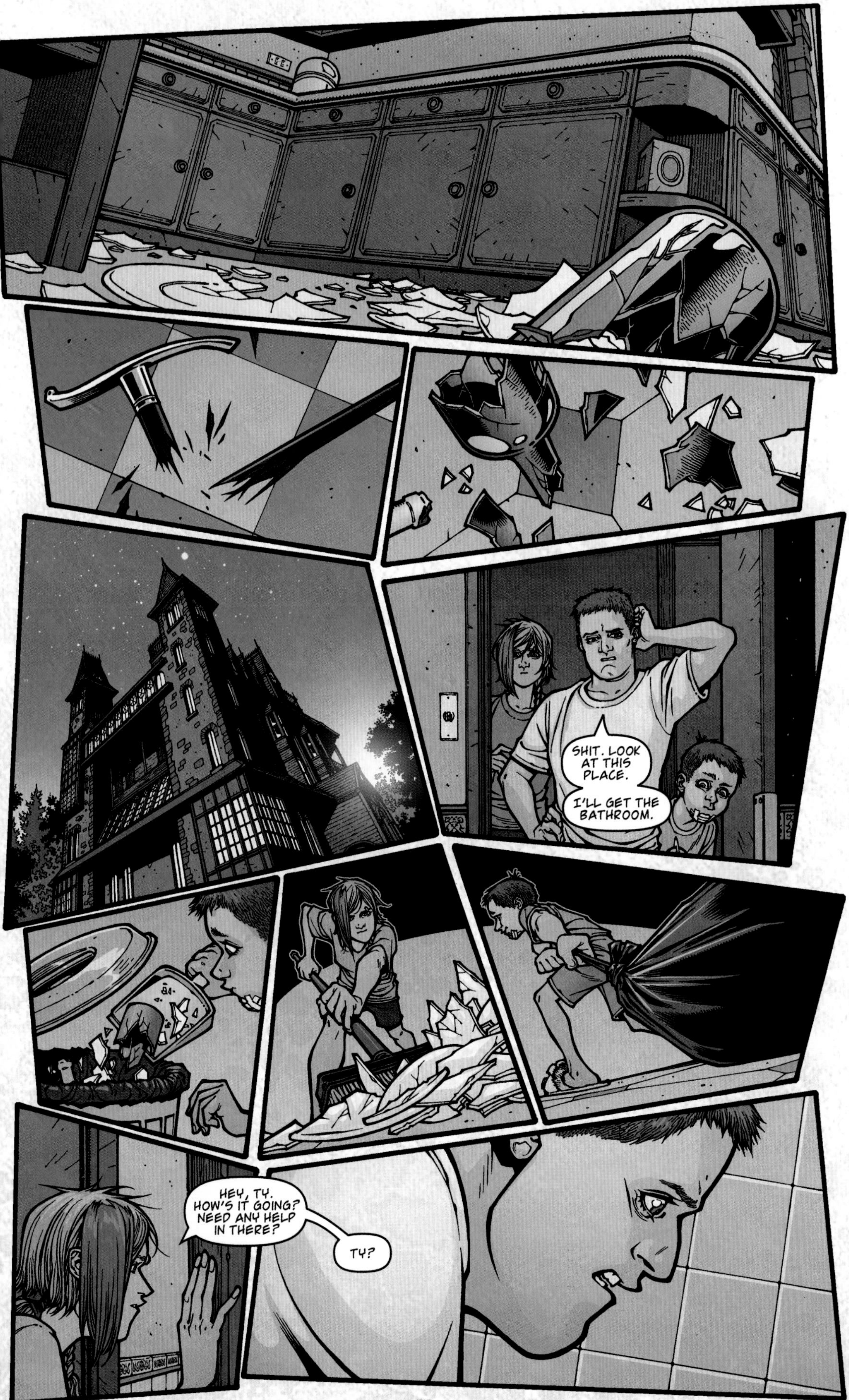
SHIT. LOOK AT THIS PLACE.
I'LL GET THE BATHROOM.
HEY, TY. HOW'S IT GOING? NEED ANY HELP IN THERE?
TY?

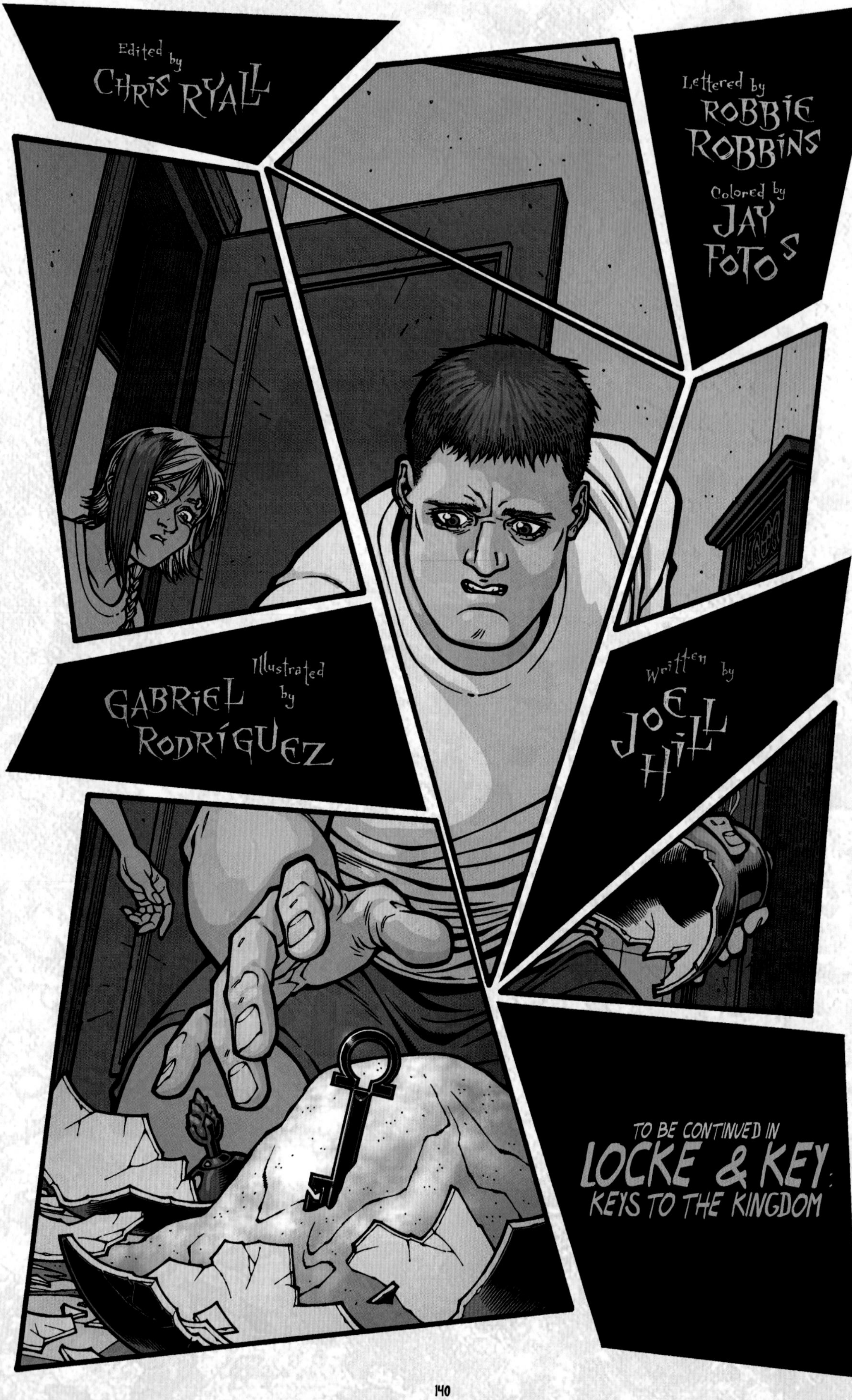
Edited by
CHRIS RYALL
Lettered by
ROBBIE ROBBINS
Colored by
JAY FOTOS
Illustrated by
GABRIEL RODRÍGUEZ
Written by
JOE HILL
TO BE CONTINUED IN
LOCKE & KEY:
KEYS TO THE KINGDOM

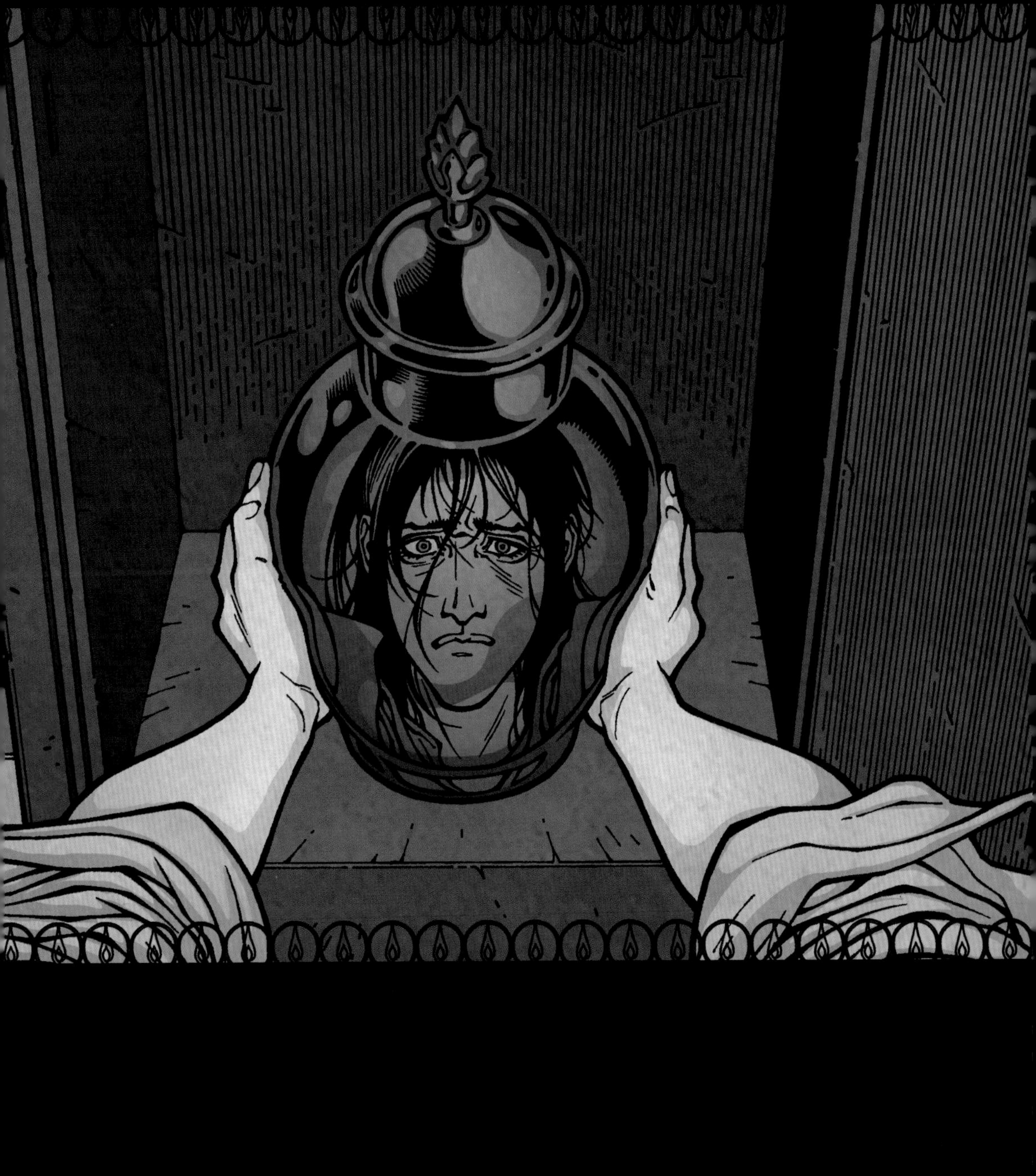

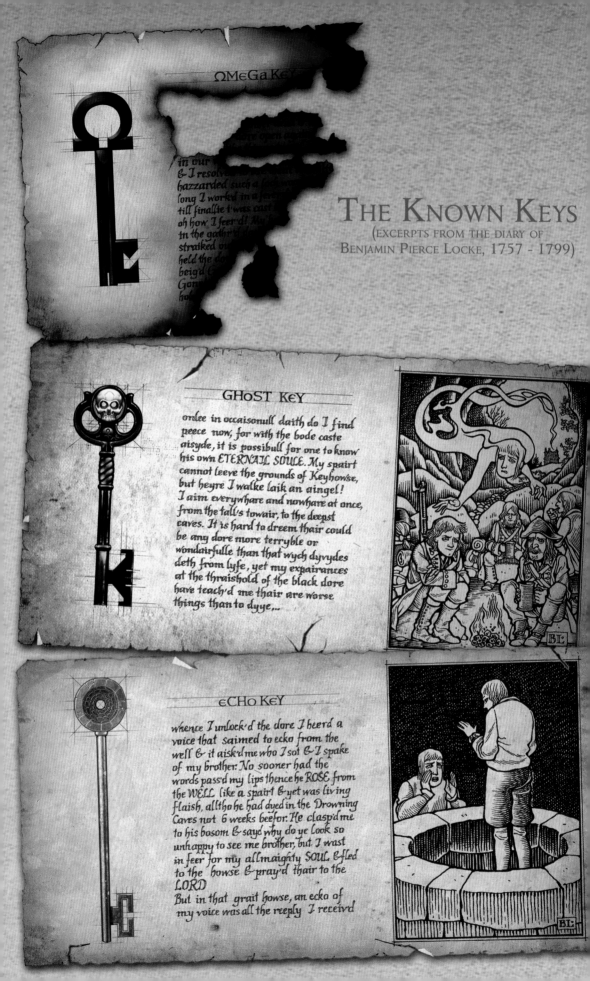

ΩMeGa KeY

THE KNOWN KEYS

(EXCERPTS FROM THE DIARY OF
BENJAMIN PIERCE LOCKE, 1757 - 1799)

in our [...]
& I resolve[d] [...]
hazzarded such a [...]
long I work'd in a fever [...]
till finalie t'was cast [...]
oh how I feer'd! [...]
in the gathr'd [...]
straiked ou[t] [...]
held the do[re] [...]
beig'd [...]
Gon[e] [...]
ho[...]

GHoST KeY

onlee in occaisonull daith do I find
peece now, for with the bode caste
aisyde, it is possibull for one to know
his own ETERNALL SOULE. My spairt
cannot leeve the grounds of Keyhowse,
but heyre I walke laik an aingel!
I aim everywhare and nowhare at once,
from the tall's towair, to the deepst
caves. It is hard to dreem thair could
be any dore more terryble or
wondairfulle than that wych dyvydes
deth from lyfe, yet my expairances
at the thraishold of the black dore
have teach'd me thair are worse
things than to dyye...

eCHo KeY

whence I unlock'd the dore I heerd a
voice that saimed to ecko from the
well & it aisk'd me who I sot & I spake
of my brother. No sooner had the
words pass'd my lips thence he ROSE from
the WELL like a spairt & yet was living
flaish, altho he had dyed in the Drowning
Caves not 6 weeks beefor. He clasp'd me
to his bosom & say'd why do ye look so
unhappy to see me brother, but I wast
in feer for my allmaighty SOUL & fled
to the howse & pray'd thair to the
LORD
But in that grait howse, an ecko of
my voice was all the reeply I receiv'd

aNYWHeRe KeY

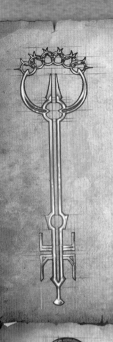

us'd the key to anyplaice againe, to return to Boston, & gaither intelaigents for Crais. Tis an act of terryble wychcraift, but better I do it, than my sister, who is obssaissed with REVENGING herself upon the RED-COATS, for thair violence agin our faither & brother & belov'd maither: Aye, my dredd of beeing called to acconnt someday by SATAN HIMSELF is a trifling concern when maiched with my desyre to rid the worlde of the devylls who taik the King's Coyne to do raip & murdur...

HeaD KeY

of alle the keys I have forged from the WHISP'RING IRON, 'tis the key that opens the human mind I most regruit. Miranda hast a pervairse fasinaytion whist the key & hast us'd ait to fill her head with all thair is to know about WAR & the SLAIYING of MEN, & she carrys an arsanall whist her whairever she goes. Yet I am less in dred of what she has put in than what she hast remov'd. Sometimes it is as if she is now without FEER and indeed is herself more man than I!

GENDeR KeY

my sister—or should I now say my brother!—fights the shadow war with Crais in the streets of Boston whilst I wait at home, like a helpless maiden, praying to the ALLMAIGHTY! for her safe return. When first I fashin'd the key, I imaguined she maight trainsform to a boy to protect her, if necessaire, from the unsavorie lusts of ENGLISHMEN should the King's foot-soldiers return to Lovecraft to abuse God fairing womain. Never did I think she wouldst WILLENGLY caist off the wardrobe of her femininitie for this ruggaid liberation among men...

SHaDoW KeY

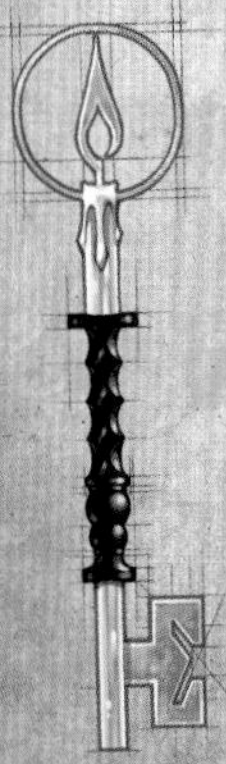

O Wycked Night! Damn'd be Crais & Damn'd be the Redcoats & Damn'd be my own foole self. Miranda tis griev'sly hurt & lingers on the thaishold of deth! The Redcoats pursued her & the tattr'd remnante of Crais's companie into the caves but I drove them back with the aide of the lyving shadows. If she dies I wouldst rather be a shadow myself than remain in thys diabollicall world, knowing she wouldst never have been at riske if not for me!

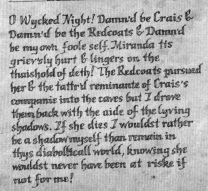

GiaNT KeY

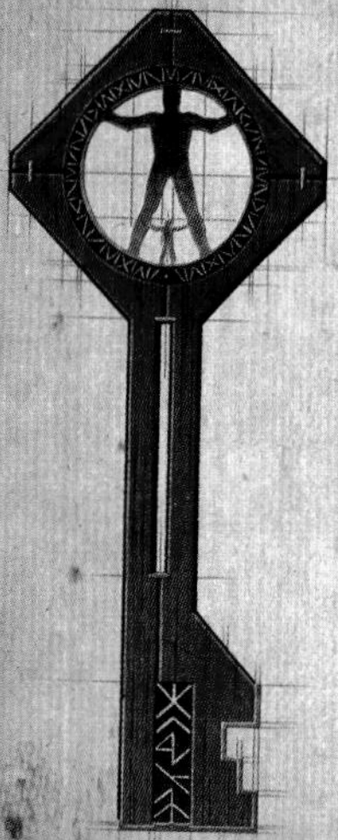

she is dying & thair is nothing I can do to save her!
The Redcoats return'd to assalle the house & claym her & I admitte I lette my fury & miserie get the better of me. I used the giant's key to multiplie my syze, so that my body was as vaste as my hayte & I turn'd upon a wholle regiment & ~ O GOD forgive me! ~ did detestably murther them alle!

MeNDiNG KeY

the Iron whispr'd to me laste night & I worked in a fever alle day, mayking a cabinet & forging a new key out of that dreadfull metal that is not metal. Yet if the devil may pervairt Holie 'Scripture to serve his purposes, so many the rihteous at times turn the DEVYLLS TOOLS to do the work of SWEET JESU! For the key & cabinet I fashin'd could be used to mend fraicturd objykts ~ shatter'd plattes, crack'd eggs & broken sistairs. Bless'd be THE LORD, Miranda hast recovr'd! I only wish she wouldst remembair her place & become the demure & modestte girlle she once was, but fear her love for Crais will emperille her againe soon enough...

ART GALLERY

ART BY GABRIEL RODRIGUEZ

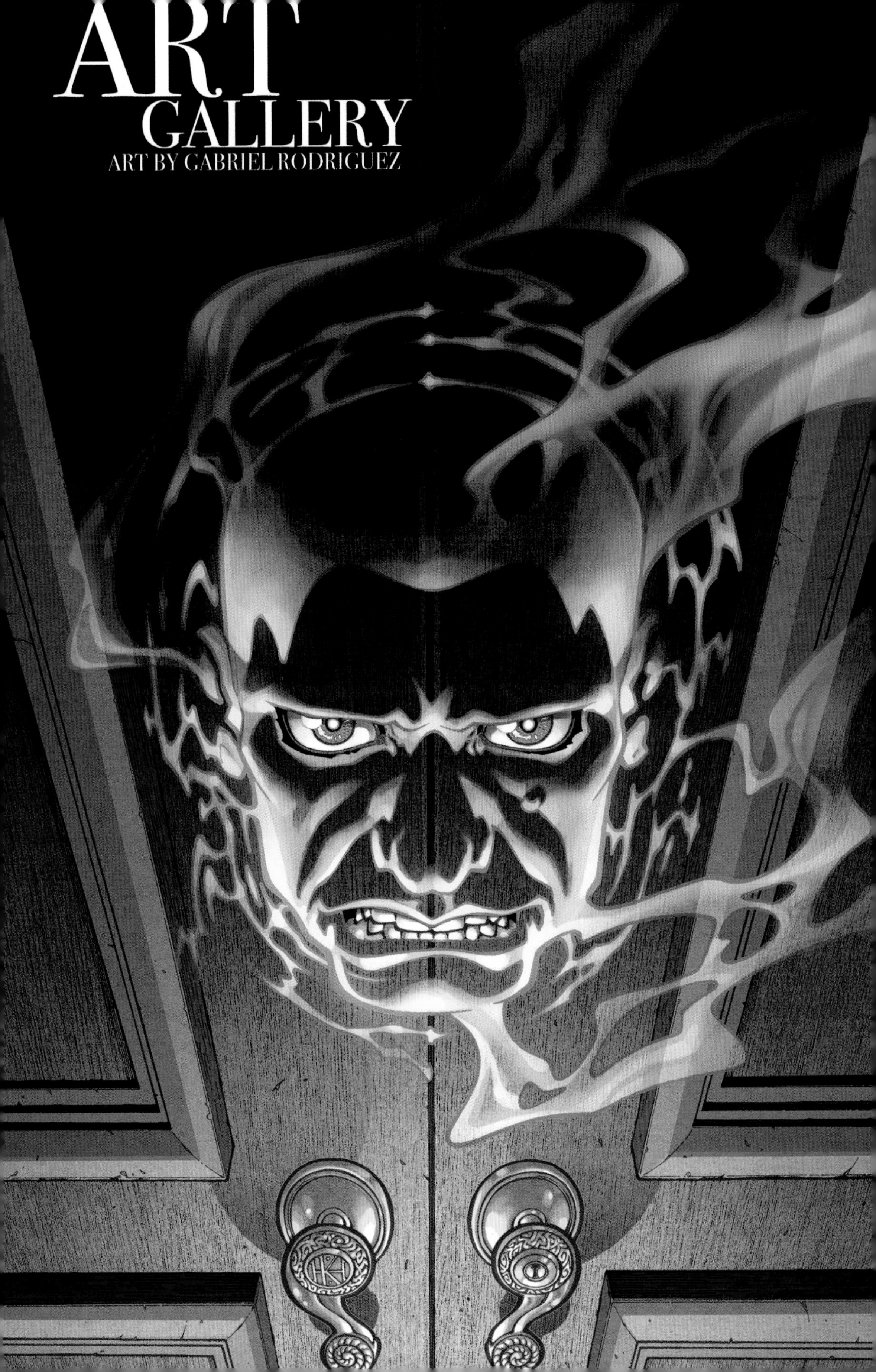

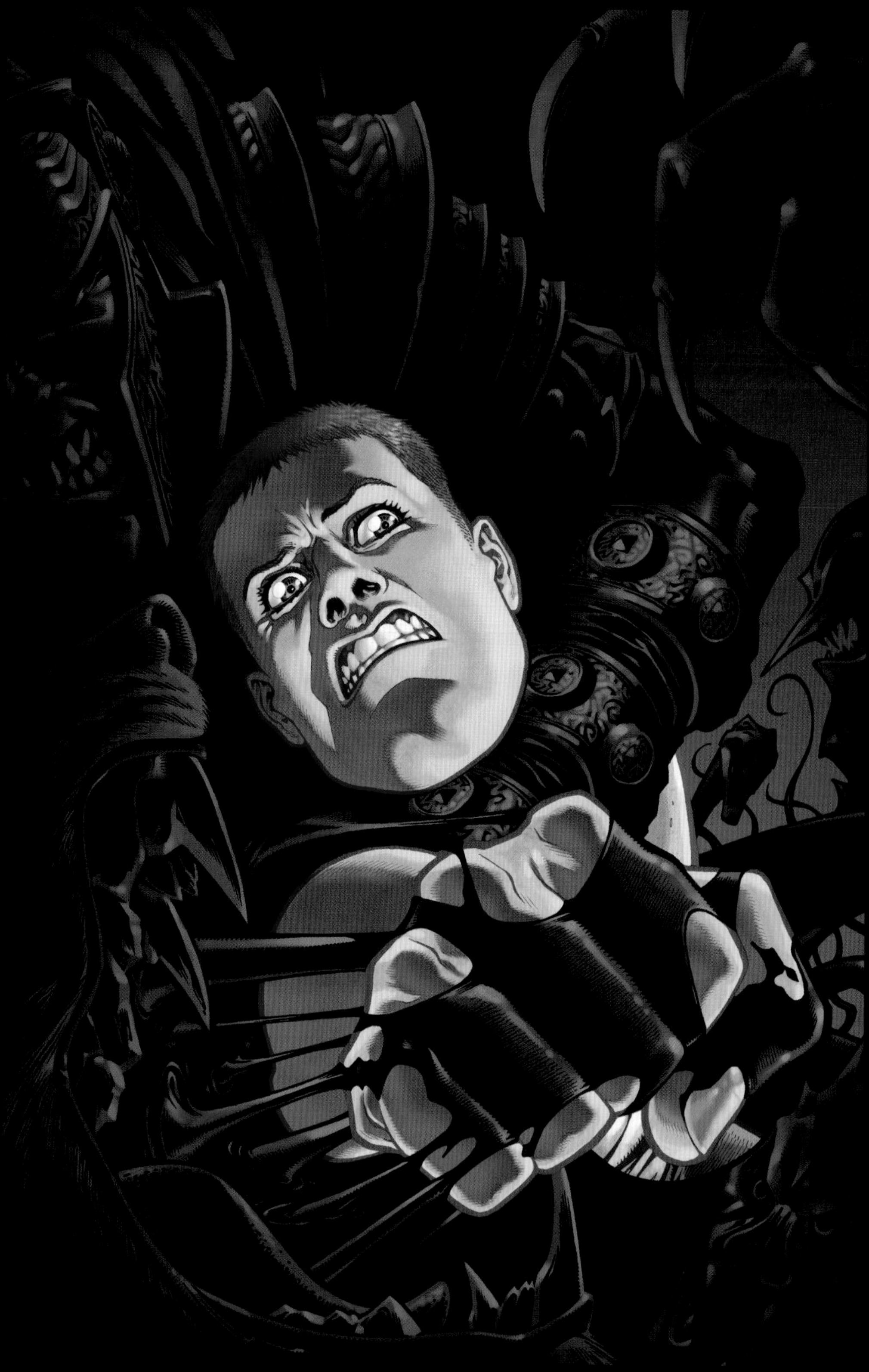

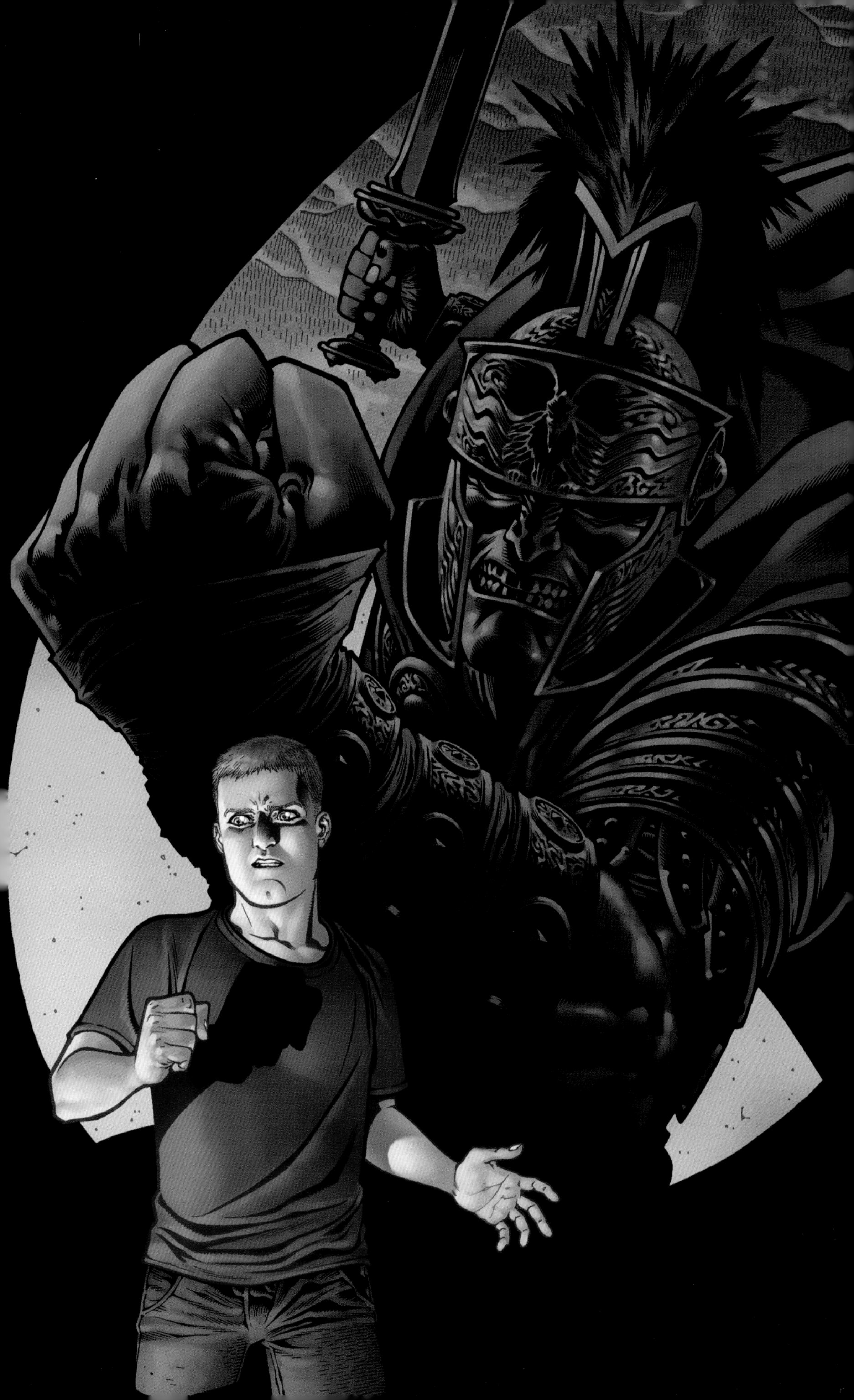

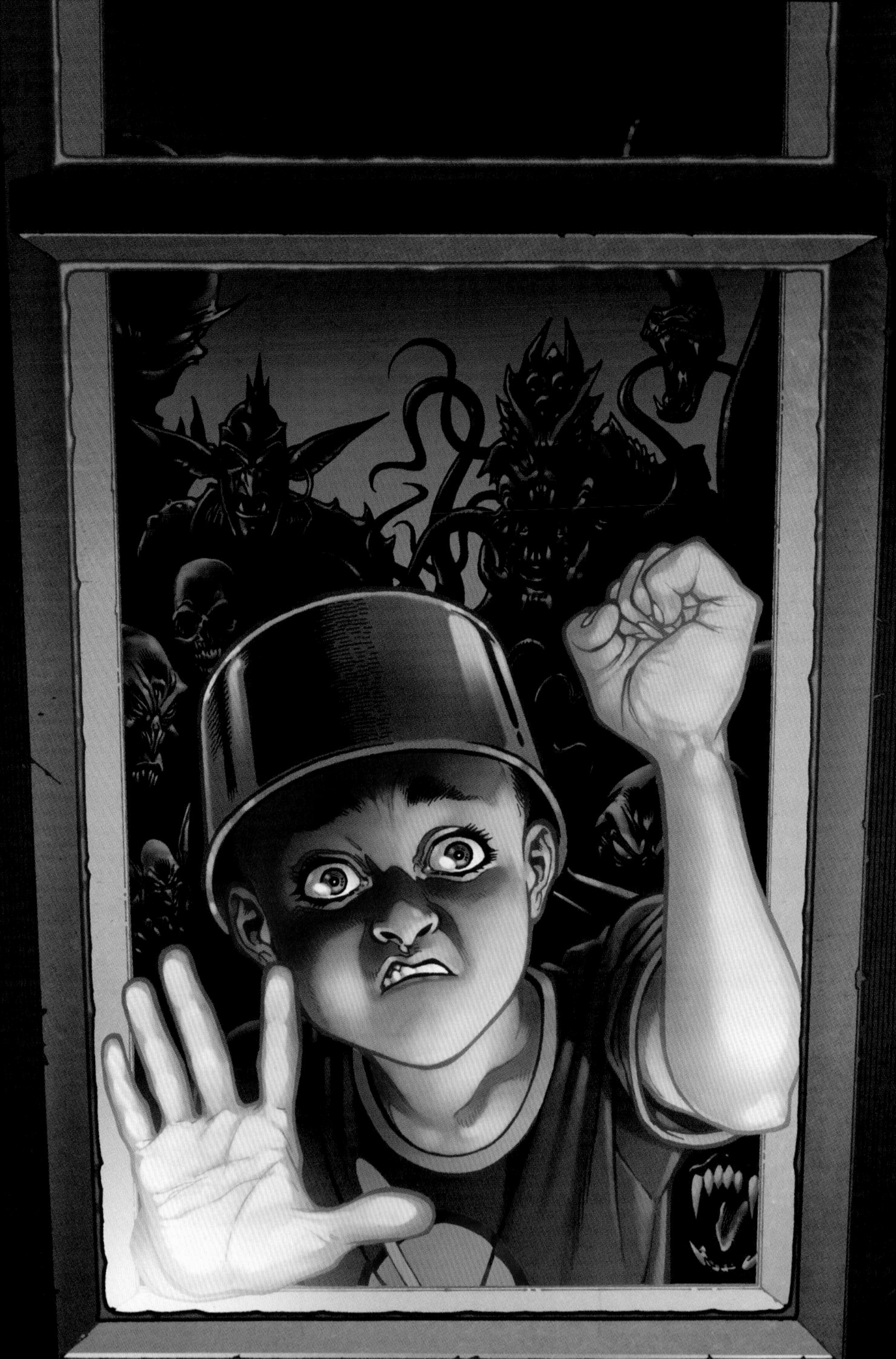

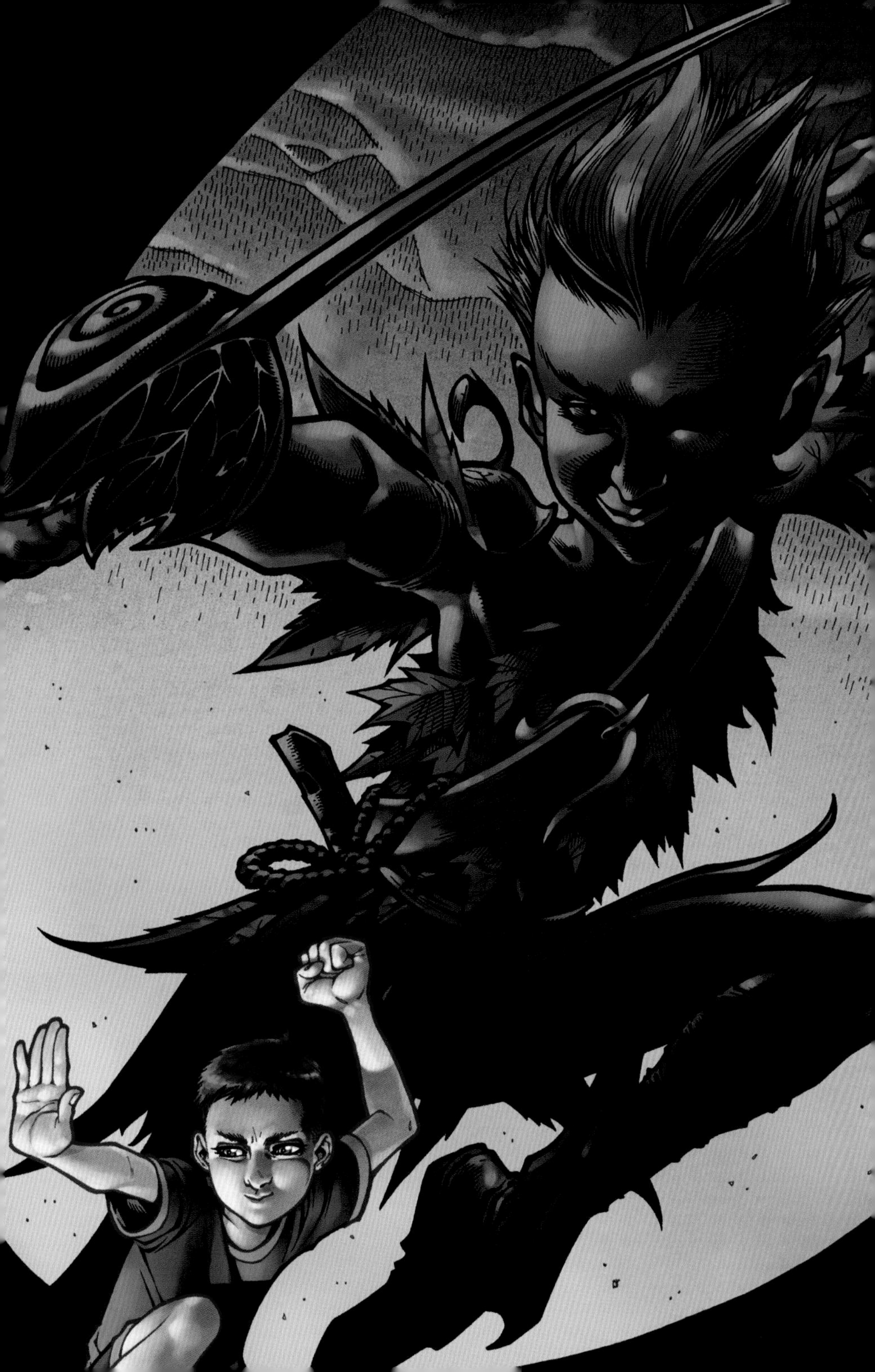

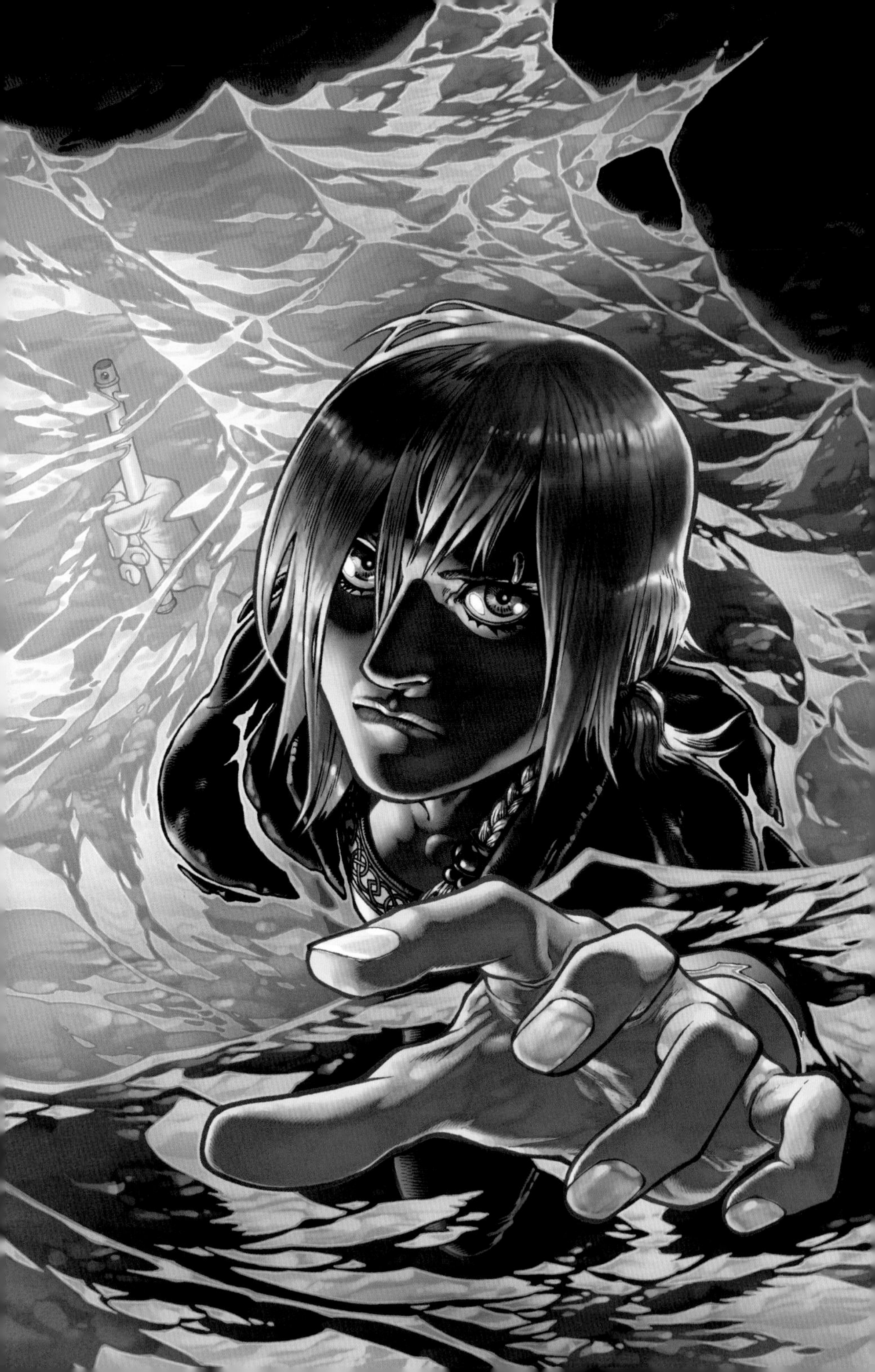

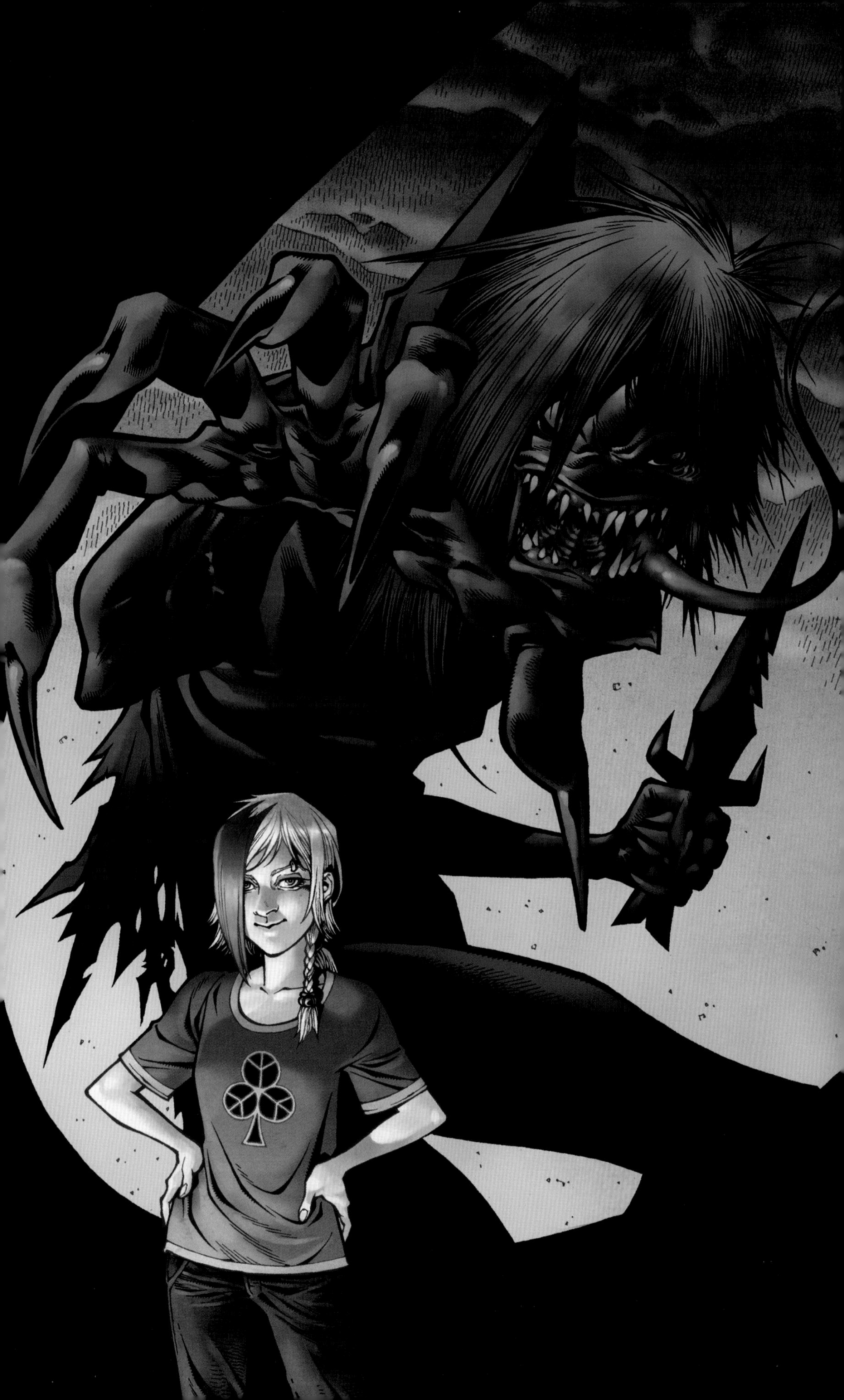

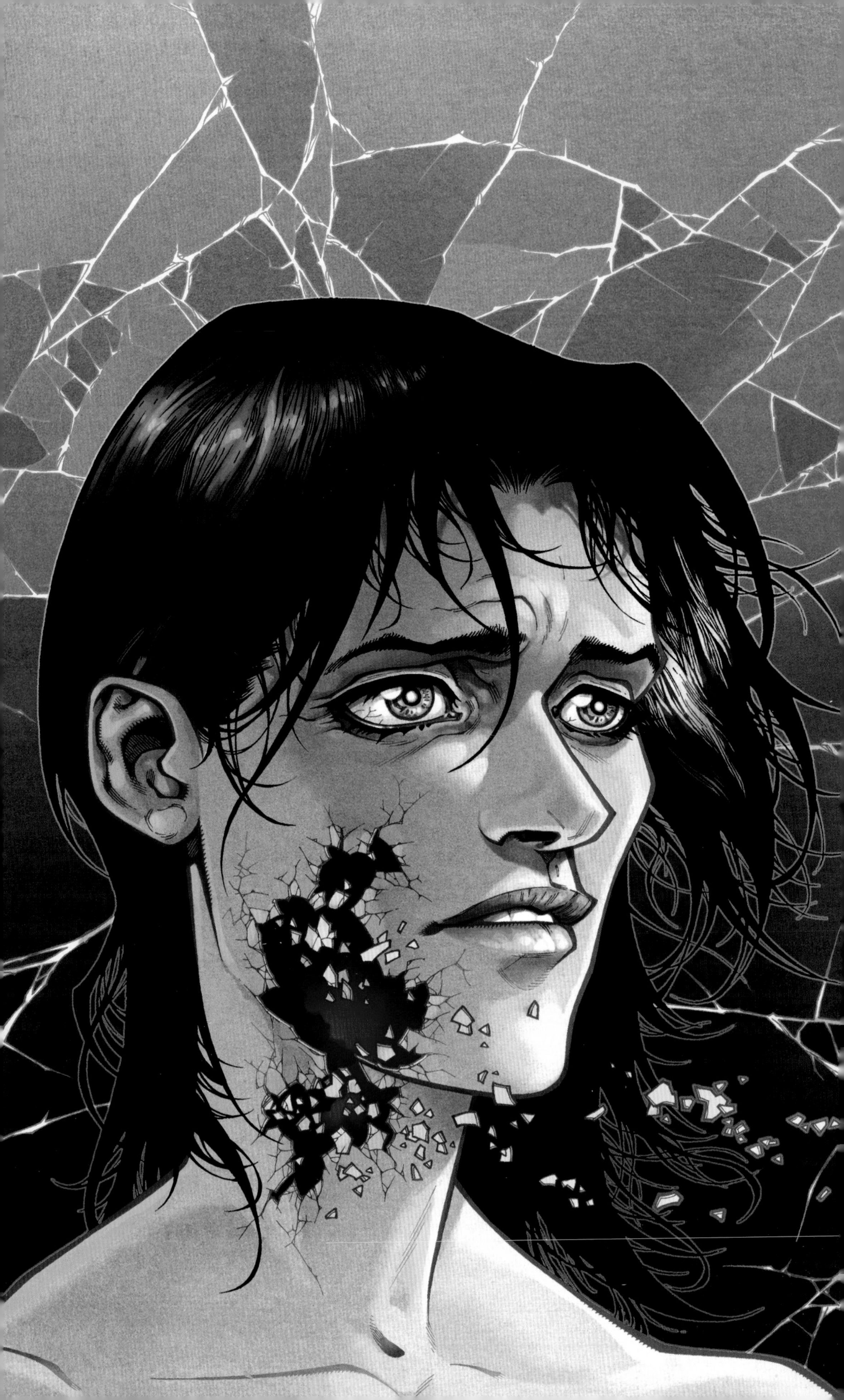